Chicago Lawyers

It is characteristic of a democracy to open wide the gates of a profession to "the average man," and then later to attack the entire profession, a part of which has thus been rendered incompetent and dangerous to the public welfare. Having first insured the utter mediocrity of judges and lawyers, it is only human nature to turn and rend them for not being extraordinary and exceptional.

—ARTHUR CORBIN,
presidential address to the
Association of American Law Schools, 1921

"The Bar" is in this country an almost meaningless conglomeration. What we have is lawyers, by their tens of thousands—individual lawyers without unity of tradition, character, background, or objective; as single persons, many of them powerful; as a guild, inert beyond easy understanding.   KARL LLEWELLYN,
in *Annals of The American Academy*, 1933

The one generalization that it may be safe to make about lawyers—except, of course, for the statistically incontrovertible one that this country has quite a few more of them than it has any need for—is that the profession includes a large number of serious eaters.

—CALVIN TRILLIN,
in *The New Yorker*, 1977

CHICAGO LAWYERS

The Social Structure of the Bar

BY

JOHN P. HEINZ

AND

EDWARD O. LAUMANN

NEW YORK   CHICAGO

Russell Sage Foundation AND *American Bar Foundation*

Library of Congress Catalog Number: 82-50355
Standard Book Number: 0-87154-378-8

10 9 8 7 6 5 4 3 2 1

To Anne,

& to Anne,

i.e., 2 (Anne).

Contents

PART I

Introduction

PART II

Lawyers' Roles: The Predominance of Client-centered Structure

PART III

*Lawyers' Lives: Social Background, Social Values,
and Career Mobility*

PART IV

Lawyers' Ties: Networks of Association, Organizations, and Political Activities

PART V

Conclusion

List of Tables

List of Figures

Foreword

Chicago Lawyers is one of the most richly detailed and systematically pursued analyses ever made of a profession. The existing literature on the legal profession—to which the Russell Sage Foundation has made a number of contributions—includes excellent studies of particular segments of the bar, such as Wall Street lawyers, and of particular issues, such as lawyers' ethical conduct. But there is no other study, I think, that offers such a theoretically disciplined examination of the full panorama of this or any profession in a complex urban setting.

The student of American society will find in *Chicago Lawyers* a comprehensive exposition of the manifold types of social differentiation and stratification within a professional community, and a consideration of the difficulties of achieving integration and cohesion in so divided a group. While the social stratification of the bar has often been noted, no other study has delineated with such detail the remarkable extent to which lawyers are channeled to specific niches of professional practice according to their socioeconomic and ethnoreligious origins and the social standing of the law schools they attended. The authors have gathered unprecedented original data on the social structure of the bar, which they display in a wide variety of tables and test with sophisticated statistical techniques to assure validity and generality.

But we are not simply presented here with documentation of the fascinating diversity of lawyers. We are also given a systematic conceptual framework that permits us not only to understand the Chicago bar but to anticipate the ways in which the social structure of the bar might differ in other cities and towns, or at other times, as social conditions change.

Such a study could have been produced only by a team with an uncommon combination of skills and training. John Heinz, a lawyer and law teacher with professional training in the social sciences, has long been occupied with social scientific research on various aspects of the legal system. Edward Laumann, a sociologist with extensive research experience in urban occupational, ethnic, and community life, has provided the outsider's eye for what is similar and different about this professional community compared to others. Together, they bring to their study an unusual scope and clarity of vision.

Although the authors take a definite and sustained interpretive stance toward their subject matter, readers are provided with sufficient information to draw their own conclusions. Awkward facts that do not quite fit are readily acknowledged. The concluding chapter is an extended interpretive essay that is frankly speculative and goes well beyond the data with which the authors are so diligently occupied in the preceding chapters. I commend this chapter to the reader's attention as an especially provocative rethinking of some of our more cherished notions about the nature of the legal profession and its role in society.

MARSHALL ROBINSON
President
Russell Sage Foundation

Foreword

THE BOOK that follows in these pages represents the fruition of a major research effort. With others, I was "in at the creation" and had something to do with inducing the authors of this book—the principal investigators in the project to study the Chicago bar—to undertake their monumental task. Perhaps the midwife can claim only modest credit for the quality of the offspring but such as is appropriate I do claim.

Others better qualified to judge the place of this work in the literature of the sociology of professions can state more accurately than I how importantly this study has contributed to knowledge in this field. I have heard enough from experts in the field, however, to be sure that the contribution has been immensely important. To me—previously almost a stranger to this discipline—it has been a continuing and valuable education.

As Executive Director of the American Bar Foundation when this foreword was written, I am proud that the Foundation has been able to sponsor and encourage the contributions to knowledge of the legal profession represented in this book and its numerous progeny. That the Foundation will continue to make contributions in this field is certain. Not only will the authors of this book be engaged—with others—in another massive undertaking now beginning, but John Heinz succeeds me as Executive Director of the Foundation and will thus be in a position to ensure and to direct the continued activity of the Foundation as a major contributor to this field.

It is my pleasant duty to recognize and to express appreciation for the financial and moral support of the Russell Sage Foundation, the co-publisher of this book, and of the National Science Foundation, in the project memorialized in part in these pages. I am sure that representatives of those institutions will recognize the propriety of my expressing very special thanks to the legal profession itself for two kinds of aid. First, there was the extraordinary amount of help the profession gave in permitting itself to be studied, especially by cooperating in an unusual manner in exposing its inmost thoughts and feelings to the searching questions of the interviewers. That level of assistance was almost unique in recent sociological study. Second, the profession, specifically through the American Bar Endowment, made a very large financial contribution to the project— dwarfing all others combined.

To all those who helped, and in particular to the authors of this book, who masterminded a successful and exemplary research enterprise from beginning to end, I express my own personal appreciation and that of the officers and directors of the American Bar Foundation whom I represent.

SPENCER L. KIMBALL
Executive Director
American Bar Foundation
June 1982

Preface

THERE IS, it is true, a dusty quality about the law. One thinks of dusty law books and even of dusty lawyers. And lawyers often make use of the tactical dust storm, designed to obfuscate. But there is also a modicum of genuine drama in the story of the legal profession. The law, after all, deals with the clash of powerful interests; it is thought to have great impact on social policy and on the course of the economy; it stages battles of courtroom advocates that are spiced with eloquence, humor, surprise, cunning and, occasionally, intelligence; it features struggles for control of vast wealth; and it poses timeless issues of liberty, life, and death. We are having none of that. If this book succeeds at nothing else, it manages admirably to resist the urge to exploit the drama of the American legal profession. Sociological research on lawyers has not often been so resolute, so unbending.

Many of the social scientists who have studied the bar have, in fact, yielded to the natural fascination of the extreme case. The extreme is likely to be conspicuous and it often includes a disproportionate share of the profession's inherent drama, which promises to sustain the interest of the scholar who labors on the research and, perhaps (though this is less likely), of the other scholars who are obliged to read it. Even leaving aside such titillating journalistic accounts as *The Superlawyers*, therefore, studies of the legal profession have tended to concentrate on the poles of the profession's prestige hierarchy—on the Wall Street lawyers,[1] at the top, or on criminal lawyers,[2] personal injury lawyers,[3] or solo practition-

1. Erwin O. Smigel, *The Wall Street Lawyer: Professional Organization Man?*, 2d ed. (Bloomington: Indiana University Press, 1969).
2. Arthur L. Wood, *Criminal Lawyer* (New Haven: College and University Press, 1967).
3. H. Laurence Ross, *Settled Out of Court: The Social Process of Insurance Claims Adjustments* (Chicago: Aldine Publishing, 1970); Douglas E. Rosenthal, *Lawyer and Client: Who's in Charge?* (New York: Russell Sage Foundation, 1974).

ers,[4] at the bottom. The profession's center has not inspired a rich literature, and little information is available on the bar's overall social structure. Jack Ladinsky's study of Detroit lawyers covered all types and specialties, and it contributed substantially to our understanding, but the amount and kinds of data available to Ladinsky were quite limited.[5] Dietrich Rueschemeyer's commentary on lawyers in Germany and in the United States has a broader, comparative viewpoint and includes useful theoretical propositions, but it presents no original data on American lawyers.[6] This study attempts to supply original data by systematically describing and analyzing the social structure of the legal profession in a major city.

The methods to be used in addressing this task were by no means obvious, and we therefore considered a number of possible research designs. Some were more creative than others. You may well find that the approaches that were adopted are rather fanciful, but consider others that occurred to us. We discussed, for example, the feasibility of classifying the types of law practice by a Hardwood Index. Thus, we might have dispatched our research team about the city with tape measures, to be used to record the amounts of walnut, mahogany, oak, teak and rosewood consumed in decorating each law firm's suite. The square centimeters of hardwood per lawyer could then have been correlated with the ascribed standing of the firm to determine whether a high score on the Hardwood Index was associated with having arrived or with trying too hard. There would, of course, have been difficulty in specifying the direction of the causal arrow—that is, does success cause hardwood or does hardwood cause success? We would also have wanted to carry the analysis to another level of depth and complexity by attempting to determine whether there was an association between particular woods and particular fields of specialization of practice. The probate specialists, for example, might have been found to prefer brown

---

4. Jerome E. Carlin, *Lawyers on Their Own: A Study of Individual Practitioners in Chicago* (New Brunswick: Rutgers University Press, 1962).

5. Jack Ladinsky, "Careers of Lawyers, Law Practice, and Legal Institutions," *American Sociological Review* 28(1963): 47–54; Jack Ladinsky, "The Impact of Social Backgrounds of Lawyers on Law Practice and the Law," *Journal of Legal Education* 16(1963): 127–44; Jack Ladinsky "The Social Profile of a Metropolitan Bar: A Statistical Survey in Detroit," *Michigan State Bar Journal* 43(1964): 12–24.

6. Dietrich Rueschemeyer, *Lawyers and Their Society: A Comparative Study of the Legal Profession in Germany and the United States* (Cambridge: Harvard University Press, 1973).

oak, while blond oak might have been associated with personal injury defense work, walnut with corporate tax practice, teak with securities work, and rosewood with bankruptcy.

Less extreme variants of this general mode of analysis were also considered. It would have been a simple matter, for example, to have had our interviewers record their respondents' modes of attire. We feared, however, that the categories might turn out to look something like this: 1) three piece, chalk-striped gray flannel; 2) three piece, plain gray flannel; 3) three piece, pin-striped gray worsted; 4) three piece, plain gray sharkskin . . . and so on, until one might reach x) two piece, navy blue mohair with waist suppression. We were not sure that we wanted to know this.

There was also the matter of identifying the audience to which the study was to be addressed. The process of decision on this issue was arduous, but in the end the choices that we made were clear. This book has not been written for lawyers. Lawyers will find that they already know all of this or, to the extent that they do not, that our data are clearly wrong. Lawyers, therefore, read this at their own risk. Neither was this written for sociologists. Why should anyone write for sociologists, when sociologists do not write for anyone? And the "educated layman" already has far more reading assignments than he can possibly manage. We could not in good conscience set out to burden him further. Having concluded that it would be either inappropriate, foolhardy, or tiresome to attempt to address any of these potential audiences for the book, we opted for appealing to the one, true audience of all academics—ourselves.

But there remains the question of how we happened to develop such peculiar tastes. Why, with our separate disciplinary training and allegiances, do we not offend each other? In part, of course, we do. But, to a far greater extent, we find that we please one another. This may merely be an example of the genius of the American political instinct—if Heinz expresses enthusiasm for the work of Laumann and Laumann praises the work of Heinz, it feeds both egos and serves their mutual interest in finishing the business. It has been a happy collaboration.

The collaboration could not have avoided strife, however, without the helpful intervention at several points of many friends and colleagues. There are so many persons and institutions to whom we owe debts for assistance with this project that it is perilous even to attempt to list them all, but none could have had a more important role than Spencer Kimball, then Executive Director of the American Bar Foundation. Professor Kimball was, in many ways, the author of the project that created this book. He initiated the discussions from which the project evolved, he introduced the two principal investigators to each other, he selected them to do the work, he secured most of the funding for the project, and he supervised, encouraged and contributed to the work at every step along the way. We are enormously grateful to him.

We are deeply appreciative of the support of the Board of Directors of the American Bar Foundation, and we are greatly indebted to the American Bar Endowment, which was the principal source of the funding for the project. Funds were also provided by the National Science Foundation, through grant #SOC 77-24699, and we valued both the financial assistance and the expression of confidence in the work. The director of the Law and Social Sciences Program of NSF at the time the grant was made was H. Laurence Ross, and he and his successors in that position, Stephen Wasby and Felice Levine, gave us helpful advice and did much to ease the administrative burdens. We are grateful also for financial, scientific, and editorial support provided by the Russell Sage Foundation. Stanton Wheeler generously gave both substantive and procedural advice that was exceedingly valuable, and he shepherded the grant and resulting manuscript through the Russell Sage Foundation's processes. We are deeply indebted to him. We are also indebted to Marshall Robinson, the president of the Russell Sage Foundation, for his support, encouragement, and thoughtful understanding.

At every stage of our work, we were blessed with the assistance of an unusually talented group of associates and colleagues. The survey, itself, was ably supervised by Terence Halliday. His skill, attention to detail, and keen perception are reflected in the quality of the data set. Halliday was, as was Michael Schaalman, an active participant in the drafting of the survey instruments, and both Halliday and Schaalman made many helpful contributions to that phase of the work. Peter Marsden assisted us in the sampling design and in the earliest stages of the data analysis, and his work was done with a high degree of professionalism.

The principal data analyses on which the book rests were carried out by Charles Cappell. He also supervised the basic organization of the data set, wrote the cleaning specifications, and conducted necessary recoding. His sophistication in statistical methods was of enor-

xxii

mous benefit to the project, and his skillful hand shows clearly at a great many places in the book. During much of this work, Cappell was ably assisted by Scott Marden, to whom we are also indebted.

Margaret Troha was a key member of the research group for two years while much of the most intensive data analysis was in progress and then, again, at the very end of the project in the process of tying up the loose ends. At both times, she performed her vital role with intelligence, creativity, dedication, and meticulous attention to detail. Were it not for her superb work, this book would not exist and whatever might have been published in its stead would have far less merit.

Later in the project, substantial sections of the data analysis were carried out by Robert Nelson and by Mariah Evans, both of whom fully met the high standards of performance set by their predecessors. We were, again, most fortunate to have the benefit of the services of two scholars of such exceptional talent, training, and motivation. In addition, Karol Soltan and Michael Powell, at varying stages of the project, performed more narrow but highly important portions of the analysis with skill and perception. As the project neared completion, Nelson and Powell also provided valuable substantive advice on the interpretation of the findings.

The several interviewers who worked on the survey and the coders who prepared the data for analysis performed their assignments with precision, understanding, and dedication, and we are indebted and grateful to them.

Several of our colleagues at other institutions generously devoted their time to reading all or substantial portions of the manuscript, and we benefited greatly from their many criticisms and suggestions. A colleague who made such a contribution at several stages of the project, to a degree that went far beyond any ordinary conception of professional duty, is Richard Lempert of the University of Michigan. We are especially indebted to him. Others who provided very helpful readings are Eliot Freidson of New York University, Robert Kagan of Berkeley, Melvin Kohn of NIMH, Stewart Macaulay of the University of Wisconsin, Dietrich Rueschemeyer of Brown University, Robert Salisbury of Washington University, Richard Simpson of the University of North Carolina, Rosemary Stevens of the University of Pennsylvania, Ross Stolzenberg of the Rand Corporation, and Stanton Wheeler of the Russell Sage Foundation and Yale University. Two anonymous referees who read the manuscript for the Russell Sage Foundation also made useful suggestions, and we are indebted to them as well.

Many of our co-workers at the American Bar Foundation, the University of Chicago, and Northwestern University suffered and exulted through this with us, read portions of the manuscript, and provided us with intellectual guidance and spiritual support. These include, in addition to those already mentioned, at least the following: Robert Bennett, Charles Bidwell, Thomas Davies, John Flood, Mayer Freed, Anne Heinz, Morris Janowitz, Daniel Polsby, Stephen Presser, James Rahl, Harry Reese, Victor Rosenblum, Edward Shils, Francis Spalding, and Frances Zemans. We gratefully acknowledge our debt to each of them.

Near the beginning of the planning for the project, we assembled a group of scholars who met with us at length to discuss research objectives and methods. That group included Fredric Du Bow, Morris Janowitz, Jack Ladinsky, Kenneth Prewitt, and Peter Rossi. As might be expected from such a distinguished assemblage, the meeting provided many useful ideas and suggestions and we benefited greatly from it. Even earlier, before this project had been conceived, Spencer Kimball convened a group to discuss the possibilities of research dealing with the Chicago Bar Association. In addition to the authors of this book and representatives of the Association, to be mentioned below, those in attendance at that meeting included Barbara Curran and Barlow Christensen of the American Bar Foundation and Walter Blum and Stanley Katz of the University of Chicago. This project, as well as some others, grew out of that meeting and all of those who were present made continuing contributions to the project. We therefore owe a special debt to those who were there at the genesis.

A number of other lawyers and law professors, including many leaders of the organized bar, provided exceedingly valuable information and advice at various stages of the project. We are, of course, indebted to each of them for taking the time and trouble to contribute to the enterprise. These included: James Connelly, Thomas Eovaldi, Milton Gray, David Hilliard, Jordan Hillman, William Hood, Robert Howard, Arnold Kanter, James Kissell, John McBride, Dennis Mayer, Bernard Meltzer, Norval Morris. Nathaniel Nathanson, Gary Palm, Marshall Patner, Alexander Polikoff, John Schmidt, and George Rothschild. We are also exceedingly grateful to the more than 800 Chicago lawyers who took the time to be interviewed in one or another of our surveys and pretests.

We owe a special debt to Alex Elson, Richard Phelan, and Edgar Vanneman, the three lawyers who chaired a Chicago Bar Association subcommittee that provided the original impetus for this research. They strongly supported the project from the beginning, and they provided advice and assistance that made the job possible. No doubt they did not quite foresee the course that the project would take—as none of us did at the outset—but it would not have happened without their vital role. Other members of the CBA's Committee on the Development of the Law also provided welcome guidance and encouragement in the early stages of the project.

Similarly indispensable to the project was the enthusiastic support of the deans of the authors' schools. Deans James Rahl and David Ruder of Northwestern Law School provided research assistance, released time, and thoughtful understanding of the rigors and needs of research. We are grateful for their wisdom and their fine sense of values.

The editors who worked on the manuscript at various stages and in various versions are also to be commended and gratefully thanked for their understanding, gentleness and compassion, as well as for their high degree of professional skill. Bette Sikes, the Director of Publications at ABF, not only supervised publication of the chapters that first appeared as articles in the *ABF Research Journal*, but also did the initial copy editing on the entire manuscript. As always, she performed her work with precision, taste, and intelligence. Priscilla Lewis, the Director of Publications at the Russell Sage Foundation, was an equal joy. She steered the manuscript through the several steps toward publication with good judgment, good sense, and good humor in spite of much that might have tried a less steady and skilled hand. Marcia Wilk made many valuable editorial contributions to the articles that became chapters 4 and 8, as did the editors of the *Michigan Law Review* to the article that became chapter 3.

Several cohorts of law students at the Northwestern Law School provided perceptive and skillful research assistance over the course of the project. Among the more recent of them were Michael Solimine, Barry Taylor, Daniel Bacastow, Jeffrey Carter, George Watson, Robert Stout, and James McDonough. We are indebted to them and to their predecessors for much that helped to make this a better book.

Finally, we have been assisted by a succession of highly skilled secretaries who consumed reams of paper and burned up several keyboards. Though many had a hand in processing all of these words over the long life of the project, those who played the most vital roles were Earlene Franklin, Glenda Hargrove, Jan Madsen, Helen Saldana, Brenda Smith, and Conray Weathers. They all did their work ably, accurately, and with unfailing good will, and for that we are most grateful.

There is no point in trying to absolve all of these many persons from their responsibility for this book. It is too late for that. Not that we could get away with shifting full responsibility onto them, but neither can they avoid a measure of accountability. Some are more responsible than others. They know who they are. And they will have to live with it.

PART I

Introduction

Chapter 1

THE SCOPE AND NATURE

OF THE STUDY

IT HAS BEEN apparent for some time that the simple view of the bar as a single, unified profession no longer fits the facts. First of all, lawyers, of course, are not merely lawyers. They are advisors to businessmen and are businessmen themselves; they are politicians, lobbyists, and judges or potential judges; they are real estate and insurance salesmen, claims adjustors, facilitators of zoning variances, scholars, and rich lie-abouts. But even those roles that are usually thought of as lawyers' work, more narrowly defined, display considerable variety.

The division of labor has proceeded in the law as it has in most other fields of endeavor, and a number of distinct types of lawyers are now clearly identifiable. A form of the old general practitioner survives in small towns and in some city neighborhoods, but these are a minority of the profession—in 1970, about 62 percent of American lawyers lived in cities of over 100,000 population,[1] and

1. Bette H. Sikes, Clara N. Carson, and Patricia Gorai, *The 1971 Lawyer Statistical Report* (Chicago: American Bar Foundation, 1972), page 5, table 1. In the same year, only about 9 percent of all lawyers resided outside the U.S. Census's "urbanized areas" (U.S., Department of Commerce, Bureau of the Census, *1970 Census of Population*, [Washington, D.C.: Government Printing Office, 1973] part 1, Sec. 2, table 222, "Detailed Occupations of Employed Persons by Residence and Sex," p. 725; for definition of "urbanized areas," see appendix A, p. 9, of report.) A lawyer might well, of course, *reside* in a small town or suburb, but *practice* in a city. In 1980, more than 22,000 of the 37,100 lawyers registered with the Supreme Court of Illinois resided in

relatively few of these city lawyers probably served primarily a neighborhood clientele.[2] In large cities like Chicago, the focus of this book, the differences among the several sorts of lawyers are dramatic. The lawyer who commutes to Brussels and Tokyo and who spends his time negotiating the rights to distribute Colonel Sanders throughout the world will have little in common with the lawyer who haunts the corridors of the criminal courts hoping that a bailiff will, in return for a consideration, commend his services to some poor wretch charged with a barroom assault. Both of those private practitioners will differ from the government-employed lawyers who prosecute criminal cases or who practice public international law in the employ of the State Department, as the two sorts of government-employed lawyers differ from one another. And all of those types will be distinguishable from the partner of the large law firm who devotes his days to advising corporations on the probable tax consequences of several alternative real estate acquisition strategies, who in turn will differ from another sort of tax lawyer, the sort who fills out individual income tax forms as April 15 approaches. Then there are the patent lawyers, many of whom prepared for law school not with the traditional liberal arts, prelaw courses but with training in engineering or some other scientific discipline and who may spend much of their time analyzing mechanical drawings; and the divorce lawyers, who may choose to process their cases quickly or to become family counselors or semiprofessional psychotherapists; and the personal injury plaintiffs' lawyers, who devote their ingenuity to devising dramatic ways of making clear to juries what it means to be paralyzed from the waist down; and the personal injury defense lawyers, who are retained by insurance companies to make the same juries understand that insurance rates will go up if they allow themselves to be overwhelmed by emotion; and the civil rights lawyers, whose long hair flies behind

---

(continued)

Cook County (Chicago) (Annual Report of Attorney Registration and Disciplinary Commission for 1980 [1981]). Moreover, small-town lawyers usually handle far less than the full range of legal work—they do not often get the most sophisticated corporate work, antitrust cases, securities work, or complex issues of corporate tax. Their practice might, therefore, be thought of not as truly general but as a type of limited specialization, a sort of "family practice."

2. Only 3 percent of our sample of Chicago lawyers report that more than half of their clients come from their own residential neighborhoods (see appendix A, question A5E).

them as they stride into battle for the public good. One could posit a great many legal professions, perhaps dozens, and to some degree there are perceptible distinctions among all of these types of lawyers.

But how significant are these differences? Does the differentiation of the lawyers' roles have important implications for the nature of the profession or for the broader society, or is a lawyer still basically a lawyer, drawing upon a tradition and an arcane body of knowledge shared in common by all or most members of the profession whatever the varying applications of their shared principles and skills to different sorts of problems? Are available professional personnel assigned to particular tasks by idiosyncratic personal predilections or by adventitious factors such as proximity, or are lawyers selected for different roles by orderly social processes or by standard criteria that have social meaning and consequences? And what is the significance in sheer quantitative terms of each of these types of legal work? That is, how large are each of these subdivisions of the bar? Are some so small as to be inconsequential in any consideration of the general characteristics of the profession, while the volume of work and the numbers of lawyers engaged in other areas of practice are so great as to have overwhelming weight in determining the overall social structure of the bar? And are all of these types of work clearly distinct from one another, or do some of the same lawyers perform several of the roles, doing one sort of work one day or week and another the next? What are the patterns of overlap or of separation among the various kinds of law practice? These questions concerning the nature and extent of the differentiation of the various roles performed by urban lawyers are among the first issues addressed in this book and, using data drawn from an extensive survey of Chicago lawyers, we provide at least partial or tentative answers.

Interesting as the differentiation of lawyers' roles may be, however, those questions are themselves of less consequence than the issue of whether the different roles are organized into some sort of hierarchy reflecting or determining the allocation of status, power, economic rewards, or whatever is valued. The analyses presented in the book turn next, therefore, to the relationship between the division of labor and the structure of social inequality in the legal profession. Mere social differentiation need not imply social inequality, of course, though it often does. The question of whether differentiated social positions (in this case, the different lawyers' jobs) get systematically different amounts of what there is to get,[3] and, if so, how and why, has been a matter of primary concern to generations of social theorists. One school, including such scholars as Kingsley Davis and Wilbert E. Moore[4] and Talcott Parsons,[5] has emphasized the functional utility of inequality in the maintenance of social systems. Another major school, including theorists such as Ralf Dahrendorf[6] and Karl Marx, has stressed the disintegrative or conflict-producing tendencies of social inequality. Though the explanations of the link between social differentiation and social inequality that are offered by these two schools differ markedly, we believe that both perspectives are useful and we do not find it necessary to reject the insights of one in order to benefit from the other. We draw upon both schools, for example, in our analyses of the means through which social differentiation is converted into inequality in the distribution of rewards, privileges, and social honor or deference. From the functionalist school, we adopt the suggestion that the social values embraced by the members of a community will influence their evaluations of the importance of the various roles of lawyers and that they will thus reward the roles differentially and will come to assign high esteem to some and to hold others in lower regard. If the community member attaches special importance to the protection of individual rights and liberties, such as freedom of speech, he will be likely to evaluate relatively highly the lawyers who are perceived as serving such goals; if he especially values economic enterprise and the production of goods and services, he will hold in regard the lawyers who are thought to advance those ends. But we also use, in our analyses, an alternative or complementary view of the process through which social differentiation is converted into patterned social inequalities, a view that derives from the so-called conflict school. Those theorists stress the differences in the

3. With elegant simplicity, Harold Lasswell defined "the influential" as "those who get the most of what there is to get" (*Politics: Who Gets What, When, How* [New York: McGraw-Hill, 1936], p. 3).

4. Kingsley Davis and Wilbert E. Moore, "Some Principles of Stratification," *American Sociological Review* 10(1945): 242–49.

5. Talcott Parsons, "Equality and Inequality in Modern Society, or Social Stratification Revisited," in Edward O. Laumann, ed., *Social Stratification: Research and Theory for the 1970s* (Indianapolis: Bobbs-Merrill, 1970), pp. 13–72.

6. Ralf Dahrendorf, *Class and Class Conflict in Industrial Society* (Stanford, Cal.: Stanford University Press, 1959); "On the Origin of Inequality Among Men," in *Essays in the Theory of Society* (Stanford, Cal.: Stanford University Press, 1968), pp. 151–78.

amounts of power possessed by the incumbents of the several social roles, and they argue accordingly that these power differences permit some social positions to exact greater rewards for their contributions than can others. Thus, lawyers whose advice is sought by powerful corporation executives and whose decisions therefore have far-reaching ramifications in the society at large might secure greater rewards for their efforts than would lawyers who advise the poor and dispossessed.

The first objective of this book, then, is to analyze the nature and extent of social differentiation among Chicago lawyers and to attempt to identify its generative mechanisms. The second is to evaluate the means by which this differentiation is converted into inequality in the distribution within the legal profession of income, organizational resources, access to leadership positions, and honor or deference.

The third and final large theme of the book is an examination of the kinds and degree of social bonds among the various sorts of Chicago lawyers. That is, given the differentiation and inequality within the bar, does the legal profession constitute a true community of common fate or collective goals, or does it consist merely of a disaggregated array of individuals and activities? Does the bar possess mechanisms for achieving social integration of the profession or for sustaining an overarching consciousness of kind among lawyers in spite of their differentiation and inequalities, or do the different types of lawyers live separate lives, seldom coming into contact and adopting conflicting stances on matters of public policy affecting the profession, on basic social values, or on issues of professional ethics? Do the patterns of association among lawyers follow the lines of some intraprofessional logic, or do they correspond to categories that have salience in the broader social world—for example, categories such as political affiliation or ethnoreligious identification? That is, is the bar (or even some portion of it) a primary reference group for most lawyers, or do they seek and find their principal identities in extraprofessional roles? Are common positions on basic social and political issues (especially those that are of particular relevance to the law) widely shared throughout the profession? Does the organized bar speak for all or most members of the profession? Do political activities or other sorts of community work serve as a meeting ground for lawyers and thus as a means of integrating the profession, or do they merely provide competing foci, alternative and conflicting causes that serve further to divide the profession? If systematic strata exist within the profession, to what extent do individual lawyers manage to transcend those barriers in interpersonal relationships, in organizational activities (as in the achievement of a leadership position in the organized bar), or in career mobility across the strata? Such answers as we are able to provide to this set of questions are even less complete and more tentative than our answers to the previous questions. These issues of collective identity and of the social bases of joint activity are exceedingly complex, and it is very difficult to marshall evidence that addresses them directly.[7] Nonetheless, we believe that we also have some worthwhile observations to offer on these points.

In analyzing the nature of interpersonal association and the structure of joint political activity within the Chicago bar, we use techniques that had been previously employed in community power studies to analyze the roles and constituencies of various sorts of elites and other political actors in several cities and towns.[8] Thus, in a sense, we conceive of Chicago lawyers as a community[9] with its own set of elites and its own criteria for inclusion in such categories, its own lines of cleavage that define constituencies, its mechanisms of social integration, and its sets of divisive issues and of personal loyalties and enmities that will tend to produce dissensus. To say that it is conceived of as a community does not, therefore, imply that the bar is monolithic any more than students of the power structure of cities assume that those communities are undifferentiated. Treating the bar as a community does, however, imply that there is some discernible boundary between that set of social actors and others surrounding them in their environment. We are not prepared to offer evidence that there is any such boundary. Indeed, we regard the point as problematic. The assumption of the existence of a community is merely that—an assumption that provides a starting point for the research but that may, itself, be drawn into question by the findings.

7. See S. F. Nadel, *The Theory of Social Structure* (London: Cohen and West, 1957).
8. See Edward O. Laumann and Franz Urban Pappi, *Networks of Collective Action: A Perspective on Community Influence Systems* (New York: Academic Press, 1976) pp. 11–12. See also John Walton, "A Systematic Survey of Community Power Research," in M. Aiken and P. Mott, eds., *The Structure of Community Power* (New York: Random House, 1970), pp. 443–64.
9. See William J. Goode, "Community Within a Community: The Professions," *American Sociological Review* 22 (1957): 194–200.

In all, we aim to provide a reasonably comprehensive analysis of the social structure of Chicago's bar and, insofar as possible, of the processes that determine that structure.

The Data Set

The data presented in the book are drawn from personal interviews with 777 Chicago lawyers, randomly selected from among the full range and variety of the city bar. The information gathered includes the nature of the respondents' legal practice and clients, their personal background characteristics, their attitudes on major political and legal issues, and their memberships and participation in various professional, civic, and social organizations. The interviews were conducted in the spring and summer of 1975 by our own staff, averaged sixty-six minutes in length, and were almost always conducted at the respondent's place of work during business hours.

The population universe included all lawyers with office addresses within the city limits of Chicago, as listed in either *Sullivan's Law Directory for the State of Illinois, 1974–75* or *Martindale-Hubbell Law Directory, 1974*. We used two directories to increase the coverage and to avoid biases of individual directories. (This procedure would not, of course, eliminate biases that the directories may share.) We then drew a true random sample from these lists.[10] Our 777 completed interviews represent 82.1 percent of our original target sample. Only 8.4 percent of our potential respondents explicitly refused to grant an interview; we missed the remaining 9.5 percent because of scheduling problems, time constraints, the subject's illness, and the like. An examination of the known characteristics of those lawyers we failed to include, for whatever reasons, suggests that we may slightly underenumerate lawyers who are not members of the Chi-

10. The sample was drawn by strict random sampling procedures intended to eliminate systematic distortion or bias. For a full description of the sampling method, see Peter Marsden, "Sampling Procedures, Chicago Lawyers Cross-Section Study" (unpublished memorandum, February 17, 1975, available in the files of the American Bar Foundation). The total number of names drawn randomly from the lawyer directories, *Sullivan's Law Directory for the State of Illinois, 1974–75* and *Martindale-Hubbell Law Directory, 1974*, was 1,142. Of those, 196 proved to be deceased, to have moved from Chicago, or otherwise to be ineligible for inclusion in the population. That left 946 lawyers as the total meeting the criteria that were used to define the sample universe.

cago Bar Association and lawyers engaged in solo practice, especially those who maintain only accommodation addresses in the city.[11] This underenumeration, however, is sufficiently small that for most purposes we can treat the completed sample as representative of the defined population universe.[12] We might turn, then, to a presentation of some of the basic characteristics of that sample.

Some Characteristics of Chicago Lawyers

Figure 1.1 (see pp. 12–13) is a presentation of the frequencies with which certain characteristics occurred in our sample of Chicago lawyers. For those who prefer words to pictures, however, we will summarize these distributions briefly, noting features that require explanation or warrant emphasis.

The lawyers in our sample are overwhelmingly white and male. The respondents include 747 whites (97.1 percent of the sample), 21 blacks (2.7 percent), and 1 Oriental (0.1 percent).[13] (All percentages

11. An indication of the reasons why we were unable to schedule interviews with some of the lawyers in the sample may be gleaned from the following article that appeared in the *Chicago Sun-Times:*

> The 100 N. La Salle Building is full of lawyers. On the 21st floor there are a half-dozen lawyers' names on the door, painted gold on little wooden plaques. But none of them is ever in. The switchboard is among the busiest in town, but the answer is always the same: "Mr. Sherman isn't in," or "Mr. Wilson isn't in, would you like to leave a message?" Because it's not really a lawyer's office at all—it's Telephone Secretaries Unlimited, one of the 200 answering services in the Chicago area. It's run by Rosee Torres, who answers the phone for 4,000 Loop lawyers. "We also have 50 doctors," she said. "We're just starting on doctors." It's a busy office.
> She also rents out office space, beginning at $10 an hour, to lawyers who are from out of town or who have just got out of law school and don't have their own offices yet. "Our offices are set up like a law office and no one can tell the difference," she said, and she is right. "If they look at the switchboard, they might think there are hundreds of offices back there." Rosee has helped many young lawyers get started. "When they're just out of law school, they'll rent an office here for an hour and then try to interview as many clients as possible during the hour, not realizing that it takes hours to really sit down and interview a client nicely and get everything they need to know," she said. . . . [Paul McGrath, "Answering Services Go Beyond Call of Duty," *Chicago Sun-Times,* September 5, 1976, p. 5.].

12. While 64.7 percent of the respondents included in our sample were members of the Chicago Bar Association, for example, 60 percent of the nonrespondents were members, according to their listings in the *Martindale-Hubbell* directory. Forty-six percent of our respondents had attended one of four local schools, while 51 percent of the nonrespondents had attended those schools, again according to *Martindale-Hubbell.*

13. Information regarding the race of the respondent was missing in eight instances.

given have been adjusted to exclude the instances of missing information. Because of rounding error, however, the percentages for the individual categories do not always total exactly 100 percent.) Only 30 respondents, or 3.9 percent of the sample, are women. The number of women enrolled in law schools had increased dramatically in the few years preceding our survey,[14] but that recent trend had not then been in progress long enough to have much impact on the traditional male dominance of the Chicago bar. Another of the heralded changes in legal education in the decade before the survey was the increased effort at many law schools to recruit students from minority groups,[15] but our findings indicate that the rise of affirmative action also had not yet had much effect on the racial composition of the bar. Though both the women and the blacks in our sample tend to be somewhat younger than the average respondent, suggesting that both of the developments were beginning to be felt, we do not have sufficient numbers of either to have much confidence in our estimates of the characteristics of those groups in the general population of Chicago lawyers.

Roughly equal numbers of our respondents—just more or just less than 30 percent—fall into each of three age ranges, under 35, 35 to 45, and 46 to 65. Fewer than 10 percent of the lawyers were over 65.

We asked our respondents for two different political affiliations, local and national, because the Democratic party in Chicago was then divided into rather distinct factions. (It still is, to some degree, though the situation now is even more complex and fluid.) At the time of our survey, Mayor Richard J. Daley was still alive. Often referred to as the last of the old-style city political bosses, Daley was also chairman of the Cook County Democratic Central Committee. Respondents who told us that they were "Regular Democrats," in local terms, can be assumed to have been more or less loyal to Mayor Daley's political organization, customarily referred to as the "Regular Democratic Organization."[16] The term "Independent Dem-

14. See Cynthia Epstein, Women in Law (New York: Basic Books, 1981); Robert B. Stevens, "Law Schools and Legal Education, 1879–1979," 14 Valparaiso University Law Review 179–259 (winter 1980), p. 254.
15. Stevens, supra note 14, pp. 252–53. See also James P. White, "Law School Enrollment Continues to Level," 66 American Bar Association Journal 724–25 (June 1980).
16. Three books provide information on contemporary Chicago politics. Two of them, Mike Royko, Boss: Richard J. Daley of Chicago (New York: E. P. Dutton, 1971) and Len O'Connor, Clout: Mayor Daley and His City (Chicago: Henry Regnery, 1975), are quite explicitly anti-Daley, and the other, Milton L. Rakove, Don't Make No Waves—Don't Back No Losers: An Insider's Analysis of the Daley Machine (Bloomington: Indiana University Press, 1975), is more sympathetic to the Regulars.

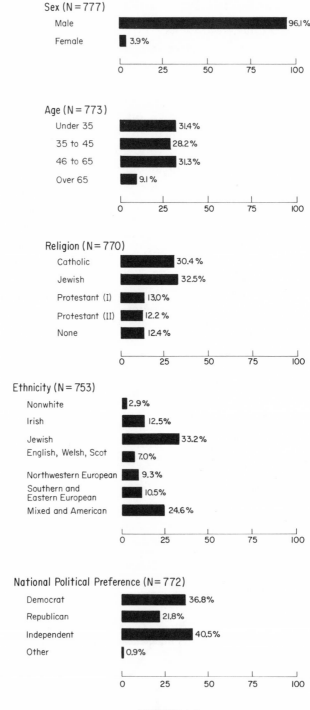

FIGURE 1.1
Selected Characteristics of Chicago Lawyers

Chicago Political Preference (N = 773)

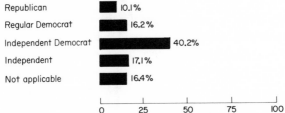

Republican	10.1%
Regular Democrat	16.2%
Independent Democrat	40.2%
Independent	17.1%
Not applicable	16.4%

0   25   50   75   100

Law School (N = 768)

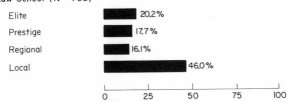

Elite	20.2%
Prestige	17.7%
Regional	16.1%
Local	46.0%

0   25   50   75   100

Practice Setting (N = 772)

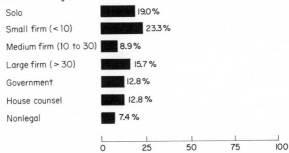

Solo	19.0%
Small firm (< 10)	23.3%
Medium firm (10 to 30)	8.9%
Large firm (> 30)	15.7%
Government	12.8%
House counsel	12.8%
Nonlegal	7.4%

0   25   50   75   100

Law Practice Income (N = 724)

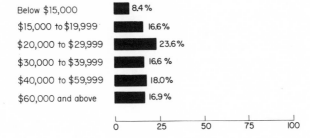

Below $15,000	8.4%
$15,000 to $19,999	16.6%
$20,000 to $29,999	23.6%
$30,000 to $39,999	16.6 %
$40,000 to $59,999	18.0%
$60,000 and above	16.9%

0   25   50   75   100

ocrats" refers to an even looser conglomeration that was generally more liberal and reformist. It was a coalition of these independent Democrats, sympathetic to the presidential candidacy of Senator George McGovern, that unseated the Daley delegation to the 1972 Democratic National Convention. Of those who are "Independents" with respect to Chicago political preference, 72 percent also labeled themselves "Independent" with respect to their national preference. The respondents in the "Not Applicable" category under Chicago Political Preference prefer the Republican party nationally in disproportionate numbers. Most of these respondents live in the suburbs (though they have offices in the city) and probably declined to express a *Chicago* political preference because of their lack of concern with or involvement in Chicago politics. It is interesting to note that a profession that is often thought to be conservative and establishmentarian includes so few Republicans and so many Independent Democrats (in local terms) or Independents (in national terms). These results may be attributable to the fact that our survey was conducted not long after the Watergate revelations, within a year of the resignation of President Nixon. They may also reflect the generally debilitated state of the Republican party within the City of Chicago.

Our respondents were asked a series of questions about their religious and ethnic identifications. Those who said they were Jewish, in response to either set of questions, are included in that category under both the Religion and the Ethnicity headings in figure 1.1. That is, ethnic Jews have been included in the Jewish religion category, and vice versa.[17] The Protestant denominations have been divided into two groups that are often distinguished in the sociological literature.[18] The denominations in group 1 tend to include

17. As the data are presented here, then, respondents of "northwestern European" origin and "southern and eastern European" origin mean non-Jewish respondents of such descent. Our data also permitted us to distinguish, if the analysis appeared to require it, among Orthodox, Conservative and Reform Jews. A majority of our Jewish respondents were Reform, another large group were Conservative, and only a small minority were Orthodox. Analyses making this distinction are reported in chapters 5 and 6. In some analyses not reported in the book we distinguished between western European Jews, primarily German Jews, and eastern European Jews, primarily Russian and Polish Jews, but that distinction adds little that is of use for our purposes. Some of the analyses reported in chapters 5 and 6 distinguish among Catholics of Irish, other northern and western European, and southern and eastern European origin.

18. Bruce L. Warren, "Socioeconomic Achievement and Religion: The American Case," in Edward O. Laumann, ed., *Social Stratification: Research and Theory for the 1970s* (Indianapolis and New York: Bobbs-Merrill, 1970), pp. 130, 152; Liston Pope,

disproportionate numbers of persons of higher socioeconomic status, from older immigrant stock—most numerous in this category
are Presbyterians, Episcopalians, and Congregationalists.[19] The largest number in group 2 are Lutherans, Methodists, Baptists, and Protestants who did not express any denominational preference. Respondents included in the final line of the Ethnicity category are
those who were of mixed national origin, being unable to choose
any nationality as predominant in their ancestry, or who told us
that they were "just American."

In addition to these social background variables, we asked respondents about their education and the nature of their legal work.
The broadest outlines of these professional characteristics are also
summarized in the bar graphs.

We found that nearly half of our sample of Chicago lawyers had
attended one of four local law schools—Chicago Kent, De Paul, Loyola,
and John Marshall—located in the central city. Other law schools are
grouped here in categories that are intended to reflect general repute or
prestige. Though all such categorizations are to some extent arbitrary
and though all are also certain to be distasteful to some, it is necessary to
combine the schools for purposes of analysis because of the small
numbers of respondents attending most of the schools. We believe that
our categories reflect the general standing of the schools at least as well
as any alternative scheme. Only six schools are included in our elite
category: Chicago, Columbia, Harvard, Michigan, Stanford, and Yale.
These six schools ranked at the top of the ratings by law school deans
that were reported by Peter M. Blau and Rebecca Z. Margulies in 1974–
75.[20] The lowest ranking of these schools, Stanford, was rated as among
the top five law schools in the country by 45 of the 104 deans responding to the survey; the next highest school had received only 19 such
ratings. Though other ratings of law schools have appeared since the
Blau and Margulies report, they are quite consistent with the use of
these categories.[21] The largest number of graduates of these elite

"Religion and the Class Structure," *Annals of the American Academy of Political and Social Sciences* 256 (March 1948): 84, 89.

19. Ibid.

20. Peter M. Blau and Rebecca Z. Margulies, "A Research Replication: The Reputations of American Professional Schools," *Change in Higher Education* 6 (winter 1974–75): 44.

21. The various ratings of the law schools are collected in E. Epstein, J. Shostak,
and L. Troy, eds., *Barron's Guide to Law Schools*, 4th ed. (Woodbury, N.Y.: Barron's, 1980), pp. 39–59.

schools in our sample are from the University of Chicago and, next, Harvard. Among the schools included in our prestige category, graduates of Northwestern are by far the most numerous, while the University of Illinois predominates in the regional grouping. Other schools represented in the prestige category are Georgetown, Wisconsin, and Virginia, together with one graduate of the University of Pennsylvania and one from New York University. The regional category includes the remaining law schools of the Big Ten Conference universities and those of Notre Dame and George Washington.[22]

The distribution of our respondents across the various practice settings, which is only one of many possible ways to categorize general types of law practice, reflects the long-term reduction in the proportion of solo practitioners among the bar and the continuing growth in the numbers of both corporate house counsel and government-employed lawyers.[23] These phenomena—the decline of the individual, general practitioner who makes his living through service to a number and variety of clients, and the great increase in the full-time employment of lawyers by a single client, usually either a corporation or a government agency—are probably the most significant changes in the nature of law practice in this century.[24] Many of the lawyers who would formerly have gone into solo practice undoubtedly contribute to the size of the small firm category here. And, though our findings reflect the often-remarked growth during the twentieth century of large law firms,[25] it is important to note

22. Of the 126 respondents in the regional category, 48 attended the University of Illinois, 12 went to Notre Dame, 7 to George Washington, and 6 to Iowa. The remaining respondents in that category attended a total of 33 other law schools, each represented in our sample by 5 or fewer graduates.

The prestige category is even more heavily dominated by graduates of Northwestern; 107 of the 135 respondents in that category attended Northwestern, 12 went to Georgetown, 8 to Wisconsin, and 6 to Virginia.

In the elite school category, there are 67 graduates of Chicago, 49 from Harvard, 21 from Michigan, 12 from Yale, 5 from Columbia, and only 1 from Stanford.

Among the local schools, our sample includes 155 graduates of De Paul, 76 from John Marshall, 67 from Chicago Kent, and 55 from Loyola.

23. The "government" category here includes 21 judges and judicial clerks. In many of the analyses reported later in the book, we deal only with "practicing lawyers." For purposes of those analyses, we do not include judges or their clerks. Thus, combining the 57 lawyers found to be doing "nonlegal" jobs with 21 judges and clerks, we get a total of 78 "not practicing law," leaving a remainder of 699 practicing lawyers. It is that base of 699 that we use in most of the analyses presented in chapters 2, 3, 4, and 6.

24. Sikes, Carson, and Gorai, *supra* note 1, pp. 10 and 11.

25. Ibid.

that only about a sixth of all Chicago lawyers worked in firms with more than thirty practitioners. The respondents included here in the nonlegal category were not presently engaged in the practice of law on a regular basis.[26]

Finally, we asked all of our respondents to indicate the amount of the income that they received from law practice. As might be expected, a larger number of our respondents refused to answer that question than any other in the interview. Of the 777 lawyers interviewed, 724 did respond, but we have no way of assessing whether there is systematic bias in the failure to respond and few ways of evaluating the validity or truthfulness of the answers that we received. It is plausible that some may have exaggerated their incomes as a form of boasting, while others may have understated theirs through modesty or from fear of the Internal Revenue Service. (Though our interviewers did not much resemble IRS agents, some respondents might have thought it desirable for their responses to be consistent with their tax returns.) And we cannot be certain that either possible bias in their answers is not systematically related to other variables in the respondents' background or practice characteristics. Therefore, we report these findings with more than the usual degree of caution. Nonetheless, our findings appear to be generally consistent with such other data as are available on lawyers' incomes.[27] That more than half of our respondents reported income from law practice alone of $30,000 or more per year would indicate, of course, that the lawyers were earning far more than was the average Chicagoan in 1975.[28]

Having summarized some of the major characteristics of our sample of Chicago lawyers, let us note some of the general features of the legal profession nationally and call particular attention to the ways in which it has changed in recent years.

26. The "nonlegal" group includes 10 teachers of law.
27. See B. Peter Pashigian, "The Number and Earnings of Lawyers: Some Recent Findings," 1978 *American Bar Foundation Research Journal* 51–82 (winter).
28. In 1975, median family income in the U.S. in current dollars was $13,719. Only 5 percent of U.S. families in that year had incomes exceeding $34,138, again in current dollars. In 1977, the median income of families in metropolitan areas of more than 1,000,000 population was $18,196. U.S., Department of Commerce, Bureau of the Census, *Social Indicators III* (December 1980), pp. 480, 486–87, tables 9/13 and 9/20. See also, U.S., Department of Labor, Bureau of Labor Statistics, *Area Wage Survey* "Chicago Metropolitan Area, May 1975" (Bulletin 1850–32, September 1975), pp. 3–30.

The Profession: Context

The social differentiation within the bar that this book seeks to analyze has occurred despite official endorsement of a holistic conception of the profession. Unlike the medical profession, which formally recognizes and certifies many specialities, the legal profession enshrines the myth of the omnicompetent practitioner. Until very recently, the profession's ethical rules forbade lawyers to represent themselves as specialists except in three small, abstruse fields: patents, trademarks, and admiralty.[29] In the last few years, some states have begun to certify legal specialists in a few fields, but these initial steps in the formal recognition of specialization have been halting and tentative, being formally labeled "experimental."[30] Illinois still has not adopted any scheme of specialty certification.[31] Moreover, certain legal institutions buttress the resistance to specialization. The bar examinations, for example, require some minimal level of competence in all of the major, traditional fields of law as a condition of entry into the profession. And yet, in spite of the continuing vitality of the myth of omnicompetence, the inexorable advance of the division of labor within the legal profession has been too obvious to ignore. Nearly fifty years ago, Karl Llewellyn said of the "modern metropolitan bar": "Most of its best brains, most of its inevitable leaders, have moved masswise out of court work, out of a general practice akin to that of the family doctor, into highly paid specialization in the service of large corporations."[32] While specialization was occurring at the individual level, however, a process of integration was taking place in the organizational contexts within which the law is practiced. Industrialization, the rise of large corporations, and the consequent growth of government regulation of

29. See American Bar Association Code of Professional Responsibility, DR 2–105(A)(1) (1977); see also Richard Zehnle, "Specialization in the Legal Profession," in *Legal Specialization,* American Bar Association, Specialization Monograph no. 2 (Chicago, 1976), pp. 20–33. (The Zehnle paper was also published separately by the American Bar Foundation, 1975.)

30. See Zehnle, *supra* note 29. See also Jerome A. Hochberg, "The Drive to Specialization," in Ralph Nader and Mark Green, eds., *Verdicts on Lawyers* (New York: Thomas Y. Crowell, 1976), pp. 118–26; Marvin W. Mindes, "Proliferation, Specialization, and Certification: The Splitting of the Bar" 11 *University of Toledo Law Review* 273–301 (winter 1980).

31. See John H. Dickason, "What Is Specialization?," 68 *Illinois Bar Journal* 714–15 (July 1980).

32. Karl N. Llewellyn, "The Bar Specializes—With What Results?" *Annals of the American Academy of Political and Social Science* 167 (1933): 177.

economic enterprise have for at least a century steadily increased the consolidation of law practice into larger and larger firms. Though two-thirds of the lawyers in private practice at the end of World War II were individual entrepreneurs, or solo practitioners, the solos had declined to half of the private practitioners by 1970 and the trend was even more pronounced in large cities.[33] Moreover, the number of private practitioners of all sorts, including lawyers in firms, declined from 89 percent of the bar in 1940 to 73 percent in 1970 as a result of large increases in the numbers of salaried lawyers employed by corporations as "house counsel" or by the various levels of government.[34] There is reason to believe that these trends have continued since 1970 (see figure 1.1).

These developments have taken place in the context of a rapid increase in the overall size of the profession. In the last few decades, the estimated number of lawyers in the nation has increased steadily; there were about 220,000 in 1951, 285,000 in 1960, 355,000 in 1970, well in excess of 400,000 in 1975, and in 1980 the estimate was slightly more or slightly fewer than 500,000 American lawyers.[35] Though the population of the country has also grown during this period, the number of Americans per lawyer has declined from 696 persons per lawyer in 1951 to 572 per lawyer in 1970, and 440 in 1979.[36] In 1970, there were about 14,000 lawyers with offices in the City of Chicago, the population analyzed in this book.[37] Though it is very difficult and perhaps misleading to compare numbers of lawyers across national boundaries because of great differences in the roles included within the category "lawyers," as well as because of the usual imprecision in the collection of such data, the best esti-

33. Sikes, Carson, and Gorai, *supra* note 1, p. 10; Jack Ladinsky, "The Impact of Social Backgrounds of Lawyers on Law Practice and the Law," 16 *Journal of Legal Education* 127, 139 (1963).

34. Sikes, Carson and Gorai, *supra* note 1, p. 10.

35. Sikes, Carson, and Gorai, *supra* note 1, p. 5, is the source of the 1951, 1960, and 1970 figures. The 1975 and 1980 figures are ABA estimates.

36. Sikes, Carson, and Gorai, *supra* note 1, p. 6, for the 1951 and 1970 estimates. The 1979 figure is from Murray Schwartz, "The Reorganization of the Legal Profession," 58 *Texas Law Review* 1269, 1270 (1980).

37. According to the U.S. Census, there were 13,400 lawyers and judges in the city of Chicago in 1970, out of only 16,087 in the entire State of Illinois; U.S., Department of Commerce, Bureau of the Census, *1970 Census of Population*, "Illinois Census" (Washington, D.C.: Government Printing Office, 1973), pp. 997 and 1011. The *1971 Lawyer Statistical Report*, however, published by the American Bar Foundation, counted 14,375 Chicago lawyers in 1970 and a total of 22,036 for the state. The ABF also reported that the *Martindale-Hubbell* directory listed 13,281 Chicago lawyers in that same year. See Sikes, Carson, and Gorai, *supra* note 1, pp. 22 and 55.

mates are that in the mid-1970s the numbers of lawyers per unit of population in the United States were twice those of Canada and England, about seven times those of France and the Netherlands, and about fourteen times that of Japan.[38]

The expansion of the legal profession in the United States and the simultaneous decline of the solo practitioner has meant that the social roles of lawyers have also changed. C. Wright Mills's characterization of the nineteenth-century advocate may be compared to what we know about the modern urban lawyer:

> Before the ascendancy of the large corporation, skill and eloquence in advocacy selected nineteenth-century leaders of the bar; reputations and wealth were created and maintained in the courts, of which the lawyer was an officer. He was an agent of the law, handling the general interests of society, as fixed and allowed in the law; his day's tasks were as varied as human activity and experience itself. An opinion leader, a man whose recommendations to the community counted, who handled obligations and rights of intimate family and life problems, the liberty and property of all who had them, the lawyer personally pointed out the course of the law and counseled his client against the pitfalls of illegality. Deferred to by his client, he carefully displayed the dignity he claimed to embody. Rewarded for apparent honesty, carrying an ethical halo, held to be fit material for high statesmanship, the lawyer upheld public service and was professionally above business motives.[39]

Though Mills's picture is probably exaggerated or idealized, it does seem likely that the prespecialized lawyer dealt with a greater range of human problems—all of the problems, save those of health and of the soul, that were of greatest consequence to the individual. They dealt with, in Mills's phrase, "the liberty and property of all who had them." The modern lawyer, by contrast, encounters a much smaller range of problems, and those are unlikely to be the intimate problems of an individual or his family. Apart from financial woes, relatively few lawyers now confront human suffering in the course of their work. While it is hard to believe that the nineteenth-century bar can have been so pure (or, indeed, so "professional") as Mills would have it, it is plausible that the modern, specialized lawyer may be less involved with his community than was the old general practitioner. In part, this may simply be a concomi-

---

38. See Marc Galanter, "Larger than Life: Mega-law and Mega-lawyering in the Contemporary United States," (unpublished paper, 1980) n. 36.

39. C. Wright Mills, *White Collar: The American Middle Classes* (New York: Oxford University Press, 1951), p. 121.

tant of urbanization, a difference between the ethos of the big city and of the small town. But the same result might also follow from the process of specialization. From whichever cause, then, and notwithstanding the obvious continuing prominence of lawyers in politics,[40] the urban lawyer is now probably more likely to be a technician and less likely to be the gentleman advocate who maintains both professional and social distance from his clients, less likely to play the role of sage, a quasi-judicial figure who personally resolves disputes within families, within church congregations, or between the Lions and the Elks. In spite of this change in the social roles of most lawyers, however, we believe that the importance of the roles of the modern, specialized lawyers fully justifies the attention given them in this book.

Talcott Parsons and some generally like-minded theorists, including Joseph Ben-David and William J. Goode, have argued that the growth of the professions is one of the most important features of modern industrial societies.[41] In the introduction to his last book, a retrospective on over forty years of scholarly work, Parsons commented:

> [T]he penetration of the professional complex beyond the more academic parts of the university into many branches of the organization of society . . . may be regarded as an important aspect of a principal structural change in modern society. . . . The central process has been the emergence of . . . the "cognitive complex" into a new position of structural salience in Western societies, in part superseding the previous position of the economy. For this reason (among others) a predominantly economic interpretation of the course of development of modern societies is unacceptable to me. . . .[42]

The occupations included by these theorists within the "professions" were all lines of work that emphasized involvement with the "cognitive complex"—that is, in a sense, the emphasis was on the

40. See generally Heinz Eulau and John D. Sprague, *Lawyers in Politics: A Study in Professional Convergence* (Indianapolis: Bobbs-Merrill, 1964); Michael Cohen, "Lawyers and Political Careers," 3 *Law and Society Review* 563–74 (May 1969); Irwin H. Bromall, "Lawyers in Politics: An Exploratory Study of the Wisconsin Bar," 1968 *Wisconsin Law Review* 751. For more recent scholarship, see Paul L. Hain and James E. Pierson, "Lawyers and Politics Revisited—Structural Advantages of Lawyer-Politicians," *American Journal of Political Science* 19 (February 1975): 41–51.

41. See esp. Talcott Parsons, "Professions," *Encyclopedia of the Social Sciences*, vol. 12 (1968), pp. 536–47; Joseph Ben-David, "Professions in the Class System of Present Day Societies: A Trend Report and Bibliography," *Current Sociology* 12 (1963–64): 247–330; William J. Goode, *supra* note 9, pp. 194–200.

42. Talcott Parsons, "Introduction to Part I," *Action Theory and the Human Condition* (New York: Free Press, 1978), p. 13.

"learned" in the term "learned profession." The professions thus were seen as rising to prominence naturally or almost inevitably because they were functional to the needs of complex, urbanized, modern societies.

Though even the scholars who are counted as adherents of this functionalist view of the professions differ on the specific list of attributes that are said to distinguish the professions from other occupations, most would agree on the primacy of the professional's possession of a body of arcane knowledge, acquired only after an extended period of specialized training, and they also tend to agree substantially on other general characteristics of the professions, including some or all of the following: professionals enjoy an unusual degree of independence or autonomy vis-à-vis their clients in work decisions (this autonomy is said to occur because the knowledge professionals possess is not shared by the clients); professionals are generally accorded elevated social standing or prestige, and tend to be compensated accordingly; the professions manifest devotion to public service rather than to narrow self-interest; and, associated with this emphasis on duty, the professions inculcate in their members special standards of ethical conduct, which are far more specific and exacting than are the common norms of the society.

There is, however, an opposing view, the lines of division of opinion corresponding generally to the split between the functionalist and the conflict schools of thought, to which we have already referred (see p. 6). The functionalists believe that it is possible to identify sets of characteristics that distinguish the professions from other occupations—the characteristics that serve their functions. The conflict or "power" theorists, on the other hand, contend that no such set of traits that account for the social standing of the professions has been or can be defined. This view has been succinctly put by Magali Larson in her influential book, *The Rise of Professionalism:*

> [T]he professional phenomenon does not have clear boundaries. Either its dimensions are devoid of a clear empirical referent, or its attributes are so concrete that occupational groups trying to upgrade their status can copy them with relative ease. For instance, it is often emphasized that professional training must be prolonged, specialized, and have a theoretical base. Yet, as Eliot Freidson ironically points out, it is never stated *how* long; *how* theoretical, or *how* specialized training must be in order to qualify, since all formal training "takes some time," is "somewhat specialized," and involves some attempt at generalization. The ser-

vice orientation is even more problematic: it is, undoubtedly, part of the ideology and one of the prescriptive norms which organized professions explicitly avow. Yet the implicit assumption that the behavior of individual professionals is more ethical, as a norm, than that of individuals in lesser occupations has seldom, if ever, been tested by empirical evidence. . . .

The most common ideal-type of profession combines heterogeneous elements and links them by implicit though untested propositions such as the proposition that prestige and autonomy flow "naturally" from the cognitive and normative bases of professional work.[43]

The conflict theorists thus argue that the status of an occupation as a profession is not determined by its possession of some identifiable set of objective characteristics but rather that such status is politically determined—that the claim of professional status is a claim of entitlement to legitimacy or a form of power, asserted by many occupational groups with more or less success depending upon the extent to which they can mobilize various sorts of resources.

Quite apart from the obvious divergence in ideological preconceptions, some of the difference in these two perspectives on the professions may be accounted for by methodological style. The vantage point of the functionalists is typically quite remote from workaday professional practice, stressing instead the macrostructural features of the society, very abstractly conceived, and focusing on the sweep of major institutional changes over lengthy historical periods. Detail is obviously lost at such a distance. The conflict view has more often arisen in the context of close-up studies of rank-and-file practitioners making their daily livings. This approach was originally identified with the field work of the "Chicago School" of sociology, particularly with the work of Everett C. Hughes[44] and his students, including Eliot Freidson[45] and Jerome Carlin.[46] Carlin's classic book, *Lawyers on Their Own*, which is based on interviews with one hundred Chicago solo practitioners, gives the flavor of the daily scramble to hustle clients and to make ends meet, and it notes the conflict between these lawyers and the more prestigious practitio-

---

43. Magali Sarfatti Larson, *The Rise of Professionalism: A Sociological Analysis* (Berkeley: University of California Press, 1977), p. xi.

44. See esp. Everett C. Hughes, *Men and Their Work* (Glencoe, Ill.: Free Press, 1958).

45. Eliot Freidson, *Profession of Medicine; A Study of the Sociology of Applied Knowledge* (New York: Dodd, Mead, 1970); idem., *Professional Dominance; The Social Structure of Medical Care* (New York: Atherton Press, 1970).

46. Jerome E. Carlin, *Lawyers on Their Own: A Study of Individual Practitioners in Chicago* (New Brunswick, N. J.: Rutgers University Press, 1962).

ners in the large corporate law firms who were seen as dominating the organized bar. Questioning the self-satisfied pretensions of the elite and instead adopting the viewpoint of lowly "outsiders" is a hallmark of the early Chicago School's approach to the study of the occupations of urban America. More recently, the conflict-oriented writings on the legal profession have adopted an explicitly Marxian approach.[47]

Works that attempt some theoretical synthesis or historical analysis of the nature of the legal profession have in fact been more numerous than have efforts to collect primary data on the social organization of the bar.[48] With the exception of Ladinsky's pioneering work on social stratification among Detroit lawyers[49] and Carlin's Chicago study, most of the primary research on the bar in the last

47. See, e.g., Larson, *supra* note 43; Richard Abel, "The Rise of Professionalism," 6 *British Journal of Law and Society* 83–98 (1979); "Socializing the Legal Profession: Can Redistributing Lawyers' Services Achieve Social Justice?" 1 *Law and Policy Quarterly* 5–51 (1979); Maureen Cain, "The General Practice Lawyer and the Client: Towards a Radical Conception," 7 *International Journal of the Sociology of Law* 331–54 (1979).

48. In addition to Larson, *supra* note 43, and the articles of Richard Abel, *supra* note 47, the theoretical works include most especially Dietrich Rueschemeyer, *Lawyers and Their Society: A Comparative Study of the Legal Profession in Germany and the United States* (Cambridge: Harvard University Press, 1973), a thoughtful and suggestive work on the two systems. Brian Abel-Smith and Robert B. Stevens, *Lawyers and the Courts: A Sociological Study of the English Legal System, 1750–1965* (Cambridge,: Harvard University Press, 1967), and Michael Zander, *Lawyers and the Public Interest: A Study in Restrictive Practices* (London: Weidenfeld and Nicolson, 1968), are incisive analyses of the English legal profession, both of them quite critical in intent. More general descriptions and analyses may be found in Quintin Johnstone and Dan Hopson, Jr., *Lawyers and Their Work: An Analysis of the Legal Profession in the United States and England* (Indianapolis: Bobbs-Merrill, 1967); and in Albert P. Blaustein and Charles O. Porter, *The American Lawyer: A Summary of the Legal Profession* (Chicago: University of Chicago Press, 1954).

Important historical studies of American lawyers include J. Willard Hurst, *The Growth of American Law: The Law Makers* (Boston: Little, Brown, 1950); Lawrence Friedman, *A History of American Law* (New York: Simon and Schuster, 1973); and Jerold S. Auerbach, *Unequal Justice: Lawyers and Social Change in Modern America* (New York: Oxford University Press, 1976).

Additional primary data on Chicago lawyers are reported in Frances Zemans and Victor Rosenblum, *The Making of a Public Profession* (Chicago: American Bar Foundation, 1981). Though that study is primarily concerned with legal education, its findings about the characteristics of Chicago lawyers are quite consistent with ours. Their data were collected by mailed questionnaires in the fall of 1975, just after our survey, and their response rate was 66.4 percent. The Zemans and Rosenblum book was a part of the American Bar Foundation's larger program of research on legal education, which was conducted under the general direction of Spencer Kimball and Felice Levine.

49. Jack Ladinsky, "Careers of Lawyers, Law Practice and Legal Institutions," *American Sociological Review* 28 (1963): 47; idem., "The Impact of Social Backgrounds of Lawyers on Law Practice and the Law," 16 *Journal of Legal Education* 127 (1963); idem. "The Social Profile of a Metropolitan Bar: A Statistical Survey in Detroit," 1964 *Michigan State Bar Journal* 12 (February).

two or three decades has focused either on a specific problem or policy area or on lawyers in a limited type of practice. Among the former, noteworthy examples include Carlin's subsequent research on the ethical conduct of New York private practitioners,[50] Douglas Rosenthal's work on the relationship between lawyer and client,[51] Stewart Macaulay's study of lawyers' handling of consumer law matters in Wisconsin,[52] Richard A. Watson and Rondal G. Downing's book on the roles of Missouri lawyers in judicial selection,[53] and Frances Zemans and Victor Rosenblum's recent work on legal education.[54] Among the studies of lawyers in particular specialties, we would note Erwin O. Smigel's early and excellent study, *The Wall Street Lawyer*,[55] Hubert J. O'Gorman's work on divorce lawyers,[56] Arthur L. Wood's book on criminal lawyers,[57] and the recent national survey of legal services lawyers conducted by a group of scholars at the University of Wisconsin.[58] Valuable as all of these major pieces of research are for what they tell us about their specific areas of concern, they give us only a sketchy and rather disjointed picture of the overall social structure of the legal profession in any geographic area. This book attempts to provide some of that missing detail for one major city and to fill in some of the gaps in the analysis.

50. Jerome E. Carlin, *Lawyers' Ethics: A Survey of the New York City Bar* (New York: Russell Sage, 1966).
51. Douglas Rosenthal, *Lawyer and Client: Who's in Charge?* (New York: Russell Sage, 1974).
52. Stewart Macaulay, "Lawyers and Consumer Protection Laws," 14 *Law and Society Review* 115 (1979).
53. Richard A. Watson and Rondal G. Downing, *The Politics of the Bench and the Bar: Judicial Selection Under the Missouri Nonpartisan Court Plan* (New York: John Wiley, 1969).
54. Zemans and Rosenblum, *supra* note 48.
55. The study, first published in 1964, has been published in a second edition, which includes a chapter updating the original data; Erwin O. Smigel, *The Wall Street Lawyer: Professional Organization Man?*, 2d ed. (Bloomington: Indiana University Press, 1969).
56. Hubert J. O'Gorman, *Lawyers and Matrimonial Cases: A Study of Informal Pressures in Private Professional Practice* (New York: Free Press of Glencoe, 1963).
57. Arthur L. Wood, *Criminal Lawyer* (New Haven: College and University Press, 1967).
58. Joel F. Handler, Ellen Jane Hollingsworth, and Howard S. Erlanger, *Lawyers and the Pursuit of Legal Rights* (New York: Academic Press, 1978).

The Plan of the Book

The book deals with three severable ways of looking at the structure of the bar and then, in a concluding essay, weaves those three strands of analysis together in comprehensive interpretation of the nature of the social worlds of Chicago lawyers. Part two of the book, "Lawyers' Roles: The Predominance of Client-centered Structure," adopts an untraditional approach. Rather than focus on the individual lawyers, their characteristics and careers, it uses fields of law as the primary units of analysis. The fields are conceived as a set of distinct roles performed by lawyers, and the objective is to analyze the structure of the profession in terms of these roles—the division of labor of the bar (chapter 2); the differentiation of lawyers' roles by social background characteristics, education, types of tasks performed, and organizational context of practice (chapter 3); and the allocation to the roles of systematically varying levels of prestige or derogation within the profession (chapter 4). All of these analyses suggest a thesis that emerges as the major theme of the book: that the social structure of the legal profession is not primarily determined by the cognitive base of the profession, by the doctrinal categories of the law or by the types of arcane training or skills used by the lawyers, nor by other interests or values that arise within the profession itself, but rather by the character of the clients served by the different sorts of lawyers and by ties to related social groupings external to the profession, including ethnoreligious and political groups.

Part three of the book, "Lawyers' Lives: Social Background, Social Values, and Career Mobility," shifts the level of analysis to a focus on individual lawyers. In chapter 5, we analyze lawyers' social and political values. The literature on the formation of values suggests that social background and early socialization experiences will be important determinants. Our findings are consistent with these general observations, but we also find that lawyers' values tend to correspond to the interests of the clients they serve. We then address the issue of whether this correspondence between lawyers' values and their clients' interests results from a process in which lawyers come to identify with the positions of their clients over the course of years in the service of those interests or whether the values come first and the affinity thus occurs because lawyers enter areas of practice that serve interests congenial to their preexisting values. In analyzing the course of lawyers' careers, chapter 6 carries some of these same themes a step further and adds substantial additional data. The chapter documents the influence of social background on placement in initial career positions and traces the continuing effects of background characteristics (particularly, ethnoreligious identification) on subsequent career mobility. The overall picture that emerges in this part of the book is of lawyers with distinctly different values following quite separate career paths in the service of fundamentally different types of clients.

Part four, "Lawyers' Ties: Networks of Association, Organizations, and Political Activities," shifts the focus yet again. The three chapters in this part of the book all deal not with fields of law nor with individual lawyers' professional careers but with the relationships among lawyers—their friendships with both lawyers and nonlawyers, their professional relationships, their joint activity in bar associations, and their connections with various constituencies within the bar. These analyses, while confirming the role of client interests in structuring the relationships among lawyers, also point to the salience of other group loyalties (principally, political and ethnic group affiliations) in which the bar is enmeshed.

The concluding chapter reviews some of the findings, but it makes no attempt at a comprehensive summary. Rather, it proposes a sustained interpretation of the processes that underlie the social structure of Chicago's bar.

Is Chicago Typical?

The importance of ethnicity in our analyses of Chicago lawyers could reflect general characteristics of the legal profession, at least as the bar is constituted in large cities, or it could be peculiar to Chicago. In his classic essay on Chicago's social system, A. J. Liebling, the Henry Mayhew of American urban sociology, commented on the city's ethnic segregation:

> Communication between the residents of the different wards is further limited by the pronounced tendency of immigrant groups in Chicago to coagulate geographically. In Chicago, a man known as a Pole or Norwegian may not have been in Poland or Norway, or of parents born there. If even only his grandparents were so born, he refers to himself as a Pole

or a Norwegian if he wants to sell coffins or groceries or life insurance to others like himself. A national identification is absolutely essential if he wishes to enter politics. A Chicago party ticket is an international patchwork, like Europe after the Treaty of Versailles. Most of the members of the Chicago national blocs, however, think of Europe as it was cut up by the Congress of Vienna. The great waves of immigration that carried them or their forefathers to their jobs in this country ended with the beginning of the First World War. . . . The national blocs are as entirely cut off from Europe as they are from the rest of America—or from the next ward. And the division between the Negro wards and the white is even more drastic.[59]

On the other hand, much the same was true of other large American cities in the early 1950s, when Liebling's ethnography was published.[60] The salience of religious background in the patterns of stratification among Detroit and New York lawyers, documented by Ladinsky[61] and Carlin,[62] respectively, are generally consistent with our own observations. If we were to replicate our study in other major American cities that vary along a social stability dimension—with, perhaps, Boston, Philadelphia, Baltimore, and St. Louis near one end of the continuum and Houston, Phoenix, Atlanta, and Los Angeles closer to the other—we would expect to find that Chicago lies somewhere between the extremes, particularly with respect to the rigidity of its patterns of social stratification. But that research has not been done.

Until replications have been completed in other cities, we will not be sure of the extent to which Chicago lawyers are typical. We believe, however, that Chicago is an important and interesting case in its own right, and we know of no reason to believe that its bar will be unrepresentative in fundamental respects of those in other large American cities with diversified economies.

59. A. J. Liebling, *Chicago: The Second City* (New York: Alfred Knopf, 1952), pp. 96–100.
60. See Stanley Lieberson, *Ethnic Patterns in American Cities* (New York: Free Press of Glencoe, 1963), pp. 44–91.
61. Ladinsky, *supra* note 49.
62. Carlin, *supra* note 50.

PART II

Lawyers' Roles:
The Predominance of
Client-centered Structure

INTRODUCTION: DEFINING THE FIELDS OF LAW

SOCIOLOGICAL studies of the legal profession have customarily used the individual practitioner as the unit of analysis. This is true both of the conventional analyses of cross-sectional survey information[1] and of the accounts of lawyers at work, whether in large law firms, divorce courts, or solo practice.[2] What could be more natural or commonsensical than to encapsulate lawyers as identifiable persons with interesting biographies? But the assumption that the individual is the proper unit of analysis may lead us to neglect the import of a hard-won sociological insight—that it is not persons as totalities but persons in roles, engaged in regular transactions with

---

1. E.g., Jack Ladinsky, "Careers of Lawyers, Law Practice, and Legal Institutions," *American Sociological Review* 28 (1963): 47; idem., "The Impact of Social Backgrounds of Lawyers on Law Practice and the Law," 16 *Journal of Legal Education* 127 (1963); idem., "The Social Profile of a Metropolitan Bar: A Statistical Survey in Detroit," 1964 *Michigan State Bar Journal* 12 (February); Jerome E. Carlin, *Lawyers' Ethics: A Survey of the New York City Bar* (New York: Russell Sage, 1966); Joel F. Handler, Ellen Jane Hollingsworth, and Howard S. Erlanger, *Lawyers and the Pursuit of Legal Rights* (New York: Academic Press, 1978).

2. E.g., on large law firms, Erwin O. Smigel, *The Wall Street Lawyer: Professional Organization Man?*, 2d ed. (Bloomington: Indiana University Press, 1969); on divorce courts, Hubert J. O'Gorman, *Lawyers and Matrimonial Cases: A Study of Informal Pressures in Private Professional Practice* (New York: Free Press of Glencoe, 1963); on solo practice, Jerome E. Carlin, *Lawyers on Their Own: A Study of Individual Practitioners in Chicago* (New Brunswick: Rutgers University Press, 1962).

other persons performing related social roles, who are the constitutive elements of a social system.[3]

In complex societies, people occupy many social positions simultaneously. If we are to understand the confusing and fluid social reality, rarely demarcated with unambiguous natural markers setting off one field of social activity from another, we must seek to identify those aspects of an actor's social behavior that define his membership in a particular social system. This analytic delineation, indicating where one social role ends and another begins, must ultimately be arbitrary, however, both as a theoretical and as an empirical or practical matter. There has long been debate over the "proper" roles, responsibilities, and privileges of the lawyer with regard to clients, fellow lawyers, the public, and the courts.[4] Even with the relative crystallization in recent decades of the rules of entry into the bar, requiring specialized training and examinations, ambiguities remain about when a person is functioning as a lawyer, as a business or marital advisor, or as a concerned citizen. The lawyer's role is still the product of an ill-defined process of social and self-labeling.

The disparate social roles or positions whose incumbents constitute the class lawyers are linked to very diverse role partners (e.g., personal and corporate clients, fellow attorneys, court officials, or the public at large), and the several lawyers' roles require quite different skills. Many of them require mastery of esoteric or arcane legal knowledge, but others have little to do with formal legal training. Some can be distinguished from other occupational role incumbents—such as real estate agents, bankers, or tax accountants—only with great difficulty, if at all. One of our key conceptual and empirical tasks, then, is to define the nature of these diverse work tasks in a manner that characterizes the social roles of lawyers. These role positions, and not the individuals who perform them, will be the unit of analysis in the discussion to follow. Since no description of these positions can hope to pay exhaustive attention to every variant detail of their activities, the identification of the set

3. Talcott Parsons, *The Social System* (Glencoe, Ill.: Free Press, 1951); Robert K. Merton, *Social Theory and Social Structure*, rev. and enlarged ed. (New York: Free Press, 1968).
4. See J. Willard Hurst, *The Growth of American Law: The Law Makers* (Boston: Little, Brown, 1950); Magali Sarfatti Larson, *The Rise of Professionalism: A Sociological Analysis* (Berkeley: University of California Press, 1977).

of generalized role positions to which incumbents may be assigned is a crucial step of empirical abstraction. We will use the *fields of law* as these generalized role positions, as the primary analytic units, to which individual practitioners are variably assigned.

Analysis of the social structure of the profession presupposes some description of the extent to which groups of lawyers differ in the tasks they perform, in the functions they serve, in the values they hold, or in other social characteristics. Insofar as they differ in work they perform as a part of what is socially labeled as their professional activity, we may say that they occupy distinct legal roles. The categories of lawyers' work employed in our analysis were, therefore, intended to be a set of these distinct roles, but until we had collected our data we did not know which fields of law were, in fact, socially distinct. Our approach to this dilemma was to begin with categories that consisted of commonly used labels for types of legal work—that is, we accepted for test and examination a set of preexisting, socially defined categories. One goal of our research, then, was to determine the extent to which these categories that are in common use describe roles that are, in fact, distinct. If our analysis should disclose that the social characteristics of two or more fields are substantially identical, we would conclude that, for our purposes, these categories collapse into one, more general role.

Many of the recognized fields of law correspond to bodies of doctrine that are generally regarded as distinct legal subjects and are taught as separate courses in law school—for example, crimes, real estate, commercial transactions, personal injury, tax, labor, corporations, antitrust, and securities. But the practicing bar commonly distinguishes between two sides of many of these doctrinal areas, sides that serve adverse clients—for example, criminal defense versus prosecution, personal injury plaintiffs' work versus personal injury defense, and labor law on the union side versus the management side. Other fields divide into parts that, though not necessarily adverse, are nonetheless distinct. Corporate tax planning differs from personal income tax work, real estate development work from home mortgage preparation and title searching, and corporate litigation from a general trial practice that may encompass bits of divorce, commercial, personal injury, or even criminal work. As these examples make clear, lawyers are accustomed to think in terms of categories of work that distinguish, within broader doctrinal areas, fields or subfields defined by the types of clients served.[5]

Generalizing, we may say that a field of law is a set of doctrines that is directed toward the regulation of a particular category of persons or corporate actors, sometimes further differentiated by the adversary system into specialties that serve only one side of the case. (Included within the meaning of the term "doctrine" as it is used here are the procedural rules dealt with in the practice of the field—the rules governing the jurisdiction of the federal courts, for example.) Thus, the boundaries among the fields of law are not the products of pure intellectual invention. Admiralty and labor law were not created as distinct fields by ratiocination alone. The dividing lines are defined by the needs of types of clients—that is, by the existence of categories of actors, varying in size and inclusiveness, who have been subjected to legal regulation or who make or defend claims cognizable at law. The law itself sometimes has a role in creating these specialized groupings of actors or in labeling them as a distinct group. The antitrust laws (the Sherman Act and the Clayton Act), for example, created a new potential type of clients, firms contemplating mergers that might be thought to constitute "monopolies" or "combinations in restraint of trade." New clients were also created by the Wagner Act (National Labor Relations Act), which gave legal recognition to labor unions as collective bargaining agents.

The categories of actors dealt with by the various fields of law are, of course, overlapping, and they differ in size or inclusiveness. The criminal law, for example, is addressed to the whole society (in form, at least), while other fields are directed toward much more narrowly defined groups such as the shipowners and charterers who are subject to the admiralty law. Specialized courts or regulatory agencies may be created to deal with these more narrow fields, regulating a strictly delimited constituency—the Federal Communi-

5. Indeed, the type of client may even determine in good measure the recognized doctrinal categories. And doctrinal areas with no corresponding type of client—constitutional law, for example—may not produce any distinct specialty of field of practice. By noting that the fields of practice often correspond to courses taught in law school, we do not intend to imply that the treatment of a subject as a unit of law school instruction establishes that it is proper to regard that subject as a coherent body of doctrine, analytically severable from other bodies of legal theory. Law schools may well organize their curricula in response to demand, which may in turn be structured by client type. For further consideration of the relative roles of doctrinal affinity and of client demand in organizing the practice of the fields of law, see pp. 55 and 79-83.

cations Commission to regulate broadcasters, for example—and these narrow specialties may then be practiced in a particular institutional setting almost exclusively.

A first step in our analysis, therefore, is to ascertain the extent to which the operational definitions of the customary categories of legal work—which may themselves influence the structure of the profession—are determined by corresponding categories of client types rather than by doctrinal categories or other systematic theory.

Chapter 2

THE ORGANIZATION

OF LAWYERS' WORK*

THE ALLOCATION among lawyers of the various sorts of tasks that the profession is called upon to perform is an important determinant of the other patterns of social differentiation within the profession and thus of its degree of social integration. In this chapter we analyze three interrelated characteristics of the fields of law practice. The first deals with the amount, or volume, of effort devoted to each of the fields. What are the relative amounts of "lawyers' effort"—the work that lawyers do qua lawyers—expended in the various fields of law? To answer this question will require us to allocate the effort exhaustively across the fields, which will not be easy. The fields surely differ greatly, however, in the volume of attention they receive from lawyers considered either collectively or as individual practitioners. Some fields, such as eminent domain

*This chapter is based on our article "The Organization of Lawyers' Work: Size, Intensity, and Co-Practice of the Fields of Law," that appeared in 1979 *American Bar Foundation Research Journal* 217–46 (spring). A version of this paper was also presented at the annual meeting of the American Sociological Association, San Francisco, September 1978. The chapter has been extensively revised, however, and some of the data analyses presented here differ from those in the article. The data have been further scrutinized and cleaned, and additional coding errors have been detected and corrected. Some of the numbers differ slightly from those in the article, therefore, but the general findings are little changed. The only substantial difference derives from a misclassification of practitioners in the real estate area in the earlier analyses. The result is that both the "personal" and "business" real estate fields have fewer practitioners than previously indicated.

and admiralty, are relatively small; there is simply little demand for those services. Other fields, such as real estate or tax, command some of the attention of large numbers of lawyers but occupy only a small fraction of their practitioners full-time. Yet other fields, such as patents, have modest numbers of practitioners but command the more or less exclusive attention of many of them. To compute the relative amounts of effort devoted to the fields, therefore, we will need to take into account both the numbers of their practitioners and the varying degrees of exclusivity with which they are practiced.[1]

The second issue to be analyzed is the exclusivity itself—the extent to which the fields differ systematically in the proportions of work time that their practitioners devote to them. The subject matter and technical procedures of patents or labor union work may be so lacking in generalizability or so time-consuming to master that part-timers will be at a severe competitive disadvantage. By contrast, the fundamental doctrines of fields such as probate and real estate will have been acquired by most lawyers in the course of their law school training and, thus, clients may believe that the work can be done by nearly all lawyers. The latter fields will be dominated by generalists; the former by specialists.[2]

The third characteristic of the organization of the fields that we wish to assess, the varying interdependencies among them, is an obvious consequence of the fact that most lawyers are active in at least two fields. Thus, we want to direct attention to the various subgroupings of the fields according to the differential likelihoods of their co-practice by the same persons. Lawyers doing probate work, for example, are likely to do some real estate or personal tax work as well, but they are much less likely to do securities or antitrust work. Conversely, lawyers doing antitrust defense work are much more likely to be active in other corporate fields than in fields that serve individuals. Because fields that share many of their personnel are likely also to share work tasks, clienteles, and practice

1. Specification of levels of effort by field of practice could well be a useful element in the comparison of professional communities or in the analysis of changes in patterns of practice. One might compare, for example, the allocation of effort by field among the bars of Chicago, Boston, and Houston to gain some insight into the differing bases of their concerns. Identification of points of stability and change in those patterns of allocation at differing times would be a good indicator of developments in the markets for lawyers' services.

2. Michael T. Hannan and John Freeman, "The Population Ecology of Organizations," *American Journal of Sociology* 82 (1977): 929.

contexts, examining the patterns of co-practice may provide insight into the social organization of the legal profession as a whole. In particular, we may identify the major "faults," or cleavage lines, in the profession. These cleavages occur where few, if any, practitioners are found who do work in fields located on opposite sides of the line. The explanation of why these cleavages occur where they do is one of the principal objectives of our analysis.

With these preliminaries in hand, let us turn to a brief description of the character of the information gathered. The first item in our survey (see appendix A) presented the respondents with a list of thirty fields of legal work. One of the sources consulted in compiling this list was Carlin's study of solo practitioners in Chicago,[3] which used a list of fourteen specialties. Though some of our categories are identical to Carlin's, many are considerably more narrowly defined, and we added some fields that have emerged only recently (e.g., environmental law).[4] Each respondent in the survey was then asked to indicate the percentage of his professional time that he devoted to each of the thirty types of work during the past twelve months—less than 5 percent, 5 to 25 percent, 25 to 50 percent, or more than 50 percent.[5] The answers to this question were used to identify the practitioners in

3. Jerome E. Carlin, *Lawyers on Their Own: A Study of Individual Practitioners in Chicago* (New Brunswick: Rutgers University Press, 1962).

4. We used relatively fine-grained categories with the intention of combining them if our sample proved to contain insufficient numbers of respondents in any field to permit separate analysis. Some of the fields, although expected to have few practitioners, were included because they are traditionally recognized as distinct specialties (e.g., admiralty) and others because we were particularly interested in one or more of their characteristics (e.g., condemnations, where a successful practice is reputed to depend heavily on good political connections).

5. There are a number of ways one might have framed this question, each with some important advantages and disadvantages. After some pilot work, we chose to ask the question in terms of the past year because we found that a shorter time period (e.g., the past week or month) tended to elicit a misleading degree of concentration of effort. A single matter—e.g., trying a major case or negotiating a merger—might well consume the lawyer's time for a week or even a month. From the perspective of a year, however, the practitioner was often seen to have handled a variety of cases in several fields of law. Thus, we were willing to sacrifice the accuracy of recall of recent events for a somewhat less reliable but substantively more significant characterization of a practitioner's work life.

Instead of asking for an estimate of the percentage of total time devoted to each field, we might have asked our respondents to estimate the number of days worked on each field over the past year. But this would not have solved the problem of comparability of the units—work days are not of standard length or uniform efficiency or quality. Using hours might have been a better alternative. The units would, at least, have been of standard length. But over a span of a year recollections of numbers of hours devoted to particular subject matter would necessarily become rough estimates, and thus be little, if any, more informative than the percentages that we used. Asking for actual hours might also have increased considerably the

each of the various fields. Respondents who reported spending less than 5 percent of their time in a field were not regarded as active in the field. Since there was, unavoidably, some overlap among the categories of work, there is certainly some degree of imprecision in the manner in which our respondents classified their tasks. The defense of a person charged with a crime, for example, might in some cases be classified as "civil liberties" work just as plausibly as "criminal defense."[6] Such imprecision should tend to diminish the clarity of our findings. The findings are, nevertheless, striking.

The Distribution of Lawyers' Effort Among the Fields of Law

Table 2.1 indicates the total number of practitioners who spent at least 5 percent of their professional time in each of the fields and an

---

burden of this question on our respondents and on the scarce interview time available. Lawyers bill for their time in hourly units, and most of them thus keep records of how they spend their hours. If we had asked for hours, there would probably have been a strong tendency for our respondents to reach for their records or to say that they could not answer the question without consulting records. Moreover, simple aggregation of the categories employed in the records probably would not have sufficed to answer the question—the billing records show the work by *client*, of course, not by *field*, and one client may well require work in different fields. It seemed to us that all of this would consume more time than it was worth; we had a number of other questions that we also wanted to ask.

6. Several other such sources of ambiguity exist. The most important one, undoubtedly, is the "civil litigation" category, which may include litigation in any of the fields other than criminal. This problem is compounded by the fact that "litigation time" may well include not only the actual time in court but also the time spent preparing for trial or attempting to negotiate a settlement. It seemed advisable to include litigation as a separate field, however, because many large firms have separate litigation departments and many lawyers think of themselves as "litigators" of a variety of types of cases.

Since we asked a number of other questions concerning the respondent's activities, we are in a position to make somewhat finer distinctions within certain selected fields of law. We have distinguished between those attorneys who handle corporate tax matters and those who handle personal tax matters, between those who handle corporate real estate transactions and those who primarily handle residential real estate matters, and between litigators who represent corporations and those who litigate private claims against corporations, governmental units, or other individuals. For those practitioners who reported doing any tax, real estate, or litigation work, we determined whether they received 80 percent or more of their professional income from corporate clients. Persons receiving the bulk of their income from such clients were designated as being active in corporate tax, corporate real estate, or corporate litigation. All others were assigned to the "general" tax, real estate, or litigation categories.

TABLE 2.1

Number of Practitioners and Estimated Percentage of Total Effort Expended in Various Fields of Law by Chicago Lawyers

Fields of Law	Cluster N	No. of Practitioners in Field[a]	Estimated Percentage of Total Legal Effort[b]
A. Corporate client sector		541	53
1. Large corporate	242		
Antitrust (defense)		47	2
Business litigation		56	3
Business real estate		80	4
Business tax		51	3
Labor (management)		39	2
Securities		53	2
Cluster total			16
2. Regulatory	110		
Labor (unions)		18	1
Patents		45	4
Public utilities and administrative		52	4
Cluster total			9
3. General corporate	396		
Antitrust (plaintiffs)		24	1
Banking		60	3
Commercial (including consumer)		102	3
General corporate		262	11
Personal injury (defendant)		73	6
Cluster total			24
4. Political	46		
Criminal (prosecution)		20	2
Municipal		30	2
Cluster total			4
B. Personal/small business client sector		421	40
1. Personal business	287		
General litigation		53	2
Personal real estate		153	5
Personal tax		57	3
Probate		195	8
Cluster total			18
2. Personal plight	296		
Civil rights		41	2
Criminal (defense)		91	5
Divorce		153	6
Family		84	3
Personal injury (plaintiffs)		120	6
Cluster total			22
C. General, unspecified legal work	248	248	8
Total		699	101

NOTES: a. The number of practitioners is defined as all the persons who report devoting at least 5 percent of their work to the field.

b. See text and note 8 for explanation.

estimate of the percentage of total legal effort expended by Chicago's metropolitan bar in each of the fields. We have divided the fields into two broad categories, corporate versus personal and small business. These categories are further subdivided into clusters of fields that disproportionately share practitioners, as we shall demonstrate below when we discuss the interdependencies among fields.[7] While there is nothing especially problematic about the numbers of practitioners, our estimates of legal effort expended are considerably more conjectural; they rest on assumptions about the data that reasonable persons might well find questionable. We thus offer these results as a first approximation only, in the hope that they will provoke more adequate treatment of a matter of considerable theoretical import.

Any attempt to assess the relative amounts of legal effort expended in diverse fields by a specified professional community assumes that it is sensible to conceive of a total volume of work that may be subdivided into mutually exclusive parts. This total volume of effort is, of course, no more than a simple summation of the individual contributions of the actors. The most critical simplification we have made is to assume that all lawyers' contributions of effort are equal—that is, Lawyer A's work year is assumed to be equivalent in time, efficiency, effectiveness, and intensity to Lawyer B's work year. While that is patently false when comparing specific individuals, it is less troublesome if one thinks of averaging many practitioners so that individual idiosyncracies tend to cancel one another.

Perhaps the more important caveat about our estimates is that the amounts of work that lawyers do may be systematically biased by their fields of practice. One might point, for example, to "undoubted" differences between the intensity of effort that litigators as a group expend in their work compared to the presumably more leisurely pace of attorneys handling probate or residential real estate transactions. With hindsight, we regret that we gathered no information on the number of hours per week put in by different kinds of practitioners—one among several obvious (though surely not foolproof) ways to evaluate the validity of this objection. We know of no study that reports such information. The magnitude of the differences among the fields is sufficient that, even allowing for a considerable margin of error, the calculations presented give one an idea of the relative levels of effort devoted to the various fields.

7. Chapter 3 will also consider some of these matters.

Only very substantial and systematic deviations of effort by *fields* would seriously modify the aggregate picture. We caution the reader, however, not to overemphasize the size of particular proportions but instead to focus on the overall structure of relative shares of effort. To extract the maximum information about an individual's allocation of effort across fields, we created an elaborate set of coding rules that took into account both the total number of fields checked and the amount of time reported for each field that was checked.[8]

On the basis of these calculations, we estimate that somewhat more than half (53 percent) of the total effort of Chicago's bar is devoted to the corporate client sector, and a smaller but still substantial proportion (40 percent) is expended on the personal client sector.[9] More than half of the lawyers in Chicago spend some of

8. Every practitioner was first assigned 20 tokens, each worth 5 percentage points of his working time in a year, to "spend" on various fields of law. Tokens were allocated to a field according to the following schedule:

Percentage of Time Allocated to Field	Tokens (k)
0–4	$k = 0$
5–25	$k = 1$ to 4
25–50	$k = 5$ to 9
More than 50	$k = 10$ to 20

Two examples may illustrate the procedure. Suppose, first, that a respondent checked 3 fields as follows: field 1 = 5–25 percent, field 2 = 5–25 percent, field 3 = 25–50 percent. The following number of tokens would be assigned: $k_1 = 4$, $k_2 = 4$, $k_3 = 9$. Seventeen of this respondent's tokens were thus assigned to specified legal work; the remaining 3 tokens were assigned to a "general" category. In the second example, a respondent checked 3 fields as follows: field 1 = 5–25 percent, field 2 = 5–25 percent, field 3 = 50 percent or more. Tokens would be assigned as follows: $k_1 = 4$, $k_2 = 4$, $k_3 = 12$. In this case, the maximum number of tokens is assigned to the first 2 fields, subject to the constraint that at least 10 tokens are assigned to field 3. This token assignment rule may understate somewhat the extent of "specialization" since more units are assigned to the smaller categories (fields with lower percentages). On the other hand, the rule is also biased against the allocation of tokens to the general category, and in this respect its tendency will be to overstate the degree of specialization.

9. This finding is generally consistent with the evidence presented in Pashigian's work on lawyers' incomes, which suggests that about half of the total earnings of the legal service industry comes from individuals and the other half from businesses or governments. See B. Peter Pashigian, "The Number and Earnings of Lawyers: Some Recent Findings," 1978 *American Bar Foundation Research Journal* 51, 77–81, tables 10 and 11.

It may be that, if the effort of persons other than lawyers were considered, the share of total effort devoted to the legal work of corporations would more greatly exceed that devoted to individuals and small businesses. The large law firms that serve corporate clients have very sizable staffs of supporting personnel, often far larger numbers than the number of lawyers in the firm. (A few years ago, the ratio of staff to lawyers in the big firms often approached two to one. With the growth in the

their time in one or more of the fields in the "general corporate" cluster, and 627 of the 699 practicing lawyers devote at least some fraction of their effort to either general corporate or "personal business" work, or both, fields that share a concern with business activities or financial transactions. This common experience must serve as an important integrative underpinning for subjective identification with the broader profession as a community of common fate and purpose. On the other hand, these two substantial segments of the profession are largely separate. Only 56 of our respondents devoted as much as 25 percent of their time to a personal business field *and* at least 25 percent to a general corporate field—these overlapping lawyers are fewer than 17 percent of the total number of respondents who practice in those fields at least 25 percent of their time. The relatively small degree of overlap in the practice of these two groups of fields is, perhaps, surprising when we consider that the substance of legal work for personally owned businesses may not be far different from work for small corporations. The separation of the corporate and individual client sectors of practice is explored further in the third major section of this chapter, "Patterns of Co-practice Among Fields of Law" (see p. 48).

Level of Specialization in the Fields of Law

Only one field of law commands the exclusive attention of as many as half of its practitioners.[10] That field is criminal prosecution.[11] Of the others, only patents even comes close to this criterion of special-

---

use of memory typewriters and word-processing equipment, staff efficiency has increased greatly; a more usual ratio now appears to be about one and one-half to one.) These support personnel include paralegals of various sorts, secretaries skilled in the use of legal forms and the preparation of documents, librarians, private investigators, computer technicians, file clerks, and expert consultants in several fields. The solo practitioners who serve many individual clients may, by contrast, get by with one part-time secretary. (Two or more lawyers, not necessarily joined in a formal partnership, often share a single suite and a single secretary. Some lawyers even hire offices and secretaries only by the hour; see chapter 1, note 11.) The total manpower purchased by corporate clients might, therefore, be thought to outweigh that allocated to individuals by a considerable margin. But Pashigian's evidence is that, at least as measured by compensation in the marketplace, any additional effort devoted to corporate clients is either only a minor increment or not very highly valued.

10. The measure of "exclusive attention" used here is that the respondents counted as full-time specialists in a field must have checked the "more than 50 percent" time category for that field and must have checked no additional field. Under this criterion, a respondent might have devoted up to 5 percent of his time to each of a

ization of effort, with 40 percent of its practitioners doing that work exclusively. Corporate tax comes in a very distant third, 22 percent of its practitioners reporting full-time activity. All the other fields tend to cluster fairly tightly around the average of 5 to 6 percent full-time practitioners. The median number of fields of practice to which our respondents devoted as much as 5 percent of their time was 2.7. It is important to note this diffusion of individual effort across the fields of law, but a more systematic exploration of the varying effort given to the different fields may prove to be illuminating, both empirically and theoretically.

The data in hand, of course, provide only a somewhat crude indication of the amounts of time that individuals devote to one or another field of law, but they do provide a satisfactory basis for distinguishing among those individuals who spend relatively little time in a field (i.e., 5 to 25 percent of their professional time), those who spend moderate amounts of time (25 to 50 percent), and those who devote the majority or all of their time to the field. Since our analytic purpose is to characterize the differences among the fields of law and not to account for the differences in participation by individual lawyers, the aggregation of these individuals permits us to compare the relative levels of concentration that the fields appear to command from their practitioners.

These variations among the fields are, no doubt, determined by the demand for and supply of the services provided by each of the fields. We may think of the demands as being arrayed on a continu-

---

(continued)
number of other fields. This measure is probably the best approximation possible, given the categories available in our data.

11. It may surprise some lawyers to find that criminal prosecution is not always a full-time job. But only 9 of our 18 respondents who reported devoting some time to criminal prosecution did not also report at least 5 percent of their time being devoted to some other category of work. There are several explanations for the time allocation patterns of the other nine. Two of them were employed by federal agencies other than the U.S. attorney and did some enforcement work that they coded as criminal prosecution, as well as doing administrative law work and civil litigation. One was a supervisory official in the office of the state's attorney and was responsible for overseeing some criminal prosecution as well as civil litigation. One was an assistant state's attorney who did some consumer fraud work that he reported in the "consumer law" category, and another was an assistant state's attorney who had started the job within the past year so that a portion of the time period covered his previous work as a solo practitioner. Another respondent had moved in the other direction during the reporting period—from a position as a prosecutor to private practice in a firm. Three assistant state's attorneys were "moonlighting," doing small amounts of divorce, real estate, and "general family" practice on the side for private clients.

um of generality, breadth, or inclusiveness of client eligibility. At one end of this continuum are the fields serving needs that are likely to arise during the course of the daily affairs of most individual or corporate actors. For example, one would expect most persons of even moderate means, as well as business concerns of whatever size, to engage in the sale or purchase of real property, the preparation of tax returns, the transmission of wealth, the establishment of contractual obligations, and the resolution of the consequences of accidents or other misadventures. The demand for such legal services is large and dispersed throughout society. At the other extreme are fields serving the needs of a highly circumscribed and identifiable set of actors who will often have been made the objects of special legal regulation. Defendants in admiralty claims, inventors and authors, corporate actors subject to special statutory provisions—such as labor unions, corporations offering securities or those with antitrust problems, or manufacturers discharging environmental pollutants—are but a few examples of sources of narrowly defined demands for specialized legal services.

As to the supply side, we can again conceive of a continuum of available professionals capable of meeting these differentiated demands. The standardization of legal training in law schools, with core curricula required of virtually all law students pursuing degrees, and the requirement of a standard examination for admission to practice assure that some limited skills are shared by most practitioners, no matter how wanting the level of competence may be. Lawyers are certified as generalists, each being licensed to serve all the legal needs of his clientele. Practitioners exposed to the traditional fields of law in their professional training may feel little hesitancy in practicing these if the occasion arises. But other fields require extensive specialized training and experience that is often not acquired in law school. Real estate syndication and much corporate litigation are probably examples of the latter sort of field.

At the risk of oversimplifying a complicated situation, we have dichotomized both the demand and the supply continua in order to create the following fourfold table (table 2.2), which is intended as a heuristic device for what we shall call the JUG theory of specialization. The entries in the table describe the pattern of practitioners' time commitments that would be expected to correspond to the fields' supply and demand characteristics.

The JUG theory is derived from an ecological perspective on the

TABLE 2.2

Generalist and Specialist Fields as a Function of Characteristics of Their Supply and Demand

		Demand for Legal Services	
		Clientele Broadly Dispersed and Endemic to Most Individual/Corporate Settings	Clientele Highly Circumscribed as to Eligibility and Need
Supply of legal services	Skills generally acquired in course of training	Generalist (G) fields (negatively sloped or reversed J-curve)	Mixed generalist/ specialist fields (bimodal/U-shaped)
	Specialized knowledge and experience acquired after entering practice	Mixed generalist/ specialist fields (bimodal/U-shaped)	Specialist (J) fields (positively sloped or J-shaped curve)

differentiation of populations sharing a territory,[12] but we are using it here as a more general theory to account for the emergence of specialized or generalized role positions in social systems. In this formulation, the types of demand for and supply of a field are the ecological conditions that constrain the form of provision of legal services—generalist, specialist, or mixed. The form that prevails will tend to be the one that is optimally adapted to successful competition in that field. The central thrust of our argument, then, is that generalists and specialists have differing competitive advantages and disadvantages in serving clients, depending on the nature of the supply of the relevant skills and on the nature of the client demands. A specialist must invest substantial amounts of time and effort to master knowledge that has little application to other legal matters. Handling cases outside the specialist's area of expertise is costly because it fails to utilize his investment. On the other hand, because a specialist has arcane knowledge readily available, he can handle cases within his area much more efficiently than can a generalist, whose knowledge of the relevant law and procedures is likely to be sketchy or out of date. The generalist can provide service efficiently only if the matters handled are relatively routine and of frequent occurrence. Once a matter begins to pose issues that arise infrequently, the generalist rapidly loses the competitive advantage to the specialist; it then becomes inefficient for the generalist to invest the time to acquire the necessary knowledge.

12. See Hannan and Freeman, *supra* note 2, esp. pp. 939–56; see also Howard Aldrich, *Organizations and Environments* (Englewood Cliffs, N.J.: Prentice-Hall, 1979).

Clients thus need a mechanism for locating appropriate lawyers, and the specialists need to be put in touch with clients who require their esoteric services. The narrower the range of clients demanding such services or the more difficult it is to identify them, the more the specialists come to depend on the existence of reliable means for linking them to their clientele. Specialists usually achieve this link either through connections with a network of other lawyers who will refer cases to them or by securing a position in a large law firm that has a sufficient volume of legal business to permit internal specialization.

Table 2.2 provides an interpretive framework within which to explore the findings portrayed in table 2.3. Since we have no independent measures of the demand and supply characteristics of the fields, we relied upon our own judgment to make these distinctions. The data presented in table 2.3 can thus be regarded only as illustrating our general argument rather than as providing an independent test of our theory. The reader should "test" our theory with his own judgments about the demand and supply characteristics of the field.

The first four columns of table 2.3 are self-explanatory: they provide the total numbers of practitioners in each field (col. [1]) and the percentages of those practitioners who devote each of the categories of time to the field (cols. [2]-[4]). The final column indicates the shape of the curve of the practitioners' time allocations. G denotes a *generalist* pattern in which most of the practitioners devote only 5 to 25 percent of their time to the field. J denotes the *specialist* pattern, where the modal participation in the field is at the level of more than 50 percent of a practitioner's time. U denotes a bimodal pattern—the practitioners devoting only 5 to 25 percent of their time *or* in excess of 50 percent of their time occur much more often than the intermediate category, those spending 25 to 50 percent of their time in the field. (To be designated a U-shaped distribution, we followed the rule of thumb that each of the two other categories had to be at least 75 percent larger than the intermediate category.) Broadly speaking, we found considerable congruence between our predicted pattern of time commitment and the empirically observed pattern.

TABLE 2.3
Concentration of Effort in Selected Fields of Law by
Individual Practitioners: Percentage Distribution

Fields of Law	Total No. of Practitioners (1)	Percentage of Practitioners in Each Time Category			Shape of Time Distribution (5)
		5–25 (2)	25–50 (3)	50+ (4)	
A. Corporate client sector					
1. Large corporate					
Antitrust (defense)	47	57	15	28	U
Business litigation	56	45	20	36	U
Business real estate	80	48	16	36	U
Business tax	51	41	20	39	U
Labor (management)	39	44	13	44	U
Securities	53	58	13	28	U
2. Regulatory					
Labor (unions)	18	28	17	56	J
Patents	45	24	7	69	J
Public utilities and administrative	52	44	14	42	U
3. General corporate					
Antitrust (plaintiffs)	24	58	21	21	G
Banking	60	45	33	22	G
Commercial	102	63	26	11	G
General corporate	272	40	33	18	G
Personal injury (defendant)	73	42	19	38	U
4. Political					
Criminal prosecution	20	25	5	70	J
Municipal	30	40	30	30	G
B. Personal client sector					
1. Personal business					
General litigation	53	54	24	21	G
Personal real estate	153	60	24	16	G
Personal tax	57	44	32	25	G
Probate	195	49	34	17	G
2. Personal plight					
Civil rights	41	66	15	20	G
Criminal defense	91	52	12	36	U
Divorce	153	63	24	13	U
Family	84	68	20	12	G
Personal injury (plaintiffs)	120	48	21	31	G

Patterns of Co-practice Among Fields of Law

As we argued in the introduction to part II, "Defining the Fields of Law," (see pp. 31–35), at least two hypotheses about the nature of the determinants of the patterns of co-practice of the fields of law should be considered. First, one could entertain the *hypothesis of cognitively based connectedness*—that there are conceptual affinities in the knowledge and modes of reasoning utilized by certain sets of fields that may influence the patterns of co-practice. A number of fields have historical and intellectual roots in the English common law tradition (e.g., torts, contracts, real property, and the law of trusts and estates). Other fields are allied because they result from new regulatory codes that create a body of administrative procedure and practice, subjecting specific sets of actors to legal control (e.g., regulation of broadcasting, natural gas, railroads, or airlines). Though the human and corporate actors subject to regulation may be diverse, the argument is that the shared underlying principles of the common law versus the new administrative law create a systematic distinction among the fields and organize co-practice accordingly. There is an analogous logic of co-specialization in medical practice where the developing theory and empirical knowledge about biology and disease tends to group specialist fields into various clusters.[13] Thus, one finds some surgeons and internists doing specialized work on gastrointestinal problems, others concerned with cardiac and vascular problems, and still others specializing in neurological disorders.

Second, one could advance the *hypothesis of client-centered organization of legal problems.* This hypothesis would assert that the primary determinant of the lawyer's allocation of time to the various fields of practice is the need to serve the interests of an identifiable set of clients. Thus, the neighborhood lawyer, serving individuals and small businesses, would seek to handle all of the matters that commonly confront his clientele—income tax, home sales, marital problems, automobile accidents, wills, and perhaps even some criminal charges. He would have an incentive to provide "full service" to his clients rather than refer them to another lawyer. The lawyer representing a large corporation, on the other hand, might or might not attempt to serve all the corporation's legal needs. The corporate lawyer and his client might well find that the client's interests would be better served by the lawyer's specialization in a limited set of tasks requiring arcane knowledge (e.g., tax, labor relations, or public utility rate making). The large law firm that serves corporate clients may, through the

13. Cf. Rosemary Stevens, *American Medicine and the Public Interest* (New Haven: Yale University Press, 1971).

specialization of "departments" or of individual lawyers within the firm, seek to achieve something like the full service provided by the neighborhood practitioner—and probably for the same reason.

In evaluating the relative merits of these deceptively simple and straightforward alternative explanations of co-practice, we pursued several strategies that differed in key theoretical and substantive assumptions, but the results converged so strongly that we feel justified in serving brevity by reporting here only one set of results. (For a full description of the methods used, see the appendix to this chapter.) To identify localized regions or clusters of fields according to the varying probabilities of co-practice, we used a method of analysis that creates successively more and more inclusive clusters of specialties on the basis of their conditional probabilities of co-practice until we reach only one cluster containing all the fields.[14] A specialty is added to a cluster when it has at least a stipulated minimum probability of being linked with all the other fields in that cluster. The investigator can then examine and seek to interpret the resulting nested hierarchy of clusters. Figure 2.1 presents a graphic summary (called a dendrogram). Reading the dendrogram from right to left, the reader can observe where specialties were successively added to particular clusters as the conditional probabilities linking given fields declined in value.

The use of conditional probabilities to link fields had recommended itself to us originally because of the intuitively obvious substantive interpretation of the measure. At the one extreme, two fields are clearly separated from each other when there is *no* likelihood that work in one field is associated with work in the other. At the other extreme, if there is a 100 percent probability of doing work in one field given that one does some work in the other, it is difficult to imagine maintaining a real distinction between the fields.[15] Choosing cutting points between these two extremes is, of

14. This technique is known as a hierarchical clustering analysis. The specific method used was the "minimum average diameter method." See Stephen C. Johnson, "Hierarchical Clustering Schemes," *Psychometrika* 32 (1967) 241; Kenneth D. Bailey, "Cluster Analysis," in *Sociological Methodology: 1975*, ed. David R. Heise, Jossey-Bass Behavior Science Series (San Francisco: Jossey-Bass, 1974), p. 59; Ronald S. Burt, "Power in a Social Topology," in *Power, Paradigms, and Community Research*, ed. Ronald J. Liebert and Allen W. Imershein (London: Sage Publications for the International Sociological Association, 1977).

15. When very high average conditional probabilities occur between fields, one would want to know the asymmetric conditional probabilities because one would suspect that the field with fewer practitioners is a more specialized subfield of the larger field.

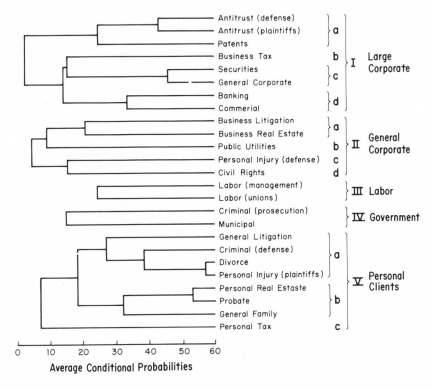

FIGURE 2.1

Hierarchical Clustering of Joint Activity Using Average Conditional Probabilities, Diameter Method (5 Percent or More Time in Each Field)

course, not so easy. The choice will depend on the analyst's purpose in differentiating among the fields.

Figure 2.1 reveals that there are five distinct clusters, indicated by roman numerals, that are distinguished by the fact that there is virtually *no* likelihood of their mutual co-practice. Cluster I includes a set of fields that are exclusively concerned with business transactions, usually involving corporations of substantial size. Using an arbitrary cutoff at .20, this broad cluster can be further subdivided into four subclusters: (*a*) antitrust and patents; (*b*) business tax; (*c*) securities and general corporate; and (*d*) banking and commercial. These subgroups probably reflect patterns of internal specialization within large law firms and in the offices of house counsel working for corporations. Of these fields, business tax is the least closely

51

connected to any of the others, and it is probably the field that is most likely to be practiced within a separate, specialized department of a large law firm or house counsel's office, or in a specialty firm devoted more or less exclusively to such work.

In Cluster II we find the balance of the corporate law fields. Of these, only business litigation and business real estate join at the .20 level, and these are the two fields within the cluster that are most likely to be found in large law firms, again often in separate departments within those firms. The other fields in the cluster are relatively free-standing specialties that are more often practiced outside the confines of the large, corporate firms and are done instead by government lawyers, house counsel, or smaller specialty firms. The services of litigators and real estate lawyers, like those of tax specialists, are likely to be required at one time or another by many of the corporate clients of a large law firm, but since these fields cut across nearly the full range of the firm's clients they may be less tightly connected to any particular subset of clients. Cluster III is quite straightforward: it includes both the union and management sides of the practice of labor law. Though lawyers who represent unions seldom also work for management, and vice versa, there is a third side to labor law work that tends to pull these two fields together. Labor law is also practiced by government lawyers and by professional mediators or arbitrators who stand between unions and management. When we asked these lawyers about the fields in which they worked, they responded that they worked in both sides of labor law, thus creating overlap. Cluster IV is, again, quite clear. It consists of the two fields of practice where municipal governments are the primary clients. The final cluster includes all of the fields that are primarily devoted to the service of individual persons and small business. Within this personal client cluster, there are three subdivisions if we use the .20 cutoff criterion. The first includes the fields most characterized by litigation on behalf of persons. The second consists of the fields (other than tax) that are most concerned with personal financial transactions or the transmission of personal wealth. And the third is personal tax, which—like business tax—appears to be a separate specialty that does not have a great affinity for any other field, in particular, but that cuts across the other fields insofar as they may involve tax issues.

In sum, though there is some clustering of the fields according to their cognitive similarities, the primary structure of co-practice appears to be client centered. That is, co-practice appears to be organized by the demands of distinct groupings of clients who have distinct sets of legal problems and who establish relationships with distinct types of lawyers.

Conclusion

Chicago's lawyers spread their work over a broad range of activities, none of which commands a very large percentage of the total legal effort. Even the two largest fields—general corporate and probate—claim a mere 11 and 8 percent, respectively, of the total (see table 2.1). None of the other twenty-two fields receives more than 6 percent. On the other hand, the numbers of practitioners in both of the largest fields constitute substantial portions of the profession—37 percent of all practicing lawyers characterize at least some of their work as "general corporate." But only a few fields of law receive the undivided attention of as many as 10 percent of their practitioners; only criminal prosecution gets the undivided attention of as many as half of its practitioners.

If we shift from the field of law to the individual lawyer as the unit of analysis, however, we get a somewhat different view of the matter. About 22 percent of our respondents indicated that they practiced in one field exclusively, while another 39 percent devoted more than half of their time to a single field but also did some work in one or more other fields. (This is consistent with the distribution across fields because the time of these lawyers that was not devoted to their fields of specialization and the time of the nonspecialists was spread across a variety of fields.) Thus, from the point of view of the individual lawyer, there is a substantial degree of specialization in the work of most Chicago practitioners. We asked our respondents whether they considered themselves "specialists," and 70 percent replied that they did. (Fewer than three-quarters of these self-labeled specialists, however, devoted as much as half of their practice time to a single field of law.) But the firms in which many of these lawyers work no doubt offer a broader range of services to their clients; one of the principal efficiencies of the large law firm is the division of labor that it makes possible, and one of the main attractions of such firms to the client is the range of service that is available. Though the individual lawyer may see his work as specialized, therefore, the client may perceive himself as dealing with a general practice firm and may talk primarily with a senior partner who is a general practitioner in the sense that he bridges the firm's departments. And it is important to reemphasize that few of the fields are dominated by specialists. Unless the specialists are aggregated into *roles* that have social meaning, their individual patterns of specialization may have little consequence. If the fields of law are an adequate set of lawyers' social roles (or, at least, of some such roles), the relative lack of specialization in most of the fields is the important social fact.

A majority of the work of Chicago lawyers is devoted to corporate clients (see table 2.1), and the profession's overall preoccupation is with business transactions, transfers of wealth, and the defense of property rights (including work in the personal business fields). Though about 42 percent of all lawyers do spend at least some time in fields concerned with the alleviation of personal "plight" (see cluster B2 in table 2.1), only 22 percent of the total effort is directed to these activities. The personal plight fields rank at the bottom of the profession's prestige hierarchy (see chap. 4), and we find that all of these fields are heavily dominated by part-timers (see table 2.3). Whether these fields are disvalued because few practitioners devote exclusive attention to them or whether few lawyers specialize in them because of their disvalued standing in the profession is a matter for speculation or further research, but the latter seems more plausible. Practitioners dividing their activities among several fields may well identify more closely with those that enjoy higher social standing among their colleagues and may try to minimize their involvement with the lower status field.

Particular types of clients tend to be afflicted with particular congeries of legal problems, and the lawyer has an incentive to deal with as broad a spectrum of these needs as is consistent with the reasonably efficient provision of service to the client. A law firm that does estate planning for rich clients is likely to handle their real estate transactions as well; a lawyer who settles divorce cases for clients from the lower middle class may also find himself called on to handle consumer credit problems or even to negotiate a plea to a criminal charge. This does not mean that the majority of Chicago lawyers, those who practice in firms with ten or more lawyers or who are employed by corporations or governments, do not manage to limit their work to a narrow range of fields and to allocate most of their time to one, principal area of practice—as we have seen, they do. But it is our thesis that the scope of that area of practice will be shaped to accommodate their clients' range of needs, broad or narrow.

To what extent, then, do our findings suggest that the patterns in the organization of lawyers' work correspond, in fact, to client type rather than to doctrinal substance or to similarities in the tasks that lawyers perform (e.g., litigation versus office practice)? Some doctrinal areas coincide so closely with one type of client that the lawyers who give more or less exclusive service to those narrow classes of clients (e.g., broadcasters or labor unions) are also likely to be specialized by task type or doctrinal substance. The issue is, therefore, the extent to which lawyers generally tend to deal within broader but mutually exclusive social groupings of clients. We can provide an answer to at least one important question that is relevant to this issue: what fraction of the profession regularly represents both corporations and individuals? Our data show that only about a seventh of all practicing lawyers do any substantial amount of work both for corporate clients and for individuals or small businesses. Of 777 respondents, 699 of whom were actively practicing, 101 devoted at least 25 percent of their professional time to one or more of the fields in the corporate sector *and* at least 25 percent to one or more of the fields in the personal sector.[16] From these data and the patterns of overlap in the practice of the fields (see fig. 2.1), we are inclined to argue that, while the organization of lawyers' work surely reflects affinities of doctrine and of task type, the Chicago bar is even more clearly specialized by type of client. Personal injury work done for plaintiffs (usually individuals) is, for example, quite separate from that done for defendants (usually insurance companies). And the clustering of fields according to the overlaps among them in lawyers' patterns of practice quite clearly shows that corporate law fields tend to group together, regardless of doctrinal substance, as do personal client fields and fields where governments are the primary clients.

The set of fields that we defined at the beginning of this study (see pp. 32–35) may, therefore, depend too much on substantive cat-

16. Tables 2.1 and 2.3 list the fields of law that are included in these broader "sectors." The figures presented in the text here, however, were derived by a separate analysis rather than from the analyses presented in those tables.

egories. Our findings suggest to us that lawyers' roles are determined less by doctrinal distinctions among tasks and more by social distinctions among clients. Rather than the role of antitrust defense practitioner, the lawyer may occupy the position of counsel to large corporations that have antitrust problems. There is, however, an important skill difference that distinguishes two broad classes of lawyers, the litigators and the office lawyers. It may be that, except for a few true specialties (the fields with J-shaped curves in table 2.3), we would reflect reality best by assigning lawyers' roles to one of four categories: corporate litigation, corporate office practice, litigation for individuals and small businesses, and office practice for individuals and small businesses.

Specialization within the legal profession is not so much a division of labor as a division of clientele. Lawyers tend to specialize in the representation of limited, identifiable types of clients and to perform as broad or narrow a range of tasks as their clientele demands.

Appendix to Chapter 2: Methods Used to Analyze the Patterns of Co-practice of the Fields of Law

To assess the patterns of overlap in the practice of the several fields of law, we constructed a 25-by-25 matrix of the fields, each row and corresponding column representing the practitioners in a given field. (In fact, two matrices were constructed according to two different criteria. The first included lawyers who spend as little as 5 percent of their time in each field, and the second required that the lawyers spend at least 25 percent of their time in the field in order to be included. Since the results for the second matrix were essentially identical to those of the first, the results reported are based on the "5 percent plus" matrix because it has substantially larger numbers in each field and thus is more statistically reliable.) For each cell in the matrix, we then calculated the frequencies for the fourfold table on p. 57.

The conditional probabilities of doing work in one field given that one does work in another are asymmetric, that is, $\Pr(X \mid Y) \neq \Pr(Y \mid X)$. They are also heavily influenced by discrepancies in the relative sizes of the two fields. In the above example, $\Pr(X \mid Y) = d/(b + d)$

	No Work in Field Y	Work in Field Y
No Work in Field X	a	b
Work in Field X	c	d

and Pr $(Y \mid X) = d/(c + d)$. A hypothetical example should clarify the difficulty.

Let us suppose, for sake of simplicity, that the general corporate field has 200 practitioners while the "admiralty" field has only 10 practitioners,[1] and 5 of these lawyers practice in both fields. Since 5 of the 10 lawyers who do admiralty also do some general corporate work, the "conditional probability" that one who practices admiralty will practice in the general corporate field as well is 50 percent (5 ÷ 10 = .5). The "condition" in this example is that one practices admiralty. But let us look at it the other way around. What is the probability of practicing admiralty given the condition that one does general corporate work? It is 5 divided by 200, or .025. Thus, in assessing the degree of co-practice between the admiralty and general corporate fields, the direction from which we look makes a great difference. Merely dividing the number of lawyers who practice in both fields (5 in this case) by the number of practitioners of the larger of the two fields (200 in general corporate) gives a misleading or, at best, one-sided view of the extent of the relationship between the fields. Where one field is a great deal larger than the other, this procedure would seriously and systematically understate their affinity. The sheer magnitude of the general corporate field overwhelms admiralty so that, rather than observe the extent of the attraction of one field to practitioners of the other, what we see is mostly the "size effect." The .025 probability that we calculate from the perspective of the larger field obscures the fact that fully half of the admiralty lawyers do general corporate work. On the other hand, it is true that the size effect also exists in the real world—that is, the small size of the admiralty field greatly limits the opportunities for general corporate practitioners to do admiralty work.

1. In fact, our sample includes 259 practitioners in the "general corporate" field at the "5 percent plus" level of activity and 133 at the "25 percent plus" level, but only 6 and 1 in admiralty at the 5 and 25 percent levels, respectively.

In our analysis, we wished to preserve some of the impact of differences in the sizes of the fields on opportunities for their co-practice without masking the affinities among the fields that we had set out to assess. As a compromise, therefore, we "split the difference." Our solution was simply to average the conditional probabilities that were computed from the vantage point of each field—that is, from each "condition" or direction. In our example, therefore, we would add .5 and .025, divide by 2, and obtain .2625 as the *average conditional probability* of joint practice of the two fields. To say that this solution is a compromise is not to say that it is arbitrary; the measure has substantive meaning. If the simple, unaveraged conditional probability that is computed from one field's standpoint is a measure of the view that practitioners in field X have of the opportunities presented by field Y, the average of the two conditional probabilities (X to Y and Y to X) is an assessment of the crossover opportunities between fields X and Y that is composed equally of the point of view of the practitioners of field X and that of the practitioners of field Y. An alternative approach would have been to use statistical manipulations appropriate to dealing with asymmetric probabilities, but to have done so would have rendered the presentation of our data unduly complex.[2] It would also have made it impossible for us to use certain data reduction techniques that we have found helpful in providing insight into the meaning of the findings.

2. An alternative to this procedure would be to calculate Yule's Q, a nonparametric, symmetric measure of the degree of association, for each of the original fourfold tables. Hubert M. Blalock, *Social Statistics*, 2d ed. (New York: McGraw-Hill, 1972); Leo A. Goodman and William H. Kruskal, "Measures of Association for Cross Classifications," *Journal of the American Statistical Association* 49 (1954): 732. We have done so for both the "5 percent plus" matrix and the "25 percent plus" matrix with results quite comparable to those reported here.

Chapter 3

SOCIAL DIFFERENTIATION
WITHIN THE PROFESSION*

IN THE previous chapter we argued that the needs of a particular type of client usually dictate the character and the diversity or homogeneity of the work of a lawyer or a law firm. The practitioner who serves a neighborhood's small businesses will often also handle the personal income tax returns of the owners of those businesses, will file their divorces, and will settle their automobile accident claims. The large firm that deals with a corporation's antitrust problems is also likely to handle its real estate acquisitions, its securities issues, and its corporate tax returns. But a lawyer who represents labor unions in one case is unlikely to represent management in another, and in this country a lawyer may not both prosecute and defend criminal cases simultaneously (though many young prosecutors later become defense lawyers). This tendency of lawyers' work to address congeries of problems associated with particular types of clients organizes the profession into two broad types of lawyers: those serving corporations and those serving individuals and indi-

*This chapter is based on our article "The Legal Profession: Client Interests, Professional Roles, and Social Hierarchies," that appeared in 76 *Michigan Law Review* 1111–42 (1978); an early version was also presented as a paper at the 1978 Annual Meeting of the Southern Sociological Society, New Orleans, March 1978. As was the case with chapter 2, however, the chapter has been extensively revised, and some of the data analyses presented here differ from those in the article. Though the data set used here was "cleaner" than that available when the article was written, we do not believe that this results in any important substantive differences.

viduals' small businesses. In this chapter, we explore the extent to which differences in the social characteristics of lawyers follow the same lines of cleavage as this division of labor or division of clientele. Do the patterns of social differentiation within the bar correspond to the organization of work? That is, are the different sorts of clients served by different sorts of lawyers?

We begin this analysis by considering some of the mechanisms—beyond the incentive for lawyers to serve a broad range of the needs of their particular clients—that could determine the structure of the relationships among the fields of law. What social processes might tend to bring two fields into contact or to make them more alike in their characteristics or, perhaps, to separate other fields, to drive them apart?

The referral system through which lawyers find clients and clients find lawyers is surely one mechanism that creates contacts and ties among the fields. Patent lawyers, for example, may maintain close ties with counsel for corporations likely to invent patentable products, and lawyers specializing in commercial litigation may seek connections with office lawyers who represent commercial enterprises. Thus, the common interest of lawyers and clients in the facilitation of their contacts may bring together doctrinally and organizationally differentiated fields of law, but note that these fields will share a concern with the same sort of client. By contrast, other types of lawyers—criminal prosecutors, for example—may not need to seek clients, and this will deprive those fields of one incentive for decreasing their social isolation from professional colleagues in other fields of practice.

Similarly, referral networks among graduates of particular law schools may bind together some fields and separate others. To the extent that practitioners of the most elite forms of corporate law graduated from the same few law schools, while personal injury or criminal lawyers studied at less prestigious, local law schools, "old school tie" networks may increase the social distance[1] between

1. There are two kinds of "social distance"; see Edward O. Laumann, *Prestige and Association in an Urban Community* (Indianapolis: Bobbs-Merrill, 1966); David McFarland and Daniel Brown, "Social Distance as a Metric: A Systematic Introduction to Smallest Space Analysis," in Edward O. Laumann, ed., *Bonds of Pluralism: The Form and Substance of Urban Social Networks* (New York: John Wiley, 1973), pp. 213–53. One is the extent to which two or more phenomena (in our case, the fields of law) differ on any number of social variables. Thus, this sense of the term simply describes the degree to which the phenomena are socially distinct. For an indication of this type of social distance among the fields of law, see figure 3.1. The other kind of social dis-

these types of practice. This phenomenon is part of a more general tendency toward equal status contact.[2] That is, lawyers in fields that enjoy similar levels of prestige within the profession will be more likely to associate with one another than will lawyers from fields with widely differing prestige.[3]

Obviously, these mechanisms reinforce one another. Practitioners in fields concerned with corporate clients' legal problems may recruit at the same law schools, participate in the same client referral networks, and share similar prestige within the profession. The tendency of all these factors will be the same: to forge relationships among the fields of corporate law practice and to separate them from noncorporate fields.

But characteristics more intrinsic to the practice of the various fields of law may also contribute to the degree of their social differentiation. Similarities in the legal doctrines, statutes, or regulatory schemes dealt with by two fields might, thus, beget a kinship that could increase social proximity. So might their general modes of analysis or the strategic problems they characteristically address. Some fields of law, for example, involve "symbol manipulation" and others "people persuasion." The former category might include preparing securities registration statements or similarly complex, technical documents; divorce, criminal, or personal injury work might fall into the latter category.

There are also some more specific differences in the types of tasks performed. The practitioners in some fields are nearly always in court or preparing for it, while those in other fields are almost exclusively engaged in office practice. And within both litigation and office practice, further fundamental distinctions may be drawn. Within litigation, important distinctions of status and task type exist between state court and federal court litigation and between trial and appellate work. Within office practice, lawyers in some fields primarily advise clients (on possible tax or antitrust consequences of alternative courses of action, for example, or on techniques of real

---

tance refers to the extent of social interaction among specified persons or groups. The first kind of social distance may, of course, influence the second. Thus, the differences or similarities in the fields' substantive law, in their characteristic tasks, in the settings of their practice, in their practitioners' social origins, or in their clients may serve to increase or decrease the social interaction among the practitioners of those fields. We analyze this latter form of social distance in chapter 7.

2. See Laumann, *supra* note 1, pp. 134–35.

3. For a discussion of the prestige of the fields of law, see chapter 4; for the extent of association among lawyers by field, see chapter 7.

estate acquisition). Lawyers in other fields, such as matrimonial law, devote much time and energy to the emotional needs of clients, to personal counseling, or to smoothing ruffled feathers. Practitioners in still other fields characteristically spend considerable time drafting legal documents such as wills, trust agreements, debentures, or contracts. To the extent that these distinct tasks call for distinct skills, the mobility of lawyers among fields requiring dissimilar skills is inhibited. The probability that a lawyer will do a substantial amount of work in two fields of law is, of course, one measure of the social distance between the fields. Once that probability exceeds a certain point, we would say that no social or behavioral distinction exists between the two fields and that any distinction between them is purely conceptual or doctrinal.

For similar reasons, the fields of law that deal with statutory or regulatory codes may be more insular than those that work primarily with older common law. Every lawyer learns the basic principles of the common law in law school and, thus, may accept a simple tort or contract case even though he principally attends to some other field. By contrast, lawyers may be less confident of their skills, or less willing to invest the time necessary to acquire them, in fields such as broadcast regulation or labor law, and there may be less tendency to accept the occasional case in that kind of field. Much of the innovation in regulatory law, with the consequent growth of multivolume codes, has occurred at the federal level, spawning entirely new specialties in federal regulatory law. Because these new fields share some common elements or common skills (and also because of the types of clients, the networks among clients and lawyers, and the differences between federal and state procedural rules), the distinction between federal practice and state practice also tends to create social distance among the fields—federal law tends to involve larger, corporate clients and to enjoy higher prestige within the profession.

Finally, fields of law that process large numbers of individual clients through the state courts may tend to be socially distant from the fields that often require several man-years of lawyers' time on each case (antitrust work, for example). But it is exceedingly difficult to separate the consequences of this difference among the fields from those of a corresponding, fundamental socioeconomic difference. High volume cases and the lawyers who handle them are unlikely to resemble the processing or the processors of "unique" legal problems, but the discovery of a unique issue is likely to be a function of the amount of time that lawyers devote to a case and, thus, of the amount of money that the client spends on lawyers. If the stakes are high, the problems can become very complex; if the client lacks money, his problems are likely to be routine. The consequent difference (perceived or real) in the levels of intellectual challenge presented by the varying fields of law may well, then, affect their relative levels of prestige within the profession and thus serve as yet another basis for differentiation among them. This possibility is considered, and the data relevant to the issue are analyzed, in chapter 4.

These mechanisms of differentiation will probably create divisions within the legal profession in spite of the endorsement by the courts and the organized bar of the myth of the omnicompetent practitioner.[4] In fact, many distinct fields of legal work do exist.

As described in chapter 2 (see pp. 38–39), we asked each respondent to indicate whether he devoted less than 5 percent, 5 to 25 percent, 25 to 50 percent, or more than 50 percent of his professional time to each of the thirty fields of law that we had listed. The respondents who reported that they devoted 25 percent or more of their professional time to a field are the practitioners whose responses were used in computing the characteristics of the fields that are reported here. For example, we derived the attributes of probate law and of its practitioners from the responses of 100 lawyers who estimated that they spend at least a quarter of their legal effort on that field. Obviously, this criterion is largely arbitrary and, because our categories unavoidably overlap, our respondents' classifications of their work must be imprecise.[5] If we had set the inclusion level at 50 percent of legal effort, we would have had purer categories— categories less contaminated by the responses of practitioners not

4. See chapter 1 at notes 29–31.
5. Since we also asked the respondents several other questions about their practices, we can distinguish somewhat more finely within certain fields of law. Within the tax field, for example, we can distinguish between corporate tax attorneys and personal tax attorneys. Similarly, we can distinguish between lawyers who handle corporate real estate transactions and those who primarily handle residential real estate matters, and between litigators who represent corporations and those who represent individuals. To accomplish this, we determined whether practitioners who reported doing tax, real estate, and litigation work received 80 percent or more of their professional income from business clients. If they did, we designated those lawyers as active in business tax, business real estate, or business litigation. We assigned all others to the personal tax, real estate, or litigation categories. Government lawyers in these fields were assigned to a residual category.

strongly committed to or involved with the field—but we would also have lost data and our findings would have been based on smaller numbers. Had we chosen the 5 percent level, we would have been more inclusive, but we would also have had a weaker, more contaminated measure of the field's characteristics. At the 25 percent level, of course, the respondents we counted in a given field may be even more active or involved in one or two other fields of law, where they will also be counted in our data.[6] This is, then, a conservative measure of the degree of differentiation among the fields of law.

The Degree of Differentiation

Notwithstanding the conservatism of our measure of the differentiation among the fields of law, we found that differentiation to be quite substantial. We analyzed the set of twenty-five fields on forty variables—an even thousand observations—but we will spare the reader here and present our data somewhat more parsimoniously in only two simple tables and one rather more complex figure.[7] The nuance lost by reducing the data is compensated for by the increased comprehensibility of the overall structure. The first table displays the differentiation among selected fields of law on a number of social variables; the second examines the hierarchical structure of that differentiation, on the same variables, across a set of categories that includes all of the fields; and the figure graphically represents the structure of the relationships among the twenty-five fields of law, simultaneously accounting for several kinds of social variation among them.

Table 3.1 presents the findings for six selected fields of law on twenty variables. The variables, which were drawn from several types of data, include characteristics of the fields' clients and of the patterns of the practitioners' relationships with clients, the tasks performed in the fields, the nature of the social organizations or institutions in which the fields are practiced, the types of law schools attended by the fields' practitioners, and some information about the practitioners' social origins.

6. The extent of this double counting is discussed briefly on pp. 72–73, and chapter 2 deals in detail with the extent of overlap among the fields of law.

7. These tabulations are presented in their entirety in appendix B.

TABLE 3.1
Differentiation Among Six Selected Fields of Law

Fields	No. of Practitioners (1)	Clients				Task Type					Practice Setting			Law School		Personal Characteristics					
		Mean % Blue-collar Clients (2)	Mean % Business Income from Major Corporate Clients (3)	Mean % Stable Clients (4)	Median No. Clients per Year (5)	Median No. of State Court Appearances per Month (6)	% High Encroachment on Practice (7)	% High on Negotiating and Advising (8)	% High on Professional Expertise (9)	% High Specialization of Work (10)	% Solo Practitioners (11)	% Firms of More Than 30 Lawyers (12)	% Corporate House Counsel (13)	% Attended Elite Law Schools (14)	% Attended Local Law Schools (15)	% Type 1 Protestants (16)	% Catholic (17)	% Jewish (18)	% Metropolitan Origin (19)	% Mean Age (20)	Prestige Score (21)
Securities	22	0	61	60	26	0	36	23	86	72	0	77	9	45	14	36	9	14	68	39	68
Public utilities	29	3	46	92	2	0	36	54	55	72	10	10	24	24	17	17	21	31	83	45	59
General corporate	135	6	39	72	35	1	35	37	62	30	19	21	16	30	34	13	27	38	73	45	59
Criminal prosecution	15	Government is only client				19	20	18	50	53	All Government employees			0	67	7	53	20	87	39	44
Probate	100	14	22	70	60	5	37	44	49	26	30	13	9	23	44	17	35	22	72	51	58
Divorce	57	38	4	42	102	15	52	57	36	23	61	0	0	11	65	0	26	56	94	45	35
TOTAL SAMPLE	699	13	35	67	35	3	30	40	52	45	21	17	14	20	45	13	30	33	78	44	50

TABLE 3.1 (continued)

Differentiation Among Six Selected Fields of Law

NOTES: In the explanations of the column headings, numbers prefixed with "A" indicate the question numbers in the interview schedule (see appendix A).

(1) Number of Practitioners: This is the number of respondents who devoted at least 25 percent of their time to a field (table 3.1) or a group of fields (table 3.2). All other entries in the row rest on this sample base, but are reduced by the small numbers of respondents who did not provide the information reported in a given column.

To determine the lawyer's distribution of time across fields, we asked:

A1. While a lawyer's time is often spread over many different areas of the law, we wish, for comparative purposes, to characterize those areas in which you spent the major part of your time during the last twelve months. [Respondent then was handed a card listing thirty fields of law.] In which of the listed areas have you spent: a. more than 50 percent of your time? b. between 25 percent and 50 percent of your time? c. between 5 percent and 25 percent of your time?

For purposes of analysis, the thirty fields were reduced to twenty-five. Four fields were excluded because of insufficient numbers of practitioners (admiralty, environmental defense, environmental plaintiff, and condemnations). Three areas were redefined to include fields that, by themselves, had insufficient cases (family law was redefined to include general family practice-paying clients, general family practice-poverty level clients, and consumer-buyer law; commercial law was redefined to include consumer-seller law; real estate was redefined to include landlord/tenant). Lawyers who spent time in tax, real estate, and civil litigation were classified as follows: if they derived 80 percent or more of their income from business clients, they were classified as business real estate, business tax, and business litigation; if they derived less than 80 percent from such sources or if this information was missing, they were classified as personal real estate, personal tax, and general litigation.

(2) Mean Percentage of Blue-collar Clients: These percentages were derived from answers to the following question:

A5C. Would you now think about the clients for whom you have handled personal matters in the last twelve months. [Respondent was handed a card listing five occupational categories.] What proportion of your clients fall into the occupational categories . . . ? Professional, Technical, Managerial; Sales and Clerical; Blue Collar Workers; Unemployed; Retired, In-School, Keeping house.

House counsel, government lawyers, and lawyers who spent less than 10 percent of their time on "personal matters" (defined as legal work for persons rather than for businesses) were not asked this question, and we therefore assigned a value of zero for their percentages of blue-collar clients.

(3) Mean Percent of Business Income from Major Corporate Clients: This is the mean percentage of law practice income reported by respondents who indicated that they received 10 percent or more of their income from work for businesses and who then answered the following question:

A5B. What proportion of your business income would come from the following size business clients?

The categories were major corporations (those with sales over $10,000,000 per year), medium-sized firms, or small businesses (those with sales of less than $250,000 per year). Government-employed lawyers were recorded as deriving 100 percent of their income from major corporate clients. Government-employed lawyers were recorded as deriving no income from major corporate clients.

(4) Mean Percentage of Stable Clients: These are the averages of respondents' estimates given in answer to the following question:

A7. What proportion of your clients have you represented for three years or more?

We did not ask house counsel or government lawyers this question, and we assigned them a value of 100 percent on this variable. Those who responded that they were employed as corporate house counsel were employed as deriving 100 percent of their income from major corporate clients.

(5) Median Number of Clients per Year: This is based on responses to the question:

A4. During the past twelve months, approximately how many clients have you done some work for—more than just going through a file, or turning over a file to another lawyer?

Again, house counsel and government lawyers were not asked this question; they were assigned a value of 1.

(6) Median Number of State Court Appearances per Month: This is the median number of state trial and appellate court appearances per month over the past year, as reported by respondents. See ABA

A9.   Different kinds of law require different kinds of professional activities. [Respondent received card listing seven pairs of statements.] Each pair represents polar opposites. Please circle the number which best represents your position in relation to the two opposites. If the situation in your practice is midway between poles, circle code 3; if your situation is at one or the other extreme, circle 1 or 5; if your position leans somewhat to either pole, circle 2 or 4.

The percentages reported in cols. (7)–(10) are based on the two values closest to the specified extreme (that is, either values of 1 or 2, or values of 4 or 5).

(7) *Percentage with High Encroachment on Practice*: This is the percentage who chose the following description of their legal practice: "There are aspects of my professional work which are being encroached upon by other occupations." The opposite was: "No other occupation is engaging in the kinds of legal matters with which I am primarily concerned."

(8) *Percentage High on Negotiating and Advising*: This is the percentage who chose the following description of their practice: "My specialty and type of practice requires skills in negotiating and advising clients, rather than detailed concern with technical skills." The opposite was: "My area demands skills in handling highly technical procedures rather than skills in negotiation and advising clients."

(9) *Percentage High on Professional Expertise*: This is the percentage who chose the following description of their practice: "The type and content of my practice is such that even an educated layman couldn't really understand or prepare the documents." The opposite was: "A para-professional could be trained to handle many of the procedures and documents in my area of the law."

(10) *Percentage with High Specialization of Work*: This is the percentage who chose the following description of their practice: "The area of law in which I work is so highly specialized that it demands I concentrate in just this one area." The opposite was: "The nature of my legal practice is such that I can handle a range of problems covering quite a number of different areas of legal practice."

(11)–(13): Respondents were asked, in the following question, about the type or form of organization of their law practice:

A3B.   Which category best describes [your] job? [Respondents received card with ten types of practice: solo; firm; federal, state, municipal/county or military government; corporate, insurance, banking, or railroad house counsel; or other.]

The four house counsel subcategories are here combined into one category (column [13]). Respondents were then asked: "How many lawyers are in your firm/office now?" Column (12) reports the percentages of respondents in firms with more than thirty lawyers.

(14) *Percentage Attended Elite Law Schools*: This is the percentage who received law degrees from Chicago, Columbia, Harvard, Michigan, Stanford, or Yale. (See chapters 1 and 6 for discussion of categories of law schools.) See A40E.

(15) *Percentage Attended Local Law Schools*: This is the percentage who received law degrees from De Paul, Kent, Loyola, or John Marshall, all located in Chicago. (The other two schools in Chicago—Northwestern and the University of Chicago—were included in the "prestige" and "elite" categories, respectively.) See A40E.

(16)–(18): The general question on religious background was:

A43.   Do you have a religious preference? That is, are you either Protestant, Roman Catholic, Jewish, or something else?

We then asked Protestants to specify their denominations and Jews to specify whether they are Orthodox, Conservative, or Reform.

(16) *Percentage of Type 1 Protestants*: This is the percentage who indicated affiliation with the following denominations: Congregational, Presbyterian, Episcopal, and United Church of Christ. (See chapter 1.)

(17) *Percentage of Catholics*: This is the percentage who indicated that they were Roman Catholics.

(18) *Percentage of Jewish Practitioners*: This is the percentage who either expressed a preference for Judaism in response to question A43 or indicated that they were of Jewish origin in response to: "What nationality background do you think of yourself as having—that is, besides being American?" See A46A.

(19) *Percentage of Metropolitan Origin*: This is the percentage reporting that they had lived during high school in a metropolitan area with a population over 250,000. See A38.

(20) *Mean Age*: This is the average age of respondents in the field or group of fields.

(21) *Prestige Score*: Standardized prestige scores of the fields of law were computed, based on the responses of a subsample to the following question:

On the following specialty list, would you please indicate the general prestige of each specialty within the legal profession at large?

These findings are presented and discussed in chapter 4, at table 4.1.

Even a cursory inspection of table 3.1 discloses large differences among the fields on many of the variables. Client volume, for example, ranges from a median of 2 in public utilities to 102 for divorce. (A field not presented here, personal injury plaintiffs' work, has an even higher client volume: a median of 149 clients represented in the past year.) The percentage of lawyers in each field who are solo practitioners ranges from 0 to 61 percent, and for those who practice in firms with more than thirty lawyers the range is from 0 to 77 percent. (This range of variation occurs among only five fields, excluding criminal prosecution.) Similarly, the percentage of lawyers who attended elite law schools ranges from 0 to 45, that for local law schools ranges from 14 to 67, and the three religion categories have ranges of 36 to 44 percentage points separating the high and low scores. Thus, the fields are highly differentiated on these important variables. Moreover, we will argue that this striking differentiation is highly ordered, that it is organized in a consistent hierarchy.

The pattern of the differences among the fields on many of the variables seems clear and interpretable. The mean percentage of blue-collar workers among the clients of these six fields ranges from 0 to 38, while the mean percentage of income received from major corporate clients—the other side of the socioeconomic scale—ranges from 4 to 61 percent. Disregarding criminal prosecution, where by definition government is the only client,[8] the rank orders of the fields on these two client type variables are, without deviation, exactly reversed. Many of the other variables reproduce this same rank order to a greater or lesser degree. If we measure the adherence of the other variables to this order by the rather stringent criterion that no more than one field may depart from it and that field may depart by no more than one position in the rank, we find that the following additional variables qualify:

- the volume of clients served by the field; *i.e.*, median number of clients represented during past year
- the percentage of practitioners who say that their work demands a high degree of professional expertise
- the degree of specialization by practitioners in the field; *i.e.*, percentage of respondents indicating high specialization

8. If the respondent changed jobs within the reporting year, however (or was engaged in moonlighting), a prosecutor might report work for some other sort of client.

- the percentage of lawyers in the field who are solo practitioners
- the rating of the prestige of the field within the legal profession

Several more of the variables, while less strongly associated with this rank order, nontheless share it to an obvious degree.

If we inspect the intercorrelations among four of the variables included in table 3.1—the percentage of blue-collar clients, client volume, the percentage of solo practitioners, and the percentage of practitioners who attended local law schools—computed across the full set of twenty-five fields, we find that the six correlation coefficients in the matrix range between .63 and .91. Since these are correlations of aggregated data (that is, they are performed on the averages or composite scores for whole fields rather than for individual respondents), we would expect relatively high coefficients, but these are high by almost any standard. In fact, one of the most vexing problems we confronted in analyzing these data is that the variables are so highly associated with one another, either positively or negatively. That is, the variables have the statistical property of multicollinearity.[9] This makes it difficult, at the least, to distinguish each variable's independent effects, but the point to note here is that a strong, overarching structure appears to organize these variables when they are analyzed at the level of the fields of law. It is less important for our purposes to state precisely each variable's effect on the legal profession's overall social structure than it is to observe their coincidence. The variables appear to reflect interrelated social processes that reinforce one another to produce an impressively persistent and highly coherent structure; the legal profession, in our view, is what quantitatively oriented sociologists call an "overdetermined" social system. We will argue that the types of clients served—the characteristics of the clients and of their use of lawyers—are the primary explanatory variables that organize and control the others, but such proofs as we will be able to offer are necessarily less statistical than sociological.

To facilitate our observation of this structure of differentiation within the profession, we present a second table utilizing data on all twenty-five fields grouped into six hierarchical categories. Table 3.2 is similar in form to table 3.1 and includes the same set of variables, but, rather than report values at the level of individual fields

9. See Hubert M. Blalock, *Social Statistics*, 2d ed. (New York: McGraw-Hill, 1972), pp. 454–64; Robert A. Gordon, "Issues in Multiple Regression," *American Journal of Sociology* 73 (1968): 592, 596.

TABLE 3.2
Differentiation Among Six Groups of Fields of Law and Generalists

Groups	No. of Practitioners (1)	Blue-collar Clients Mean % (2)	Mean % Business Income from Major Corporate Clients (3)	Stable Clients Mean % (4)	Median No. Clients per Year (5)	Median No. of State Court Appearances per Month (6)	% High Encroachment on Practice (7)	% High on Negotiating and Advising (8)	% High on Professional Expertise (9)	% High Specialization of Work (10)	% Solo Practitioners (11)	% Firms of More Than 30 Lawyers (12)	% Corporate House Counsel (13)	% Attended Elite Law Schools (14)	% Attended Local Law Schools (15)	% Type 1 Protestants (16)	% Catholic (17)	% Jewish (18)	% Metropolitan Origin (19)	% Mean Age (20)
Large corporate	151	2	62	69	25	1	30	33	62	53	6	44	24	28	32	15	29	28	72	41
Regulatory	77	6	50	83	20	0	26	40	60	75	12	6	18	19	32	19	23	27	71	45
General corporate	226	6	43	71	33	2	31	35	57	35	15	24	17	27	36	13	31	33	75	44
Political	32	3	11	84	3	9	19	26	55	38	0	3	0	12	59	16	44	25	78	40
Personal business	165	18	18	64	75	6	38	42	43	30	34	12	5	22	47	12	35	29	76	49
Personal plight	171	34	10	49	100	15	34	52	42	36	42	3	2	12	64	4	33	42	92	44
"Generalists"	86	15	41	71	50	5	25	41	49	33	27	13	21	17	52	16	26	35	78	45
Total Sample	699	13	35	67	35	3	30	40	52	45	21	17	14	20	45	13	30	33	78	44

NOTE: See notes to table 3.1

of law, it presents scores for larger groupings of the fields. As table 3.1 indicates, our sample includes relatively few practitioners in many of the fields, and the groupings of fields thus provide larger, more stable numbers for analysis.

Because the groups contain fields that differ substantially, the aggregation of the fields suppresses the degree of variance, as compared with that at the level of the individual fields. Nonetheless, the differentiation among the groups that we observe in table 3.1 remains quite substantial. Very large ranges still occur on the two variables relating to socioeconomic type of client, client volume, frequency of state court appearances, type of practice organization, and percentage of high status Protestants among the practitioners. Five more of the variables have a range of at least 100 percent; that is, the maximum value at least doubles the minimum. These are the "encroachment on practice," "negotiating and advising," and "specialization" variables, and the law school types. Thus, thirteen of the nineteen variables exhibit differences among the groups of at least this magnitude.

Four of the groups of fields lie in the corporate sector of the profession; the remaining two are in the sector that primarily represents individuals or small businesses. We have distributed the fields among the groups as shown on p. 73.[10]

We intend the groups of fields to comprehend cognate areas of practice. As indicated above, we believe that the types of clients served primarily define these areas. We have refrained, however, from simply using statistically generated clusters of fields to maximize homogeneity in the client type data; though those data informed our categorization, we did not derive the groups solely by empirical methods. Instead, we also took into account conceptual notions about the nature of the fields, including subjective characteristics of the clients and of the substance of the work.[11]

10. By design, the 6 fields of law presented in table 3.1 include 1 from each of the 6 groups listed, in the same order.

11. Thus, the "regulatory" group is distinguished from the "general corporate" by a substantive concern with economic enterprises that are regulated by independent or quasi-independent governmental agencies, and the "political" group includes fields concerned with formal governmental functions, fields in which a successful practice or career reputedly depends upon good political connections. (For our purposes, governments and labor unions are corporate bodies.) See James S. Coleman, "Loss of Power," *American Sociological Review* 38 (1973): 1–17.

The "large corporate" group includes those fields we thought most likely to serve the largest business corporations. In the mean percentage of practice income received from "major" corporate clients, however, personal injury defense work ranks higher

The tables also include a category of "generalists"—86 respondents who did not devote as much as 25 percent of their time to any one field and thus are included in none of the fields or groups of fields. Seventy-eight more respondents (10 percent of our random sample) were not then practicing law; the tables include only the responses of the 699 practicing lawyers. As noted above, we double-counted some of those respondents in ascertaining the characteristics of the individual fields.[12] Many respondents qualify for inclusion in more than one field within the groups used in table 3.2, but

---

(continued)
than some of the fields that we included in the large corporate group. Nonetheless, our categories seem appropriate. Though the insurance companies represented by personal injury defense lawyers are certainly corporations with large assets and dollar volume, the law and the facts involved in personal injury cases distinguish their problems from the legal problems of large corporations per se. Securities and antitrust defense problems are, by contrast, the sorts of legal matters that afflict large corporations almost exclusively. Though businesses of all sizes are concerned with taxes, both the complexity and the consequences of tax problems tend to be directly proportional to a corporation's size. A corporation is also likely to be sizable if it is concerned with the legal problems involved in real estate development, and only large corporations can afford to use litigation regularly as a corporate strategy.

We might well have placed the practice of labor law for management clients in the "regulatory" group with the representation of unions, but we included it in the large corporate group instead because the companies with union difficulties sufficiently serious to warrant hiring a labor lawyer are likely to be quite large employers. In their study of the Missouri bar, Watson and Downing treated union representation as a distinct specialty but included labor work on the management side in their general corporate law category; see Richard A. Watson and Rondal G. Downing, *The Politics of Bench and Bar: Judicial Selection Under the Missouri Nonpartisan Court Plan* (New York: John Wiley, 1969), pp. 24–25.

Our division of the personal client sector into two groups rests upon a similar distinction in the substance of the work. The "personal business" group includes fields concerned with the financial transactions of individuals (or of small businesses owned by individuals or families), while the "personal plight" group includes fields concerned with emotional issues, with personal freedom or liberty, or with personal anguish. We do not mean to suggest that the latter fields have no financial consequences for the clients. Significant financial burden may accompany personal anguish—especially in personal injury work, general family practice, or divorce—but the distinguishing characteristic of the "personal plight" fields is their emotive content.

Several hierarchical cluster analyses (diameter method) (see Stephen C. Johnson, "Hierarchical Clustering Schemes, *Psychometrika* 32 [1967]: 241) were performed using selected combinations of the client characteristic variables described in table 3.1. In each case, the first two principal components of a factor analysis of the relevant intercorrelation matrix were used as proximity estimators for the clustering routine. The cluster structure was quite consistent across the various solutions. In devising the clusters used in this chapter, however, for substantive reasons we decided to assign labor union law to the corporate client sector rather than leave it with the personal client fields with which it was clustered. Similarly, we moved civil rights from the corporate client sector to the personal plight cluster for definitional reasons (see *infra* note 18.)

12. See p. 64.

Corporate Sector	Personal Sector
Large Corporate Group	Personal Business Group
Antitrust (defense)	General litigation
Business litigation	Personal real estate
Business real estate	Personal tax
Business tax	Probate
Labor (management)	Personal Plight Group
Securities	Civil rights
Regulatory Group	Criminal (defense)
Labor (unions)	Divorce
Patents	General family practice
Public utilities and	Personal injury (plaintiffs)
administrative law	
General Corporate Group	
Antitrust (plaintiffs)	
Banking	
Commercial	
General corporate	
Personal injury (defense)	
Political Group	
Criminal (prosecution)	
Municipal	

in computing group scores we counted each respondent within the group only once. A respondent who devoted at least 25 percent of his time to fields in two or more groups, however, was included in the analysis of each of those groups. With the 25 percent time criterion, therefore, a respondent might theoretically be included in as many as four fields. We discuss overlap among the fields in detail in chapter 2, but we may note here that, of the 699 practicing lawyers, the 86 generalists are included in none of the groups, 390 respondents are counted in only one group, 190 in two groups, and the remaining 17 in three groups. In general, this double counting has the conservative effect of understating differentiation among the fields of law.

The Dimensions of Differentiation

We have noted the magnitude of the differences among the fields of law on several variables and have observed the more obvious patterns of those differences, but it is difficult to grasp the overall structure of the differentiation by pondering numbers in a table. If we consider simultaneously several kinds of similarities and differences in the fields and group the fields accordingly, what will be the resulting structure? In a graphic representation of that structure, will the fields be grouped by type of client or will some other dimension or dimensions appear to determine the structure?

Multidimensional scalogram analysis is one approach to answering these questions.[13] Figure 3.1 depicts the relationships among the fields of law, representing them as points in two-dimensional space and accounting for their positions on a number of variables. Fields with similar profiles lie in close proximity (that is, share a region of Euclidean space); those with greater differences on the variables lie at greater distances from one another.[14]

13. Specifically, we have used MSA-1. See James C. Lingoes, ed., *Geometric Representations of Relational Data* (1977) (hereafter cited as *Geometric Representations*); Edward O. Laumann and James House, "Living Room Styles and Social Attributes: The Patterning of Material Artifacts in a Modern Urban Community," in E. Laumann et al., eds., *The Logic of Social Hierarchies* (Chicago: Markham, 1970), p. 195.

14. The Euclidean distances are assumed to be a monotonic function of an underlying multidimensional construct, "legal role," that creates social distance among the fields of law because of dissimilarities in some specialized set of their characteristics. We have already argued in chapter 2 that we can conceptualize the fields of law as a set of differentiated social roles and that an individual lawyer may occupy a number of these roles simultaneously.

In the multidimensional scalogram analysis, our interval level data were transformed into ordinal data. (MSA-1 requires, in fact, only nominal level data. See *Geometric Representations, supra* note 13.) The derived Euclidean distances represented in the figure are, of course, metric and fully at the interval level of measurement, but the data used to derive these distances were at the ordinal level. That is, we specified the rank order of the fields on each variable but not the distances between fields.

The algorithm required a reduction in the number of values used on each of the variables. Therefore, we collapsed the range on each variable into 2 to 4 categories of fields. For example, we converted the percentages of Jewish practitioners in the fields into a four-point scale. We gave 6 fields with percentages of 10 to 15 a value of 1, or "low"; 5 fields with percentages from 21 to 30 a value of 2, or "medium low"; 7 fields with percentages ranging from 30 to 40 a value of 3, or "medium high," and the remaining 7 fields with percentages above 40 a value of 4, or "high." Except where extreme outlying cases occurred, we preserved natural breaks in the distributions. We simply dichotomized the percentages of government employees in the various fields. We gave the 15 fields with 0 to 5 percent government employees the value 1, and the remaining 10 fields, all having 10 percent or more, the value 2. Four of the variables were trichotomized. For example, in the percentage of income received from business clients, we classed as "low" the 10 fields with scores of less than 50 percent, as "medium" the 8 fields with 50 to 80 percent, and as "high" the remaining 7 fields with over 80 percent. The input matrix thus consisted of the 25 fields in the rows and 9 columns of variables having entries of "1," "2," "3," or "4" corresponding to the respective field's position on each scale.

Figure 3.1 portrays the two-dimensional solution, which had a very satisfactory coefficient of contiguity of .994 (a perfect fit would be 1.00) after only 12 iterations. The one-dimensional solution does not reach .99 (though it comes close) even after 50 iterations, and its fit is no longer improving appreciably at that point.

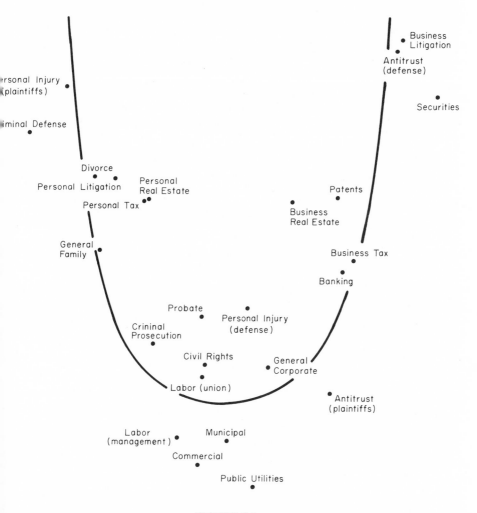

FIGURE 3.1
Multidimensional Scalogram Analysis of Twenty-five Fields of Law on Nine Selected Variables

The nine variables used in this analysis are:

1. Business clients (mean percentage of income received from clients who are businesses rather than persons)
2. Stability of practice (mean percentage of clients represented for three years or more)
3. Lawyer referrals (mean percentage of clients obtained through referrals from other lawyers)

4. Freedom in choice of cases (percentage of practitioners indicating wide latitude in selecting clients)
5. Negotiating and advising (percentage of practitioners indicating their work often involves negotiating and advising rather than the use of highly technical procedures)
6. Government employment (percentage of practitioners employed by federal, state, or local government)
7. Local law school (percentage of practitioners who attended any of four local law schools in Chicago)
8. High-status Protestants (percentage of practitioners who state a preference for one of the Type I Protestant denominations)
9. Jewish origin (percentage of practitioners who report either Jewish religion or ethnicity)

Three criteria determined the choice of these nine variables. First, to minimize the redundancy built into the model, we sought to avoid choosing highly intercorrelated variables. Because of the multicollinearity in the data set, this was particularly important and difficult.[15] Given the structured nature of the data—and, presumably, of the social system under study—we could have avoided substantial intercorrelations completely only by choosing variables of tangential relevance or doubtful substantive significance. Second, we sought to represent the full range of data in the variables chosen and to avoid overrepresenting any one type. Thus, the nine variables include data on client type, sources of clients, task type, practice setting, schooling, and social origins. Finally, and perhaps most importantly, we required that the variables chosen have substantive significance. There is a persuasive case that each of the variables used might have important influence on the social distances among

15. The intercorrelations among the 9 variables used in this solution are relatively modest. We did not use some interesting and important variables (e.g., the percentage of blue-collar clients) because they are too strongly associated with one or more of those included in the solution. Of the variables used here, the pair that is most highly correlated is percentage Jewish with percentage Type I Protestants. Pearson's coefficient for that pair is −.53, which means that one variable accounts for 28 percent of the variance in the other.

In a previously published article, we presented a different version of this solution, using 12 variables (see 76 *Michigan Law Review* 1111, 1129–30 [1978]). The number of variables is reduced here in order to lessen further the problem of intercorrelation. The 3 variables dropped from the analysis are the volume of clients, the frequency of state court litigation, and the "size of practice organization" (median number of lawyers in the firm or other organization in which practitioners work). It is interesting to note that though these variables were dropped the solution is nonetheless structured in such a way that the patterns of these variables are still evident. The general structure of the solution presented here is, in fact, highly similar to the previous, 12-variable version.

the fields. Those arguments have, in fact, already been summarized at the beginning of this chapter.

As we see from the figure, the relationships among the fields form a structure that may be interpreted as roughly U-shaped. (The U-shaped line is not a part of the statistical solution. We have drawn it in to aid interpretation.) The fields that serve corporations lie to the right, fields that serve persons lie to the left. Fields that serve either a mixture of the two or special sorts of corporations such as governments or labor unions fall toward the lower middle.[16] The reader will recall that only one of the nine variables used in the multidimensional scalogram analysis explicitly measures the type of client—though, as we have already noted and argued, some of the other variables correlate with client type.

The vertical dimension of the structure appears to be related to the distinction between litigation and office practice. The fields with higher rates of court appearances tend to be higher in the space. Other general patterns in the structure are perhaps less striking, but they are surely discernible. The median size of the law firm or other practice organization increases as one moves from the upper left counterclockwise around the U. Client volume and the percentage of practitioners who attended a local law school both move in the opposite direction, increasing as one proceeds clockwise around the U. The percentage of stable clients generally increases as one moves toward the bottom of the figure. The most prestigious fields of law are at the upper right of the U and the least prestigious are at the upper left. Prestige, in fact, decreases in a very orderly clockwise fashion; the correlation between our measure of the prestige order of the fields and their order on the U is .9.[17]

The groupings of fields used in table 3.2 also tend to be reflected

16. Recall that the field labeled "Public Utilities" on the figure includes "Administrative Law" and other sorts of government regulation work. It has, in fact, one of the highest percentages of government employed lawyers (see appendix B).

17. One might wonder why litigation fields should be high on both ends of the U—meaning that corporate litigators have higher prestige than many of the other corporate fields, while litigators in the personal sector have lower prestige than other personal client fields. It may be that the greater visibility of litigators enhances their prestige if the substance of their cases is regarded as prestigious and enhances their derogation if the kinds of cases and clients with which they deal are derogated; see Robert Merton, chapter on "Continuities in Reference Group Behavior," in *Social Theory and Social Structure*, revised and enlarged ed. (New York: Free Press, 1968).

The prestige rankings reported in chapter 4 used a somewhat different list of fields than that employed in this chapter. Specifically, the prestige rankings did not differentiate between the "personal" and "business or corporate" sides of the tax, civil litigation, and real estate fields. To compare the prestige rankings with the

in the figure. A small cluster of high status fields representing the largest corporations lie at the upper right of the U. Generally, the work for larger business corporations appears to be concentrated higher on the right side of the U, and the size of the businesses represented usually decreases as one moves down. Moving clockwise, we encounter a group of fields dealing with financial transactions, particularly those regulated by government. Farther clockwise, a more diffuse cluster contains the remainder of the corporate sector. The field of probate law—which, of all the personal client fields, most deals with the transmission of wealth and thus with the wealthier personal clients—is a part of this general cluster but is on its upper left periphery, nearest to the balance of the personal client fields. The other fields in our personal business group are included in the next cluster of points in the figure, still moving clockwise. Finally, we find four of the five fields of the personal plight group in the upper left quadrant of the U. The fifth, civil rights, is a special case. Because half of its practitioners are full-time government employees, we could in fact define civil rights work as a governmental function and place the field in the political group of the corporate sector, which is about where it appears in the figure.[18]

(continued)
order of the fields on the U-shaped multidimensional scalogram analysis, therefore, we had to generate prestige scores for both sides of each of these three fields. We did so by computing a regression model, using characteristics of the fields as the variables, that explained 80 percent of the variance in the prestige scores of the original list of fields. We then used that model to create prestige scores for the new fields according to their observed values for the same set of characteristics, as weighted by the regression equation. Finally, we calculated a Spearman rank-order correlation of the fields' prestige ranks, including the newly created prestige scores, with their ranks along the U structure. This correlation is .90, significant at and beyond the .01 level. We determined the ranks on the U by placing the fields on the smooth U curve depicted in figure 3.1 at the intersections with the curve of the shortest lines that could be drawn from the fields' points to the curve. We are indebted to Scott Marden and Margaret Troha for their assistance in this analysis.

18. Including civil rights work among the personal plight fields greatly increases the heterogeneity of that group on most of the variables. The civil rights field is atypical in that a substantial portion of the cases are handled as a public service without fee (*pro bono publico*). Ideological motivations may thus attract to this work lawyers who are unlikely to be found in the other personal plight fields (see chapter 5 for a more extensive discussion of this point). For example, the distribution of civil rights lawyers among law school types looks much more like that of a field from the "large corporate" group than like any of the other fields in the personal plight group—the percentage of civil rights lawyers who attended elite schools is more than twice that of the next highest personal plight field.

Still, the substance of its work seems to dictate the placement of civil rights. The civil rights field probably exemplifies par excellence the sort of legal work that deals with personal liberty and freedom. A plausible argument can be made, however, for placing civil rights work in the corporate sector. Outlining that argument illustrates

Conclusions

These findings suggest that even though the measures used to determine the characteristics of the fields of law (principally, the 25 percent time criterion) generate rather weak or contaminated categories, the variables display a consistent structure based primarily

---

how the variables interrelate and shed light upon the interpretation of one another.

It is commonly believed that most of the practitioners doing civil rights work are corporate lawyers from large firms who handle a few such cases on a *pro bono* basis. As an elite of the bar committed to the protection of civil liberties, these lawyers are thought to include disproportionate numbers of Jews and higher status Protestants. Arthur Corbin asserted as early as 1922 that the profession's elite were more likely to serve "the poor and the friendless" than were lower status lawyers; see Arthur Corbin, "Democracy and Education for the Bar," 4 *American Law School Review* 725, 732 (1922). While some elite lawyers may devote small amounts of their time to civil rights law, however, the data on the 14 lawyers in our sample who devote 25 percent or more of their time to work that they label "civil rights" suggest that this assumption should be examined. Because of the small number of these civil rights lawyers in our sample, most of the differences in representation of ethnic groups among the 14 lawyers are not statistically significant. Nonetheless, it may be worthwhile to take a look at the differences.

Both Jews and high status Protestants are represented among these civil rights lawyers in *less* than their percentages of the total population of lawyers, Catholics are represented in about the same percentage as in the total sample, and both lower status Protestants (Type II) and the nonreligious are substantially overrepresented. Some of the lower status Protestants are probably blacks, who are overrepresented in the civil rights practice by a factor of more than five times their percentage in the bar (14 percent versus 2.5 percent). About twice the normal percentage of southern and eastern Europeans are found in civil rights work. The distribution of civil rights work by practice setting probably explains these findings. Half of the lawyers who report devoting 25 percent or more of their time to civil rights work are government employees, and almost another third (29 percent) practice in firms of fewer than ten lawyers. Only 13 percent of these civil rights lawyers are from large firms with more than 30 lawyers, and only 7 percent are from corporate law departments. Solo practitioners apparently cannot afford to do civil rights work; they are not represented at all. Nor, indeed, are lawyers from medium-sized firms. Thus, Catholics and southern and eastern Europeans may have disproportionate shares of civil rights work because they are overrepresented among government lawyers.

We do not wish to make much of all this, especially since our sample includes only 14 civil rights lawyers at the 25 percent level of activity, but the general pattern seems reasonably clear. Perhaps the most interesting point to be noted here is that civil rights work, rather than being motivated by noblesse oblige, appears to be in large part a public function, performed by government employees who are compensated by tax funds. Accordingly, we could with almost equal justification place the civil rights field in the corporate client sector with other government work. Though this reclassification would increase the sectors' homogeneity on several variables, the conceptual reasons already advanced have induced us to sacrifice this tidiness. The work of the profession is, in fact, a bit untidy in places, and it is important to note where points of ambiguity or overlap occur. The civil rights field presents one of the relatively rare opportunities for full-fledged corporate lawyers to practice law that deals with personal plight, with human suffering. Thus, the civil rights field, with a few others, is a point of intersection in the profession. Though quite a small field, it is one of those special places where residents of the profession's two hemispheres may meet one another.

on the nature of the clients served by the fields. Because particular types of clients are often associated with corresponding types of legal issues, however, it is often difficult to determine whether some aspect of the structure of the fields of law is more plausibly attributed to the nature of the clients served or to the knowledge or skills used in the fields. For example, in analyzing the overlap among the fields of law in the allocation of lawyers' time in chapter 2, we found a small, tight cluster consisting of patent law and the two sides of antitrust law. What common attributes of patents and antitrust enhance the likelihood that a lawyer who practices one will also practice the other? Broadly, both fields involve legal doctrines that in some way regulate competition, and they share common origins in English legal history.[19]

But this overlap in the doctrines of the fields corresponds to an overlap in the types of clients served. We may often think of patent lawyers as dealing with an "inventor," and we may also think of inventors as individual entrepreneurs, independent, idiosyncratic, obsessive, and quirky. This is, of course, a romantic, nineteenth-century view of the inventor, fostered by juvenile fiction of the Tom Swift genre. However quirky they may be, most commercially significant inventors are now surely organization men in the research and development departments of major corporations, and most valuable patents are now owned by large corporations or exploited by them under license. As with antitrust specialists, therefore, patent lawyers' principal clients are corporations. The patent lawyers in our sample estimated that they derived an average of 95 percent of their practice income from businesses rather than persons.

Moreover, the historical importance of using patents as a means of monopolizing further exacerbates this confounding of knowledge base and client type. One of the methods used by the classic trusts to monopolize an industry was acquisition of the patents for

---

19. During the sixteenth century, the Crown increasingly granted favored individuals monopoly privileges or exclusive licenses through proclamations known as "letters patent" (that is, open or public letters). The Statute of Monopolies (1623, 21 Jac. I, c. 3) curbed this practice. It voided the licenses or "patents" previously granted and provided that persons injured by a monopoly in the future could sue for treble damages, but it excepted patents granted to "the first and true inventor or inventors of . . . manufactures." Thus, Holdsworth observes that the Statute of Monopolies was "the foundation of the patent law of the present day" (William Holdsworth, *A History of English Law* [London: Methuen, 1924], vol. 4, p. 353). See also James Rahl and Ronald Kennedy, *Cases and Materials on Antitrust Law*, multilithed (Northwestern University Law School, 1978).

the key manufacturing processes.[20] The clients who owned the patents became, then, the clients charged with restraint of trade, and the legal issue became whether the scope of the patent-granted monopoly privilege conflicted with the scope of the antitrust laws.[21] Today, litigation brought by the Justice Department, the Federal Trade Commission, and private plaintiffs often charges illegal restrictive practices in the licensing or use of patents. Patent infringement claims are also met with antitrust counterclaims or a defense of misuse of the patent; that is, the defendant in the infringement action charges that the plaintiff used the patent to restrict competition in violation of the antitrust laws or of the policy favoring competition. Thus, both the doctrines and the types of clients served by the two fields merge at some points.

To attempt to distinguish the independent effects of client type and of knowledge base on the structure of the fields would, in such circumstances, be not only difficult but artificial and misleading. We should, instead, appreciate that the two are inextricably entwined and then seek to understand their relationship and how the legal and social systems produced it.

In some areas of the law, however, the adversary system provides a natural control of the two variables. In criminal law, labor law, or personal injury work a rather rigid division separates practitioners serving opposing sides of the cases—with their corresponding, distinct types of clients—while the substance of the law is constant within each area. Therefore, where one doctrinal area of the law contains specialized fields of practice that are dictated by the type of client, we may want to examine the extent to which those fields are socially differentiated. How socially distant is labor law work for unions from the representation of management, criminal prosecution from criminal defense, or plaintiffs' antitrust or personal injury work from defendants'? We may, of course, look at the differences between those pairs of fields on any variables that particularly concern us, but the multidimensional scalogram analysis summarily measures the extent of their social distance. Inspecting figure 3.1, we find the two sides of labor law located relatively close together at the base of the U. The other pairs, however, lie

20. See, e.g., United States v. United Shoe Mach. Co., 247 U.S. 32, 52–55 (1918) (United Shoe's acquisition of key patents by merger with and acquisition of companies holding those patents did not violate the antitrust law). In addition, see Justice Clark's dissenting opinion, 247 U.S. 77–78.
21. See, e.g., United Shoe Mach. Co. v. United States, 258 U.S. 451, 460–64 (1922).

quite a bit further apart: criminal prosecution and defense are both on the left side of the figure but they are sufficiently separated to be clearly distinct; similarly, antitrust defense is considerably higher on the right side of the U than is antitrust plaintiffs' work; and personal injury plaintiffs' work reaches the far upper left corner, while personal injury defense falls into the general corporate cluster located near the lower middle of the U.[22] In some cases, therefore, differences in the clients served apparently produce clear social distinctions between the fields even though the fields' knowledge bases are substantially identical.

We would argue, in fact, that the more the clients of two fields differ, the more socially distant the fields will tend to be. Consider, for example, the comparisons just made between these pairs of fields. Though labor unions and the corporations that battle them doubtless differ in many significant ways, both are usually large organizations with substantial assets. The differences between criminal defendants and the government officials whom prosecutors consider their clients are probably greater (though the two kinds of clients do on occasion coincide), and greater yet are the differences between clients of the pairs more widely separated in figure 3.1. The two sides of antitrust work appear to serve distinct sorts of businesses—the defense lawyers serve very large corporations, while the plaintiffs' lawyers serve the individuals and smaller businesses that sue the "trusts." Antitrust defense lawyers report that they derive 77 percent of their practice income, on the average, from major corporations, while an average of only 22 percent of the income of antitrust plaintiffs' lawyers comes from major corporations. Of these four pairs of fields, however, the difference in the clients is probably greatest between the two sides of personal injury work. The clients of the personal injury defense lawyers are almost exclusively insurance companies—major corporations with very substantial assets.[23] By contrast, the clients of the plaintiffs' lawyers are usually individuals, and although doubtless drawn from a range

22. Similarly, if we compare "personal litigation" with litigation for business clients, thus holding the task type constant, we find business litigation at the far upper right but personal litigation diagonally across the space at the middle left. In this case, however, the substantive law no doubt differs systematically with the kind of client.
23. The personal injury defense lawyers in our sample reported that on the average 60 percent of their income from business clients came from "major" corporations (which we had defined in the survey as corporations with sales in excess of $10 million annually). This percentage may sound modest, but it is quite large when

of social classes, they are from the lower classes far more often than are the clients of most lawyers.[24]

As was the case in chapter 2 with respect to the organization of lawyers' work, therefore, we conclude that the most plausible interpretation of the findings is that the nature of the clients served by the fields primarily determines the structure of social differentiation among the fields. This reading of the data raises an issue that we address from several different perspectives in the remaining chapters: given the tendency of the profession's structure to respond to interests and demands of clients—that is, of parties external to the profession—how much autonomy does the legal profession enjoy in defining professional roles, in determining which lawyers will perform which services for which clients, and in organizing the delivery of those services?

---

compared with most fields—"general corporate" lawyers, for example, reported an average of only 39 percent of their income from major corporations—and it is roughly equal to the average percentage of the corporate litigators, who reported 57 percent from major corporations.

24. Personal injury defense lawyers derived 25 percent of their law practice income from work for persons (rather than businesses); for personal injury plaintiffs' lawyers, the figure was 76 percent. The percentage of blue-collar workers among the clients of personal injury plaintiffs' lawyers was 43 percent—the highest in any field. (see appendix B, table B.1)

Chapter 4

HONOR AMONG LAWYERS*

IN THE preceding chapters, we have noted the strong relationship between the types of clients served by the fields of law and the nature of the social organization of those fields. We have also suggested, in the concluding paragraph of chapter 3, that clients or other parties outside the legal profession might determine the allocation of lawyers to different sorts of work, thus affecting both quantity and quality in the distribution of legal services. But the law is a high status profession, and the desire for elevated professional standing is presumably a part of the motivation that induces persons to enter the occupation. In choosing the fields of law in which he will practice, therefore, a lawyer may seek the work that will maximize his prestige within the bar.[1] Such prestige might cor-

---

*This chapter is a revised version of an article that appeared in the 1977 *American Bar Foundation Research Journal* 155–216 (winter), under the title, "Specialization and Prestige in the Legal Profession: The Structure of Deference."

After publication of the original article, we made corrections in the data tape that reflected several recodings of the respondents' practice and personal characteristics, but the only substantial change involved the classification of real estate practitioners, as described in the note at the beginning of chapter 2. Because of the costs in time and data-processing expenses that would be incurred in redoing the entire analysis with the revised tape, we have decided to retain the tables and figures used in the original published report. For this reason, there will be some discrepancies between the data reported here and those given in most of the other chapters. (Only this chapter and chapter 8 are based on the original tape. All other data reported in the book incorporate the recodes and are thus mutually consistent.) We have, however, run some of the key analyses reported in this chapter using the revised tape and have confirmed our expectation that none of the substantive conclusions drawn in this chapter need to be changed as a result of the recoding.

1. Social standing outside the profession, of course, may not be identical to that within it. Some of the lawyers who enjoy the highest repute—or, at least, the great-

respond to the differences among the types of clients served, following the division of labor and the patterns of social differentiation among the fields noted earlier. Service to the rich and the powerful might well earn one prestige in many circles (and some of the money and power might rub off as well, probably with no deleterious effect on prestige), while service to the poor and powerless might be less highly regarded. But the conferring of honor or deference is in its nature a process that is highly charged with symbolic content, and it might therefore be influenced less by economic and power considerations and more by norms or values. Learned professions are, after all, said to embrace values that set them apart from ordinary occupations—values that emphasize the importance of intellectual skills and devotion to public service (see pp. 21–22). If this is so, honor and deference might be accorded by the bar to those lawyers' jobs that are most characterized by conformity to these values, and thus prestige within the profession and its consequent impact on the distribution of legal services might be determined by the standards and criteria of the profession itself rather than by the clientele or by other factors external to the profession.

Yet another possibility exists: lawyers might simply try to make money. That is, in selecting among the available work, they may seek to maximize profit.[2] Or there may be some trade-off between prestige and profit, some optimal level of each with respect to the other. The necessity of choosing between profit and prestige will be avoided, however, to the extent that the sorts of work that enjoy greatest prestige within the profession are coincidentally those that are also most highly paid. If high income should bring high pres-

---

est fame—among the public at large may not be so highly regarded within the bar, while others may be "lawyers' lawyers"; see Andrew Abbott, "Status and Status Strain in the Professions," *American Journal of Sociology* 86 (1981): 819. The prominence of a Lee Bailey or Melvin Belli or even of a Dean Acheson or Cyrus Vance is not what we mean by prestige, however. We are not concerned with cases of conspicuous individuals. Sociological usage restricts the term "prestige" to the evaluation of the standing of a general social position when compared with others (each of which has a number of incumbents). The esteem in which a given individual is held in the legal community is a combination of the prestige of the several social positions that he simultaneously occupies (including his work specialties, ethnic group membership, seniority, etc.) and the social evaluation of the personal competence and skill with which he occupies them. Thus, we are concerned here only with the general social evaluation of legal roles or the fields of law and not with the relative esteem or personal reputation of individual lawyers.

2. The amount and range of choice that lawyers enjoy in selecting their cases will always be more or less constrained, of course, demand being both limited and structured.

tige or (no matter how remote the possibility may seem to a professor) if high prestige should command high pay, or if service to the rich and powerful should earn one both honor and riches, such a result would follow. But that may or may not be the case. If the values of the profession do, in fact, emphasize the duty of public service or the desirability of intellectually challenging work, prestige within the profession might be expected to reflect those values, and there might not then be a close correspondence between wealth or social power and honor among lawyers.

In their discussion of the theoretical and methodological difficulties of current empirical work on occupational prestige, John H. Goldthorpe and Keith Hope note that prestige has classically been defined as "a particular form of social power and advantage that is of a symbolic rather than of an economic or political character, and which gives rise to structured relationships of deference, acceptance and derogation."[3] They thus emphasize that prestige judgments are functionally autonomous from the hierarchies of wealth and power—that they are, instead, subjective responses rooted in generally shared value orientations. As they observe, while it is common to speak of a person's possessing "naked power," or wealth through which his will may be enforced, it is meaningless to speak of a person's "naked prestige" because giving deference to another ultimately requires the complicity of the lower status person. Goldthorpe and Hope assert that "advantage and power in the form of prestige remain distinctive in that they entirely depend upon the existence of some shared universe of meaning and value among the actors concerned."[4]

They also suggest a number of reasons why the prestige judgments elicited by the usual survey questions, of the sort we used, may not tap this classical conception of prestige. On the contrary, these judgments may merely provide a more or less adequate summary of general socioeconomic status or of the general "goodness" or social desirability of given occupations (so far as goodness is related to economic rewards, cleanliness of work, and other extrinsically or intrinsically rewarding features of particular occupations). But not all occupations enjoying social and economic rewards are

3. John H. Goldthorpe and Keith Hope, "Occupational Grading and Occupation Prestige," in Keith Hope, ed., *The Analysis of Social Mobility: Methods and Approaches* (Oxford: Clarendon Press, 1972), pp. 19, 21.
4. Ibid., p. 25.

prestigious in the classical sense of engendering deferent behavior from nonincumbents and of regulating intimate associations between incumbents and nonincumbents.

While possessing merit, the Goldthorpe and Hope argument can be overstated. As we have indicated above, there are good reasons to expect a fairly high correspondence between the hierarchies of wealth and power in a society and the prestige-oriented behavior of deference or derogation.[5] Only in situations where the population's commitment to values and beliefs legitimating the social order is completely out of phase with the processes generating wealth and power differentials in the society, as in times of revolutionary upheaval, would we expect marked disjunctures among the three systems. Now, it is true that the prestige judgments elicited by survey questions are not in themselves evidence of the attractiveness or repulsiveness of incumbents of particular occupations for social intercourse—admittedly a key issue in classical discussions of prestige. Some research not noted by Goldthorpe and Hope, however, has shown substantial correlations between the prestige of occupations (as measured, for example, by the Duncan Index of Socioeconomic Status) and people's subjective social distance reactions toward them,[6] as well as a marked patterning of actual choices of partners for friendship and other intimate relations according to the principle of equal status contact.[7]

Goldthorpe and Hope's contention that prestige depends upon the existence of shared values is consistent with Edward Shils's theory that the prestige of social positions is determined by the degree of their association with the "core values" of the society.[8] Pursuing

5. See Edward Shils, "Deference," in J. A. Jackson, ed., *Social Stratification* (Cambridge: Cambridge University Press, 1968), p. 104.

6. Cf. Frank R. Westie, "Social Distance Scales: A Tool for the Study of Stratification," *Sociology and Social Research* 43 (1959): 251; Edward O. Laumann, *Prestige and Association in an Urban Community: An Analysis of an Urban Stratification System* (Indianapolis: Bobbs-Merrill, 1966); Edward O. Laumann and Richard Senter, "Subjective Social Distance, Occupational Stratification, and Forms of Status and Class Consciousness: A Cross-National Replication and Extension," *American Journal of Sociology* 81 (1976): 1304.

7. Cf. Richard F. Curtis, "Differential Association and the Stratification of the Urban Community," *Social Forces* 42 (1963): 68; Morton B. King, Jr., "Socioeconomic Status and Sociometric Choice," *Social Forces* 39 (1961): 199; Laumann, *supra* note 6; Lois M. Verbrugge, "Adult Friendship Contact: Time Constraints and Status-Homogenetity Effects, Detroit and Jülich, West Germany" (Ph.D diss., University of Michigan, 1974); Karl-Heinz Reuband, "Differentielle Assoziation and Soziale Schichtung" (Ph.D. diss., University of Hamburg, 1974).

8. Shils, *supra* note 5.

his classic distinction between the society's center and periphery, Shils argues that deferent behavior is elicited in response to various "entitlements," most notably the roles of the positional incumbents in controlling, mediating, or allocating the society's core values. The closer a social position is to the putative power centers at the societal level, the higher its prestige. Such an argument is a useful reformulation of Kingsley Davis and Wilbert E. Moore's earlier functional theory of social inequality[9] because it moves away from the more objectionable features of a theory that assumes that a structure, to be functional, must contribute to the survival of a society. In this reformulation, we need not assume that a functionally important position is awarded high prestige, among other rewards, but merely that a position believed to serve core values will be highly regarded and its incumbents deferred to. If these values should change, for whatever reason, so as to lower their core legitimacy, then the position should lose prestige to those who serve the newly legitimated core values more closely. The issue of the society's survival is thus avoided.

Broadly speaking, theories of prestige conferral may be distinguished according to whether they have a macrostructural or a microstructural focus. Some macrostructural theories of prestige generation attempt to account for the patterning of prestige and deference in terms of a functionalist model of society in which the society's members make differing valuations of social activities according to what is usually assumed to be a widely shared value system.[10] Prestige or its opposite, derogation, in this view becomes expressive of the deep-seated feelings about the core symbols or meanings that constitute the very definition of that society's identity and basis of existence. Other macrostructural theorists, following a more conflict-oriented perspective that questions the broad value consensus postulated by the functionalist,[11] tend to regard prestige

9. Kingsley Davis and Wilbert E. Moore, "Some Principles of Stratification," *American Sociological Review* 10 (1945): 242.

10. Cf. Talcott Parsons, "Equality and Inequality in Modern Society, or Social Stratification Revisited," in Edward O. Laumann, ed., *Social Stratification: Research and Theory for the 1970s* (Indianapolis: Bobbs-Merrill, 1970), p. 13; Davis and Moore, *supra* note 9; Shils, *supra* note 5; Piotr Sztompka, *System and Function: Toward a Theory of Society* (New York: Academic Press, 1974).

11. Ralf Dahrendorf, "On the Origin of Inequality Among Men," in his *Essays in the Theory of Society* (Stanford, Calif.: Stanford University Press, 1968), p. 151; Alvin W. Gouldner, *The Coming Crisis of Western Sociology* (New York: Basic Books, 1970); Randall Collins, *Conflict Sociology: Toward an Explanatory Science* (New York: Academic Press, 1975).

as a more manipulative or instrumental strategy of those who hold power positions, employed to bolster their domination by eliciting the voluntary compliance of the persons who occupy subordinated positions in the system. Prestige here alludes to its original Latin meaning of creating illusion or bedazzlement. Both the functionalist and conflict perspectives, despite their radical differences in the underlying processes postulated, imply almost identical predictions with regard to which positions will enjoy high or low prestige (although, admittedly, prestige in the conflict perspective tends to be a more precarious phenomenon).

Microstructural perspectives on theories of prestige conferral, on the other hand, direct attention to the social-psychological processes by which individuals come to make their subjective evaluations of the relative standings of various social positions according to some specified valuational criteria. Concern here is with identifying the various factors an individual takes into account in making such judgments, how the judgments are affected by detailed information or ignorance about a particular position or by personally held values and social attributes of the judges, such as age, sex, race, class, and so on.[12] Because they are based much more on empirical, quantitative work than are the macrostructural theories, microstructural approaches tend to be descriptively oriented, to be tied to particular techniques of measurement, and to avoid more qualitative interpretations of why certain individual-level variables are more predictive than others of relative prestige standing.

12. Cf. Albert J. Reiss, Jr., *Occupations and Social Status* (New York: Free Press, 1961); Robert W. Hodge, Paul M. Siegel, and Peter H. Rossi, "Occupational Prestige in the United States: 1925–1963," in Reinhard Bendix and Seymour Martin Lipset, eds., *Class, Status, and Power*, 2d ed. (New York: Free Press, 1966), p. 322; Paul M. Siegel, "Prestige and the American Occupational Structure" (Ph.D. diss., University of Chicago, 1971); Goldthorpe and Hope, *supra* note 3; Paul M. Siegel, "Occupational Prestige in the Negro Subculture," in Edward O. Laumann, ed., *Social Stratification: Research and Theory for the 1970's* (Indianapolis: Bobbs-Merrill, 1970), p. 156; Anthony P. M. Coxon and Charles L. Jones, *The Images of Occupational Prestige: A Study in Social Cognition* (New York: St. Martin's Press, 1978). Of course, there is yet another important microstructural tradition growing most recently out of Erving Goffman's work, *The Presentation of Self in Everyday Life* (Garden City, N.Y.: Doubleday, 1959), and his *Interaction Ritual: Essays in Face-to-Face Behavior* (Garden City, N.Y.: Doubleday, 1967); Collins, *supra* note 11, sensitively portrays the dynamic interplay between status display and deference-demanding or -avoiding behavior in face-to-face interaction. This approach requires a set of data-gathering and analytic techniques radically different than those employed here. It is very much our impression, however, from our extended informal observations of lawyers with different practice characteristics, that the empirical results generated by the two approaches are broadly compatible and mutually reinforcing.

In the following analyses, we draw on several of these differing perspectives in our efforts to account for the levels of prestige accorded by the respondents to the various fields of practice.

The Prestige Order

A randomly selected, one-in-four subsample of our survey respondents was asked to rate the "general prestige within the legal profession at large" of each of thirty fields of law. The ratings used a five-point scale, ranging from "outstanding" to "poor."[13] The resulting prestige scores of each of the fields, converted to a standard scale (see table 4.1, n. 2), are presented in table 4.1, where the fields are listed in rank order of declining prestige.[14]

The degree of consistency among the respondents in their prestige evaluations, especially with respect to the impact of their own fields of law on their allocations of prestige, is a matter of considerable theoretical import. If lawyers active in the fields that rank low in the overall prestige standing tend to invert the order of prestige of the fields or if those in higher prestige fields tend to inflate the prestige of their own fields to an exaggerated degree, then a key assumption of the analysis—namely, that deferent behavior requires the voluntary complicity of the subordinate participant in the transaction—is cast into serious doubt.

We have examined the data in a number of ways to determine the degree of agreement on prestige evaluations and the extent to which there are systematic departures in prestige evaluations as functions of the judges' own field status and personal values. For example, lawyers espousing strong civil libertarian and social welfare values might accord prestige to fields serving these values, while lawyers holding strong pro-business values might rate highly fields serving business interests and give lower standing to more welfare-oriented fields.

Summarizing these analyses, if we divide the fields into three

13. Cf. National Opinion Research Center, "Jobs and Occupations: A Popular Evaluation," in Reinhard Bendix and Seymour M. Lipset, eds., *Class, Status and Powers: A Reader in Social Stratification* (Glencoe Ill.: Free Press, 1953), p. 411; Hodge, Siegel, and Rossi, *supra* note 12.

14. In the survey instrument, the fields were listed in alphabetical order (see appendix A, question A1).

broad prestige levels—high, middle, and low—we find high rank-order correlations between the mean prestige ratings assigned by respondents practicing in each of these three groups of fields and the overall evaluations of the sample as a whole. These correlations range between .85 and .97. With respect to evaluations of particular fields, however, there are some statistically significant differences between the ratings of practitioners in high-ranked and in low-

TABLE 4.1

Prestige Ranking of Thirty Fields of Law[1]

Rank Order	Fields of Law	Prestige Score[2]	Rank Order	Fields of Law	Prestige Score[2]
1.	Securities	68	16.	Labor (unions)	49[b]
2.	Tax	67	17.	Environmental (defendants)	49[c]
3.	Antitrust (defendants)	65	18.	Personal injury (defendants)	48
4.	Patents	61	19.	Environmental (plaintiffs)	47
5.	Antitrust (plaintiffs)	60	20.	Civil rights/civil liberties	46
6.	Banking	59[a]	21.	Criminal (prosecution)	44
7.	Public utilities	59[b]	22.	General family (paying)	42
8.	General corporate	59[c]	23.	Criminal (defense)	41
9.	Probate	58	24.	Consumer (creditor)	40
10.	Municipal	56	25.	Personal injury (plaintiffs)	38[a]
11.	Admiralty	55	26.	Consumer (debtor)	38[b]
12.	Civil litigation	54	27.	Condemnations	37[a]
13.	Labor (management)	53	28.	Landlord-tenant	37[b]
14.	Real estate	51	29.	Divorce	35
15.	Commercial	49[a]	30.	General family (poverty)	34
				TOTAL SAMPLE	50

NOTES: 1. Note that there are some discrepancies between the labels for the fields of law used in table 4.1 and those used in the preceding two chapters. The thirty fields used here are the original list presented to the respondents in the survey (see appendix A, question A1). After the data were in hand, we were in a position to create more inclusive fields of practice when there were too few respondents in the more narrowly defined fields to sustain statistical analysis, or to differentiate broadly inclusive fields into more homogenous subfields. In the latter case, for example, we could distinguish between personal and corporate real estate or between personal and corporate tax work by taking into account other information the respondents gave us about their typical clients. We have, thus, aggregated and disaggregated some of these thirty fields in other analyses.

2. A random subsample (N = 224) of our total sample of Chicago lawyers was asked, "On the following specialty list would you please indicate the general prestige of each specialty within the legal profession at large." The respondents rated each specialty on a 5-point scale, from "outstanding" to "poor." We then computed the mean rating for each field. To facilitate comparing the prestige ratings, we calculated a standard score for each field by determining the grand mean of the thirty field means and its standard deviation and then subtracting the grand mean from each field mean and dividing by the standard deviation. To eliminate decimal points and negative numbers, we multiplied the standard score by 100 and added 50 to the result. Thus, 50 represents the average mean prestige rating, with 10 points being the standard deviation. To illustrate: "Securities," the most highly regarded field, is 1.8 standard deviations above the average mean prestige rating, while "General family (poverty)," with its score of 34, is 1.6 standard deviations below the average mean.

a, b, c—Differentiate the prestige scores of fields of law that are tied when rounded to nearest full point.

ranked fields. Moreover, there is a discernible pattern of these differences, respondents in low-ranked fields tending to assign higher prestige to such fields and, conversely, those from high-ranked fields assigning disproportionately high prestige scores to high-ranked fields. But the overwhelming tendency is for judges at all prestige levels to concur on the general prestige rank order of the fields, providing evidence that the lower status lawyers understand the general hierarchy of the fields in the distribution of deference.

As a more concrete illustration of this general tendency, consider the fact that practitioners in the five fields ranked highest in prestige rate the following as the six most prestigious fields (in declining order): securities, antitrust defense, tax, general corporate, banking, and antitrust plaintiffs' work. By comparison, the top six fields as rated by practitioners of the bottom five fields in overall prestige are: securities, tax, probate, civil litigation, antitrust defense, and banking. Four fields are thus included in both lists of six. Similarly, practitioners of the five highest prestige fields assigned the six lowest places on the prestige scale to consumer (buyer), landlord-tenant, condemnations, family (poverty), personal injury plaintiffs' work, and divorce (again in declining order), while practitioners in the five lowest prestige fields chose for those same positions personal injury plaintiffs' work, condemnations, family (poverty), landlord-tenant, consumer (seller), and consumer (buyer). Here they agree on five in each list of six fields. Thus, even raters who practice at the respective extremes of the prestige order display a high degree of similarity in their prestige ratings. Whether they like it or not, practitioners in the lower status fields know which positions get the prestige, and their recognition of that hierarchy is, in itself, a form of complicity in the existing distribution of deference.

Turning to the characteristics of the prestige order itself, let us initially note some of the most striking general properties of the scores presented in table 4.1. First, the top of the prestige ranking is quite clearly dominated by fields that might be characterized as "big business" law. Of the first eight fields in the rank order, only tax is a type of work that is likely to be done for individual as well as for business clients, and the great predominance of tax work that lawyers do is almost certainly done for businesses or well-to-do individuals. The respondents spending 25 percent or more of their time doing tax work indicated that they derived 38 percent of their income from individuals—somewhat less than average—and that, of these individual clients, 70 percent were in the highest status (professional, technical, or managerial) category. Not until we reach probate work, ranked ninth in prestige, do we come to a type of legal work that is done exclusively for individuals, and it may be significant to note that it is by its nature concerned with the transmission of wealth.

At the other end of the prestige ranking, we find the sorts of legal work that are characteristically done for individuals—general family practice, divorce, personal injury, consumer, and criminal law. Some of these types of practice may be derogated not only because of the lower socioeconomic status of the clientele but because of the "distasteful" or "unsavory" nature of the work. Divorce work involves emotionally charged, embarrassing personal situations, the clients are often at their worst, and the fate of children often hangs in the balance; personal injury work deals with grisly facts and with claimants who are badly maimed; and criminal work often requires the lawyer to associate with persons who are less than pleasant. Thus, the low prestige of these fields may be seen as analogous to the derogation of refuse collectors, coal miners, and others whose work involves untidy, burdensome tasks.[15]

Toward the middle of the prestige ranking, we find types of work that are done to some degree by large numbers of lawyers (e.g., real estate, civil litigation, and commercial work) and that might, thus, be seen as mediating fields. A type of work done by a great many lawyers, with widely differing characteristics, is unlikely to be regarded as either particularly high or particularly low in prestige. There are also some fields near the middle of the ranking that might be regarded as problematic; they possess ambivalent characteristics and may thus be inconsistently valued. For example, the practice of labor law (both for unions and for management) involves considerable financial stakes, but it also involves association with blue-collar workers or their representatives. Similarly, the lawyers who represent defendants in personal injury cases usually work for high status clients, since those defendants are typically insurance companies, but their work also involves unsavory fact situations.

The nature of the clients represented by the fields thus immediately appears to be an important determinant of field prestige, but

15. Shils, *supra* note 5; Goldthorpe and Hope, *supra* note 3.

this may bear further analysis and some alternative hypotheses might also be considered.

The Structure of Prestige

In attempting to account for the ways in which Chicago lawyers allocated prestige among the fields, we have used two structure-revealing techniques; smallest space analysis and hierarchical clustering. As the first step in our analysis, we computed the product-moment correlations of the respondents' prestige evaluations for every possible pair of fields. A high positive correlation between the prestige scores given any two fields tells us that the respondents tend to see the two fields as having similar prestige standing in the profession. A negative correlation, on the other hand, tells us that lawyers who evaluate one field as having a high prestige standing in the profession tend to regard the other as having lower social standing. A lack of correlation (i.e., a coefficient approximately zero in value) indicates no relationship in the evaluations of the fields under consideration.

These correlation coefficients can be treated as estimating the relative proximities of fields with respect to their prestige standings: fields similarly evaluated and thus having comparatively high positive coefficients are more proximate than are fields that are dissimilarly evaluated and that thus have either zero or negative coefficients.[16] These latter fields would appear to be farther apart in the minds of the judges. Note, however, that in comparing these proximities with one another, we do not expect them to order them-

16. Peter Rossi has brought to our attention the fact that interpretations of correlation coefficients of this nature are somewhat ambiguous. If, on the one hand, all the judges agreed on their prestige evaluations of the fields there could only be small correlations between judgments across fields. This is so because correlation is based on covariation and, in this case, covariation would be minimal. Such small correlations among the prestige evaluations of a cross section of occupations in the labor force are, in fact, typically observed. On the other hand, when judges are in agreement concerning the attributes on which they evaluate fields (e.g., type of client) but disagree in the evaluations they make on the basis of these attributes, substantial correlations of the sort observed in our study are the result. Other analyses we have done support this speculation. For example, in examining the data using analysis of variance techniques, we found that characteristics of the judges themselves, including such things as their type of field, law school, and value orientations, were related to systematic differences in their prestige judgments. See Charles Cappell, "Differential Evaluations of the Status of Legal Specialties: A Detailed Analysis with Theoretical Implications" (unpublished paper, American Bar Foundation, 1977).

selves automatically along a single or unidimensional prestige ranking unless prestige is, in fact, a unidimensional variable—as
income, for example, would be. The patterning of the coefficients
could indicate the presence of several divergent dimensions or
bases underlying the generation of prestige judgments. Thus, our
conceptual framework and method of analysis permit prestige to be
a multifaceted, subjective phenomenon that need not fit neatly into
a single prestige hierarchy.

The structure of the resulting 30-by-30 matrix of correlation coefficients, which contains 435 coefficients, is obviously very difficult
to discern by visual inspection of the matrix itself. Fortunately,
however, a number of techniques have recently been developed to
facilitate the recovery of the underlying structure of such a matrix.
Because we were prepared to make only ordinal assumptions about
our measures, rather than some of the more restrictive assumptions
required to employ factor analytic techniques,[17] we turned to smallest space analysis.[18] This technique was designed to represent such a
matrix graphically in the fewest possible dimensions of a Euclidean
space. Most readers will be familiar with such representations from
their exposure to plane and solid geometry in high school or college.[19] Perhaps an analogy will help to clarify the procedure and its
purpose. If one were to perform a smallest space analysis of the

17. Because of the relative crudeness with which we have measured prestige differences among the fields, we certainly do not want to assume that our prestige scale
is as precise, valid, and invariant a measuring device as the use of a yardstick would
be in measuring physical distances between points in physical space. While we are
prepared to assume that the fields can generally be reliably arranged in a rank order
from high to low prestige standing, we are not prepared to say that the interval
separating the top-ranked and second-ranked fields is equal to the interval between
the third- and fourth-ranked or the twenty-ninth and thirtieth fields, or that field X
has twice the prestige of field Y. This, among other things, is what is meant when we
say that we can treat the prestige scale used to rank fields as meeting the ordinal or
ranking assumption about scale measurement but that it does not meet the much
more restrictive assumptions of interval or ratio scales. Factor analysis ideally requires scale measurement at the level of interval scales, although this is often violated in practice.

18. Cf. Louis Guttman, "A General Nonmetric Technique for Finding the Smallest
Coordinate Space for a Configuration of Points," *Psychometrika* 33 (1968): 469; David
D. McFarland and Daniel J. Brown, "Social Distance as a Metric: A Systematic Intro-
duction to Smallest Space Analysis," in Edward O. Laumann, *Bonds of Pluralism: The
Form and Substance of Urban Social Networks* (New York: John Wiley, 1973), p. 213;
James C. Lingoes, *The Guttman-Lingoes Nonmetric Program Series* (Ann Arbor, Mich.:
Mathesis Press, 1973).

19. In principle, one can always represent exactly the interpoint distances among
n points in *n* minus 1 dimensions in a Euclidean space. Of course, since we cannot
physically represent a space having more than three dimensions, we are usually interested in seeing if it is possible to sacrifice some accuracy of representation for a

mileage chart presenting the distances between all the principal cities of the United States, he would obtain the conventional two-dimensional map of the United States on which the locations of the individual points—representing the cities—are so arranged that they accurately reflect, according to a specified scale, the distances between any given city and every other city. Similarly, the original matrix of correlation coefficients among prestige judgments estimates the relative (i.e., rank order) distances between each field and all of the others in terms of their similarities (or systematic differences) in eliciting prestige judgments.

Figure 4.1 presents the three-dimensional smallest space solution with a coefficient of alienation of .129, indicating a satisfactory fit.[20] In considering how this picture can best be interpreted, we should first emphasize that three dimensions were, in fact, required to achieve an adequate representation of the original matrix of correlations. The one-dimensional solution had a very high coefficient of alienation. This indicates that a representation with only a single dimension, presumably arranging the fields from highest to lowest prestige, would distort the more complex order present in the original data beyond acceptable limits. The respondents thus appear to have rated the fields on the basis of a more complex conception of their similarities and differences with respect to prestige or deference entitlements.[21] It is true, however, that the locations of the fields on the first axis of the three-dimensional solution are highly

---

(continued)
minimum number of dimensions, ideally three or fewer, consistent with an acceptable level of distortion between the "real world" distances and those represented in the smallest space model of the real world. Two-dimensional world maps are examples of representing a three-dimensional object, the earth, in a more convenient and easily comprehended form. Note, however, the distortions necessitated by adopting such an expedient.

Similarly, smallest space analysis tells us whether we have found an acceptable goodness of fit between the original matrix of proximity estimates, treated here as providing information only about the rank order of the distances among the points, and the calculated Euclidean distances between the points of a particular smallest space solution; cf. Peter V. Marsden and Edward O. Laumann, "The Social Structure of Religious Groups: A Replication and Methodological Critique," in Samuel Shye, ed., *Theory Construction and Data Analysis in the Behavioral Sciences* (San Francisco: Jossey-Bass, 1978), pp. 81–111. When the coefficient of alienation (the measure of goodness of fit) is zero, it indicates a perfect congruence between the real world proximities and the distances portrayed in the smallest space solution. As the coefficient increases in value, it indicates growing distortions or discrepancies between the real world data and the smallest space solution. Experience has shown that a coefficient of alienation of .15 indicates a satisfactory or acceptable smallest space solution.
20. See discussion of SSA-1 in Lingoes, *supra* note 18.
21. Cf. Shils, *supra* note 5.

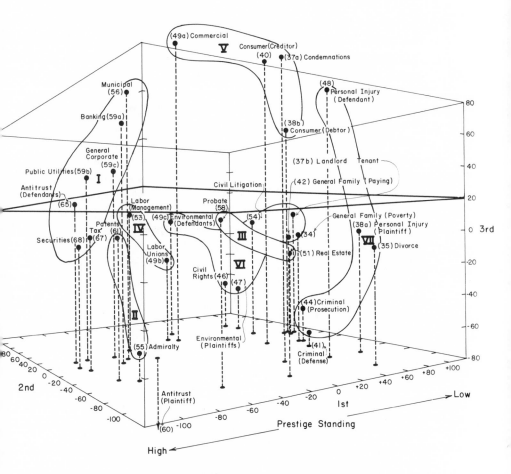

FIGURE 4.1

*Three-dimensional Smallest Space Solution for Prestige Judgments of
Legal Specialities*

correlated (−.89) with the standardized prestige scores given in table 4.1, indicating that general prestige standing accounts for the
lion's share of the ordering of the fields on the first axis.[22]

Quite clearly, generalized prestige standing has a powerful influ-

22. Of course, because the data used to construct the standard prestige scores are
the same as those used to calculate the original matrix of correlation coefficients,
there is a sense in which the two are not strictly independent, despite the very different manipulations of the data involved in the two procedures. Lacking any independent fine-grained estimates of the prestige order of the specialties, we must run
the risk of some circularity in our reasoning on this point. In our defense, however,

ence on the location of fields in the spatial solution. Also apparent, however, is the operation of other factors in determining perceived prestige similarities among the fields that are not so easily organized according to a single dimension. One of the special attractions of smallest space analysis over other data reduction techniques is the fact that one is not limited to using unidimensional ordering principles in interpreting the spatial configurations.[23] It is, for example, quite permissible to look for localized regions in the space in which the points are relatively homogeneous with respect to some nominal or qualitative characteristic distinguishing them from all other points in the space; this may be thought of as sector differentiation.[24] Another aspect of the configuration that may be interpretable is the relative distances of the points from the centroid of the solution[25]—that is, points in peripheral locations may differ in systematic ways from more centrally located points.[26]

In interpreting the smallest space solution, it is helpful to be able to give some labels to particular regions of the space—that is, to identify clusters of points that seem to have something in common. To accomplish this by criteria more objective than visual impressions, we submitted the original matrix of correlation coefficients to a hierarchical clustering analysis, using the minimum average diameter method that was described in chapter 2. Figure 4.2 presents the dendrogram summarizing the results of this analysis. Reading

---

(continued)

we should stress the high face validity of the prestige order and its congruence with orderings used by other researchers (e.g., Ladinsky, Carlin, Watson and Downing, and Smigel, see pp. 23–25) and also point out that the high correlation between the first axis and the standard scores—whether or not it is, in part, artifactual—is not crucial to our subsequent analysis.

23. The coordinates of the smallest space solution are themselves completely arbitrary and can be rotated to any other orientation without changing the order of the Euclidean interpoint distances—a feature that facilitates interpreting the generating principles organizing the space (cf. Edward O. Laumann and Franz U. Pappi, *Networks of Collective Action: A Perspective on Community Influence Systems* [New York: Academic Press, 1976], pp. 6–9). Being arbitrary, the coordinates are not always substantively interpretable (although, for the case in hand, the first axis of the solution happened to be substantively interpretable in terms of a general prestige rank order).

24. Cf. Edward O. Laumann and Franz Urban Pappi, "New Directions in the Study of Community Elites," *American Sociological Review* 38 (1973): 212, 221–23.

25. A physical analogy gives an intuitive sense of the meaning of the "centroid" of a smallest space solution: if all points in a two-dimensional smallest space solution were a set of equal weights resting on a weightless plane, the centroid would be that point on which the plane would balance. For a technical discussion, see E. Roskam and J. C. Lingoes, "A Mathematical and Empirical Study of Two Multidimensional Scaling Algorithms," *Michigan Mathematical Psychology Program* 1 (1971): 1.

26. Cf. Laumann and Pappi, *supra* note 24, pp. 221–23.

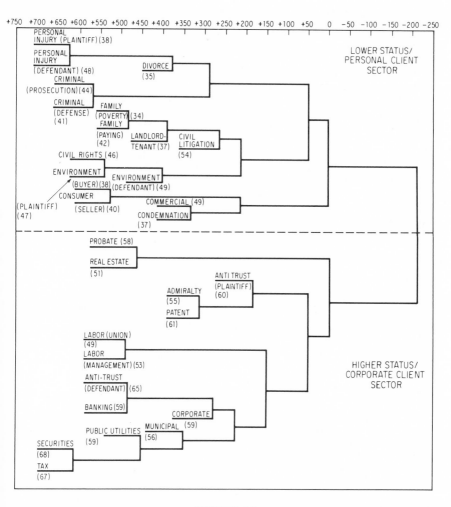

FIGURE 4.2
*Hierarchical Clustering Solution for Correlations Among Prestige Ratings
of Fields of Law*

the dendrogram from left to right, the reader can readily see how
fields were successively added to particular clusters as the correlation coefficients linking given fields declined in value.

Inspection of the dendrogram suggests that a minimum value of
.20 would provide a meaningful cutoff point for identifying the
clusters and, for ease of reference, these are listed in table 4.2 (and
indicated in figure 4.1 by roman numerals and encircling lines

Lawyers' Roles: The Predominance of Client-centered Structure

around the relevant points). Note, however, that most of the fields in a given cluster are much more highly correlated with one another than this minimum. The average correlation of the pairs of specialties in the big business cluster (I), for example, is .40. Table 4.2 also indicates that these seven clusters can be grouped into two mutually exclusive clusters, that is, higher status fields with predominantly corporate clientele versus lower status fields with small business or individual clients, labeled clusters A and B, respectively. Indeed, this penultimate clustering is finally joined in the last step of the hierarchical clustering (in which all points are put into one all-inclusive cluster) with a negative correlation of −.21, indicating that prestige evaluations of fields in one cluster are negatively correlated with those of fields in the other.

Within Cluster A, one can discern an internal order among the component clusters from those fields serving establishment, big business, and government clients to those serving relatively less esteemed clients in the corporate world—namely, the labor unions. Similarly, Cluster B appears to be internally ordered from fields serving "respectable" small business and personal clients to those having to do with more unsavory and disreputable clients.

TABLE 4.2

Prestige Clusters Identified by Hierarchical Clustering Analysis of Original Matrix of Correlation Coefficients

	Cluster No.	Cluster Label	Specialties in Cluster (with Standardized Prestige Score)[a]
(A) Higher status / corporate clientele clusters	I	Big business	Securities (68), tax (67), antitrust (defendants) (65), banking (59a), general corporate (59), public utilities (59b), municipal (56)
	II	Classic specialties	Patents (61), admiralty (55)
	III	Property	Probate (58), real estate (51)
	IV	Labor	Labor (management) (53), labor (union) (49b)
(B) Lower status / small business / individual clientele clusters	V	Small business / commercial	Commercial (49a), consumer (creditor) (40), consumer (debtor) (38b), condemnations (37a)
	VI	Public interest & litigation	Civil litigation (54), environmental (defendant) (49c), environmental (plaintiff) (47), civil rights (46), family (paying) (42), landlord-tenant (37b), family (poverty) (34)
	VII	Unsavory litigation	Personal injury (defendant) (48), criminal prosecution (44), criminal defense (41), personal injury (plaintiff) (38a), divorce (35)

NOTE: a. Antitrust (plaintiff) (60) was not assigned to any of the above clusters at the criterion specified.

The smallest space analysis, presented in figure 4.1, tells essentially the same story as the dendrogram but with the added advantage of showing how the clusters are related to one another. (Remember that the closer two points are in the space, the more highly correlated they are and the more similar are their profiles of correlations with all the other points.) The seven clusters (plus the one nonclusterable field, antitrust plaintiffs' work) all roughly fall on the surface of a sphere. Using the first axis of figure 4.1 as an orientation for examining the spatial arrangement, we can divide the sphere into hemispheres with the left-hand hemisphere containing Cluster A and the right-hand hemisphere mapping Cluster B. Roughly the upper half of the globe consists entirely of commercially oriented fields, whether the clients are major corporations or small businesses (note how personal injury defendants' work in Cluster VII is pulled into this region because its clients usually are corporations), while the lower half of the globe consists of fields serving individual clients. Thus, these analyses provide additional support for the hypothesis that client type is the primary determinant of the prestige structure of the fields, just as it was of the division of labor and of the social differentiation of the fields, but this cannot be the end of our inquiry.

Correlates of Prestige: Imputed Characteristics

Of the many characteristics of the fields that might be thought to affect their prestige, some—such as the levels of income earned by practitioners in the fields, for example—are capable of more or less "objective" measurement (leaving aside issues of the reliability or validity of such measures). Other characteristics that may be associated with prestige, however, are more subjective in character, or at least it would be much more difficult and expensive to devise objective measures of them—the degree of "intellectual challenge" presented by the fields, for example. Like prestige, such characteristics are themselves more a matter of repute, but this does not mean that they may not reflect "real" differences among the fields. To assess the extent and distribution of such differences in characteristics that are less amenable to objective measurement, we have relied upon ratings made by a panel of experts. This panel consisted of fifteen Northwestern University professors in various fields of law and four lawyer-researchers on the staff of the American Bar Foundation. We sought experts who were not active in the practice of law in the hope that this would minimize bias or defensive reactions,[27] and we asked them to rate all thirty fields on five characteristics. The averages of their judgments, converted to the same sort of standardized scores used for the prestige ratings made by the subsample of practioners, are presented in table 4.3.

All five of these "imputed characteristics" of the fields were hypothesized to have significance for the prestige structure of the types of legal work. The first, intellectual challenge, might be expected to be highly valued within a community that characterizes itself as a learned profession. If, as the question we presented to the raters put it, "the legal doctrines, cases, statutes, and regulations involved in some types of practice are characteristically more difficult, complex, and intellectually challenging than are those in others," then we would expect the fields that are regarded as more demanding to command a higher degree of respect and, thus, of prestige. Similarly, the second imputed characteristic, rapidity of change, was also intended to address a factor that would make the practice of a field more difficult and, therefore, more entitled to respect. If the substantive law involved in an area of practice changes only seldom or slowly, the practitioner will not have to work as hard at keeping up with developments in the law, and his practice is likely to become more routine. By contrast, the practitioner in a rapidly developing field will have to devote more effort to keeping abreast of the field, he is likely to have more opportunities for creativity in his work, and he may thus be regarded as more deserving of deference. The third imputed characteristic, referred to in table 4.3 as the public service score, was intended to measure the degree to which work in the specialty tends to be done *pro bono publico*, or for altruistic or reformist motives, as opposed to being

27. An alternative research strategy would have been to have the practitioners who rated prestige also rate these characteristics, thus permitting us to compare their prestige judgments to their ratings of the individual characteristics. To have done so would have greatly extended already crowded interviews, however, and it was thus not practical to pursue this strategy. We do not regard this as a great loss. We are not so much interested in analyzing the interrelationships among various evaluations by the individual rater—i.e., among the individual's ratings of field prestige and his ratings of the fields on other evaluative dimensions. Rather, we were concerned to examine whether some "real" properties of the types of work might be discovered that would help account for the differences among field prestige at the aggregate level. Thus, we used independent experts to judge the presence or absence of these properties.

TABLE 4.3
Imputed Characteristics of Fields of Law Practice

Public Service Field	Intellectual Challenge Score[1]	Rapidity of Change Score[2]	Public Service Score[3]	Ethical Conduct Score[4]	Freedom of Action Score[5]
1. Securities	63	62	44	57	39
2. Tax	67	66	43	55	46
3. Antitrust (defendants)	64	56	40	53	39
4. Patents	56	44	45	62	47
5. Antitrust (plaintiffs)	65	57	46	47	65
6. Banking	47	42	42	58	35
7. Public utilities	55	53	48	56	39
8. General corporate	51	48	44	59	41
9. Probate	45	32	44	57	46
10. Municipal	44	38	45	56	41
11. Admiralty	52	34	42	62	48
12. Civil litigation	52	48	51	45	55
13. Labor (management)	52	53	45	46	38
14. Real estate	45	37	43	48	50
15. Commercial	52	48	46	55	48
16. Labor (unions)	53	53	51	47	42
17. Environmental (defendants)	61	65	47	51	43
18. Personal injury (defendants)	33	42	43	38	46
19. Environmental (plaintiffs)	61	65	72	58	66
20. Civil rights/civil liberties	61	65	77	64	70
21. Criminal (prosecution)	48	56	56	47	53
22. General family (paying)	38	41	52	54	55
23. Criminal (defense)	51	57	57	33	64
24. Consumer (creditor)	50	60	46	43	41
25. Personal injury (plaintiffs)	35	43	43	25	64
26. Consumer (debtor)	52	59	65	50	62
27. Condemnations	35	36	43	39	49
28. Landlord-tenant	43	47	55	41	52
29. Divorce	30	45	50	30	54
30. General family (poverty)	38	51	76	61	64
TOTAL SAMPLE	50	50	50	50	50

NOTES: 1. An expert panel of nineteen persons, composed of Northwestern Law School professors and American Bar Foundation research specialists on the legal profession, answered the following question for the thirty fields: "The legal doctrines, cases, statutes, and regulations involved in some types of practice are characteristically more difficult, complex, and intellectually challenging than are those in others. Would you say that the degree of intellectual challenge presented by the *substance* (as opposed to the strategic considerations) of this type of work is: very great, higher than average, average, lower than average, or very little." The resulting means were standard scored, following the procedure described in table 4.1, note 2. A high score indicates a field above average in intellectual challenge.

2. The expert panel was asked: "The substantive law involved in some areas of practice changes more rapidly than it does in others. The practitioner, thus, may find it more difficult to keep up with developments in the former specialties than in the latter. Would you say that the law involved in this type of work: changes very rapidly, changes relatively quickly, changes at a moderate or average pace, changes relatively slowly, or changes very little or seldom." The resulting means were standard scored, following the procedure described in table 4.1, note 2. A high score indicates field above average in rapidity of change.

3. The expert panel was asked: "Some types of legal work are more often done *pro bono publico*, or for

motivated primarily by a desire for profit. Our hypothesis was, of course, that altruism or dedication to public service might be positively valued and, thus, might enhance the prestige of fields where such motivations are characteristic. The ethical conduct dimension also represents a quite straightforward hypothesis, in some respects similar to the hypothesis concerning altruistic motivation. A reputation for rectitude may be thought to enhance prestige and power,[28] and a field that is thought to have a high incidence of unethical conduct or sharp practice may, conversely, be derogated. Finally, the freedom of action characteristic refers to the degree to which practitioners in the field are free to pursue the courses of action suggested by their own professional judgments, as opposed to being constrained by knowledgeable clients or by organizational superiors who supervise and guide their decisions. Autonomy has often been proposed as one of the characteristics that distinguishes the professions from other occupations.[29] In addition to the value given to independence in society generally and in the other professions, the legal profession might be thought to give special weight to the ideal of the individual advocate fighting lonely, gallant battles, as opposed to the lawyer as bureaucrat, as a small cog in a large machine. Thus, we hypothesized that freedom of action might also enhance the prestige of a field.

Let us now examine in some detail the ways in which each of

28. Harold D. Lasswell and Abraham Kaplan, *Power and Society: A Framework for Political Inquiry* (New Haven: Yale University Press, 1950).

29. See, e.g., Ernest Greenwood, "Attributes of a Profession," *Social Work*, July 1957, p. 45; Richard H. Hall, *Occupations and the Social Structure* (Englewood Cliffs, N.J.: Prentice-Hall, 1969).

---

altruistic or reformist motives, while other sorts of legal work much more clearly involve a profit motive. Would you say of this type of work that it is: highly money- or profit-oriented, substantially profit-oriented, neither or average, substantially *pro bono*, or mostly *pro bono*." The resulting means were standard scored, following the procedure described in table 4.1, note 2. A high score indicates a field above average in public service motivation.

4. The expert panel was asked: "Some types of legal work have a reputation for 'sharp practice' or for a higher incidence of unethical conduct than is common in some other types of legal work. Would you say of this type of work that its reputation for ethical conduct is: very good, above average, average, below average, or poor." The resulting means were standard scored, following the procedure described in table 4.1, note 2. A high score indicates a field above average in ethical reputation.

5. The expert panel was asked: "In the practice of some types of law, the pratitioner is, to a considerable degree, a 'free agent,' free to pursue whatever strategic course of action his own professional judgment may suggest. By contrast, the freedom of action of a practitioner of some other types of law is more highly constrained by knowledgeable clients or by organizational superiors who supervise and guide his decisions. Would you say that the practice of this type of law is characterized by: a high degree of freedom of action, above average freedom of action, average, below average freedom of action, or little freedom of action." The resulting means were standard scored, following the procedure described in table 4.1, note 2. A high score indicates a field above average in freedom of action.

these characteristics is related to prestige in our findings. In order to focus on the nature of the fields, as well as on the individual characteristics—that is, on the rows as well as on the columns of table 4.3—we have selected five fields for particular attention, though we will not be slavish about following them through all of their characteristics. These five are more or less evenly spaced along the prestige ranking; securities, the highest in prestige; public utilities, which has a moderately high prestige rating; real estate, which ranks near the middle; criminal defense, which has a moderately low rating; and divorce, which is the lowest prestige specialty for which we have a large enough number of respondents to make generalization sensible. These particular types of work have not been chosen, then, because of any special substantive significance but rather because they represent a range of positions in the prestige order. We will also call attention to other fields that are particularly noteworthy on one or more of the dimensions.

Beginning with the first variable in table 4.3, we find that securities work ranks fourth in degree of intellectual challenge. Its score is exceeded only by those of tax and of antitrust plaintiffs' and defendants' work. Thus, the four highest intellectual challenge scores are held by fields that rank among the top five in prestige. The consistency of this tendency throughout the ratings is reflected in the fact that the intellectual challenge and prestige scores are correlated at .65.

Securities work is concerned with the legal requirements and regulations governing the distribution and resale of stocks, bonds, and other securities. The sorts of matters dealt with include the registration of securities being sold by corporations; the disclosure of information by corporations; insider trading; corporate takeover and proxy solicitations; and the regulation of underwriters, broker-dealers, securities exchanges, investment companies, and other entities involved in the securities industry. As such, it deals with a complex set of federal statutes and regulations. It is interesting to note that all four of the fields rated highest in intellectual challenge and all of the top six in the prestige ranking deal predominantly with federal rather than state law and that all of them require their practitioners to deal with federal regulatory boards, commissions, agencies, or departments (as well as, potentially, with the federal courts). Thus, involvement with the federal government would appear to enhance prestige. This observation is strengthened by noting that the correlation between the prestige of a field and the frequency of appearances by its practitioners in the state courts is −.68. (The frequency of appearance in state courts is also correlated at −.65 with the intellectual challenge scores of the fields.) At the other end of the scale, we find that divorce is assigned the lowest intellectual challenge score of all the fields. Other fields with notably low scores on this dimension are personal injury work (for both plaintiffs and defendants) and condemnation law (eminent domain), all of which also rank relatively low in the prestige order.

All of the four fields rated highest in intellectual challenge also have rapidity of change scores that are well above average, with the tax field again receiving the highest score. Keeping up with developments in a rapidly changing specialty may make that field more demanding than it would otherwise be, or slow change may make it less so. Probably for this reason, the rapidity of change and intellectual challenge scores are correlated at .69. The other high scores on the rapidity of change dimension were assigned to environmental law (plaintiffs and defendants) and to civil liberties work, which have been areas of rapid and substantial change in public policy in recent years. The lowest change scores went to probate and admiralty law, both of which are fields with very long histories and traditions.

On the dimension that dealt with the extent to which work in the fields is motivated by altruism as opposed to a desire for profit (the public service score), we find that securities work received one of the lowest scores, as did the other high prestige fields. The only fields with lower public service scores were antitrust defense, banking, admiralty, and real estate. Real estate work deals with the transmission of property or with real estate development, both of which pretty clearly involve the profit motive—as do banking law, the defense of companies charged with antitrust violations, and the representation of shipowners or insurers in admiralty cases. Divorce work, by contrast, received one of its higher scores on this dimension—it reached the mean, 50. By comparison, it may be interesting to note that the personal injury lawyers were not given much credit for altruistic motivation—the field received a score of 43, tied with real estate—while criminal defense work was scored substantially above average. The highest public service scores were assigned to civil liberties work, understandably enough, and to general family practice with poverty level clients, the field ranked lowest in prestige. More generally, the public service score is negatively correlated with prestige at −.51. If altruistic motivation is highly valued within the legal profession, then the weight given it does not seem to be sufficient to offset the value attached to other factors that influence prestige judgments.[30]

The ethical conduct score behaves very differently than the public service score, and ethical behavior appears, therefore, to be seen as quite separate from altruistic motivation. This would be consistent with the role conception of the lawyer as a "hired gun" who provides professional representation, within the ethical rules, for anyone who is able to afford his services. Securities work, like most of the high prestige fields, has an ethical conduct score that is well above average. Though the highest ethical conduct score was assigned to civil liberties work, as was the case with the public service dimension, and one of the highest scores went to general family work for impoverished clients, most of the high ethical conduct scores were assigned to fields that represent big business clients and, particularly, to the more traditional of those fields such as patents and admiralty. The lowest ethics scores were given to fields that represent individuals in the sorts of cases that have already been characterized as "unsavory"—personal injury plaintiffs' work, divorce, and criminal defense. That is, the circumstances of the cases are unsavory, by hypothesis, for reasons quite distinct from the unethical conduct of practitioners in the field. There may be a tendency, then, to see work that is "dirty" in one respect as dirty in

30. Note that the question on which the public service dimension is based did not ask for an assessment of the "social worth" or "contribution to the public good" of each field. Such a question would be even more difficult to answer than the one that we did, in fact, pose. Rather, our question asked the panel of scholars to judge the extent to which practitioners in each field were likely to undertake the work because of the money to be made in it rather than because of "altruistic" or "reformist" motives. Thus, the distinction is whether the work of the field is more often motivated by the practitioner's desire for profit or by ideological motives, e.g., those addressed to "law reform," to more general social or political reforms, or to "service" apart from personal gain. We recognize (and think it safe to assume that our panel of scholars did, as well) that the choices open to any lawyer may well be limited both by opportunity and by personal circumstances. Some lawyers may take relatively low-paying work—criminal prosecution or real estate title searches, for example— because it is the only type of work open to them. Nonetheless, some lawyers no doubt choose to take the types of cases that will earn them only small fees (or a small salary) or no fee at all. And it may well be, to pursue our examples, that decisions to go into criminal prosecution are more likely to reflect such a choice than are decisions to do real estate title searches. Our panel of scholars thought that such altruistic or reformist motivations were even more common in civil rights work and in poverty law, and this makes sense to us.

another, or the labeling process may lead to unethical conduct in work that is already derogated for other reasons.[31] The score of personal injury plaintiffs' work on this dimension, for example, is particularly striking: 25, the lowest score that any of the fields received on any of the dimensions. The image of the "ambulance chaser" apparently remains quite vivid. The ethical conduct score is correlated with prestige at .53.

The freedom of action score summarizes the scholars' judgments of the extent to which practitioners in the field are free to pursue their own courses of action, rather than being constrained by clients or superiors. Both securities work and public utilities work, for example, have quite low scores on this dimension. These kinds of work are typically carried out in large organizations, with senior lawyers supervising juniors, and the clients are highly knowledgeable. A large percentage of the lawyers who devote at least 25 percent of their time to public utilities work are house counsel in either corporations or governments, and 77 percent of the securities lawyers practice in the largest firms, those with more than thirty lawyers (see appendix B, table B.3). The practice of securities law is, in fact, reputed to be confined largely to a few major urban centers where the securities underwriters are located. The only fields with lower freedom of action scores than securities and public utilities are banking and the management side of the labor law practice, both of which serve very sophisticated clients who are capable of assessing the situation and guiding the lawyers' actions. Thus, the higher prestige fields serving business clients tend to have low freedom of action scores: consequently, this dimension is correlated negatively with prestige (−.54).

Criminal defense work has a very high score on this dimension. This may reflect not only the large number of solo practitioners among criminal defense lawyers but also the characteristic lack of sophistication and influence of their clients, persons charged with crimes. The only fields with higher freedom of action scores than criminal defense are civil liberties, environmental plaintiffs', and antitrust plaintiffs' work. In the case of civil liberties, the powerlessness of the clients may be one of the factors accounting for the score, but another contributing factor may well be the inherent cre-

---

31. See Edwin M. Lemert, *Human Deviance, Social Problem, and Social Control* (Englewood Cliffs, N.J.: Prentice-Hall, 1967), pp. 40–64, on "secondary deviation."

ativity or lack of legal structure of the field, which permits the civil liberties lawyer great freedom of action in devising the theory and strategy of his case. This explanation may also apply to environmental plaintiffs' work, which is a new and relatively unstructured field.

The other field receiving a high score, antitrust plaintiffs' work, is a very interesting deviant case. That field ranks fifth in prestige and has a freedom of action score of 65—not until we descend to nineteenth position in the prestige order (environmental plaintiffs' work) do we find another freedom of action score in the 60s. The lawyers who represent the plaintiffs in antitrust cases must have all the same knowledge and abilities as do those who represent the large corporations that are the defendants in these cases. In addition, however, the plaintiffs' lawyers have the task of creating novel theories on which to base antitrust treble damage actions—in recent years, some of these have involved class actions on behalf of large numbers of consumers[32]—and the fact that they search out their clients, rather than being presented with a problem by a client, enhances their freedom of action. The antitrust plaintiffs' lawyers tend to be seen by other lawyers as, in a sense, "traitors to their class." They have all the special skills of the antitrust lawyers, but they misuse those skills by making them available to the "wrong" sort of client (and profit handsomely by doing so, if they are successful). The profession's view of the antitrust plaintiffs' lawyer as a species of pariah may also be reflected by the field's score on the ethical conduct dimension, which is substantially lower than would be anticipated from its prestige rank.

Correlates of Prestige: Practitioner Characteristics

Chapter 3 explored the extent of differentiation among the fields of law, as reported by their practitioners, and the literature on "deference entitlements" suggests that several of the differences that we noted there might have an impact on field prestige. At least four

32. Cf. Benjamin S. DuVal, Jr., "The Class Action as an Antitrust Enforcement Device: The Chicago Experience (I)," 1976 *American Bar Foundation Research Journal* (Summer): 1021, 1032.

broad categories of characteristics of the fields are worthy of examination:

1. Social origins of the practitioners. Persons of higher social origins are expected to gravitate toward more prestigious work while persons of derogated origins are relegated to the less attractive work tasks. In an important sense, this is a result of a prestige hierarchy rather than a cause, although one would expect a differential distribution according to esteemed and derogated social origins to reinforce perceptions of the prestige differences among positions.
2. Work context and task characteristics. Such aspects as the size of the employer organization have implications for predictability and routinization of work flow, for the range and variety of tasks performed, for the dependence of one's goal achievement on the satisfactory performance of others, and so on.[33]
3. Client characteristics. The social evaluation of the relative importance (in power or social status) of the organizations and persons for whom services are being rendered might also affect prestige. This rests on the proposition of honor or derogation by association with the high and the mighty or the lowly and despised.
4. Rewards. Finally, there is reason to think that prestige might be affected by the characteristic levels of extrinsic and intrinsic rewards associated with practice in the fields, including direct financial rewards, the quality of working conditions (such as office furnishings and space or access to secretaries and other work assistants), and the personal job satisfaction arising from the presence or absence of monotony, excitement, risk taking, or challenge in one's work.

These broad categories of variables, and their possible effects on prestige, vary considerably in their empirical or analytic independence from one another and in their sensitivity to the hypothesized construct underlying a particular basis for deference entitlement, but each may be of significance. Let us examine a few variables that exemplify each of these categories. In the analyses discussed here, as in those reported in chapter 3, the description of the characteristics of each of the fields and of its practitioners is based on the responses of lawyers who said that they devoted at least 25 percent of their time to the field.[34]

33. Cf. Davis and Moore, *supra* note 9; James D. Thompson, *Organizations in Action: Social Science Bases of Administrative Theory* (New York: McGraw-Hill, 1967).
34. As pointed out in the introductory footnote to this chapter, the analyses discussed here differ in minor respects from those reported in chapter 3. These differences arise because we employed different rules in assigning particular persons to fields of law and because the prestige analysis used a somewhat different list of fields. For a more complete listing of the characteristics of each of the fields, see appendix B.

The extent to which the practitioners in a field have their origins in a metropolitan community has a strong negative correlation with the prestige of the field ($-.69$). That is, lawyers who resided during their high school years in cities with populations in excess of 250,000, or in suburbs of such cities, make up a larger percentage of the practitioners in the lower prestige fields than in the types of work enjoying higher prestige. Securities work, for example, has one of the lowest percentages of practitioners of metropolitan origin. The only fields with lower percentages are two of the other top prestige fields, antitrust defendants' work and patents. By contrast, many of the lowest prestige fields have very high percentages—in divorce, criminal defense, and personal injury plaintiffs' work the proportion of practitioners who were raised in cities exceeds 90 percent.

We find, then, a process of selection in the recruitment of practitioners to the various fields that results in a negative correlation between metropolitan origin and the prestige of the fields. Some of this may well be self-selection. Our sample was drawn only from lawyers with offices in the city of Chicago, and persons of rural or small-town origin who have chosen to practice law in such a large city might be expected to be highly motivated for success or "upward mobility." The recruitment of lawyers for the high prestige fields may also be more wide-ranging, resulting in a greater diversity of origin of the practitioners. The large law firms and corporations that employ disproportionate numbers of the lawyers in the high prestige fields are likely to recruit at the top national law schools (see pp. 112–13) and to select students with high academic achievement, regardless of whether they grew up in the firm's locality. In the lower prestige fields, by contrast, the lawyers tend to be solo practitioners or to be in smaller firms. The sorts of contacts that are facilitated by the kinship and acquaintance networks of locals may be more important to survival in these fields—that is, the flow of legal work to these lawyers is not so likely to be guaranteed by affiliation with a large, ongoing organization.

The percentage of Jewish practitioners in each field and the percentage of Republicans appear to be almost mirror images of one another. Securities work has a relatively low percentage of Jews and a relatively high percentage of Republicans, which is the general tendency for the higher prestige fields—though the Republican percentage is more strongly correlated with prestige (.67) than is the Jewish percentage (−.45).[35] Divorce and consumer work both have relatively high percentages of Jewish practitioners and relatively low percentages of Republicans, as is the case with the other lowest prestige fields.

The meaning of these findings seems straightforward, if unpleasant. Jews are, perhaps, the most derogated of the ethnic groups that are represented in the bar in any substantial numbers,[36] and the Republicans tend to be, conversely, high on deference entitlements such as family wealth and social origins.[37] These factors may bias both the actions of the gatekeepers who limit entry into the high prestige fields and the perceptions of the prestige of the fields that have high concentrations of the derogated or privileged group. Thus, two complementary tendencies may reinforce one another here. Jews have tended to be excluded from the high prestige fields and Republicans (or persons with the sort of social origins, family wealth, and connections that Republicans tend to possess in disproportion) to be welcomed in them, leaving the Jews with only the less prestigious work available if they choose to practice law and leaving the Republicans free of the necessity of doing such work. The presence of Republicans in the higher prestige fields may then serve further to enhance the prestige of those fields by association, and the presence of Jews in the lower prestige fields may serve further to depreciate the prestige of those fields in the eyes of lawyers who derogate that ethnic group.

A phenomenon that is in some respects similar may be observed in the data on the percentage of practitioners in each of the fields

35. Though all respondents were asked their religious preferences and their ethnic or national origins (see pp. 14–15), only the percentage of Jewish practitioners in each field is reported here because the "percentage Jewish" had a stronger negative correlation with prestige than did any of the other religious and ethnic categories, and it is, in our opinion, the most interesting and important of those variables. There is considerable literature on anti-Semitism within the bar; see especially, Jerold S. Auerbach, *Unequal Justice: Lawyers and Social Change in Modern America* (New York: Oxford University Press, 1976). "Percentage Catholic" was also negatively correlated with prestige, though not to a statistically significant degree, and "percentage Protestant" had a strong positive correlation with the prestige of the fields (.67, even stronger than the negative correlation of "percentage Jewish"). Too few nonwhites appear in our sample to permit separate statistical analysis of that category. The fact that there are so few nonwhites in our random sample of the Chicago bar is itself, of course, of substantive importance.

36. Cf. Nathan Glazer and Daniel Patrick Moynihan, *Beyond the Melting Pot: The Negroes, Puerto Ricans, Jews, Italians and Irish of New York City* (Cambridge: MIT Press, 1963); Laumann, *supra* note 18.

37. E. Digby Baltzell, *Philadelphia Gentlemen: The Making of a National Upper Class* (Glencoe, Ill.: Free Press, 1958).

who attended one of six elite American law schools (see p. 15). Forty-five percent of the securities lawyers had graduated from these schools, while only 11 percent of the divorce practitioners, 8 percent of the personal injury plaintiffs' attorneys, 4 percent of the criminal defense lawyers, and none of the criminal prosecutors had done so. The two sides of antitrust work both have high percentages of elite school graduates, which is consistent with both their high prestige and their intellectual challenge scores. Noteworthy here is the substantial correlation of .65 between the percentage of elite law school graduates practicing in a field and the intellectual challenge score assigned to the field by our panel of scholars.

An intriguing finding on this dimension is that one of the highest percentages of elite school graduates is found in the civil rights/civil liberties field. (Since this field has one of the smallest case bases, however, we should be cautious regarding this result.) Civil rights ranks only twentieth in prestige on the original list of thirty fields. Given the high percentage of elite law school graduates practicing civil liberties law, what might account for its relatively low prestige? There is not a great deal that is noteworthy about the other characteristics of the lawyers practicing in the field, except that the percentage of solo practitioners who do civil liberties work is zero in our sample, a fact that would also tend to be associated with high prestige. We have already noted, however, that civil liberties was ranked highest on three of the five imputed characteristics— the public service score, the ethical conduct dimension, and the freedom of action score—and near the top of the ratings on the other two. Of those scores, particularly extreme ratings occurred on the freedom of action and public service dimensions (where the scores were 70 and 77, respectively) and these two imputed characteristics are the ones that are negatively correlated with prestige. On the face of these data, then, one interpretation might be that the prestige of civil liberties work suffers because its practitioners enjoy too much autonomy in their work and have an unseemly reputation for altruistic motivation! But perhaps it would be well to be tentative about this conclusion, having a decent regard for the limitations of our data—in particular, the sample size. We will have more to say about these general issues at the conclusion of this chapter.

Moving from data that concern demographic and recruitment characteristics of practitioners in each of the fields, we turn to characteristics of the work context of the fields. These include the nature of the organizations within which the fields are practiced, the type of clients served, and the stability of the attorney-client relationship in each of the fields. We might begin with four of these characteristics that constitute two more pairs of mirror images. The percentage of solo practitioners in a field tends to be inversely related to the percentage of the specialists who practice in firms with more than thirty lawyers, and the two are correlated with prestige at −.58 and .63, respectively. (These are, of course, only two among several possible practice settings—the others include positions in smaller firms, as corporate house counsel, or as government lawyers at the federal, state, or local level. All of these other possibilities, however, have smaller correlations with prestige.) A similar relationship exists between the percentage of law practice income that the practitioners in the field receive from major corporations (defined as corporations with more than $10 million in sales per year, in 1975 dollars) and the percentage of their clients who are persons of lower social status. These two variables are correlated with prestige at .54 and −.86, respectively. (These are again, of course, only two among several possible client types, but these categories are mentioned because of their extremity of type rather than the degree of their correlations with prestige. The percentage of income derived from major corporate clients has, in fact, the lowest correlation with prestige of the five client type categories.)[38]

The securities field has one of the largest percentages of lawyers who practice in large firms and in our sample its percentage of solo practitioners is zero. Its percentage of large firm lawyers is surpassed only by that of the antitrust defendants' lawyers, another of the highest prestige fields. These two fields are among those with the highest percentages of practice income derived from major corporate clients and the lowest percentages of clients who are blue-collar workers. The low prestige fields, by contrast, reverse this pattern. Divorce, the lowest prestige field, has the highest percentage of solo practitioners, one of the two lowest percentages of large firm lawyers and of income from major corporations, and a percentage of

38. The other three client categories that we analyzed and their correlations with prestige are "mean percentage of law practice income derived from personal (versus business) clients" (−.71); "mean percentage of personal clients who have professional, technical, or managerial occupations" (.79); and "mean percentage of income from business clients that is derived from 'small businesses,' e.g., neighborhood stores, local restaurants, local real estate brokers, etc.—less than $250,000 in sales per year" (−.71).

lower status clients that is well above the mean. The pattern of the divorce lawyers is repeated, in a degree that is only slightly less extreme, by criminal defense counsel and by the other lowest prestige fields—in particular, general family practice and personal injury plaintiffs' work. The direction of these findings would certainly be anticipated, but the clarity of the pattern is impressive when one recalls that the practitioners included in these fields may have devoted up to 75 percent of their time to other types of work.

Public utilities practitioners do not fit this pattern. They include relatively small percentages both of solo practitioners and of large firm lawyers. Instead, corporate house counsel and government lawyers are substantially overrepresented among the public utilities practitioners. Public utilities work also has by far the highest percentage of clients whom the lawyer has represented for three years or more. That is, again, perhaps attributable to its high percentage of house counsel and of government lawyers. In general, the higher prestige fields tend to have greater stability of clientele, though the correlation of this variable with prestige just fails statistical significance at the .05 level (.33). Criminal defense has the lowest percentage of clients represented for three years or more, in spite of the well-publicized delay in bringing criminal cases to trial. But it is interesting to note that lawyers engaged in general family practice report that they have, on the average, represented about three-fifths of their clients for three years or more. Apparently the clientele of the neighborhood lawyer is fairly stable. As on several of the other variables, we find that the antitrust plaintiffs' lawyers are somewhat out of line here, given what one would expect from their position in the prestige order—they have one of the lower percentages of stable clients. Some of this tendency may well reflect the relative youth of practitioners in this field, as well as the nature of their work.

All of the respondents in our survey were asked to characterize the nature of the tasks involved in their legal work in terms of dimensions defined by sets of polar opposites. One of these dimensions dealt with the degree to which work in the field required arcane skills or expertise. Eighty-six percent of the securities lawyers responded that it would not be possible to train paraprofessionals to handle many of the tasks involved in their practice. Though this percentage was far higher than that of any of the other fields, there was a general tendency for the more prestigious fields to be relatively high on this dimension—it correlates .49 with prestige. The two sides of antitrust work were, however, both somewhat out of line on this dimension. In spite of their high prestige standing, a minority of each of those sorts of practitioners believed that a professional's skills were so uniformly required in antitrust work.

At the other end of the prestige order, only 31 percent of the general family practitioners believed that professional expertise was indispensable in their work. Divorce, criminal defense, and personal injury plaintiffs' lawyers were slightly more likely to feel that a professional's training was essential to performing the tasks required in their practices—about two-fifths of the practitioners in each of those fields responded that paraprofessionals could not be trained to handle much of the work. And civil liberties had, again, a position on this dimension that was inconsistent with its relatively low prestige rank—nearly 70 percent of the civil liberties lawyers believed that their work required professional expertise. This result may be related to the high percentage of civil liberties lawyers who are graduates of the elite law schools or to the high rate of change in the law of the field.

Another of these work task dimensions dealt with the extent to which the practice of each of the fields requires skill in negotiating and advising clients, rather than detailed concern with technical rules. Though this may sometimes be associated with the relative proportions of corporate and individual clients, that is not always the case. To the extent that the big business lawyer spends his time putting business deals together, as many lawyers certainly do, he functions as a negotiator and advisor. The overall tendency, however, is for the negotiating and advising tasks to be inversely related to prestige; the correlation is −.42. The largest percentages of practitioners who define their tasks as negotiating and advising are to be found in such specialties as general family practice and divorce. Securities work, by contrast, has one of the lowest percentages on this dimension, the other conspicuously low ones being antitrust plaintiff's work, banking, and criminal prosecution. (Apparently, the negotiation of plea bargains does not consume much of the prosecutor's time or attention.) Note, however, that the antitrust defense practitioners differ from those on the other side of their cases and from lawyers in the other high prestige fields in that antitrust defense has one of the highest percentages defining their tasks as negotiating and advising, as does labor management work.

A third work task dimension concerns the extent to which practitioners in the field find that the nature of their work requires them to concentrate on one field of law. This dimension is, then, a measure of the degree of specialization (or, at least, of the lawyers' perceptions of it). Securities has one of the highest percentages of practitioners reporting that their work is concentrated in one field. The only fields higher on this dimension are patents—a "classic" specialty that traditionally commands the exclusive attention of its practitioners—and labor union work, perhaps the purest of the new specialties. Divorce has one of the lowest percentages on this dimension. Other fields low on this dimension are probate, commercial work, and—especially low—general family practice. The dimension correlates .52 with prestige.

It is interesting to note that on all three of these dimensions, general family practice is found at one of the extremes. Perhaps this result is attributable to the fact that a general family practice is perceived as the sole remaining refuge of the general practitioner, the small-town lawyer in the big city. In fact, the range of problems handled by these lawyers is, no doubt, rather severely limited. They are highly unlikely to handle any antitrust law or securities or patents or municipal bond work or labor law. Still, it is no doubt true that the general family practice is as close as we come in today's major cities to the practice of law as it existed before the rise of specialization and of the large firm.

Finally, we turn to the extrinsic rewards of law practice—the percentage of practitioners in each of the fields who have incomes from law practice of $50,000 per year or more (recall that these are 1975 dollars).[39] The financial rewards of law practice do not quite achieve a significant correlation with the prestige of the fields and, when the income variable is included with others in a regression equation, it makes no additional contribution to the prediction of prestige (see table 4.4). Securities work, however, has one of the highest percentages of practitioners with incomes of $50,000 or more, and high income rates are also found in the banking, patents, and general corporate fields. The lowest percentages are found in

39. Because an individual's income tends to increase with age and higher prestige fields tend to have disproportionately younger lawyers, we were concerned to eliminate the confounding influence of age on income and prestige. To do so, we projected incomes of persons active in a particular field as if all the fields had the same age distribution. When the income distribution is thus standardized by age, its correlation with field prestige (.40) just fails to achieve statistical significance.

criminal prosecution (where there is a system constraint on income—the practitioners are full-time, salaried public employees),[40] in consumer law, and in real estate. Real estate, thus, has fewer high income practitioners than would be suggested by the more moderate prestige level of the field. The correlation of law practice income with the prestige of the fields is certainly in the expected direction, then, but it is important to note that the extrinsic reward system seems to affect the prestige judgments less than do several of the more intrinsic characteristics of the practice—including, specifically, client type, the nature of the work, and the characteristics of the lawyers engaged in the practice.

The lack of a strong relationship between income and prestige has surprised some of the lawyers whom we have informed of this finding. It may not appear so surprising, however, if we consider the possible impact of field prestige on the market for legal services. Prestige may tend to increase the supply of lawyers in the high status fields and to decrease supply in the types of work that have lower prestige. If these hypothesized effects of prestige on supply did occur, their impact on income would, of course, tend to increase remuneration in the lower status specialties and, conversely, to decrease income in the high prestige fields—producing, perhaps, a result like the one we observe. A study of the medical profession also found no significant correlation between income and the professional prestige of the medical specialties,[41] suggesting that some such general process may operate.

Multivariate Models of Prestige

Of the many possible attributes of a social position that theorists and empirical researchers have suggested might be grounds for differing prestige evaluations, we have included in this analysis only one or two representatives of each of the major varieties of defer-

40. But see chapter 2, note 11.
41. See Allan M. Schwartzbaum, John H. McGrath, and Robert A. Rothman, "The Perception of Prestige Differences Among Medical Subspecialties," *Social Science and Medicine* 7(1973): 365, 370. See also S. M. Shortell, "Occupational Prestige Difference Within the Medical and Allied Health Professions," *Social Science and Medicine* 8(1974): 1.

ence entitlements recognized in the literature. Given the limited theoretical closure in the field and the limitations on the data that we could realistically gather on the various fields, we can certainly make no claim that our list of attributes is theoretically or empirically exhaustive. The attributes imputed to the fields by the scholars whom we used as expert raters (see table 4.3) were, however, designed to tap what we thought were the most important, analytically independent characteristics of the work that might influence prestige, apart from the social characteristics of the persons who perform such work. (But we recognize, of course, that our panel's evaluations may have been "contaminated" by knowledge of the sorts of people involved in particular fields.) Four of these five attributes proved, in fact, to be significantly correlated with prestige, giving some support to our initial ideas. We can only appeal to face validity, however, to justify our claim that these five attributes are analytically independent of one another. In examining the intercorrelation matrix of the five imputed characteristics, we found that five of the ten correlations were statistically significant, but these correlations were usually of only modest strength. (Only two of the ten coefficients were larger than .55.) The correlational structure had no simple pattern, although the relative strength of specific correlations made good sense. For example, as one might have expected, intellectual challenge and rapidity of change of the law relevant to a field were correlated at .69. Similarly, we analyzed a number of measures drawn from four broad categories of deference entitlements. Most of these variables also proved to have statistically significant, zero-order associations with the allocation of prestige standing among the fields, but they too are correlated among themselves to varying degrees.

The crucial question thus becomes: given the extensive information that we have about the characteristics of the fields, many of which are known to covary with one another in highly predictable ways, can we devise a parsimonious explanation of the differential allocation of prestige among the fields? In attempting to answer this question, we constructed three alternative theoretical models of the prestige allocation process in which we specified in advance a set of characteristics that might determine prestige standing. We were then interested in calculating the net effect on prestige of each characteristic, holding constant the effects of all the other independent variables in the model. The statistical technique of multiple regression analysis is designed to do just this sort of task.[42]

Table 4.4 presents three regression models. Model I considers all five of the characteristics imputed to the fields by the scholars because we believed at the outset that they all would make analytically independent contributions to our understanding of prestige allocation. Model II considers six selected characteristics drawn from the much larger set of differentiating attributes of the practitioners and their practices. The proportions of "Jewish origin" and "elite law school attended" are intended to represent social origins; proportions "working in law firms with thirty or more lawyers" and "professional training required for practice" tap the complex of work context and work characteristics; percent "lower status clients" represents client characteristics; while proportion "earning $50,000 or more" represents the extrinsic rewards associated with the fields. Of course, all these indicators are resultants of complex social processes and cannot, consequently, be expected to measure precisely only one hypothetical construct in our theoretical argument. The proportion working in large law firms, for example, is associated with the proportion reporting major corporations as clients, while the proportion in solo practice, which we have treated as a work context attribute, is associated with the proportion of Jewish origin, a putatively social origin attribute. Thus, since we expected some confounding and redundant effects among the various indicators, caution in interpreting the results is advisable. Model III is a composite that considers simultaneously the five variables in Model I and the six in Model II to construct the best predictive model.

Table 4.4 lists the variables for each model in the order of their standardized coefficients (see last column). These standardized coefficients may be compared with one another in a given model in order to determine the relative impact each variable has on the dependent variable, the standardized prestige score. The partial Fs in the third column permit one to test whether the independent variable in question still contributes significantly to the explained sums of squares once the effects of the other variables in the model have been statistically removed. The unstandardized coefficients in the first column are the b coefficients or partial slopes for the multiple

42. For a good, brief introduction to this mode of statistical analysis, see Hubert M. Blalock, Jr., *Social Statistics* (New York: McGraw-Hill, 1960), pp. 326–58.

TABLE 4.4

Multiple Regression of Selected Variables Predicting Prestige of Fields

	Unstandardized Coefficients	Standard Error	Partial F	Standardized Coefficients
Model I: Characteristics Imputed by Legal Scholars				
1. Public service	−.81	.27	9.18**	−.62
2. Intellectual challenge	.84	.32	6.80**	.62
3. Ethical conduct	.55	.32	2.95*	.33
4. Freedom of action	.16	.22	0.51	.11
5. Rapidity of change	−.15	.31	0.25	−.11
Multiple R^2 = .88; F = 24.73, p < .001.				
Model II: Selected Characteristics of Practitioners				
1. % lower status clients	−4.63	1.03	20.07**	−.73
2. % professional training	1.41	.99	2.01	.20
3. % Jewish	−1.29	1.05	1.53	−.16
4. % law income $50,000 or more (age adjusted)	1.48	1.43	1.08	.16
5. % firm larger than 30	−.45	.86	.27	−.10
6. % elite law school	.02	1.33	.00	.00
Multiple R^2 = .80; F = 10.90, p < .001.				
Model III: Composite Model				
1. Public service	−.56	.14	16.56**	−.43
2. Ethical conduct	.54	.13	15.85**	.33
3. Intellectual challenge	.44	.14	9.51**	.33
4. % lower status clients	−1.48	.85	3.04*	−.23
5. % Jewish	−1.43	.61	5.54**	−.18
Multiple R^2 = .92; F = 41.77, p < .001.				

NOTES: *Statistically significant at the .05 level.
**Statistically significant at the .01 level.

regression equation that can be used to predict the prestige scores; the second column gives the standard errors of these coefficients, providing a different way to evaluate the significance of a given unstandardized coefficient in the multiple regression equation as a whole.[43]

The reader can see that all three regression models are able to explain very high proportions of the total variance in prestige scores (the multiple R^2s range from .80, or 80 percent, for model II to .92, or 92 percent of the total variance, for model III). But in fact, in the case of models I and II only one to three variables are re-

43. If an unstandardized coefficient is less than twice its standard error, one cannot assume that it departs significantly from zero (or no association between the independent and dependent variables, net of the effects of all the other variables in the model) with a probability less than .05. Such a test is ultimately equivalent to the partial F test in the third column.

quired to achieve these high R^2s. In model I the first two variables, public service and intellectual difficulty, achieve a multiple R^2 of .80, which rises to .87 with the addition of ethical conduct. The remaining two variables, freedom of action and rapidity of change, do not make significant contributions to the explanation of the prestige scores once the effects of the first three variables are taken into account. In Model II an even more dramatic result emerges. Only the first variable, the percentage of lower status clients, is significantly involved in explaining prestige, achieving an R^2 of .74. The addition of each of the other variables does not appreciably improve the prediction. Especially noteworthy is the absence of impact of the income of the fields on their prestige standing—a negative finding of considerable theoretical import.

Model III confirms the results of the other two models by selecting only the top three variables from Model I and the top two from Model II (from the eleven it was originally given) to construct the optimal prediction of the prestige scores. It also informs us, however, that our fears about the problem of disentangling the confounding effects of the various indicators were justified.[44] The percentage

44. The following detailed statistical analysis of aggregation and multicollinearity effects was prepared by Charles Cappell:
The linear models in table 4.4. were inspected for redundancy among the independent variables. Eigenroots and eigenvectors were extracted from the intercorrelation matrices of the two sets of independent variables in Models I and II. The ratio of the first eigenroot to the sum of all the eigenroots was obtained for each solution. For Model I, this value was .3454; for Model II, .5212. This comparision indicates a greater degree of redundancy among the independent variables of Model II than among those in Model I. An inspection of the sixth eigenroot indicated that the matrices were of full rank.
The effects of this redundancy can be observed in the size of the standard errors of the betas in the models. The effects are more pronounced, as they would have to be, for the standard errors in Model II. We can be reasonably certain (statistically) about the direction of effects only for the characteristics of percent lower status clientele and percent Jewish.
The original data used in Model I consisted of 19 observations on 6 attributes for the 23 specialties. The results of a two-way analysis of variance indicated the absence of an interaction effect; and a measure of the profile similarity of the judges, R =.57, indicated a moderate degree of similarity in the judges' responses (see Ernest A. Haggard, *Intraclass Correlation and the Analysis of Variance* [New York: Dryden Press, 1958], chapters 5, 7). In regression Model I, the mean observation across judges was used as the value for the attribute on a given specialty. This linear function relates a set of experts' mean judgments on 6 attributes for 23 specialties to the mean specialty prestige score obtained from a larger sample of lawyers. In this case, inferences regarding the size of the relationship can be extended to the individual level. Evidence suggests that the relationship for individuals would not be as large and that the inflation in the aggregate R^2 is substantial even when the intercorrelations among the independent variables is moderate (see Ye-

of lower status clients, the single most powerful predictor in Model II, drops to relative insignificance when the imputed characteristics are taken into account. To a considerable degree, however, this result is probably attributable to the fact that the imputed characteristics may be themselves—like the prestige judgments—relatively abstract assessments of the goodness or social desirability of the fields.[45] They may thus be expected to be closer to prestige.[46] Moreover, it is well known that the variables that are subject to the least measurement error and contamination will tend to have the great-

---

huda Grunfeld and Zvi Griliches, "Is Aggregation Necessarily Bad?" *Review of Economics and Statistics* 42 [1960]: 1, esp. sec. 1).

In Model II a slightly more complicated problem arises. Here the measures on the independent variables were obtained by grouping and then finding the mean of the independent observations. (Individual lawyers were conceptualized as observations on fields.) The grouping criterion was the amount of time the lawyer spent on the given field. Previous observations on the effects of redundancy and aggregation apply to this model, also, but further complications arise if the grouping criterion is not random with respect to the independent variables. See Hubert M. Blalock, Jr., *Causal Inferences in Non-experimental Research* 97–125 (Chapel Hill: University of North Carolina Press, 1964); Grunfeld and Griliches, *supra;* Michael T. Hannan, "Problems of Aggregation," in H. M. Blalock Jr., ed., *Causal Models in the Social Sciences* 473 (Chicago: Aldine-Atherton, 1971). An extended multivariate analysis was not warranted; instead the extent of grouping effects was determined by inspecting the analysis of variance results obtained during the grouping operation. Intraclass correlation coefficients indicate the effect grouping had on the variance of the attribute for the grouped specialists compared with the variance of the attribute for the sample. In only a few instances did the intraclass correlation exceed .10. This indicates that, for the most part, the assumption of random grouping with respect to the independent variables seems reasonable. Extrapolating the findings to the individual level, one can infer that the relative strength of the betas would be maintained.

However, a subtle substantive difference results from shifting levels of analysis in Model II. In this model at the grouped level, the mean of an attribute for a group of practitioners, not judges, is related to the mean field prestige score. This implies, at the individual level, that an individual, in allocating prestige to fields, may be doing so on the basis of a vector of attribute means for each of the fields. He must, therefore, be aware of the central tendency of each of the attributes for each of the fields. Given the highly indirect nature of this allocation process (and the degree of redundancy among the attributes), the ability of Model II to fit the prestige scores is surprising.

45. See Goldthorpe and Hope, *supra* note 3, and discussion in the text following note 4.

46. Indeed, if the general good or bad repute of the fields had substantial impact on the ratings of these characteristics made by our panel of scholars, then these imputed characteristics would, to that extent, not be "independent variables"—i.e., they would not be independent of the general prestige of the fields. But the correlations of the individual imputed characteristics with the prestige judgments are relatively modest and thus suggest that this is not the case. (Three of the five correlations are about .5; one, rapidity of change, is .08; and the fifth, intellectual challenge, is a. 65.)

est explanatory power in a given regression analysis.[47] For this reason also, then, the relative predictive contribution of the client type variable and of the other practitioner responses may be, in a sense, understated. Moreover, the lower status client variable is clearly associated with several of the imputed characteristics of the fields, and perceptions affecting the prestige of the fields that serve lower status clients are probably measured more directly by these more abstract, imputed characteristics. The sorts of cases that lower status clients bring to their lawyers, for example, often call only for relatively routine legal procedures, however much these cases may be of great personal moment to the clients. But this fact about the nature of practice for lower status clients may be measured more directly by the inclusion of the intellectual challenge variable in the composite model. Similarly, we have noted that certain types of cases—for example, personal injury, criminal defense, and divorce—are perceived as more likely to be handled by lawyers who employ sharp practices that are contrary to the prevailing ethical norms of the profession. These cases, too, tend more often to involve lower status clients, but our measure of ethical conduct more directly addresses the issue. Finally, lower status clients, being persons of limited financial means, are likely to be involved in the less profitable sorts of litigation and legal work—at times even requiring *pro bono* service. As Model III shows, such public service is negatively associated with the prestige of the fields of law. Indeed, according to the standardized coefficients, it plays the strongest role in predicting the prestige scores (see p. 132). We tentatively conclude, then, that the percentage of lower status clients is better treated as a compound indicator that is a complex function of variance in intellectual challenge, ethical conduct, and profitability.

The negative impact of the percentage of practitioners of Jewish origin, a nonsignificant variable in Model II but of some importance in Model III, appears to be tapping an aspect of the prestige of legal specialties that is no longer masked by the effects of the other variables in the model. The negative impact on prestige standing of high concentrations of Jews in a specialty is probably due to the past and possibly continuing discrimination against the entry of

47. Cf. Paul M. Siegel and Robert W. Hodge, "A Causal Approach to the Study of Measurement Error," in Hubert M. Blalock, Jr., and Ann B. Blalock, eds., *Methodology in Social Research* (New York: McGraw-Hill, 1968), p. 28; Robert A. Gordon, "Issues in Multiple Regression," *American Journal of Sociology* 73 (1968): 592.

Jews into the higher status specialties that serve major corporate clients.[48] But since our data measure the state of affairs at only one point in time, we cannot be certain of whether this reflects a historical process that has run its course.[49]

48. "The Jewish Law Student and New York Jobs—Discriminatory Effects in Law Firm Hiring Practices," *Yale Law Journal* 73 (1964): 625–60; Jerold S. Auerbach, *Unequal Justice: Lawyers and Social Change in Modern America* (New York: Oxford University Press, 1976); Jack Ladinsky, "Careers of Lawyers, Law Practice, and Legal Institutions," *American Sociological Review* 28 (1963): 52–54; idem., "The Impact of Social Backgrounds of Lawyers on Law Practice and the Law," *Journal of Legal Education* 16 (1963): 137–38; idem., "The Social Profile of a Metropolitan Bar: A Statistical Survey in Detroit," *Michigan State Bar Journal* 43 (1964): 19–20.

49. Though no amount of mock cohort analysis can fully substitute for the absence of longitudinal data (see pp. 161–64 and 178), it may be instructive to examine the types of practice engaged in by Jewish respondents of differing ages. Thus, if prestigious areas of practice were formerly closed to Jews but more recently have become open to them, we would expect to find that the observed tendency for Jewish lawyers to be overrepresented in the less prestigious jobs differs with the age of our respondents, the effect being much stronger among older lawyers than among younger ones.

A superficial look at some of our data might suggest strong support for this hypothesis of age difference. Thus, the percentage of Jewish respondents who are solo practitioners (a reasonably good proxy variable to use as a summary indicator of lower status practice) declines markedly with age. If we divide our respondents into three age categories that produce approximately equal numbers of Jews in each age range—age 46 and older (includes 78 Jewish respondents), age 34 to 45 (includes 74 Jews), and age 33 and younger (also 74 Jews)— we find that 42 percent of the Jewish respondents in the oldest group are solo practitioners, as compared to 26 percent of those in the middle group and only 12 percent in the youngest group. Similarly, if we use employment in a large law firm (30 or more lawyers) as a proxy for a high status position, we find that only 5 percent of the Jewish respondents in the oldest group are in such firms, but that this increases to 10 percent in the middle group and 19 percent in the youngest group. This would appear, then, to be evidence of a substantial improvement in the position of Jews in the Chicago bar in recent years.

On the other hand, if we look somewhat more closely at the data, we find that these trends are very substantially due to decreases and increases, respectively, in those types of practice generally—that is, the trends reflect an overall growth in the share of the profession that practices in firms of 30 or more lawyers and a precipitous decline in the solo practice. The proportion of solos decreases from 33 percent of the oldest group to 19 percent of the middle group and only 8 percent of the youngest lawyers, while the large firm share of the total bar increases from 12 percent of the oldest group to 18 percent of the middle group and 26 percent of the youngest.

If we examine instead, then, the ethnoreligious composition of the total number of lawyers in each of the practice settings by age, we find that the percentage of Jews in the large firm category does indeed increase across the age groups, but that the percentage does not yet come close to equaling their percentage of the total profession, even in the youngest age group. The Jewish share of the total Chicago bar increases steadily across the three age groups, from 30 percent of the oldest group to 33 percent of the middle group and 38 percent of the youngest, while the comparable percentages of Jews in the large firm category are 13, 18 and 28. The degree of underrepresentation thus decreases from 17 percentage points in the oldest group to 15 points in the middle group and 10 percentage points in the youngest group. While the gap narrows appreciably in the youngest group, then, even in that age category Jewish respondents are still substantially underrepresented in the large firms. At the other end of the status hierarchy, the picture is even less supportive of

More generally, the regression models are best regarded as providing at this stage of research only some broad clues to understanding the empirical processes generating prestige judgments. The most serious limitation of our analysis is the widely varying measurement status of the several indicators considered. The relatively weaker roles that variables based on the responses of practitioners played in the regression analysis when compared with the imputed characteristics of the scholar judges is probably due to the fact that they are compound indicators of diverse social processes, sharing at least some common functional dependencies, in contrast to the analytically more homogeneous and empirically abstracted judgments of the legal scholars (see n. 44). We should not, therefore, take too seriously the results regarding the relative impact of the different variables in explaining prestige differences. But, however tentative we must remain in assessing the relative importance of these variables, we should add on a more positive note that these several models do indicate that we have succeeded in identifying a relatively small set of theoretically interesting variables that are remarkably powerful in explaining the allocation of prestige.

(continued)
the hypothesis that opportunities have opened up—the percentage of solo practitioners who are Jewish actually increases in the younger age categories, from 39 percent in the oldest group to 43 percent in the middle group and 53 percent in the youngest. One should exercise great caution in giving weight to this finding, however, because the decline in the solo practitioners' share of the total profession means that there are few respondents in the younger categories. In absolute numbers, there are 33 Jewish solo practitioners in the oldest age category and only 9 in the youngest.

In sum, while there appears to have been some improvement in the position of Jews within the Chicago bar, that improvement has not been as great as one might have expected. Even in the youngest age group, Jewish respondents exceed their percentage of the total profession only in the solo practice and in the small and medium-sized firm categories and exceed it most among the solos and small firm practitioners. The greatest improvement in the access of Jews appears to have come in the medium-sized firms, where they increase from 17 percent among the oldest group to 46 percent in the youngest. While the percentage of Jewish respondents in the large firms increases in the younger groups, Jews are still underrepresented—by a full 10 percentage points, even in the youngest age group. The increase among house counsel has been less steady, but is quite substantial in the youngest group. Even there, however, Jewish respondents remain underrepresented by 11 percentage points. From these data, it would be hard to argue that the vestiges of anti-Semitism have disappeared.

For additional analyses of career patterns by ethnoreligious background, see chapters 5 and 6, especially table 6.6.

Conclusions

Though it is difficult to sort out the elements of prestige within the legal profession because of the high degree of intercorrelation among several of the hypothesized independent variables, some interpretations of the findings seem relatively clear. The general pattern of the prestige ranking, with fields serving big business clients at the top and those serving individual clients (especially clients from lower socioeconomic groups) at the bottom, is unambiguous. Here again, however, we may run up against a confounding of effects. The degree of intellectual challenge of the fields is highly correlated not only with their prestige (.65) but also with their percentages of lower status clients (−.59). Thus, what may appear to be an effect of client type on the prestige rankings might, instead, be in large part an effect of peer opinions of the intellectual demands of the different sorts of practice, or vice versa.

Rather than resorting to further techniques of multivariate analysis to attempt to unravel the confounding of intellectual challenge and client type, a condition that may well exist in the real world, let us simply look at a few specialties where the degree of intellectual challenge is held constant. Our list of thirty fields includes six where the adversary system creates clearly distinguishable specialties representing the two sides of the case—antitrust, labor, environmental, personal injury, criminal, and consumer law. The intellectual challenge ratings of the two sides of each of these six areas are, of course, substantially identical.[50] (Dealing with the legal substance of a case requires the lawyer, on whichever side of the case, to anticipate and respond to the law on the other side.)[51] In each of

50. The differences between the intellectual challenge scores of each of these pairs are, in fact, very small, ranging from 0 to 3 points. In the five comparisons in which there is a difference in the intellectual challenge scores of the two sides of the case (in environmental law, the scores are identical), however, the difference is always in the same direction—the higher score is given to the "nonestablishment" side of the field. Thus, the direction of the differences suggests that the scholars who served as our judges of intellectual challenge were not biased by the "establishment" view of the prestige of the fields. The tendency in their ratings could, of course, indicate some bias in the opposite direction, but it also might reflect a perception that differences in the resources available to the two sides make the tasks of the lawyers for the nonestablishment side systematically more demanding. See *infra*, note 51.

51. Differences in the burden of proof or extralegal differences in the resources available to the lawyers might make it consistently easier to try one side of the case than the other, but the direction of these differences, if any, will usually tend to

these six fields of law, the side that represents the more "establishment" client is consistently rated higher in prestige. That is, those who defend criminals are given less prestige than those who prosecute; labor union lawyers rank lower in prestige than do the labor lawyers who represent management; lawyers who represent plaintiffs with personal injury, environmental, or antitrust claims are assigned lower prestige scores than the lawyers who represent the insurance companies and other businesses that are the defendants in such actions; and the advocates for buyers of consumer goods have less prestige than do those who represent the sellers. The consistency of result in these comparisons seems to us to be rather persuasive support for the hypothesis that client type has an effect on prestige that is independent of the intellectual difficulty of the subject matter. And that effect is, quite clearly, to enhance the prestige of work done for corporate, establishment, or big business clients and to derogate that done for small businesses or for individuals, particularly those from the lower classes.

In the practice of law—as on the assembly line and in many other sorts of work—an almost inevitable consequence of the division of labor has been a routinization of tasks for most of the workers.[52] There are few kinds of law practice where a high proportion of the problems call for truly creative solutions, and these jobs are likely to be at the top of the prestige ladder, in the service of the most influential, most wealthy clients; unique problems and unique solutions are more likely to be generated when the stakes are high, and high for more than a few people.

Service to individuals is often repetitious and dull. Although a divorce, a limb wasted by an automobile accident or by medical malpractice, a home mortgage foreclosure, a sanity hearing, a criminal charge, a lost job, or an adoption or child-custody proceeding may all involve anxiety and suffering for the client, the specialized

---

(continued)
make the jobs of the lawyers on the establishment side less demanding. That is, the greater resources are likely to be on the establishment side. In criminal cases, the burden of proof will be favorable to the defense rather than to the establishment (government) side, but in all of the other pairs of fields, which are civil, the establishment sides, as the defense, will usually also have the benefit of the burden of proof. Insofar as these differences exist between the two sides of the fields, therefore, the tendency of these differences will not explain the higher prestige of the establishment sides as attributable to a greater degree of intellectual challenge. Rather, if anything, the differences will usually cut in the opposite direction.

52. Cf. Robert E. Blauner, *Alienation and Freedom: The Factory Worker and His Industry* (Chicago: University of Chicago Press, 1964).

lawyer finds most such cases routine. Thus, the value placed on intellectual challenge in the allocation of prestige within the legal profession has an inherent elitist tendency—that is, because the depth of the clients' pockets determines, in important part, the complexity of the legal issues with which their lawyers will be permitted to deal, the value placed on intellectual challenge will tend to lead lawyers into the service of a socioeconomic elite. In this respect, the legal profession differs from medicine. An exotic medical problem may afflict rich or poor (though such a problem is no doubt more likely to be detected in the well-to-do), and prestige within the medical profession may not, therefore, correspond so closely to the wealth of patients. Even poor people can have prestigious diseases.

The association between the public service scores of the fields and their prestige is similarly entwined with the nature of the clients served by the fields. The clients who receive legal services at no fee or at greatly reduced fees (the recipients of *pro bono* work) are, of course, likely to be either persons of lower social status who cannot afford service at the going rate or politically or ethically controversial clients who are served as a matter of principle. Thus, the highest public service scores were assigned to civil rights/civil liberties, poverty law, work for plaintiffs in environmental cases, and work for debtors in consumer cases. By contrast, the fields that receive the lowest public service scores, banking law and antitrust defense,[53] serve powerful corporate clients. While we doubt that altruism is directly or consciously derogated, even in the practice of law, it may well be that the profit motive and the values associated with it are given some weight in the allocation of prestige within the profession. The American legal profession seems to be preoccupied with economic enterprise—Karl Llewellyn observed long ago that the "main work" of the metropolitan bar was "in essence the doing of business," and he drew some further conclusions.

53. Note, however, that personal injury plaintiffs' work also received one of the lowest public service scores, even though it is disproportionately likely to serve lower status clients. The service to impecunious clients in that field is not usually done on a no fee or reduced fee basis, but rather on a contingent fee that is intended to be highly profitable to the lawyer. Note also that though personal injury plaintiffs' work ranks at the high prestige end of the public service scale (i.e., the lower end), its prestige score is, in fact, among the lowest. That is, its prestige corresponds not to its public service score but to the social status of its clients—it serves persons of low status and it has low prestige within the profession.

Now, any man's interests, any man's outlook, are shaped in greatest part by what he does. His perspective is in terms of what he knows. His sympathies and ethical judgments are determined essentially by the things and the people he works on and for and with. . . . Hence the practice of corporation law not only works for business men toward business ends, but develops within itself a business point of view—toward the work to be done, toward the value of the work to the community, indeed, toward the way in which to do the work.[54]

We do not mean to suggest that the many lawyers who are primarily concerned with the facilitation of business do not perform useful social functions—they obviously do. The values they serve are the core economic values of our society,[55] and the more a field of law serves these values, the higher its prestige will be within the profession.

In addressing theories of prestige generation in the professions more generally, Andrew Abbott has commented on our findings and has put the subject in an interesting light.[56]

Intraprofessional status is in reality a function of professional purity. By professional purity I mean the ability to exclude nonprofessional issues or irrelevant professional issues from practice. Within a given profession, the highest status professionals are those who deal with issues predigested and predefined by a number of colleagues. These colleagues have removed human complexity and difficulty to leave a problem at least professionally defined, although possibly still very difficult to solve. Conversely, the lowest status professionals are those who deal with problems from which the human complexities are not or cannot be removed. The theoretical origins of this argument lie in anthropology. . . . [P]urity and contagion taboos are an extension of cultural systems. The impure is that which violates the categories and classifications of a given cultural system. Through amorphousness or ambiguity it brings together things that the cultural system wishes to separate. Nearly all writers agree that the application of esoteric knowledge to particular cases is characteristic of professions. . . . [P]roblems that fundamentally challenge basic professional categories are impure and professionally defiling. It is at once clear why Laumann and Heinz (1977) find that legal practice involving corporations in nearly all cases stands above that involving private individuals. The corporation is the lawyers' creation. The muck of feelings and will is omitted from it *ab initio*. Where feelings are highest and cli-

54. Karl N. Llewellyn, "The Bar Specializes—With What Results?" *Annals of American Academy of Social and Political Sciences* 167(1933): 177.

55. Cf. Francis X. Sutton et al., *The American Business Creed* (Cambridge: Harvard University Press, 1956).

56. Andrew Abbott, "Status and Status Strain in the Professions," *American Journal of Sociology* 86 (1981): 819.

ents most legally irrational—in divorce—intra-professional status is lowest.

Over time, professional knowledge develops a system of such relative judgments of purity and impurity. All these judgments follow the same pattern. The professionally defined or definable is more pure than the undefined or undefinable. . . . The barrister stands above the solicitor because he works in a purely legal context with purely legal concepts; the solicitor links the law to immediate human concerns. The free-lance or associated professional stands above the employed professional because his work is not conditioned by employer policy. The academic professional's high status reflects his exclusively intraprofessional work.[57]

We find this an intriguing and appealing argument, and we believe that it merits further examination. It is, in fact, quite consistent with some of our observations (see pp. 102–8). Abbott suggests, however, that our data provide an adequate test of his thesis. We doubt this. In an extended footnote to his article, Abbott asserts that our study "provides striking confirmation of the purity thesis." He continues:

The best correlate of prestige in their legal data is the degree to which a specialty implies work for altruistic or reformist motives (*pro bono* work). Such service for non-legal ends is a strong negative correlate of specialty status, while a subfield's legal (intellectual) challenge and reputation for professional ethicality are strong positive correlates. It is clear that professional ethicality, at least, is an aspect of professional purity. The low ethicality ratings of personal injury, criminal defense, and divorce lawyers reflect the profession's fear that their judgment will be corrupted by client concerns. The low status of *pro bono* work is a similar disparagement of extralegal motives.[58]

After noting that our definition of the intellectual challenge variable specifically distinguished the legal or doctrinal substance of the work from the "strategic considerations" and dealt only with the challenge presented by the former, Abbott argues:

Since only legal complexity is measured, the variable of professional purity is implicitly included. Given that issues of the exclusion of the non-professional seem to sustain the other two correlates of prestige, parsimony suggests their importance in this correlation as well. Given that these correlates account for 87 percent of the variance in intraprofessional prestige rankings, Laumann and Heinz's study seems strong evidence indeed for the place of purity in determining that status.[59]

57. Ibid., pp. 823–24.
58. Ibid., pp. 825–26.
59. Ibid.

One difficulty with this line of argument is that it is an incautious use of our regression analyses. As we noted, the relative contributions of the several variables to the prediction of prestige cannot be taken at face value.[60] Because of the nature of the variables and their measurement and because of statistical properties of regression analysis itself, it is almost inevitable that the more abstract, imputed characteristics of the fields, as rated by a small group of scholars, will do better in the regression equations than will the "real life" characteristics of clients and practitioners, as obtained from our interviews with 777 randomly selected respondents. Indeed, the remarkable fact is that the client and practitioner characteristics do as well as they do (see pp. 122–26). Moreover, Abbott points to the public service score as the "best correlate of prestige," presumably referring to the regression analyses, but by far the strongest simple, bivariate correlation with prestige is that of the percentage of the field's clients who are persons of lower social status—a correlation of −.86. If one were primarily interested in parsimony, therefore, one could do quite well in predicting the prestige of a field just by knowing the proportion of its clients who are blue-collar workers. And Abbott's thesis does not account for the consistently higher prestige of the establishment sides of the split fields[61]—that is, personal injury plaintiffs vs. personal injury defense; criminal prosecution vs. criminal defense; consumer/creditor vs. consumer/debtor, etc.—unless he wishes to argue that the corporate side of a given field or case is consistently more professionally pure than the personal client side (of the same field or case). If one takes this latter position, the professional purity thesis becomes very similar to the client type thesis of the generation of professional prestige. It really amounts to a contention that the mixture of client type with public service, ethicality, and intellectual challenge, in our terms, cannot be decomposed.

Whatever the explanation of this distribution of prestige within the profession, however, it is important to inquire into whether it can be translated into more generalized influence, either within or outside the profession. Public office would, of course, provide one sort of opportunity for such influence. Another type of influence is almost a necessary consequence of the role of adviser to big business. Lawyers who influence the expenditure of many millions of

60. See *supra*, notes 44–47, and accompanying text.
61. See pp. 127–28.

dollars, who determine whether corporate acquisitions or mergers will or will not take place, undeniably have an important sort of power. But there is also the sort of influence that may come from control of the pattern maintenance institutions of the profession, especially the bar associations. That is, who is given the authority to speak in the name of the profession as a whole? We have examined the extent to which lawyers in the several fields have held positions of leadership in the Chicago Bar Association (CBA), the principal professional association in Chicago, and we find that the percentage of practitioners in a field who have held such positions correlates .56 with the prestige of the field. More than 20 percent of the securities, patent, and public utility lawyers in our sample had been CBA leaders, for example, while 5 percent or fewer of the criminal defense and of the personal injury lawyers had held such positions. The direction of the causation (if any) seems quite clear. It is not very plausible that the proportion of CBA officers in a field would enhance its prestige appreciably. Rather, it seems more likely that lawyers are chosen for CBA office on the basis of their personal prestige, some of which is attributable to the prestige of the sorts of work they do. Thus, there is evidence that the prestige of the field of law may be convertible into influence, at least within the profession.

Another important consequence of the prestige structure may well be its effects on the recruitment of lawyers into the various fields. Most of us value deference, and there will thus be an incentive to enter the types of legal work that will earn one that deference. Many of the lawyers who practice in the fields that serve persons of moderate means[62] are probably not as highly qualified as are those who serve the large corporations, and many probably entered the lower prestige fields more from necessity than from choice. As we have noted, the proportion of practitioners who attended the most prestigious law schools is much higher in corporate practice than it is in the fields serving individuals and small businesses. The other side of this coin is that the percentage who attended law schools of only local repute ranges from a high of more than 70 percent in criminal defense and personal injury plaintiffs' work to a low of less than 20 percent in securities, antitrust defense, public

---

62. Barlow F. Christensen, *Lawyers for People of Moderate Means: Some Problems of Availability of Legal Services* (Chicago: American Bar Foundation, 1970), pp. 92–97.

utilities work, and business litigation.[63] The local law schools have fewer resources to denote to legal education than do the elite schools,[64] and the lawyers who serve individuals are therefore likely to be less well trained than are those who serve corporations. Since the income that a lawyer receives from his practice is not significantly associated with the prestige of his field, the monetary rewards available may induce some lawyers—even some well-qualified ones—to enter a lower prestige practice. A desire for service or a desire to appear (in his own eyes or those of others) to be motivated by altruism might also lead, of course, to that same result. But to the extent that lawyers making career choices are concerned with their prestige within the legal profession—concerned, that is, with receiving deference or respect from their fellow professionals— they will tend to choose service to big business rather than to poor people.

In sum, the distribution of honor or deference among the fields of law is entirely consistent with our observations about the organization of legal work and the structure of social differentiation of the fields. All three appear to be organized by the types of clients served, and the great divide occurs between the kinds of law practice that serve primarily corporate clients and those that serve primarily individual persons or small businesses. These are the two main sectors of the legal profession. Further measures of the size of the gulf between them and further implications of the existence of this gulf are explored in the chapters yet to come.

63. These local schools are De Paul, Illinois Institute of Technology-Chicago Kent, Loyola, and John Marshall, all located in Chicago.
64. See Charles D. Kelso, "Adding up the Law Schools," *Learning and the Law,* Summer 1975, p. 38.

PART III

*Lawyers' Lives:
Social Background,
Social Values,
and Career Mobility*

Chapter 5

SOCIAL VALUES
WITHIN THE PROFESSION

IN PREVIOUS CHAPTERS we have suggested that the organization of lawyers' work, the structure of social differentiation among the fields of law, and the allocation of prestige within the profession are all principally determined by the nature and interests of the clients served. But we have thus far given little attention to the values, attitudes, or beliefs that the lawyers embrace. The daily work of doctors, engineers, or architects may be little influenced by their general social values, but the lawyer's professional role is much more directly related to issues of choice among alternative allocations of benefits in society and to competing views of the proper purposes of institutional authority. Because of this relationship between lawyers' social values and the work that they do (or that some of them do) we think it particularly important to examine the positions that lawyers take on social issues.[1]

Are lawyers' values also determined by the interests of the lawyers' clients, through a process of socialization or accommodation?

1. There have been very few empirical studies of the values and opinions of lawyers. Richard Abel's extensive recent review of the literature on the profession failed to find any such study apart from a few reports on the values of law students; Abel, "The Sociology of American Lawyers: A Bibliographic Guide," *Law and Policy Quarterly* 2 (July 1980): 335–91. Since 1977, the monthly *American Bar Association Journal* has published a "Lawpoll" section, reporting the results of survey questions of lawyers on a variety of topics of interest to the profession, but it is not of a scholarly nature.

Or do their values derive more from their social origins, childhood training, and home environments? Are common values widely shared throughout the profession? (William J. Goode cites the sharing of values within a profession as one of the characteristics of the professions that justify his treatment of them as communities.)[2] Or is there substantial differentiation among lawyers' value positions, reflecting differences in either their social origins or their clients' interests? To the extent that the values with which we are concerned deal with attitudes toward institutions such as the church, we would expect that lawyers' social origins and early religious training (or the absence of it) would have relatively greater impact on their positions than would client concerns. If we look at social values that are more directly related to the lawyers' professional roles or that have a greater nexus with client interests, however, we might expect lawyers' values to correspond more closely to the characteristics of their clients. Thus, if the value relates to the desirability of government intervention in the regulation of the economy, lawyers who serve certain kinds of corporate clients might be expected to display a characteristic predisposition regardless of their ethnic or religious origins.

Let us begin our analysis of lawyers' values, however, not with an analysis of the extent and character of the differentiation within the profession but with an analysis of the general characteristics of the value positions of our total sample of lawyers, considered as a whole. It may also help to establish a context for the analysis of lawyers' values if we compare them, so far as available data permit, with the values of other populations. To facilitate comparisons across the various attitude items used to measure economic and civil libertarian values, table 5.1 gives the percentage distributions of agreement and disagreement with the various items for the total sample of 777 lawyers.

Economic Values

Dietrich Rueschemeyer has argued that the values of American lawyers are strongly influenced by "reference groups in the business

2. William T. Goode, "Community Within a Community: The Professions," *American Sociological Review* 22 (1957): 194.

TABLE 5.1
Chicago Lawyers' Attitudes on Selected Economic and Civil Liberties Issues
(Total Sample = 777)

	Strongly Agree	Agree	Undecided	Disagree	Strongly Disagree
Economic Values					
1. The protection of consumer interests is best insured by a vigorous competition among sellers rather than by federal government intervention and regulation on behalf of consumers.	17	29	11	33	11
2. There is too much power concentrated in the hands of a few large companies for the good of the country.	16	36	17	26	5
3. Labor unions have become too big for the good of the country.	21	32	21	22	4
4. The gains that labor unions make for their members help make the country more prosperous.	3	36	26	28	8
5. Differences in income among occupations should be reduced.	5	9	12	47	26
6. All Americans should have equal access to quality medical care regardless of ability to pay.	41	46	7	6	1
7. One of the most important roles of government is to help those who cannot help themselves, such as the poor, the disadvantaged, and the unemployed.	26	52	7	13	3
8. Economic profits are by and large justly distributed in the U.S. today.	3	23	20	41	14
Civil Libertarian Values					
1. The right to associate with whom one pleases is being endangered by the excesses of civil rights legislation.	7	18	12	41	22
2. Preservation of the traditional moral values of the community in such areas as prostitution, gambling, and homosexuality is a perfectly legitimate objective of the criminal law.	8	29	13	34	16
3. The provisions of the U.S. Constitution should be construed strictly so as to implement the intent of the framers.	8	27	10	44	12
4. A group of feminists remove all their clothing in public at the site of a Hugh Hefner speech in order to protest *Playboy's* treatment of women as "sex objects." To punish them for indecent exposure would abridge their right to political expression.	7	22	12	49	11

TABLE 5.1 *(continued)*
Chicago Lawyers' Attitudes on Selected Economic and Civil Liberties Issues
(Total Sample = 777)

	Strongly Agree	Agree	Undecided	Disagree	Strongly Disagree
5. Publishing a directory of homosexuals, describing the acts that they are willing and available to perform, should be punishable as a conspiracy to corrupt public morals.	8	18	19	39	16
Religious Values					
1. To lead a good life it is necessary for a person to be guided by the teachings and beliefs of an established religious group.	10	18	12	35	25
2. Churches are necessary to establish and preserve concepts of right and wrong.	11	32	17	28	12
3. A man ought to be guided by what his experience tells him is right rather than by what any institution, such as church or government, tells him to do.	21	40	15	20	5

community" and by the fact that "sons of businessmen are the strongest background group in the American bar, and later education does comparatively little to discourage the orientations engendered by such home backgrounds."[3] Thus, Rueschemeyer suggests that lawyers' values will be influenced by both their clients' interests and their social origins, in some mixture of unspecified proportions, but that both of these influences will point in the same direction—toward a pro-business orientation. Certainly, as we speculated above, the lawyers who represent businesses might be expected to oppose government interference in business activity. But less than a majority of our respondents agreed with the proposition that "the protection of consumer interests is best insured by a vigorous competition among sellers rather than by federal government intervention and regulation on behalf of consumers." 46 percent of our sample agreed with that statement, 44 percent disagreed, and the remainder were undecided. Thus, the profession was quite evenly split on the question of whether competition or federal interven-

3. Dietrich Rueschemeyer, *Lawyers and Their Society: A Comparative Study of the Legal Profession in Germany and in the United States* (Cambridge, Mass.: Harvard University Press, 1973), pp. 111–14.

tion better serves consumers. The cynical among us may note that many lawyers have a stake in governmental regulation of the economy—it makes work for lawyers—but it is nonetheless hard to find in these results an overwhelming expression of support for the businessman's point of view.

Moreover, the proportion of lawyers who agreed with the statement was much smaller than that among two other populations that have been surveyed. At about the same time that our survey was being conducted, another group of researchers directed by Laumann polled two samples of residents of smaller towns in the greater Chicago area; the first was a cross-sectional sample, and the second was a sample of community elites consisting of business, civic, and local government leaders.[4] While 46 percent of the lawyers agreed with the proposition quoted above, expressing a preference for competition rather than federal government intervention, 68 percent of Laumann's community cross section embraced the statement, as did 74 percent of the community elite sample.[5] Because both of these latter samples were drawn from smaller cities, their differences from the lawyers may well reflect a difference between suburban and small town conservatism, on the one hand, and urban liberalism, on the other, as much or more than the difference between professionals and nonprofessionals. Nonetheless, our findings suggest that big city lawyers stand far from the extreme of support in our society for an unrestrained business ethic.[6]

4. Additional information on the two communities and how the study was executed may be found in Edward O. Laumann, Peter V. Marsden, and Joseph Galaskiewicz, "Community-Elite Influence Structures: Extension of a Network Approach," *American Journal of Sociology* 83 (1977): 598–600, esp.; Joseph Galaskiewicz, *Exchange Networks and Community Politics* (Beverly Hills, Calif.: Sage Publications, 1979).

5. Rather than the five-point scale used in our survey of lawyers, Laumann's community surveys used a six-point scale and included no middle position labeled "undecided," "neutral," or "no opinion." It used three degrees of agreement and three of disagreement ("strong," "moderate," and "weak"). Thus, that scale may have had the effect of forcing more choices than did ours, which permitted an undecided or neutral response. In comparing the results of the community surveys with the lawyer survey, therefore, we use only the percentages of community respondents reporting "strong" or "moderate" agreement or disagreement, treating those who take those positions "weakly" as equivalent to our middle position. In notes to our textual discussion, however, we will give the full distributions of Laumann's community respondents across all six of the scale positions. Here, of the community elites, 42 percent strongly agree, 32 percent moderately agree, 2 percent weakly agree, 1 percent weakly disagree, 13 percent moderately disagree, and 9 percent strongly disagree. The corresponding percentages for the community cross section were 27, 41, 6, 3, 16, and 8.

6. See Francis X. Sutton, Seymour E. Harris, Carl Kaysen, and James Tobin, *The American Business Creed* (Cambridge, Mass.: Harvard University Press, 1957).

Three of the items used in our survey had been administered to a national probability sample several years earlier;[7] the first dealt with attitudes toward large corporations, and the other two dealt with attitudes toward labor unions. The first read, "There is too much power concentrated in the hands of a few large companies for the good of the country" (see table 5.1). Almost exactly the same percentages—52 percent of our respondents and 53 percent of the national sample—agreed with that statement.[8] The lawyers included a somewhat larger percentage who expressed disagreement than did the national sample (31 percent versus 24 percent) and a correspondingly smaller percentage who were undecided or had no opinion (17 percent versus 23 percent), but those differences are relatively minor. The lawyers, thus, do not appear to differ greatly from the national cross section in the extent to which they believe that the growth of large corporations has not been in the national interest. A similar statement was presented about labor unions: "Labor unions have become too big for the good of the country"[9] (see table 5.1). Again, the responses of the two samples were very similar. Fifty-four percent of the lawyers agreed with the statement, as did 55 percent of the national sample; 26 percent of the lawyers and 27 percent of the national sample disagreed with it; 21 percent of the lawyers and 18 percent of the national sample were undecided or had no opinion.[10] The third item used in the national survey read: "The gains that labor unions make for their members help make the country more prosperous" (see table 5.1). Here, there was a greater difference between our sample of lawyers and the national cross section, with the lawyers more often expressing disagreement with the statement. While only 24 percent of the national sample disagreed, half again that percentage, 36 percent, of the lawyers did. Fifty-six percent of the national sample but only 38 percent of the lawyers agreed with the statement; a larger percentage of the lawyers than of the national sample expressed no opinion, 26 percent versus 20 percent.[11] Thus, while the national sample agreed by a margin of more than two to one with the proposition that labor

7. The Opinion Research Corporation conducted the survey in 1960. The results are reported in John P. Robinson, Jerrold G. Rush, and Kendra B. Head, *Measures of Political Attitudes* (Ann Arbor: University of Michigan, Survey Research Center, 1968).
8. Ibid., p. 196.
9. In the national survey, the item read "Labor unions have become too big *and powerful* for the good of the country" [emphasis added]. Ibid., p. 197.
10. Ibid.
11. Ibid.

unions contribute to national prosperity, the lawyers were almost evenly divided on the issue.[12]

It appears, therefore, that our sample of lawyers expressed substantially more anti-union sentiment than did the national cross section at an earlier time, but they were not markedly more pro-business than was the national sample. The lawyers were quite consistent as a whole (whatever their inconsistencies may have been at the individual level) in expressing disapproval of large concentrations of power, whether in the hands of business or of labor. Almost equal proportions agreed with the statements that large companies have too much power (52 percent) and that unions are too big (54 percent). It is possible that lawyers, being relatively clever respondents, deliberately sought to give the appearance of consistency in their responses on these issues, but the items were not worded similarly and were separated during the interview by three intervening questions.[13] In any event, such evidence as we have available provides little support for the hypothesis that lawyers as a whole display a "business mentality."[14]

Indeed, the lawyers' responses to other items in our survey suggest a surprising degree of support for what might be characterized as a welfare state mentality. While very few of the lawyers agreed with the proposition that "differences in income among occupations should be reduced," there was widespread support for redistribution of wealth and power in other respects. Given that the reduction of income differences among occupations would hit lawyers squarely in their pocketbooks, it is perhaps remarkable that only three-quarters of them disagreed with the statement. That is, of course, a substantial consensus, but the greatest consensus among the lawyers on any of the fifteen social values items that we used

12. Because the survey was administered during a mild economic recession in 1975, the language in the item about "making the country prosperous" may have had a tendency to increase the level of disagreement with the statement. It is also true that antiunion sentiment grew throughout the population generally between 1960, the date of the survey of the national cross section, and the time of our survey. This trend is strong enough to account for all or most of the difference between the two samples.

Thus, the general approval rating for labor unions fell from 68 percent in 1959 to 59 percent in 1972; the disapproval rating rose from 19 percent in 1959 to 29 percent in 1972; George H. Gallup, *The Gallup Poll: Public Opinion, 1935–1971* (New York: Random House, 1972), vol. 3, p. 1591; idem, *The Gallup Poll: Public Opinion, 1972–1977* (Wilmington, Del.: Scholarly Resources, Inc.), vol. 1, p. 82.

13. See appendix A, questions A20 and A21, which give the actual format and order of the attitude items.

14. See Rueschemeyer, *supra* note 3, p. 114.

was their response to the statement that "all Americans should have equal access to quality medical care regardless of ability to pay," to which 86 percent agreed. We do not know, of course, whether the lawyers thought that the medical care should be made available through insurance plans, through direct government subsidies, or through the largesse of physicians. It would be interesting to see whether lawyers would be similarly enthusiastic about equality of access to *legal* services.

The next highest level of agreement is also found on an item dealing with the redistribution of power or advantage in society. The statement read: "One of the most important roles of government is to help those who cannot help themselves, such as the poor, the disadvantaged, and the unemployed." More than three-quarters of our respondents agreed with that proposition; only 16 percent disagreed. This is quite widespread support for the government's role as protector of the weak, alleviating the effects of the powerlessness of the lower classes. Whether lawyers' support for this position springs from social conscience, from philosophical or professional views about the proper roles of government and of law, or from self-interested recognition of the financial stake that lawyers have in the administration of government social programs, we cannot say. It may well reflect a combination of these.

The role of social conscience in the formation of these values is, however, suggested by the positions that the lawyers took on yet another of our propositions. The statement read: "Economic profits are by and large justly distributed in the U.S. today." The lawyers disagreed by a margin of more than two to one. Only 26 percent agreed with the statement; 54 percent disagreed, and 20 percent were undecided. Thus, a solid majority of our sample of lawyers believed that the existing distribution of economic benefits in our society was, in some sense, unjust. Since the item was framed in terms of justice, agreement with it suggests that some notion of fundamental fairness is involved—that the economic system deprives a substantial segment of society of benefits to which they possess an entitlement. Given the lawyers' response to our inquiry about the role of government in assisting the "poor, the disadvantaged, and the unemployed," they may also believe that it is the duty of government to redress that inequity. And because the government's duty will presumably be carried out through the instrumentalities of the law, this view may reflect lawyers' conceptions of themselves as righters of wrongs.

Civil Libertarian Values

The law is concerned, of course, not only with financial transactions and matters of economic justice but with the protection of individual (and, increasingly, group) rights and liberties. Some of the items in our inventory of lawyers' social values dealt, accordingly, with the extent of lawyers' commitments to civil libertarianism.

We would expect to find that lawyers would be more likely than the general public to support civil liberties. As an elite, specially educated to respect the rule of law, including the Bill of Rights, lawyers should express an unusually high degree of commitment to civil libertarian values.[15] Unfortunately, however, only one of the civil liberties items used in our survey has been administered to another population, thus permitting direct comparison. That item was used in the studies of the two smaller Chicago-area communities, referred to above.[16] The findings are in the expected direction, though not so strongly as might have been anticipated. The statement read: "The right to associate with whom one pleases is being endangered by the excesses of civil rights legislation." Sixty-three percent of the lawyers disagreed, while 58 percent of the community elite and 50 percent of the community cross section declined to

15. That political elites in general support civil liberties more strongly than does the populace at large was the principal finding of Samuel A. Stouffer's classic work, *Communism, Conformity, and Civil Liberties* (Garden City, N.Y.: Doubleday, 1955); see also Herbert McClosky, "Consensus and Ideology in American Politics," *American Political Science Review* 58 (June 1964): 361–82. This broad generalization must, however, be treated with caution. A recent replication of the Stouffer study reached essentially the same conclusion, but it noted that the gap between political elites and the public was narrowing; see Clyde Z. Nunn, Harry J. Crockett, Jr., and J. Allen Williams, Jr., *Tolerance for Nonconformity: A National Survey of Americans' Changing Commitment to Civil Liberties* (San Francisco: Jossey-Bass, 1978), pp. 142–60. Moreover, of course, civil liberties do not receive uniform levels of support from all groups within the elite structure; see Herbert M. Kritzer, "Ideology and American Political Elites," *Public Opinion Quarterly* 42 (winter 1978): 484–502. Our findings regarding the differentiation of values within the legal profession, presented later in this chapter, are consistent with the latter conclusion.

16. Laumann, Marsden, and Galaskiewicz, *supra* note 4.

embrace the statement.[17] Perhaps the urban-suburban difference between the professional and nonprofessional populations, noted above, served here to reduce the margin between them. That is, the sophistication, the educational attainment, the relative affluence, and the ethnoreligious composition of the suburban populations may tend to enhance their support for civil liberties.[18] Whatever one's speculation on that matter, however, the lawyers appear to line up quite strongly on the side of civil rights legislation—at the least, they do not believe that it has yet endangered the "right of association."

It is possible, though not very plausible, that lawyers feel obligated to support civil rights legislation merely because it is part of the law on the books. The implausibility of this hypothesis is underscored by the lawyers' responses to another item in our survey. The item read: "Preservation of the traditional moral values of the community in such areas as prostitution, gambling, and homosexuality is a perfectly legitimate objective of the criminal law." In spite of the laws on the books that proscribe prostitution and gambling (and, to a lesser extent in Illinois, homosexuality), presumably intending to preserve traditional moral values, a clear majority of our respondents disagreed with this statement. Only 8 percent "strongly agreed," while twice that percentage "strongly disagreed." Thus, most Chicago lawyers do not automatically endorse existing legislation, even when the laws are part of a long tradition, as are the morals offenses. Lawyers appear to value individual liberty or privacy in these matters above conformity to established norms of moral conduct.

Later in this chapter, we provide some further analysis of the patterns of support for civil libertarian values within the bar.

17. Of the smaller community samples, 14 percent of the elite members "strongly agreed," 17 percent "moderately agreed," 6 percent "weakly agreed," 4 percent "weakly disagreed," 26 percent "moderately disagreed," and 32 percent "strongly disagreed." The corresponding percentages for the community cross section were 15, 20, 8, 6, 29, and 21.

18. Though we argued at p. 141 that suburban support for the business ethic may inflate the difference between the lawyer and nonlawyer samples on that variable, here the urban-suburban difference may operate to decrease the difference between the two samples. That is, it may tend to understate the differences between lawyers and nonlawyers on civil liberties issues (see Nunn, Crockett, and Williams, *supra* note 15, pp. 96–110).

Religious Values

The extent of lawyers' support for traditional moral values is, of course, related to their support of religion and its institutions.[19] Three of the items used in our survey dealt explicitly with religion or the church. The items approached the subject from different angles and elicited varying responses.

While most lawyers do not support the notion that adherence to established religion is a necessary condition of a good life, they are evenly split on whether churches are essential to the preservation of standards of right and wrong. The first of these statements was: "To lead a good life it is necessary for a person to be guided by the teachings and beliefs of an established religious group." The lawyers disagreed with that statement by a margin of more than two to one; 28 percent agreed, but 60 percent disagreed. Not surprisingly, Laumann's survey of the smaller community cross section produced very different results—67 percent of that sample agreed with the statement.[20] The second statement (presented several items later in the interview) read: "Churches are necessary to establish and preserve concepts of right and wrong." Many more of the lawyers were inclined to agree with this. They were nearly evenly divided on the statement, 43 percent agreeing and 40 percent disagreeing. Again, however, the lawyers' support for the church lagged behind that of Laumann's community samples. Of the community cross section, 68 percent agreed with this statement.[21] The local community elites supported it nearly as strongly, with 61 percent agreeing.[22] That a population of urban professionals would display less support for

19. The correlation between frequency of church attendance and the "traditional moral values" item is .34. The correlations between church attendance and the first two "religion items," discussed just below, are .48 and .49, respectively. When those two items are combined into a single "religiosity index," that index correlates with church attendance at .54.

20. Thirty-five percent answered "strongly agree," 32 percent "moderately agree," 5 percent "weakly agree," 5 percent "weakly disagree," 11 percent "moderately disagree," and 13 percent "strongly disagree" (see *supra*, note 5).

21. Thirty-nine percent answered "strongly agree," 29 percent "moderately agree," 9 percent "weakly agree," 2 percent "weakly disagree," 12 percent "moderately disagree," and 10 percent "strongly disagree."

22. Thirty-five percent answered "strongly agree," 26 percent "moderately agree," 15 percent "weakly agree," 4 percent "weakly disagree," 13 percent "moderately disagree," and 7 percent "strongly disagree."

religious institutions than would samples of nonprofessionals, drawn from smaller communities, was certainly to be expected.[23]

We should also note, however, that Chicago lawyers are not prone to support the authority of institutions, whether churches or governments. Another of our items read: "A man ought to be guided by what his experience tells him is right rather than by what any institution, such as church or government, tells him to do." Sixty-one percent of the lawyers agreed with this statement; only 24 percent disagreed. The local community elites surveyed by Laumann were somewhat less likely to agree.[24] (The item was not used in Laumann's survey of the community cross section.) Given lawyers' professional roles and obligations, it is a bit surprising that they so overwhelmingly endorse the propriety of following one's own lights rather than what the government tells one to do. We would have expected lawyers to feel a greater commitment to or stake in the authority of governmental institutions.

Thus, the overall picture of the profession's values that emerges from this analysis is one of substantial support for individualism and individual liberties, as against concentrations of power in large corporations or in labor unions, and as against the authority of established social institutions, including the church and even the state. While the state's role in the preservation of traditional moral values is opposed by most lawyers, there is widespread support in the profession for the use of governmental power to redistribute social benefits and to promote civil rights. But there is substantial disagreement within the profession on all of these issues, and it is to the analysis of the structure of this disagreement that we now turn.

---

23. See, e.g., Charles Y. Glock and Rodney Stark, *Religion and Society in Tension* (Chicago: Rand McNally, 1965); Nicholas J. Demerath, *Social Class in American Protestantism* (Chicago: Rand McNally, 1965); Nunn, Crockett, and Williams, *supra* note 15, esp. pp. 121–41; Gerhard Lenski, *The Religious Factor* (New York: Free Press, 1960); Howard Schuman, "The Religious Factor in Detroit: Review, Replication, and Reanalysis," *American Sociological Review* 36 (1971): 30–48.

24. Twenty-eight percent answered "strongly agree," 26 percent "moderately agree," 6 percent "weakly agree," 9 percent "weakly disagree," 20 percent "moderately disagree," and 10 percent "strongly disagree."

Value Differentiation Within the Profession

We have already observed several types of systematic differentiation within the legal profession—by tasks, by clients, by social origins, and so on. The distribution of social values throughout the profession also manifests a systematic structure. Given the nature of the fields' clients and the nature of what is at stake in many of these social issues, we would of course expect lawyers practicing in some fields of law to differ from those working in others. Lawyers who represent the largest corporations would surely be terribly guilt-ridden if they believed that large concentrations of economic power represented a threat to the republic. But, rather than go through the fields one by one on individual value items, we will describe only the most noteworthy differences among the fields in their overall tendencies toward economic liberalism[25] and civil libertarianism. As broad measures of these tendencies, we have constructed two scales, an eight-item economic liberalism scale and a five-item civil libertarianism scale.[26]

One field occupies the high end of both scales. Lawyers who represent unions in labor law matters, almost half of whom are Jewish, have the highest scores on both economic liberalism and civil libertarianism.[27] Given the traditional ideology of the labor movement, this finding is not at all remarkable. Another field that is identified with the ideology of the defense of the downtrodden and that in fact represents a high proportion of lower status clients is criminal

25. "Economic liberalism" is used here in the modern political sense of the term "liberal" rather than in the classical, nineteenth-century meaning of the term. That is, it denotes support for government regulation of the economy and the redistribution of wealth through various social welfare programs rather than support for free enterprise and reliance on the market mechanism to accomplish social justice.

26. Table 5.1 lists the items included in each of the scales. Both scales satisfied criteria for reliability. The scales are highly correlated, however, thus raising the issue of discriminant validity; (D. T. Campbell and D. W. Fiske, "Convergent and Discriminant Validation by the Multitrait-Multimethod Matrix," *Psychological Bulletin* 56 (1959): 81–105). We nonetheless decided to use the two separate scales because it seemed substantively important to attempt to relate the lawyers' values to the nature of their work, and the work of some lawyers of course deals more with economic issues while that of others involves more concern with civil liberties. For the "economic liberalism" scale, Cronbach's Alpha = .717, mean = 3.187, standard deviation = .633. For the "civil libertarianism" scale, Cronbach's Alpha = .678, mean = 3.202, standard deviation = .783.

27. Labor union lawyers also had the lowest scores of those in any of the fields on the religious values items discussed at pp. 147–48.

defense. We find that the scores of criminal defense lawyers are also significantly higher than the balance of the profession on both scales.[28] Civil rights lawyers' scores are significantly high on the economic liberalism scale; interestingly, however, their scores on civil libertarianism, although relatively high, are not high enough to achieve statistical significance.[29]

Though disproportionate support for civil libertarian values is, thus, found in some of the fields that represent the dispossessed, the other main source of support for those values appears to be the elite members of the profession. The only other field that has a score high enough to be statistically different from the balance of the profession on either of the scales is business tax (i.e., tax law practiced for business clients), which is significantly different not on economic liberalism but on civil libertarianism—and its score is significantly *high*. Other fields that are markedly high on civil liberties, though their scores do not achieve statistical significance, are the two sides of antitrust work. There is, indeed, a rather consistent tendency for the high prestige, corporate fields to have high scores on the civil libertarianism scale. The scores on that scale of all practitioners in the "large corporate cluster,"[30] considered as a whole, are significantly higher than the balance of the profession. By contrast, practitioners in the "personal business cluster" tend to have the lowest scores on civil libertarianism, significantly lower than the balance of the profession. The individual fields with the lowest scores on the civil liberties scale, probate and personal real estate, are both in that cluster. The scores of both of those fields are low enough to be statistically significant.

While the large corporation fields tend to be relatively liberal on civil liberties issues, they are divided on matters of economic liberalism—antitrust defense and securities lawyers appear to be quite conservative on economic matters, but business tax and business real estate practitioners are more liberal than the average on those issues.[31] The only field with a significantly low score on the eco-

28. Analysis of variance was used to test the differences within and between groups; F significant at .05 or better.
29. It is possible, of course, that some of the lawyers who devote significant amounts of time to "civil rights" matters may do so on behalf of clients who are charged with having violated civil rights in one manner or another. See also chapter 3, note 18.
30. For the composition of the clusters, see p. 73.
31. But the differences are not great enough to be statistically significant, given the relatively small numbers of practitioners in those fields.

nomic liberalism scale is general corporate, but a number of other fields have scores that are as low or lower. Those fields (which have fewer practitioners than does the general corporate area, thus making it more difficult for their scores to achieve statistical significance) are patents, with the lowest score of all; antitrust defense, next in line; personal tax, probate, and securities.

Practitioners in the personal business, office practice fields are more consistently conservative on both economic liberalism and civil libertarianism issues, but those in personal litigation are considerably more liberal than average on both. The most consistently liberal on both scales are the lawyers in the personal plight fields.[32]

Multiple Classification Analysis of Value Differences

While it is clear that practitioners in the various fields of law differ in their social values, it is not at all clear whether these differences are attributable to characteristics of the fields themselves, including the nature and interests of the fields' clients, or to the differential distribution across the fields of lawyers of varying social origins who have brought differing values along with them into the fields of practice. Is, thus, the low position of personal injury plaintiffs' lawyers on the civil libertarianism scale to be attributed primarily to characteristics of the field or its clients or to the presence in the field of a disproportionate number of Roman Catholics? How much of the extremity of the value position of labor union lawyers is due to the special nature of their practice and how much to the fact that our sample includes not one Roman Catholic in that field but finds a substantial overrepresentation of Jews among the lawyers who serve labor unions? To begin to address such issues, taking into account a number of social background and practice variables (including, but not limited to, ethnoreligious and field differences), we have used a technique known as multiple classification analysis.

Multiple classification analysis (MCA) is a multivariate technique used to examine the relationship between a predictor (independent) variable consisting of a set of discrete categories (such as men/wom-

---

32. The personal injury plaintiffs' lawyers, however, rank well toward the bottom of the scale on support for civil liberties, perhaps reflecting the disproportionate numbers of Roman Catholics in that field; see p. 157.

en or Protestants/Catholics) and a continuously distributed dependent variable approximating an interval scale (e.g., earned income) or to examine the relationships between each of a set of such predictor variables and a dependent variable, holding the effects of all the remaining predictors constant.[33]

For purposes of the following analysis, we shall treat economic liberalism and civil libertarianism as continuously distributed dependent variables.[34] Each will be examined in relationship to a

33. While similar to multiple regression techniques with respect to its additive assumption, multiple classification analysis is the analysis of variance with unequal cell entries (reflecting the correlations among the independent variables being considered). Its advantage over multiple regression techniques, which assume that all the independent variables are also measured by interval scales, is that the predictor variables are categorical (or qualitative distinctions) in form. The major constraints of MCA are that the dependent variable must approximate an interval scale and that no predictors should be so highly correlated that there is complete overlapping on any of the categories. Furthermore, multiple classification analysis strictly assumes that the effects of each of the predictor variables on the dependent variable are only additive. That is, it assumes that combinations of categories of the predictor variables—e.g., lawyers who are both Jewish and of working-class origin versus lawyers who are both Catholic and of middle-class origin—do not statistically interact with one another in such a way that their combined effect on the dependent variable is greater or less than it would be if the net effects of particular categories of religious and class origins, each considered separately, were simply summed together to estimate their joint effect.

To determine the relationship between an independent and a dependent variable, the computer routine yields the mean value of the dependent variable for each category of each predictor variable, thus allowing one to see whether the relationship is positive, negative, or curvilinear across the categories. The program also yields an eta coefficient (or correlation ratio), the square of which indicates the proportion of the total variance in the dependent variable accounted for by the effect of each predictor variable considered by itself. When multiple predictors are used, the program yields an adjusted mean giving the mean value of the dependent variable for each category of the predictor, controlling for the effects of the remainder of the set of predictors. Other output includes an adjusted multiple correlation coefficient, which, when squared, yields the proportion of variance in the dependent variable accounted for by all of the predictor variables considered simultaneously, the total sum of squares, the total explained sum of squares, and the residual sum of squares. From these statistics, a variety of F tests can be computed to test the statistical significance of various summary statistics, such as the correlation ratio and the net increment of an additional variable in the multivariate model.

For more technical expositions of these issues, see T. P. Hill, "An Analysis of the Distribution of Wages and Salaries in Great Britain," *Econometrica* 27(1959): 355–81; Donald C. Pelz and Frank M. Andrews, "The SRC Computer Program for Multivariate Analysis: Some Uses and Limitations" (Ann Arbor: University of Michigan, Survey Research Center, 1961): James Morgan et al., *Income and Welfare in the United States* (New York: McGraw-Hill, 1964); Frank M. Andrews, James Morgan, and John Sonquist, "Multiple Classification Analysis" (Ann Arbor: University of Michigan, Survey Research Center, 1967); James Fennessey, "The General Linear Model: A New Perspective on Some Familiar Topics," *American Journal of Sociology* 74 (1968): 1–27.

34. Both variables approximate normal distributions and meet the conventional requirements for reliable scales—i.e., they achieve satisfactory values for Cronbach's Alpha and have moderate item-to-scale correlations. Obviously, both scales are only

number of social characteristics, including father's occupation, eth-noreligious origin, and law school attended. These predictor vari-ables are most meaningfully treated as being categorical in form and are, of course, substantially correlated among themselves (which raises the question of the extent of each variable's relation-ship to the dependent variable "net" of the effects of other vari-ables that may be correlated with the independent variable under examination). Extensive testing of these data using Leo A. Good-man's log-linear method of analysis[35] assures us that there are no statistically significant two-way or higher-order interaction effects that need to be taken into account for the variables we shall consid-er. In other words, the additive assumption from which the multi-ple classification analysis proceeds is fully justified for the data we are discussing.

Table 5.2 presents the results of these analyses. Because lawyers' positions on both economic liberalism and civil libertarianism are known to vary significantly with their age and income, we have treated those two variables as "covariates." The results for the pre-diction of the lawyers' scores on the economic liberalism scale indi-cate that by using the five-variable Model I, including two social background variables and three law practice variables (law school attended and two practice type variables), we can explain 23 percent of the variance in individual differences on economic values with-out taking into account the covariation of age and income with the dependent variable. Taking that covariation into account, we ex-plain 27 percent of the variance in lawyers' positions on the eco-nomic liberalism scale. If we exclude the social background vari-ables from the analyses and use only the law practice variables—law school attended, practice setting, and field of practice (Model II)—we explain 15 percent of the variance without the covariates, or 20 percent with the covariates taken into account. Note, then, that a

at the ordinal rather than interval level of measurement, but experience has shown that multiple classification analysis of ordinal scales yields meaningful results.

35. See Leo A. Goodman, "The Multivariate Analysis of Qualitative Data: Interac-tions Among Multiple Classifications," *Journal of the American Statistical Association* 65 (1970): 226–56; idem., "A Modified Multiple Regression Approach to the Analysis of Dichotomous Variables," *American Sociological Review* 37 (1972): 28–46; idem., "A Gen-eral Model for the Analysis of Surveys," *American Journal of Sociology* 77 (1972): 1035–86; idem., "Causal Analysis of Data from Panel Studies and Other Kinds of Surveys," *American Journal of Sociology* 78 (1973): 1135–91; Peter J. Burke and David Knoke, "A User's Guide to Log-linear Models," in Robert B. Smith, ed., *Handbook of Social Science Methods* (New York: Irvington Publishers, 1980).

TABLE 5.2
Multiple Classification Analysis of Lawyers' Scores on Economic Liberalism and Civil Libertarianism Scales

Variable	Economic Liberalism Scale			Civil Libertarianism Scale		
	Unique R^2	Cumulative R^2 without Covariates	Cumulative R^2 with Covariates, Age, and Income[a]	Unique R^2	Cumulative R^2 without Covariates	Cumulative R^2 with Covariates, Age, and Income[a]
Model I: Social Background and Law Practice Variables						
Father's occupation[b]	.013	.011	.086	.001	.012	.178
Ethnoreligious origin[c]	.063	.090	.153	.083	.108	.260
Law school[d]	.020	.105	.175	.003	.125	.283
Practice setting[e]	.038	.145	.196	.037	.156	.292
Field of practice[f]	.083	.228	.272	.074	.230	.345
Model II: Law Practice Variables Only						
Law school[d]	.007	.002	.082	.004	.018	.205
Practice setting[e]	.042	.047	.110	.032	.039	.216
Field of practice[f]	.098	.145	.201	.101	.140	.287

NOTES: For the characteristics of the economic liberalism and civil libertarianism scales see note 26 (p. 149) and for the items included in each scale, see table 5.1.

The "Unique R^2" given for each variable is the additional amount of variance explained by the inclusion of that variable in the total model. That is, it is the difference between the total R^2 of the model, including that variable, and the R^2 obtained by excluding that variable from the computations but using all of the other variables of that model. It is, therefore, *not* the amount of the variance that would be explained by that variable alone—that R^2 would almost always be considerably larger because of the intercorrelations among the variables. That is, the variable might well serve as a "proxy" for one or more of the other variables, explaining some of the variance that would be accounted for by those other variables if they were included in the analysis. The Unique R^2 reported here has been computed on the total R^2 without covariates.

The columns headed "Cumulative R^2 without Covariates" and "Cumulative R^2 with Covariates, Age, and Income" present a stepwise analysis. That is, as each successive variable is added to the model it contributes additional explained variance. The total variance explained by the model is, therefore, the last figure in each column. To obtain the additional variance explained by each variable, as it is added to the model, one would subtract the R^2 immediately before that variable had been added from the R^2 listed opposite that variable (which is, of course, the R^2 with that variable included).

"R^2 without Covariates" refers to computations made without taking age and income effects into account. "R^2 with Covariates, Age, and Income" refers to computations made with those effects taken into account.

a. In constructing the income variable, the values assigned to respondents were the mid-points of the income categories indicated by them; see appendix A, question A49. Age is a simple continuous variable, the ages having been straightforwardly computed by subtracting the respondents' birth years from the year of the interviews (1975).

b. The categories used for father's occupation were (1) lawyers, (2) professional, technical, administrative and sales, and (3) clerks, craftsmen, operatives, laborers, farmers and service workers; see appendix A, questions A36 and A37.

c. The ethnoreligious categories were Irish Catholics, southern and eastern European Catholics, other Catholics, northern and western European Protestants, other Protestants, Orthodox and Conservative Jews, other Jews, nonwhite, and non-identifying; see appendix A, questions A43, A46, and A50.

d. The law school categories were those used throughout this book—elite, prestige, regional, and local (see chap. 1).

e. The practice setting categories were solo practitioners, firms with 5 or fewer lawyers, firms with 6 to 39 lawyers, firms with 40 or more lawyers, government counsel, and corporate house counsel.

f. Respondents were assigned to the set of 25 fields of law elsewhere in this book and to a residual (or "other") category and a generalist category (see appendix B). Unlike the assignment rule used in some other analyses, however, respondents were assigned to the fields on a mutually exclusive basis so that there was no overlap among the categories (see notes to table 7.1).

substantial amount of the variance that we are explaining can be accounted for by the law-related variables alone. If we include the social background variables, we add about 7 or 8 percent to the explained variance, either with or without the covariates. Since the organization of law practice is to some degree structured by these background variables,[36] however, the practice variables may explain as much variance as they do only because they serve as proxies for the social characteristics of the practitioners.

Turning to the civil libertarianism scores, we see that we are able to explain a somewhat larger percentage of the variance in the lawyers' positions on that scale. Using the same combinations of variables, we account for 35 percent of the variance with the five-variable model, including covariates, and 29 percent if we use only the three law practice variables, with the covariates. Again, then, most of the explained variance can be accounted for by the law-related variables alone. Given that we are dealing with something as idiosyncratic as individual value preferences, within a quite homogeneous and sophisticated population, this is a respectable amount of variance to explain with relatively broad, categorical variables.

The most striking finding is that the same two variables make the most important contributions to the explanation of the variance in both sorts of values. One of those two variables, ethnoreligious origin, is a social background characteristic, and the other, field of practice, deals with the nature of the respondents' legal work (and, presumably, clients). It would make good sense that, since issues of civil liberties are so charged with ideological symbolism, they would be more greatly influenced by the lawyer's social background (presumably reflecting early socialization) than would positions on economic issues that are more often of direct relevance to the lawyer's daily work. Field of practice does make a somewhat greater contribution than does ethnoreligious origin to explaining variance in economic values, and ethnoreligious origin makes the greater contribution to explaining variance in civil libertarianism, but those differences between the two variables are relatively small. Thus, both sorts of values are influenced by social background and by law practice characteristics, in roughly equal measure.

Because these two variables have emerged in the multiple classification analysis as being of principal importance, we might wish to

36. See chapter 3, esp. tables 3.1 and 3.2, and appendix B.

note their characteristics in some detail. We have already described the most significant of the values differences among the fields of practice (see pp. 149–51), but we have not yet indicated the nature and extent of the differences on both scales with respect to the other principal variable, the ethnoreligious categories. These are presented in full in table 5.3. Note that on "economic liberalism," the nonwhites have the highest, most liberal scores by a considerable margin. The next most liberal categories are the "nonidentifiers"—that is, whites who are not Jewish, either by religion or by ethnic identification, and who are also not affiliated with any of the Christian denominations—and the Jews who are affiliated with a Reform synagogue or who identify themselves as Jews only by ethnicity and not by religion. Next comes a cluster of three groups, the Orthodox and Conservative Jews, the Catholics of southern and eastern European origin, and the Irish Catholics. These are followed by the Catholics of northwestern European origin, predominately German Catholics, who stand about halfway between the Protestants and the other Catholic groups. Finally, taking the most "conservative" positions on the economic issues, we find the Protestants, both Type I and Type II.

On the civil libertarian scale, we find a somewhat different pattern. The most striking of these differences are the more moderate position of the nonwhites, who stand closest to the Orthodox and Conservative Jews near the middle of the scores on this scale, and the much more conservative positions of the Catholic groups, who join the two Protestant groups at the bottom of the scale. The top of the civil libertarian scale—that is, the most liberal position—is occupied by the nonidentifying category and by the Reform and ethnic Jews.

Further Consideration of the Impact of Economic Values

Since the economic values appear to be the more difficult to predict, further analysis of them may shed additional light on their impact on the legal profession. Again using Goodman's log-linear technique,[37] we examined the interrelationships among economic val-

37. See *supra* note 35.

TABLE 5.3
Values Scales by Ethnoreligious Categories

	Mean Score	Number
A. Economic Liberalism		
Nonwhite	3.70	19
Nonidentifying	3.41	86
Reform & ethnic Jews	3.33	136
Orthodox & Conservative Jews	3.25	100
Southern & eastern European Catholics	3.23	55
Irish Catholics	3.21	80
Northern & western European Catholics	3.04	90
Type I Protestants	2.89	89
Type II Protestants	2.88	79
Grand mean = 3.18; eta = .32, p < 0.001.		
B. Civil Libertarianism		
Nonidentifying	3.55	88
Reform & ethnic Jews	3.51	137
Orthodox & Conservative Jews	3.36	100
Nonwhites	3.32	21
Southern & eastern European Catholics	3.01	55
Type II Protestants	2.98	81
Northern & western European Catholics	2.95	86
Type I Protestants	2.93	90
Irish Catholics	2.93	76
Grand mean = 3.20; eta = .33, p < 0.001.		

ues, prestige of law school attended, field of practice, and ethnicity. To facilitate exposition, we will focus our attention here on the apparent conditioning impact of economic values on the odds of practicing in any of several "wealth-oriented" fields of law, a category that includes the fields that we thought most likely to deal with the acquisition and preservation of wealth. These fields are: antitrust defense, banking, business litigation, business real estate, business tax, commercial, general corporate, labor (management), patents, personal injury defense, probate, public utilities, and securities. We created this list of fields a priori, without consulting our findings on the positions of the fields on the economic liberalism scale, and other fields do in fact have scores that are lower (more conservative) than are some of these. Dichotomizing the fields of law in this way (i.e., into those that are wealth-oriented and those that are, perhaps, not so much so) serves to simplify both the analysis and our

presentation of it here. In addition to that dichotomous categorization, we further simplified the problem by also dichotomizing the
law school variable into more prestigious and less prestigious
schools (i.e., the "elite" and "prestige" schools versus the "regional" and "local" schools) and the ethnicity variable into white Gentiles, on the one hand, and Jews and nonwhites (as groups that are
more likely to be subject to discrimination), on the other. Because of
the central importance of the economic liberalism variable in this
analysis, however, that scale was divided into four categories rather
than merely being dichotomized. Scores that fell more than one
standard deviation above or below the mean were assigned to the
"extremely liberal" and "extremely conservative" categories, respectively, while scores within one standard deviation of the mean were
labeled "moderately liberal" or "moderately conservative."

We then computed the odds that a lawyer would practice in one
of the wealth-oriented fields given his ethnicity (dichotomized, as
indicated above) and given his attendance at a higher prestige versus a lesser law school. For example, we determined the likelihood
that white Gentiles who had attended prestigious law schools
would practice in a wealth-oriented field as compared to the odds
that white Gentiles who had attended less prestigious law schools
would practice in such fields. We did the same for the other ethnicity category and then added a further breakdown based on the positions of the respondents on the economic values items. Let us now
summarize those findings.

For our total sample, the odds that a respondent would spend as
much as 25 percent of his time in one of the wealth-oriented fields
was 1.49 to 1—that is, about 60 percent of the respondents devoted
at least a quarter of their time to one of the fields listed above,
while 40 percent of the sample practiced more exclusively in fields
dealing with government work or personal problems. For white
Gentiles who attended elite or prestige law schools, these odds increase to 2.5 to 1; for white Gentiles who attended less prestigious
law schools, the odds are 1.53 to 1. For Jews and nonwhites who
attended high status schools, the odds of practicing in a wealth-
oriented field are 1.73 to 1, but for those who attended less prestigious law schools the odds are only 0.91 to 1. Thus, in both ethnic
categories the graduates of more prestigious law schools are substantially more likely to be found practicing corporate and financial

law than are the graduates of regional and local law schools, but white Gentiles have considerably higher odds than do Jews and nonwhites of practicing in these fields given the category of law school attended. There is a strong effect between law school and field, no doubt reflecting the recruitment practices of the corporate firms, but there is also an independent, direct effect of ethnicity on field. Thus, it appears that, net of law school effects, a lawyer's ethnicity does have substantial influence on the type of law he practices.

It is certainly conceivable that lawyer's *preferences* for work in the opposing types of fields might differ systematically by their ethnic identities, reflecting the relationship between ethnicity and values. We have already speculated about this. To evaluate these possibilities, we calculated the odds that respondents from each of the two ethnicity categories would have scores on the economic liberalism scale that were one standard deviation or more below the mean—of the four categories on this variable that we used in the model, this was the definition of the most extreme conservative position. For our total sample, the odds of having such a value position are 0.19 to 1. For Jews and nonwhites, those odds substantially decrease to 0.10 to 1. For white Gentiles, they increase to 0.24 to 1. Thus, a white Gentile respondent is almost two and one-half times as likely as is a respondent in the Jewish and nonwhite category to take the most economically conservative positions. This is the direct effect observed between ethnicity and values, and it would appear to lend support to the hypothesis that different ethnic groups might choose different fields of practice because they have differing value preferences. But we have also observed a *direct* effect between ethnicity and field, net of whatever effect may flow from ethnicity through values to field. The nature of that effect is easy to comprehend if we examine again the odds that lawyers in each of the two ethnic categories will practice in a wealth-oriented field, this time while controlling for the respondents' positions on the economic values scale. We find that Jews and nonwhites having any but the most liberal of economic values[38] are substantially less likely than are white Gentiles to be found in such fields:

38. Among those with the most liberal positions on economic issues, of course, *avoidance* of practicing in a "conservative" field may well indicate that the lawyer is able to exercise greater freedom in the choice of his work.

	Odds of Practicing in a Wealth-oriented Field	
Economic Values	*Jews & Nonwhites*	*White Gentiles*
Very conservative	1.5	2.4
Conservative	1.4	2.2
Liberal	1.2	2.1
Very liberal	.7	.6

These findings suggest quite strongly that the channeling of Jews and nonwhites away from corporate law and into personal plight and government work is not attributable solely to their social values but rather reflects limits imposed on their opportunities for choice of fields for practice. Our list of wealth-oriented fields includes all of those that are most prestigious within the profession, and the desirability of acquiring prestige by association with these fields presumably does not vary greatly by one's ethnicity.

Self-selection versus Socialization

The more general issue of the extent to which lawyers' choices of fields of practice are influenced by their social values is impossible for us to assess with any certainty because we possess only cross-sectional data (i.e., data gathered at one point in time) rather than longitudinal data (data gathered at several times, which would permit us to observe changes in lawyers' values and to assess the temporal ordering of causal variables).[39] The association that we observe between lawyers' values and the types of work that they do might be caused by the influence of preconceived value positions on their decision to enter the fields, but it might also be attributable to adaptation to the fields' values after entry into the field or to some combination of these two factors. Adaptation after entry might occur through socialization to the values of the field (or of its clients) over the years of one's work in the field or through attrition from the field of lawyers whose values are not consonant with the nature of the work. If a young lawyer begins practice with the view that his clients are malefactors of great wealth, he may well either moderate

39. For a more extended discussion of this problem, see pp. 174–78 and 196–97.

those views over time or eventually become uncomfortable enough to leave the service of such clients. Because many of the lawyers that we interviewed had been practicing in their fields for several years, the association that we have observed between social values and field of practice[40] could as plausibly be attributed to the effects of this sort of adaptation as to the influence of lawyers' values on their decisions to enter the fields.

As a means of addressing this problem of interpretation, we divided our sample into broad age groups to see whether the lawyers' values corresponded to the nature of their fields even among the youngest lawyers, who will usually have practiced in the fields for the shortest periods of time, or whether the correspondence between field and values is greater among the older lawyers, who have usually been at it longer. Because we were not able to observe the same lawyers (or the same age cohorts) over several years to ascertain how their values and their fields of practice changed over the years, we cannot be sure that historical events do not account for the differences that we find among the fields and age groups. Differences in the conditions governing entry to or exit from the various fields as the profession has grown and evolved could produce differences among the age groups by field or among the fields by age group. On the other hand, we find it difficult to generate any plausible hypothesis about the kinds of historical events, developments, or conditions that might account for the patterns that we present in table 5.4.

Table 5.4 summarizes the differences among age groups on both of the values scales that we have used in this analysis—economic liberalism and civil libertarianism—segregating practitioners in fields that were clearly identified with a particular position on those scales. That is, we first identified a set of fields that is associated with the "conservative" position on the economic liberalism scale; the fields selected were antitrust defense, securities, patents, and probate. The practitioners in those fields had been observed to have among the lowest scores on the economic liberalism scale, and we also thought it likely that those fields were generally perceived by law students and by lawyers as traditionally conservative on economic issues. We then computed the mean scores on the economic

40. We do not wish to overstate the extent of this relationship. The zero-order correlation between field (defined as a dichotomy between wealth-oriented and other fields) and economic liberalism is only .114.

TABLE 5.4
*Mean Scores on Values Scales of Practitioners in Liberal
and Conservative Fields, by Age*

Age Groups[1]	Practitioners in Conservative Fields[2] Score (N)	Practitioners in Other Fields Score (N)	Difference of Conservative Fields
A. Economic Liberalism			
to 31	3.37 (41)	3.38 (131)	−.01
32–52	3.03 (71)	3.19 (275)	−.16
53–88	2.80 (46)	3.16 (103)	−.36
Age Groups[3]	Practitioners in Libertarian Fields[4] Score (N)	Practitioners in Other Fields Score (N)	Difference of Libertarian Fields
B. Civil Libertarianism			
to 32	3.75 (22)	3.55 (172)	+.20
33–42	3.69 (23)	3.33 (164)	+.36
43–88	3.24 (23)	2.81 (267)	+.43

NOTES: Practitioners in each field of law were defined as respondents who devoted 25 percent or more of their time to the field.

1. The age groupings used in the analysis of economic values were selected by inspecting the age distribution of practitioners in the economically conservative fields and then choosing break points that would keep the respective extreme categories (i.e., the eldest and the youngest lawyers) as narrow as was consistent with having an adequate number of cases in each category. That is, the bias was to assign cases to the middle category rather than to the extremes in order to minimize contamination of recent entrants and to maximize any possible effects of longevity. As a rule of thumb, forty cases was taken to be a minimally satisfactory number of cases for the categories.

2. The "economically conservative" fields are antitrust defense, securities, patents, and probate.

3. Because of the small numbers of practitioners in the "civil libertarian" fields, the age groupings used in this analysis were chosen by inspecting the age distribution of those practitioners and using age ranges that would equalize the numbers of cases in each category, thus tending to minimize statistical instability to the extent possible.

4. The "civil libertarian" fields are criminal defense, civil rights, and labor union work.

liberalism scale of the lawyers within each age group who devoted as much as 25 percent of their time to any of these four fields, and we compared their mean scores to those of the remainder of the lawyers in each age group.

A similar procedure was followed for the analysis of civil libertarian values, but the selection of a set of fields that was clearly identified with a position on civil libertarian values proved to be far more difficult. Criminal prosecutors may be generally perceived as taking conservative positions on such issues, but our finding was that their scores are above the overall mean. The fields with scores that are significantly low in the statistical sense, fields such as probate and personal real estate, are little concerned with civil liberties issues in their professional work. We wanted the set of fields chosen to have scores at one extreme or the other, but also to have face validity—to be widely perceived as taking a characteristic posture on civil liberties issues arising, in a sense, out of the very nature of their legal work. There is a small set of fields that we believe to be generally identified with prolibertarian positions and that also have high mean scores on our civil libertarianism scale, but the fields include relatively few practitioners. Those fields are criminal defense, civil rights, and labor union work. We have used them as the set and, given the clarity of the patterns that we observe in table 5.4, we do not believe that the small number of respondents in the libertarian fields presents serious problems of interpretation of the findings.

The lessons of this analysis appear in sharp focus in table 5.4. First, the older groups are consistently more conservative on both values scales—a finding about the relationship of liberalism with age that has consistently been found in surveys of cross sections of the American population as a whole.[41] Second, at each age level, on both scales, there is a difference in the predicted direction between the comparison groups of practitioners from different fields. Third, the size of the difference between these comparison groups increases steadily with age on both scales. The difference in economic values within the youngest age group is so small as to be inconsequential, but the size of the difference increases dramatically with age. On civil libertarian values, the differences between the sets of fields also increase substantially with age, but the difference is already marked even in the youngest age group—the percentage increase in the differences between the fields is not nearly so great on civil libertarian values as it is on economic values.

If we discount the effects of history on entry into the fields, the findings presented in table 5.4 suggest that, whether through so-

41. See, e.g., Stouffer, *supra* note 15; Angus Campbell, Philip E. Converse, Warren E. Miller, and Donald Stokes, *The American Voter* (New York: John Wiley, 1960); Norman H. Nie, Sidney Verba, and John R. Petrocik, *The Changing American Voter* (Cambridge, Mass.: Harvard University Press, 1976); Philip E. Converse, *The Dynamics of Party Support, Cohort-Analyzing Party Identification* (Beverly Hills, Calif.: Sage Publications, 1976); Nunn, Crockett, and Williams, *supra* note 15, esp. pp. 76–95.

cialization or through selective attrition from the fields, the older lawyers have adapted to the values of their fields.[42] With respect to economic values, there appears to be little or no difference between the young lawyers who have recently entered conservative fields and lawyers of the same ages who practice in other fields. The difference occurs only in the older age groups, among lawyers who have spent more time in their respective fields. The lack of any pronounced difference at the entry level suggests that selection into the conservative fields depends less on the distribution of value preferences among entering lawyers than on the distribution among those lawyers of opportunities for entry into the fields. That

42. We examined two plausible rival hypotheses—hypotheses that might constitute alternative explanations for the patterns observed in the table.

The first of these was the hypothesis that specialization in these fields might increase with age, so that the older practitioners would devote larger percentages of their time to their "specialties" than would the younger lawyers and thus these field categories would become "purer" as age increases. If that were true, then the increasing differences that we observe might be attributable not to age or adaptation but to the increasing "purity" of the categories. But it is not true. Among the practitioners in the economically conservative fields, the percentage that devotes larger portions of time to those fields does not increase significantly with age. In the youngest age group, 14 percent devote half or more of their time to such fields, in the middle age category the percentage devoting that much time is 11.7, and among the oldest practitioners the percentage is about the same as that of the youngest group, 15.1. Among practitioners in the civil libertarian fields, there is also no significant difference in specialization by age, and such tendency as exists is for practitioners to devote a smaller percentage of their time to those fields as age increases.

The second rival hypothesis that we examined is that ethnicity might differ with age in these field categories. Thus, if certain fields were more open or more closed to entrants from particular ethnic groups at particular points in time, lawyers of those ethnicities would have had different opportunities for entry into the fields if they began practice during one era rather than another. What appear in the table to be age effects might then instead be the effects of differential ethnic composition of the field categories in the different age groups. Of the ethnicity categories, only the Jews were in fact distributed in substantially different proportions across the age categories. And though there was a tendency for Jews to be differentially represented across the age groups in both types of fields, being found more among the younger lawyers in the economically conservative fields and more among the older lawyers in the civil libertarian fields, the magnitude of these differences was not sufficient to account for the size of the increasing values spread between the fields that we observe in the table.

In order to evaluate more formally the relative effects on values of changing ethnoreligious composition, extent of specialization, and age, we used multiple regression models to predict economic conservatism for lawyers practicing in economically conservative fields and civil libertarianism for the lawyers in civil libertarian fields. For the former, age was by far the strongest and the only statistically significant predictor of economic conservatism. For the latter, both age and ethnoreligious background were statistically significant in predicting civil libertarianism, but the extent of specialization in civil libertarian fields was not. These analyses show that adaptation to field of practice, as represented by age, has a statistically significant effect, net of other causal factors, on both sorts of values scores.

is, beginning lawyers do not appear to select themselves for the economically conservative fields, exercising their values preferences, so much as to be selected by the incumbent lawyers in the field or by the clients of the field, presumably according to criteria that serve the field's or the clients' interests. While economic values seem to play little role in decisions to enter these fields, however, we would not discount the possibility that they contribute importantly to decisions to leave—that is, though values do not influence selection *into* the fields, they may well influence selection *out*.

On civil libertarian values, attrition that is systematically related to the ideological positions embraced by the lawyers probably accounts for much of the increase with age of the differences between the sets of fields. The civil libertarian fields do not pay well, nor do they enjoy high prestige within the profession,[43] and longevity in those fields is therefore likely to reflect an unusually strong ideological commitment. Even at the youngest, entry level, however, there is a considerable values difference between practitioners in the civil libertarian fields and lawyers who do not practice in those fields. Possibly because civil libertarian ideology is perceived as more directly related to the issues and tasks involved in the daily practice of those fields of law than is economic ideology to the practice of the economically conservative fields, ideological commitment to civil libertarian values appears to play a significant role in selection or recruitment into criminal defense, civil rights, and labor union work. The difference exists from the beginning; it merely becomes greater with age. Whatever barriers to entry into these fields may exist, therefore, they would seem not entirely to frustrate the exercise of personal value preferences. If young lawyers who are found in these fields have values that differ substantially from those of their peers, that fact suggests that the lawyers were free to exercise choice in their decisions to enter the civil libertarian fields. That those fields are less renumerative and less prestigious probably helps to insure that there will be places available in them for the ideologically committed.

43. See discussion of these fields in chapter 4, table 4.1.

Conclusion

We do not find that Chicago lawyers possess a distinct set of value positions. In this respect, then, the Chicago bar does not conform to Goode's characterization of the professions as communities that embrace internally consistent values or that have an identifiable, homogeneous culture. Rather, we find that, on several of the issues examined, the legal profession in Chicago is divided into two camps of roughly equal size. We have seen in previous chapters that much of the social differentiation within the Chicago bar is hierarchically ordered, but the legal profession does not appear to be the sort of hierarchy where the values of the elite permeate the entire structure and are shared throughout the various strata.

As should be anticipated, the differences in lawyers' social origins that are associated with differences in their early socialization experiences account for much of the variance in lawyers' values. But factors relating to the nature of their legal training and practice also make a substantial contribution, approximately equal in weight to that of the social origin variables. In sum, lawyers' positions on economic and civil libertarian issues appear to be determined in substantial measure by the kinds of law they practice and by the kinds of client they serve.

Chapter 6

THE PATTERNS OF
LAWYERS' CAREERS*

TOWARD THE END of the last chapter we had occasion to begin to analyze the process through which lawyers are recruited or allocated to the varying, socially differentiated roles within the legal profession. Our objective there was limited to ascertaining the extent to which the value preferences held by individual lawyers determine the type of law that they practice or the type of client that they serve. We now wish, however, to document more fully and systematically the nature of the allocation of personnel within the profession. This chapter therefore examines the movement of individuals with different sets of social attributes, representing their starting positions in society, through the career stages of recruitment, training, and successive jobs to their eventual destinations in the bar. What we find most startling in the analysis that we are about to present is the strong influence of ethnoreligious background on the structure of careers in a major metropolitan bar that is largely concerned with facilitating the most advanced forms of modern economic enterprise.

* We wish to acknowledge our special debt to Mariah Evans, a graduate student in sociology at the University of Chicago, who performed the computer-assisted data analyses reported in this chapter and provided valuable advice on a number of important statistical issues, especially with respect to the application of demographic techniques.

In their systematic review of evidence concerning recruitment to various sorts of jobs, Harold L. Wilensky and Anne T. Lawrence observe:

[M]any scholars have arrived at the basic generalization that modern society tends toward the structural and cultural integration of minority groups. There is considerable consensus that industrialization and urbanization together foster increased equality of opportunity, if not absolute equality between races, religious-ethnic or ethnic-linguistic groups, young and old, men and women. The drift toward equal opportunity is said to reflect a shift from ascription to achievement in role assignment. Yet there is also considerable consensus that even in the richest countries many, perhaps most jobs are assigned on the basis of a combination of sex, age, and descent; that powerful barriers to social mobility for able young people from lower-class families are still more powerful for deprived minorities; and that political criteria for important posts remain important.[1]

Leon Mayhew in his classic paper, "Ascription in Modern Society," has also commented that ascription will persist in modern society, despite the strong pressures toward performance-oriented standards of personnel allocation, because "it is cheap."[2] That is, ascription dramatically reduces the costs of a search for "the best person for the job" by providing a rule that sharply limits the range of possible candidates who must be considered. In *Bonds of Pluralism*, Laumann argued further that these contradictory strains toward achievement and ascription could coexist in modern society because there was no inherent functional incompatibility between them.[3] Laumann, however, anticipated that they would be embraced to different extents depending on a person's class location. His hypothesis was that ascriptive bases for constructing informal social networks of friends, neighbors, and acquaintances would be more heavily stressed by working-class people because of their jobs, being relatively interchangeable and nondistinctive, afford few criteria for social preferences based on occupation (or performance). Middle- and upper middle-class persons, on the other hand, would tend to emphasize occupation or performance-linked criteria for selecting their informal associates, rather than ascriptive criteria such

1. Harold L. Wilensky and Anne T. Lawrence, "Job Assignment in Modern Societies: A Re-examination of the Ascription-Achievement Hypothesis," in Amos H. Hawley, *Societal Growth: Processes and Implication* (New York: Free Press, 1979), p. 202.

2. *Sociological Inquiry* 38 (spring 1968).

3. Edward O. Laumann, *Bonds of Pluralism: The Form and Substance of Urban Social Networks* (New York: John Wiley, 1973), pp. 85–98.

as shared ethnoreligious group memberships, because occupation provides such a salient and distinctive basis for their own social identities. Furthermore, Laumann found considerable evidence consistent with these suppositions in his sample of native-born white men in Detroit. He found, for example, that the working-class men were likely to have close personal friends of the same ethnoreligious group as themselves, but that middle-class men, in contrast, were more likely to have close personal friends who shared their occupational status.[4] In support of his speculation that ascriptive and achievement-based criteria are not inherently incompatible, Laumann noted that he found no correlation, positive or negative, between the degree of ethnoreligious homogeneity of a man's friends and the degree of occupational homogeneity of his friends. This means that the men studied appeared to employ these criteria of friendship choice essentially without regard to one another. If the two criteria were functionally incompatible, there should have been a strong negative correlation between the two homogeneity measures. The basic flaw in these data, however, lay in the relatively imprecise way Laumann had measured occupational status similarity. He had used a standard scheme for scoring the prestige of occupations,[5] but this scheme tends to put rather heterogeneous occupation titles together on the same prestige level. Because our study of the Chicago bar is focused on one very high status occupation, with nearly uniform educational attainment, our data permit us to examine how ascriptive solidarities insinuate themselves in manifold ways in the work life of one occupation. The data thus provide a different sort of test of Laumann's hypothesis.

A considerable literature has arisen that examines the process of status attainment in the adult labor force, a literature that received a major impetus from Peter M. Blau and Otis Dudley Duncan's classic monograph, *The American Occupational Structure*.[6] There is also a well-known, but decidedly incomplete, literature more specifically

4. Ibid.
5. Otis Dudley Duncan, "A Socioeconomic Index of All Occupations," in Albert J. Reiss, Jr., ed., *Occupations and Social Status* (New York: Free Press, 1961), pp. 109–31.
6. See Peter M. Blau and Otis Dudley Duncan, *The American Occupational Structure* (New York: John Wiley, 1967); Raymond Boudon, *Education, Opportunity and Social Inequality* (New York: John Wiley, 1974); James S. Coleman et al., "White and Black Careers During the First Decade of Labor Force Experience. Part I: Occupational Status," *Social Science Research* 1(1972): 243–70; James S. Coleman, "Flow Models for Occupational Structure," in A. Brody and A. P. Carter, eds., *Input-Output Techniques* (Amsterdam: North Holland Publishing, 1972) pp. 80 ff.; B. G. Glaser and A. L.

directed to lawyers' careers. In one of the first efforts to examine systematically the social origins of lawyers, Jack Ladinsky analyzed a sample of 207 Detroit lawyers who were interviewed in 1960.[7] His data revealed that solo lawyers more often come from minority religious-ethnic, entrepreneurial, and working-class homes, have inferior educations, and experience chaotic work histories. Moreover, religious and socioeconomic origins were shown to exert independent effects on subsequent career achievement. Focusing on "lawyers in the making," Seymour Warkov and Joseph Zelan analyzed a segment of a National Opinion Research Center (NORC) survey of 33,782 college seniors at 135 colleges and universities.[8] The students were asked in the spring of 1961 about their postgraduate plans, and Warkov and Zelan directed particular attention to those respondents who indicated an intention to attend law school in the following year. While their analyses shed light on the impact of social origins and undergraduate school experiences on the decision to

---

(continued)

Strauss, *Status Passage* (Chicago: Aldine, 1971); David L. Featherman, "A Social Structural Model for the Socioeconomic Career," *American Journal of Sociology* 77 (1971): 293–304; Christopher Jencks et al., *Inequality: A Reassessment of the Effect of Family and Schooling in America* (New York: Basic Books, 1972); Jonathan Kelley, "Causal Chains in the Socioeconomic Career," *American Sociological Review* 38 (1973): 481–93; David McFarland, "Intra-generational Mobility as a Markov Process: Including a Time-Stationary Markovian Model that Explains Observed Declines in Mobility over Time," *American Sociological Review* 35 (1970): 463–76; Robert McGinnis, "A Stochastic Model of Mobility," *American Sociological Review* 33 (1968): 712–21; William H. Sewell and Robert M. Hauser, *Education, Occupation and Earnings: Achievement in Early Career* (New York: Academic Press, 1975); Burt Singer and Seymour Spilerman, "Social Mobility in Heterogeneous Populations" in *Sociological Methodology 1973–74* (San Francisco: Jossey-Bass, 1974) pp. 356–402; Aage B. Sørensen, "A Model for Occupational Careers," *American Journal of Sociology* 80 (1974): 44–57; Aage B. Sørenson, "The Structure of Intragenerational Mobility," *American Sociological Review* 40 (1975): 456–71; Angela Lane, "The Occupational Achievement Process, 1940–49: A Cohort Analysis," *American Sociological Review* 40 (1975): 472–82; Otis Dudley Duncan, "How Destination Depends on Origin in the Occupational Mobility Table," *American Journal of Sociology* 84 (1979): 793–803; Leo Goodman, "Multiplicative Models for the Analysis of Occupational Mobility Tables and Other Kinds of Cross-Classification Tables," *American Journal of Sociology* 84 (1979): 804–19; Nancy Tuma, Michael Hannan, and Lyle P. Groenveld, "Dynamic Analysis of Event Histories," *American Journal of Sociology* 84 (1979): 820–54; Nancy B. Tuma, "Rewards, Resources, and the Rate of Mobility," *American Sociological Review* 41 (1976): 338–60.

7. Jack Ladinsky, "Careers of Lawyers, Law Practice and Legal Institutions," *American Sociological Review* 28 (1963): 47–54; see also idem., "The Impact of Social Backgrounds of Lawyers on Law Practice and the Law," *Journal of Legal Education* 16 (1963): 127–44; idem., "The Social Profile of a Metropolitan Bar: A Statistical Survey in Detroit," *Michigan State Bar Journal* 43 (1964): 12–24.

8. Seymour Warkov (with Joseph Zelan), *Lawyers in the Making* (Chicago: Aldine Publishing, 1965).

enter different types of law schools, the data obviously could tell us nothing about actual career outcomes. There are but a handful of other studies that have discussed the recruitment of lawyers to particular practice settings in one or another metropolitan area. Most notably, Erwin Smigel described the recruitment of Wall Street lawyers circa the late 1950s,[9] while Daniel Lortie and Jerome Carlin presented some suggestive data on the social origins and types of law schools attended by Chicago's lawyers in the same time period.[10] More recently, Howard S. Erlanger has examined the impact of social background on the recruitment of lawyers to work for the Legal Services Corporation, a provider of legal aid to the poor.[11]

9. Erwin O. Smigel, *The Wall Street Lawyer: Professional Organization Man?*, 2d ed. (Bloomington: Indiana University Press, 1969).

10. Dan C. Lortie, "The Striving Young Lawyer: A Study of Early Career Differentiation in the Chicago Bar" (Ph.D. diss., University of Chicago, 1958); Dan C. Lortie, "Laymen to Lawmen: Law School Careers and Professional Socialization," *Harvard Education Review* 29 (1959): 352–69; Jerome E. Carlin, *Lawyers on Their Own: A Study of Individual Practitioners in Chicago* (New Brunswick, N.J.: Rutgers University Press, 1962).

11. Howard S. Erlanger, "Lawyers and Neighborhood Legal Services: Social Background and the Impetus for Reform," *Law and Society Review* 12 (1978): 253–74.

On the basis of data from a national survey of lawyers conducted in 1973 and early 1974, Erlanger recently concluded that while entry into the profession is strongly correlated with family characteristics—notably class, religion, and national origin—these characteristics do not have substantial direct or indirect effects on attainment within the profession ("The Allocation of Status Within Occupations: The Case of the Legal Profession," *Social Forces* [1980]: 882–903). Obviously such a conclusion, even with its qualifications and caveats, is at variance with the findings reported here and in other studies of local bars. Erlanger explored several possible explanations for this discrepancy and concluded that the difference in findings is attributable to the local culture of some of the cities (see pp. 897–99). Much of the difference in results might, however, be explained by differences in the specification of the population universes and in the operationalization of key variables.

Erlanger's national data did not include lawyers in salaried positions in business and government, but instead was limited (as previous studies of the bar had been) to "private practitioners." The salaried segment of the bar, however, is one of the most rapidly growing parts of the profession and amounts to a quarter of our total sample. Our data suggest that entry into such positions is much affected by background and educational characteristics of the incumbents, and that differences might therefore be found in a sample of the total bar that would not appear in a sample of private practitioners alone. Indeed, in a footnote that discusses our findings (page 900, note 8), Erlanger notes that if one looks at the full distribution of law jobs, rather than only at the private practitioners, "the differences by religion are greater" in our data. The table in one of our earlier articles to which Erlanger refers indicates that the largest over- and underrepresentations of the religious groups across the job categories used there are the underrepresentation of Jews among both government-employed lawyers and corporate house counsel, the overrepresentation of Catholics among government lawyers, and the overrepresentation of Protestants among both house counsel and lawyers holding "nonlegal" jobs—none of these differences involving "private practitioners." (See *American Bar Foundation Research Journal* 1976: 780, table A5). Because of the particular issue that concerns him at that point, Erlang-

Though these studies hardly give us a comprehensive view of lawyers' career patterns, they do seem to converge on several central findings. First, for all the talk about the law being a major avenue of upward mobility for the socially disadvantaged, a very substantial majority of lawyers come from families of at least middle-class, if not higher, socioeconomic standing. Second, those who are from socially disadvantaged backgrounds are much more likely to end up in solo or small firm practices, with individuals as their clients and with relatively modest and uncertain incomes. Third, the conversion of the social advantages or disadvantages of one's birth into legal career achievement is accomplished by the channeling of persons into different types of law schools, which are

---

(continued)

er's discussion of our findings ("Allocation of Status," p. 897) compares only Catholics with Protestants on the firm size variable. He notes that, in our sample, Catholics (of all nationalities, considered together) are only slightly more likely than are Protestants (of all kinds, considered together) to be in solo practice, and Protestants are only slightly more likely than are Catholics to be in firms with more than thirty lawyers. The same table also reports that the distribution of Jewish lawyers, which Erlanger does not have occasion to note or discuss, is much more skewed—Jews are substantially overrepresented in firms with fewer than ten lawyers and greatly underrepresented in firms with ten or more lawyers, especially so in those with more than thirty lawyers.

Because of the limited size of Erlanger's data set, it was not possible for him to use anything other than the broadest ethnoreligious categories, and such categories may be too broad to disclose important variation. National origin, for example, was dichotomized (see p. 901), "respondents with fathers whose origin was in northern or western Europe" being opposed to all others. Similarly, the data did not permit analysis of differences among identifiable social types within the broad religious categories—Protestants, Catholics and Jews (see Edwin Scott Gaustad, *Historical Atlas of Religion in America* [New York: Harper and Row, 1962]). But such differences may be crucial. It is plausible, for example, that German Catholics are a substantial enough proportion of all Catholics, nationally, to conceal important ethnoreligious differences when all Catholics are pooled for analysis in a national sample. That is, because the relevant characteristics of German Catholics are more similar to those of Protestants than are the characteristics of other sorts of Catholics and because German Catholics are relatively more numerous in rural areas and small towns than they are in large cities, the similarity between Protestants and German Catholics may mask differences between Protestants and the other Catholics when all Catholics are grouped together. Thus, in a sample drawn from a large city, the numbers of southern and eastern European Catholics, who differ most from the Protestants, might so outweigh the numbers of German Catholics that an overall Protestant/Catholic difference would be observable, while the differences between the broad religious categories in a national sample might fail to achieve "statistical significance." In short, the relatively minor role that religion and ethnicity play in the regression analyses of the national sample may be attributable to the use of internally heterogeneous categories that conceal the real variance.

See also, Charles Cappell, "Dynamics of Organizational Decision-Making" (Ph.D. diss., University of Chicago, 1980), chapter 2.

themselves loosely organized into a hierarchical structure of top-flight law schools associated with major national universities and local law schools of less certain standing. Fourth, the impact of social origins on subsequent career attainments, while demonstrably present, should not be exaggerated. Put in other words, only a very small proportion of the total variation in career achievement is attributable to such factors. Our data do not produce any surprising reversals of these generalizations, but they do provide rich and fine-grained documentation and elaboration of these and other propositions.

While we shall exploit some of the sophisticated methodology now available to examine lawyers' careers, we shall content ourselves for the most part with presenting the data in the more familiar guise of bivariate contingency tables, noting, when appropriate, where the results from multivariate techniques provide additional support for our interpretations. Even with our sample of roughly seven hundred practicing lawyers, we often run out of cases in key cells of the tables. Rather than sacrifice interesting clues to the underlying processes of social allocation on the altar of statistical rigor, however, we shall attempt to tease out promising hypotheses that can be tested in subsequent investigations.

Introducing the Concept of Social Biography

In our analyses, we will attempt to construct "social biographies" of the practicing lawyers. From the individual's point of view, the order of changes of social locations at different ages constitutes his personal biography. Certain social locations can be entered only after others have been successfully completed. One must, for instance, complete law school and then pass the bar examination before being licensed to practice. There are, however, other sequences of status locations that are not so restrictively ordered in time. One individual, for example, may start his practice in the prosecutor's office and then enter solo practice, while another reverses this sequence. And not only may particular sequences of status incumbencies differ for different individuals, but they may be differentially likely or unlikely for different cohorts of actors.[12] Persons entering practice in the late 1940s, for instance, may well have confronted career opportunities very different from those encountered by persons entering practice in the late 1960s. The relation between an individual's personal biography and the common experiences over time of his cohort, defined as the time of entry into practice, thus poses serious analytic problems. These problems are especially severe when one is dealing, as we are, with cross-sectional data (i.e., data gathered at only one point in time) because it is difficult to determine whether an observed effect is due to the individual's maturation or to the events encountered by given cohorts of individuals. As we noted in chapter 5, the observation in a cross-section survey that age is positively correlated with socially conservative attitudes does not necessarily support the conclusion that individuals become more conservative with age. It could be the case that different cohorts of individuals—in commonly experiencing major social events of peace or war, prosperity or depression in their formative years— were more or less likely to acquire certain social attitudes. In short, the effects of aging and the cohort experiences are confounded in a single survey. Despite our respectable sample size, we only have data gathered at one time and thus can only make some crude efforts to assess the impact of the several effects.

The second major facet of social biography that concerns us is the identification of the sets of mutually exclusive statuses to which we assign individuals at the different career stages. Here we are necessarily captives of our a priori notions of what constitutes the relevant status categories and critical time junctures. (We are, of course, constrained as well by the limits of the detail in our data and by the numbers of persons to be found in particular categories.) We focus attention on two aspects of a person's status origins—his ethnoreligious group membership and his father's occupation—as they affect the likelihood of attending particular types of law schools. We then

---

12. In his classic article on the subject, Norman Ryder defines a cohort as "the aggregate of individuals (within some population definition) who experienced the same event within the same time interval"; see "The Cohort as a Concept in the Study of Social Change," *American Sociological Review* 30 (1965): 845. "In almost all cohort research to date the defining event has been birth, but this is only a special case of the more general approach. Cohort data are ordinarily assembled sequentially from observations of the time of occurrence of the behavior being studied, and the interval is age."

For our purposes, the cohort-defining event is the year of entry into practice, though this is very highly correlated with year of birth.

look at how given types of law schools raise or lower the chances of entering particular types of full-time legal jobs and conclude with a brief look at the extent to which the various types of first jobs tend to retain or expel their incumbents.

We can depict our overview of the key junctures in the social biographies of lawyers in this simple diagram:

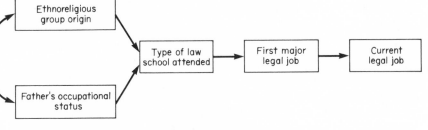

FIGURE 6.1

Causal Model of the Process of Recruitment, Socialization, and Allocation of Practicing Lawyers

The double-headed arrow between ethnoreligious group member-ship and father's occupational status indicates that we expect an as-sociation between the two, but in this study we advance no hypoth-esis about the causal direction of their relationship. A single-headed arrow between two variables indicates our guess about the causal order of the variables. In this model we postulate that all effects of social origin on current career status are mediated through their impact on the type of law school attended and, in turn, the type of law school directly determines the first legal job obtained, and so on. We shall, among other things, examine whether the assumption that there are no direct effects between social origin and final desti-nation status is consistent with the data in hand.

Life Course Trajectories in the Occupancy of Selected Statuses

Before looking at the data, however, it will be useful to know how the process of aging itself might be implicated in organizing key features of practitioner careers. We say "might be implicated" be-cause our data, being only cross-sectional, afford only limited means for disentangling the confounded effects of age and cohort. Figure 6.2 provides estimates of the age-specific likelihoods of occupying five selected status categories. To construct the figure, we simply plotted the percentages of practitioners in a particular status category by successive age intervals and connected the resulting plot with straight lines.[13] While there are more sophisticated means of estimating these curves,[14] we are only interested in certain relatively obvious features, and nothing would be gained by employing elaborate procedures that might give a sense of more precision than is warranted.

At least two caveats must be kept firmly in mind in interpreting these age trajectories. First, we have no way of estimating the age-specific exits of practicing attorneys from the Chicago bar. Our sample includes only attorneys currently listed in the directories—these are the survivors in a process of selection, and those who have dropped out, for whatever reasons, are lost from sight. Some of these dropouts may have voluntarily left to become corporate exec-

13. Occupational careers are built out of ordered patterns of transitions between roles. These transitions are typically tied fairly closely to age. Figure 6.2 is intended to capture certain aspects of lawyers' careers through cross-sectional (or period) age profiles of the prevalence of several types of status positions for practicing Chicago lawyers aged 27 to 68 in our sample.

Each line in the figure joins points representing the percentage of lawyers (at each age) who occupied the given status at the date of interview. Thus the graph shows not the actual legal biography of any one group of lawyers but, rather, a synthetic biography which yields an image of how patterns of status occupancy over the life course *would* look if the members of a group of young lawyers were to pass through their occupational careers according to the patterns prevailing in 1975. Alternatively, the graph can be viewed as a simple description of the distribution of lawyers of different ages among various status categories. Such a description is valuable in itself, but the interpretation as a synthetic legal biography is still more compelling for it affords not merely a glance at a slice of life, as it were, but a view of the typical age-specific life changes confronting a group.

Does the synthetic biography, in fact, tell us much either about the routes mature lawyers followed to arrive at their present positions or about the future course of young lawyers' careers? It may, if we are cautious about interpretation. A synthetic legal biography only gives a perfect description of the past and future if the rates (or percentages) used to generate it are constant over time. They are obviously not; the profession has expanded and has changed its structure in ways that may alter some of the rates used. For example, expansion in the sheer size of the bar may mean that young lawyers are less likely than their elders *ever* to know anyone in the professional elite. Nevertheless, the shape of the curve is of more interest than the precise levels at given ages, and there is no compelling reason to believe that recent changes have affected the shapes of the curves. In short, focusing on the shapes of the curves depicted in the synthetic biography may reveal information of importance about the characteristics of lawyers' careers.

14. E.g., by the method of averages; see Louis Henry, *Population: Analysis and Models*, trans. Etienne van de Walle and Elise F. Jones (New York: Academic Press, 1976), pp. 38–39.

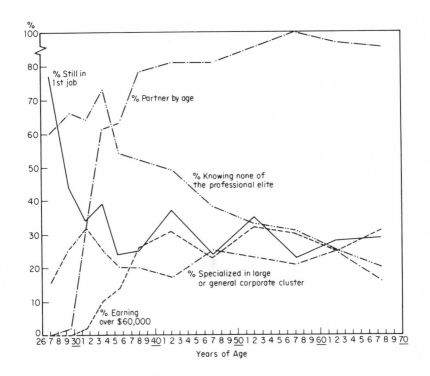

FIGURE 6.2

Status over the Life Course: Cross-sectional Estimates of Age-specific Likelihoods of Occupying Selected Status Categories in the Practicing Bar

utives or practitioners in other geographical areas, or they may have been forced to enter other occupations because they could not attract enough clients to make a living. There is thus good reason to believe that these exit rates are quite substantial, especially in the younger ages. One important implication of these unknown exit rates is known—that the age-specific percentages in figure 6.2 systematically overestimate the proportions of persons in particular status categories for the population of *all* persons who have passed the bar examination and are thus eligible to practice law in the state.[15]

15. In fact, the legal profession, like the medical profession, appears to exert an unusually strong "retention effect" over the occupational life of its practitioners, when compared to many other professions and semiprofessions. See appendix to this chapter for a more extended discussion of this neglected but important matter. Also see Mariah D. Evans and Edward O. Laumann, "Professional Commitment: Myth or Reality," in Donald Treiman and Robert Robinson, eds., *Research in Stratification and Mobility* (Greenwich: JAI Press, 1983).

The second caveat derives from the fact that age and time of entry into practice, the latter being definitional of a cohort, are almost perfectly correlated. This means that most persons over 40 entered practice before 1960, while the youngest lawyers entered practice most recently. If there are reasons to believe that time of entry into practice substantially affects the likelihood of entering government employment or of becoming a corporate house counsel, or changes the time it takes to "make partner" in large firms—for example, that the rapid growth of large firms in recent years may have induced more rapid advancement to partnership status—then the swings in the age trajectories of older versus younger practitioners are attributable to cohort effects rather than to aging or to maturation in one's profession. We can and will look for some cohort effects by creating synthetic cohorts whereby we compare the younger age groups' rates of movement into certain destination statuses with the older age groups' rates when they were at comparable ages. But figure 6.2 does not distinguish between such effects.

Let us look first at the solid line in figure 6.2 that graphs the percentages of persons at given ages who are still in the first major legal jobs with which they began practice. As one would expect, the vast majority of 27- and 28-year-olds—about 78 percent—are still in their first jobs, but this proportion rapidly drops to 34 percent by age 30 and then oscillates around 30 percent from about 34 years of age through the rest of the age distribution. This oscillating line from age 30, which hits a high of 37 and a low of 24, poses some fascinating questions of interpretation. Are these fluctuations merely statistical artifacts arising from the relatively small numbers of persons used to estimate the percentages at given age intervals? If so, then a smoothed curve running roughly along the 30 percent line after age 33 or so would represent our best guess about the expectation of the long-term job stability for attorneys who remain in practice throughout their lives. Put another way, roughly 70 percent of Chicago's practicing attorneys would be expected to have at least two legal jobs over the course of their careers.

On the other hand, if the oscillation depicted by the line truly reflects changes in the opportunities for job stability that were confronted by the different cohorts of attorneys, then one is led to a more historically circumstantial account of the conditions of practice in Chicago over the past forty years. Disregarding the very early years' high peak, which is self-explanatory, the first notable peak in first-job stability occurs at 42 years of age and corresponds to a cohort of lawyers who entered practice around 1958 and 1959, the end of the Eisenhower years of relative peace and tranquility on both the national and international scene. (Most lawyers graduate from law school and pass their bar examinations between the ages of 24 and 26.) The first trough point occurs at age 35, which corresponds to a point of entry into practice about 1965 or 1966. We need little reminder that the 1960s were a period of great social turbulence and unrest as symbolized in the two great events of the period, the Vietnam war and the Great Society programs. Attorneys entering practice during this period thus might have been more likely to change jobs as they attempted to come to terms with the new career opportunities in government, business, and large firm practice that were open to them.[16] The next high peak of job stability occurs at age 52, corresponding to an entry cohort around 1949 and 1950, which was a nonwar period some years after the dislocations occasioned by World War II. The two trough points of relatively lower job stability at ages 47 and 57 correspond to times either during or immediately after wars—specifically, the 1944-45 period, which fell toward the end of World War II, and the 1954-55 period, which followed the conclusion of the Korean War.[17]

The second curve to be discussed is the heavy-dash-and-dot line graphing the percentages of practitioners of the various ages who are partners in the law firms in which they work (as opposed to associates, lawyers who are "of counsel," and other employment categories). These percentages are calculated only on the population of lawyers working for law firms and do not include lawyers working in other practice settings. The main point here is the demarcation of the critical period of movement into partner status that oc-

16. See, e.g., Erlanger, *supra* note 11.

17. That different cohorts of practicing attorneys in Chicago have experienced different career opportunities, with their consequent implications for job stability, can be demonstrated from a variety of related analyses. Perhaps the most straightforward to present here in buttressing our interpretation stressing cohort effects is the fact readily seen in the table below that for every type of practice context the mean length of time spent in the first major legal job is longer for those who entered practice prior to 1960 than it is for those who started practice in 1960 or later. Worth stressing here is that we are now explicitly comparing the mean number of years spent in first major legal jobs for each cohort of lawyers rather than trying to infer relative job stability only from the proportion of lawyers at different ages who stayed in their first job until the time of the interview.

curs between 30 and 33 years of age, with a second surge of movement between 35 and 38. The curve then more or less flattens out at around 85 to 90 percent for the remainder of the age categories. One immediately wonders what might be causing the break in the upward movement of the curve around 33 to 34 years of age, though this could also be merely a statistical artifact. One explanation, if it is a "real" phenomenon, might be that the first rise reflects the first round of selection of associates for partnership status in the large law firms. Those associates who are not promoted at this point (after five to seven years with a firm) typically will seek placement in smaller and perhaps less prestigious firms where they may be made a partner after a short trial period, thus accounting for the second upward surge.[18]

Two pieces of evidence from the figure itself are at least consistent with this interpretation. First, note the very steep drop in the curve for "percent still in first job" precisely in the age interval 33 to 35. Second, the curve depicting the age-specific percentages of lawyers who specialize in corporate law fields also shows a more moderate drop after its peak at age 31, the curve rising again only after age 42. The rapid rise in the percentages of persons in the large corporate cluster between entry into practice and 31 years of age probably reflects the growing involvement of young associates assigned to work in teams on large corporate matters in the large law firms. As some of these persons fail to "make it" and are asked to leave around age 31 and thereafter, they may move into other practice contexts that are less involved with major corporate clients and more heavily involved with small business and personal clients. Only after they achieve some seniority in their second placement—at, say, 42 years of age or so—are they likely to begin getting the more desired corporate clients again.

The shape of the curve depicting specialization in large or general corporate practice suggests that corporate legal work is done primarily either by very junior or by relatively senior lawyers. Lawyers in mid-career (between 35 and 45 years old) are less active in corporate practice. This pattern probably arises from the way in which access to corporate clients is organized in the profession. The very junior lawyers (namely, the associates in the large law firms) are essentially hired hands assisting the senior partners who are in

18. Compare Smigel, *supra* note 9.

charge of the legal affairs of major corporate clients.[19] Because of the great importance attached to major corporate accounts, partners are usually not assigned such plums until they have fully earned their status. Younger partners (in their mid-careers) may be more likely to devote their time to their particular substantive specialties, perhaps in economic regulatory law, rather than to general corporate work.

The fourth curve to be discussed concerns the age-specific percentages of lawyers who annually earn $60,000 or more from their practices. Not surprisingly, the rate of ascent is considerably more moderate than for the other curves we discussed, achieving its first peak around age 42, which might be taken as the age at which lawyers either make it to the top of the professional tree or do not. If a lawyer has not achieved the heights by that age, he is rather unlikely to do so subsequently (though there is a second peak ten years later). The rather tantalizing fact is that this curve, between the ages 42 and 52, appears to co-vary with the curve for the percentage of attorneys still in their first jobs, but at age 52 the percentage earning $60,000 a year or more appears to stabilize and it then gently drops in the early sixties. This co-variation suggests the possibility of some cohort effect operating on the opportunities to earn higher incomes.

The final curve in figure 6.2 describes the age-specific percentages of attorneys who knew none of the professional elite.[20] We selected this indicator as an alternative measure of professional success because earned income tends to understate the relative professional standing of attorneys in salaried employment (e.g., government or house counsel). Though salaried law jobs tend to have lower ceilings on earned income than do other forms of practice, lawyers in these positions may be well regarded in the professional community and may have good connections to influential lawyers. The rise in the percentages from age 27 to age 31 amounts to almost a 14 percentage point move in the "wrong direction"— that is, one would normally expect this curve to be downwardly sloping from the onset of practice as attorneys simply have more

19. Ibid. Recall our discussion in chapter 4 and table 4.2 about the differing levels of autonomy of the fields in handling client affairs. One of the reasons that the corporate fields ranked low in autonomy is that their practice tends to involve a number of attorneys working as a team under the supervision of a senior partner.

20. See chapter 9 for an extended treatment of this group of notables.

time to get to know the leading personalities of the local bar. This odd result probably arises from two factors. First, the list of notables contained local law school deans and a young (but prominent) law professor. Attorneys who had just completed law school locally were thus likely to be acquainted with at least one notable whom they met by virtue of attending law school. Somewhat older attorneys, even only a few years out of school, may not have had the same opportunities to meet these people. Second, the time of maximum geographical mobility of lawyers occurs in the five to seven years immediately after their completion of law school. A 29-year-old lawyer who was trained in the East and moved to Chicago to accept a position as an associate in a major law firm after completing his clerkship with a federal judge will simply not have had the chance to meet the local establishment. The presence of such persons in the age category will thus dilute acquaintance with the local professional elite. The time of the most rapid acquisition of such acquaintance occurs in the early 30s (note the steep drop in the curve between ages 32 and 35) and the curve then descends more slowly as the lawyers become more senior in the local bar and their acquaintances continue to accumulate. The smoothness of the descent after age 35 argues that there are then no critical career events or cohort effects that appreciably modify the opportunities to become acquainted with the notables. Seniority in the profession after the first ten years and personal success in one's practice thus appear to be the dominant factors in accounting for the integration of lawyers into their professional community.

Evaluating the Model of the Status Attainment Process

With this perspective on the organization of lawyers' careers by age and cohort, we can now turn our attention to the components of the proposed model of recruitment, socialization, and allocation that was summarized in figure 6.1. As indicated in that diagram, we think that there are two aspects of people's social origins that are likely to play significant roles in channeling them to different sorts of law schools. The basic data relating ethnoreligious origins and law school are presented in table 6.1.

Almost from the start of empirical sociology, there has been great

TABLE 6.1
Percentage Distribution of Practitioners from Given Ethnoreligious Backgrounds by Type of Law School Attended (Whites Only)

Ethnoreligious Background	Type of Law School				
	Elite	Prestige	Regional	Local	Total
Protestant I	43.5	16.1	21.0	19.5	100.1
	(+21.5)	(−0.9)	(+5.6)	(−26.1)	(n = 62)
Protestant II	36.0	18.0	26.0	20.0	100.0
	(+14.0)	(+1.0)	(+10.6)	(−25.6)	(n = 50)
Northern & western	25.5	17.0	23.4	34.0	99.9
European Catholics	(+3.5)	(0.0)	(+8.0)	(−11.6)	(n = 47)
Nonidentifiers	20.5	16.1	12.5	50.9	100.0
	(−1.5)	(−0.9)	(−2.9)	(+5.3)	(n = 112)
Reform & ethnic	20.9	16.5	12.2	50.4	100.0
Jews	(−1.1)	(−0.5)	(−3.2)	(+4.8)	(n = 115)
Orthodox &	19.0	17.7	10.1	53.2	100.0
Conservative Jews	(−3.0)	(+0.7)	(−5.3)	(+7.6)	(n = 79)
Irish Catholics	11.3	25.8	16.1	46.8	100.0
	(−10.7)	(+8.8)	(+0.7)	(+1.2)	(n = 62)
Southern & eastern	0.0	6.7	11.1	82.2	100.0
European Catholics	(−22.0)	(−10.3)	(−4.3)	(+36.6)	(n = 45)
TOTAL	22.0	17.0	15.5	45.6	100.0
					(n = 572)

NOTE: Included in this table are lawyers aged 30 through 75 who were engaged in the practice of law at the time of the survey. Chi-square = 87.37, p < .001, Eta = .334. Numbers in parentheses are the differences between the observed and expected percentages.

interest in the role of ethnic groups in the economic, political, and social life of American cities and the assimilation of these groups into the "host" society. Beginning in 1925, Emory S. Bogardus and his students, employing the classic Bogardus Social Distance Scale, charted subjective orientations toward the manifold groups that have migrated to this country.[21] Despite some serious methodological defects in the samples employed (e.g., they were typically drawn from college student populations rather than from broader cross sections) and in the methods used to measure ethnic "prejudice," one finding that emerged consistently was the differential ranking of ethnic groups along a hierarchical dimension of social desirability and of acceptability for intimate relationships such as marriage, friendship, and common residence—a ranking that has remained

21. Emory S. Bogardus, "A Social Distance Scale," *Sociology and Social Research* 17 (1933): 265–71.

remarkably stable over time.[22] The relative position of a given ethnic group on this dimension seems to be a function of the principal time of immigration of the group's ancestors (the earlier in American history, the higher the standing of the group) and the degree to which the group approximates the cultural attributes of white Anglo-Saxon Protestants. In addition to such attitudinal studies of ethnic prejudice, a large number of studies of residential segregation of ethnic groups have found a generally parallel ranking of groups by their degree of segregation from each other.[23] Complementary (but less plentiful) studies have also demonstrated the continuing impact of ethnic origins on occupational attainment.[24]

In an important modification of the argument about the role of ethnic groups in determining worldly success, Will Herberg, drawing from Ruby Jo Reeves Kennedy's description of ethnic and religious intermarriage trends in New Haven,[25] advanced the descriptive hypothesis that the religious differences that remain in the American population fall into three broad categories, Protestant, Catholic, and Jewish, and that differences within these broad groupings, especially to the extent that they arise from ethnic differences, are relatively residual and are slowly disappearing.[26] Moreover, Herberg argues, the significance of these broad religious preferences lies in their social structural implications—that is, it lies in determining who associates with whom rather than in any fundamental differences of religious outlook or values. Among the three faiths, then, he argues that the growing tendency is to emphasize beliefs shared in

22. Emory S. Bogardus, "Measuring Changes in Ethnic Relations," *American Sociological Review* 16 (1951): 48–53; idem., "Racial Distance Changes in the United States During the Past 30 Years," *Sociology and Social Research* 43 (1958): 127–35.

23. Otis Dudley Duncan and Stanley Lieberson, "Ethnic Segregation and Assimilation," *American Journal of Sociology* 64 (1959): 363–74; Stanley Lieberson, *Ethnic Patterns in American Cities* (New York: Free Press, 1963); James M. Beshers, Edward O. Laumann, and Benjamin Bradshaw, "Ethnic Congregation-Segregation, Assimilation and Stratification," *Social Forces* 43 (1964): 482–89.

24. E.g., Oscar Handlin, *The American People in the 20th Century* (Cambridge, Mass.: Harvard University Press, 1954); Beverly Duncan and Otis Dudley Duncan, "Minorities and the Process of Stratification," *American Sociological Review* 33 (1968): 356–64; David L. Featherman, "The Socioeconomic Achievement of White Religioethnic Subgroups: Social and Psychological Explanation," *American Sociological Review* 36 (1971): 207–22; Laumann, *supra* note 3, pp. 186–98.

25. Ruby Jo Reeves Kennedy, "Single or Triple Melting Pot? Intermarriage Trends in New Haven, 1870–1940," *American Journal of Sociology* 49 (1944): 331–39; idem., "Single or Triple Melting Pot? Intermarriage Trends in New Haven, 1870–1950," *American Journal of Sociology* 58 (1952): 56–59.

26. Will Herberg, *Protestant, Catholic, Jew*, rev. ed. (New York: Doubleday-Anchor, 1955).

common and to minimize their differences. His view minimizing the significance of value differences among religious groups has been challenged by Gerhard Lenski, Charles Y. Glock and Rodney Stark,[27] and others, who argue that the empirical evidence supports the view that there are indeed important differences among and within the broad religious communities that cannot be neglected.[28]

Because we had too few cases in certain ethnic groups to sustain meaningful analysis, we decided to treat ethnic groups and religious origins simultaneously, just as Laumann had done in his study of friendship formation in Detroit.[29] We subdivided each of the three broad religious preferences into categories ordered according to their departure from the "ideal" standard of a white Anglo-Saxon Protestant. Since almost all of the Protestants reported northwestern European origins, if they claimed any ethnic identity at all, we distinguished among them only on the basis of the relative social standing or prestige of their denominational affiliations.[30] Thus, we distinguished between high-status Protestant denominations, such as United Church of Christ (Congregational), Episcopal, and Presbyterian (Protestant Type I) and all the other Protestant denominations, including the Baptists, Methodists, Lutherans, nondenominational Protestants, and the fundamentalist sects (Protestant Type II). Those who reported no religious affiliation at all (the nonidentifiers in table 6.1) are predominantly of Protestant origin since persons who claimed no religious preference of any kind but indicated Jewish ethnic affinity were assigned to the Jewish subgroup. For the Jewish subcommunity, we combined those who claimed affiliation with Reform Judaism and those expressing only a Jewish ethnic affiliation (representing, by hypothesis, the more assimilated group) and, in another category, combined the respondents claiming affiliation with Orthodox or Conservative Judaism. Finally, for the Catholics, we were able to distinguish among the Irish Catholics (who are of particular significance in Chicago local politics), other northern and western European Catholics (including the English, German,

27. Gerhard Lenski, *The Religious Factor* (New York: Free Press, 1960); Charles Y. Glock and Rodney Stark, *Religion and Society in Tension* (Chicago: Rand McNally, 1965); Rodney Stark and Charles Y. Glock, *American Piety: The Nature of Religious Commitment* (Berkeley: University of California Press, 1968).
28. See chapter 5, table 5.3.
29. Laumann, *supra* note 3, pp. 58–72.
30. See H. Richard Niebuhr, *The Social Sources of Denominationalism* (New York: Henry Holt, 1929); Nicholas J. Demerath, *Social Class in American Protestantism* (Chicago: Rand McNally, 1965); Laumann, *supra* note 3, pp. 51–58.

and French), and southern and eastern European Catholics.

The pertinence of these ethnoreligious categories for the likelihood of attending different types of law schools is demonstrated in table 6.1 where the rows, moving from high to low social status in the ethnoreligious hierarchy, order the degree of over- or underrepresentation of each ethnoreligious category's attendance at elite law schools (see the numbers in parentheses in the first column). This over- or underrepresentation is almost precisely reversed in the case of attendance at the local law schools, which are lowest in the pecking order of law schools (see the fourth column). Within each religious subcommunity, the more assimilated groups usually have somewhat higher likelihoods of attending elite schools and somewhat lower likelihoods of attending local law schools than do their less assimilated coreligionists.

Noteworthy here also is the fact that, in comparison to both the Protestants and the Catholics, both subgroups of Jews and the non-identifiers have only small, essentially negligible deviations from their expected incidences across all types of law schools. In other words, the access of Jews to different types of law schools is less biased than it is for either of the other major religious subcommunities in the sense that the Jews distribute themselves among the different types of law schools essentially as does the population as a whole. To assess the presence of cohort effects, we constructed the same table for those who entered practice prior to 1960 and those who entered practice in 1960 or afterwards. The overall pattern for each cohort is essentially identical to that observed in table 6.1, and thus we will not present the additional tables here.

When we turn to a consideration of the second major aspect of an individual's social background, his family's socioeconomic status, we find that over 73 percent of the practicing lawyers in Chicago come from solidly middle-class or upper middle-class homes (as indexed by the father's occupation at the time the son or daughter was in high school).[31] This proportion is about what one would expect for the recruitment of persons into a high status profession in a major metropolitan area. In a 1963 survey of the white adult male

31. It is worth noting here that occupational inheritance among lawyers is extremely high when compared to most other occupational groups. Only the medical profession and other high status traditional professions like the clergy and professors, as well as farmers and self-employed proprietors, attain comparably high rates of self-recruitment (see Blau and Duncan, *supra* note 6, pp. 26–48). Note that all of these occupations are historically rooted in activities stressing individualism, autono-

population of Cambridge-Belmont, Massachusetts (part of the Boston Standard Metropolitan Statistical Area), Laumann observed that almost 72 percent of the men in the top professional and managerial jobs had fathers who were in professional, technical, or managerial positions.[32] His coding of occupations was almost identical to the one used in this study. A 1962 national survey of males 25 to 64 years old (including urban and rural residents, whites and non-whites) by Blau and Duncan found that slightly over 60 percent of the self-employed professionals had fathers who were in white-collar or higher status jobs.[33] The latter survey would be expected to find a somewhat lower percentage because it used a more inclusive sample. Various studies of the social origins of the major business, political, military, and professional elites in American society tend to converge on an estimate of two-thirds to three-quarters of the members of the elites coming from lower middle-class or higher status socioeconomic origins.[34]

In the face of such social homogeneity, one would hardly expect socioeconomic origins to be a major explanatory factor in allocating persons across the different types of law schools. But the basic data on the relationship between father's occupation and school attended, presented in table 6.2, show that social origin does matter: there are significant, albeit modest, differences among schools with regard to the economic origins of their students. More than 87 percent of the lawyers who attended elite law schools had fathers in professional, technical, or managerial occupations; and 79 percent of those who attended a prestige law school had such a father; but "only" 64 percent of those who attended a local law school—still a substantial majority—had such a family background.

---

my, self-reliance, and entrepreneurship (cf. Daniel R. Miller and Guy E. Swanson, *Inner Conflict and Defense* [New York: Henry Holt, 1960]; Magali Sarfatti Larson, *The Rise of Professionalism: A Sociological Analysis* [Berkeley: University of California Press, 1977]). Some 15 percent of the respondents had fathers who were also lawyers. There is only modest evidence that attorneys with lawyer fathers differ in any systematic or substantively significant ways from attorneys with fathers who worked in other middling to high status occupations. See table 6.2.

32. Edward O. Laumann, *Prestige and Association in an Urban Community* (Indianapolis: Bobbs-Merrill, 1966), p. 79.

33. Blau and Duncan, *supra* note 6, p. 39.

34. C. Wright Mills, *The Power Elite* (New York: Oxford University Press, 1956); Donald R. Matthews, *The Social Background of Political Decision-Makers* (New York: Random House, 1954); Morris Janowitz, *The Professional Soldier: A Social and Political Portrait* (New York: Free Press, 1960); Suzanne Keller, *Beyond the Ruling Class: Strategic Elites and Modern Societies* (New York: Random House, 1963), pp. 198–226.

TABLE 6.2

Percentage Distribution of Practitioners with Fathers of Given Socioeconomic Standing
by Type of Law School Attended

Father's Occupational Status	Type of Law School				Total
	Elite	Prestige	Regional	Local	

Panel A: Respondents Aged 30 Through 75 and Practicing Law at Time of Interview*

Lawyer	23.5	26.7	10.7	9.3	15.6
	(+7.9)	(+11.1)	(−4.9)	(−6.3)	
Salaried professional, technical,	31.9	26.7	29.8	24.3	27.2
or managerial	(+4.7)	(−0.5)	(+2.6)	(−2.9)	
Self-employed professional,	31.9	25.6	34.5	30.4	30.6
technical, or managerial	(+1.3)	(−5.0)	(+3.9)	(−0.2)	
Occupation of lower	12.6	21.1	25.0	36.0	26.7
socioeconomic status	(−14.1)	(−5.6)	(−1.7)	(+9.3)	
Total	99.9	100.1	100.0	100.0	100.1
	(n = 119)	(n = 90)	(n = 84)	(n = 247)	(n = 540)

Panel B: Respondents Who Started Practice Before 1960**

Lawyer	25.8	31.1	5.9	6.0	15.2
	(+10.6)	(+15.9)	(−9.3)	(−9.2)	
Salaried professional, technical,	25.8	24.4	29.4	24.1	25.3
or managerial	(+0.5)	(−0.9)	(+4.1)	(−1.2)	
Self-employed professional,	32.3	20.0	32.4	25.9	27.2
technical, or managerial	(+5.1)	(−7.2)	(+5.2)	(−1.3)	
Occupation of lower	16.1	24.4	32.4	44.0	32.3
socioeconomic status	(−16.2)	(−7.9)	(+0.1)	(+11.7)	
Total	100.0	99.9	100.1	100.0	100.0
	(n = 62)	(n = 45)	(n = 34)	(n = 116)	(n = 257)

Panel C: Respondents Who Started Practice in or After 1960***

Lawyer	21.1	22.2	14.0	12.2	15.9
	(+5.2)	(+6.3)	(−1.9)	(−3.7)	
Salaried professional, technical,	38.6	28.9	30.0	24.4	29.0
or managerial	(+9.6)	(−0.1)	(+1.0)	(−4.6)	
Self-employed professional,	31.6	31.1	36.0	34.4	33.6
technical, or managerial	(−2.0)	(−2.5)	(+2.4)	(+0.8)	
Occupation of lower	8.8	17.8	20.0	29.0	21.6
socioeconomic status	(−12.8)	(−3.8)	(−1.6)	(+7.4)	
Total	100.1	100.0	100.0	100.0	100.1
	(n = 57)	(n = 45)	(n = 50)	(n = 131)	(n = 283)

NOTES: *Chi-square = 40.75, p < .001. Eta = .252. Numbers in parentheses are the differences between the observed and expected percentages.
**Chi-square = 33.39, p < .001. Eta = .323. Numbers in parentheses are the differences between the observed and expected percentages.
***Chi-square = 14.40, p < .11. Eta = .216. Numbers in parentheses are the differences between the observed and expected percentages.

One interesting pattern discernible in the table is that the effects of social background appear to be concentrated among respondents from lower socioeconomic origins and those whose fathers were lawyers, while the respondents who had self-employed fathers are distributed across the law schools without a pronounced bias in favor of one type of school or another. The self-employed origin group, being representatives of what C. Wright Mills and others call the entrepreneurial "old middle class,"[35] are in somewhat more precarious and generally lower socioeconomic positions than are the salaried group. Being located in the middle reaches of the socioeconomic hierarchy, then, the sons and daughters of the self-employed might be distributed by chance among the different types of law schools because they are, in a sense, equally distant from them all.[36] Status and financial considerations would then be expected to have a stronger and more systematic impact on the school choices of the children of families located at the extremes of the socioeconomic hierarchy.

A further point to be gleaned from table 6.2 is that lawyers are disproportionately recruited from entrepreneurial family origins. (An entrepreneurial family is defined as having a self-employed head of household.) In addition to those whose fathers were lawyers, another thirty percent of our practicing attorneys claim fathers who were self-employed.[37] Although it is difficult to make a precise estimate of the chance likelihood of having a self-employed father because we lack an appropriately defined cross-section survey of the current labor force in metropolitan Chicago, that likelihood surely would not exceed 8 to 12 percent.[38] A number of studies have suggested that entrepreneurial families tend to inculcate in their young a distinctive set of values stressing autonomy, individualism, a desire for freedom from supervision or other forms of social control, and attraction to risk taking. Such values would presumably make the practice of law, at least as it is perceived by outsiders, a quite attractive profession.[39]

35. Mills, *supra* note 34.
36. See Boudon, *supra* note 6.
37. See *supra* note 31.
38. See Laumann, *supra* note 3, p. 76, for an estimate for the Detroit Standard Metropolitan Statistical Area (SMSA).
39. See Daniel R. Miller and Guy E. Swanson, *The Changing American Parent* (New York: John Wiley, 1958); Miller and Swanson, *supra* note 31; Melvin L. Kohn, *Class and Conformity: A Study in Values* (Homewood, Ill.: Dorsey Press, 1969); Laumann, *supra* note 3.

Has the relationship between socioeconomic origins and type of school strengthened or weakened over time? Panels B and C suggest that is has not changed much. The patterns of under- or over-proportional attendance at the different types of law schools by category of socioeconomic origin are highly similar for the pre-1960 and post-1960 cohorts. This absence of change in the impact of socioeconomic origin on law school attended is all the more remarkable in light of the substantial growth in the numbers of lawyers over the postwar period, particularly since 1960. One might have expected that the growth rate in excess of that of the population at large would require changes in the social recruitment of aspiring lawyers to the different types of schools. If the top law schools did not expand their entering classes to keep up with these increasing numbers—and we know that they did not for the most part—then they could exercise even greater care in selecting, on whatever basis, from among the enlarged pool of applicants. A surprising finding is the change in the pattern of recruitment *toward a greater bias* in favor of the higher socioeconomic groups at the expense of the lowest socioeconomic group! Contrary to all the rhetoric in the 1960s about opening the door of opportunity for the neglected and disadvantaged groups in American society, we find in table 6.3 a decline of over 10 percentage points in the numbers of

TABLE 6.3
Percentage Distribution of Practitioners with Fathers of Given Socioeconomic Standing by Cohort of Entry

	Cohort of Entry		
Father's Occupational Status	*Pre-1960*	*Post-1960*	*Total*
Lawyer	15.3	15.8	15.6
Salaried professional, technical, or managerial	24.9	28.9	27.0
Self-employed professional, technical, or managerial	27.6	33.5	30.6
Occupations of lower socioeconomic status	32.2	21.8	26.8
Total	100.0	100.0	100.0
	(n = 261)	(n = 284)	(n = 545)

NOTE: Included in this table are lawyers aged 30 through 75 who were engaged in the practice of law at the time of the survey. Chi-square = 7.786, p < .06.

persons from lower socioeconomic origins in the greatly expanded post-1960 cohorts. This decline represents more than a 33 percent decrease in the proportion of lawyers from the working and lower middle classes in the cohort entering practice in the socially conscious 1960s and early 1970s.[40] It is also true, however, that there has been a continuing upward generational shift in the average socioeconomic status of the labor force over time. That is, changes in the occupational composition of the labor force over the past several generations have included a dramatic expansion of the numbers of persons employed in the higher status managerial, technical, and professional jobs and a sharp relative decline in the numbers of persons holding lower status unskilled and semiskilled manual jobs.[41] The effect of these shifts within the labor force is, of course, to increase the likelihood that lawyers in the post-1960 cohort will report fathers who were of higher socioeconomic status than were the fathers of the pre-1960 cohort. The available data do not permit us to assess the extent to which the downward shift in recruitment of lawyers from humbler origins arises from generational shifts in the composition of the labor force—sometimes called "structural mobility"—or from changes in the social selectivity of recruitment.

---

40. How can this recent decline in recruitment from the working class be explained? One possible explanation would first point to the declining financial returns to investment in additional years of schooling that began in the early 1960s as a result of the rapidly burgeoning labor supply due to the postwar baby boom coming to maturity. A declining marginal return on schooling would be expected to affect more adversely the schooling plans of the less financially well off. It might have less effect on the middle and upper classes because of status-linked differences in the relative burdens of education and in the evaluations of the nonfinancial, intrinsic rewards of higher education per se. Studies of middle-class youth and adults have repeatedly found that they value the nonincome returns of higher status, intrinsically gratifying occupations more highly than do working-class persons. See Morris Rosenberg, *Occupations and Values* (Glencoe, Ill.: Free Press, 1957); Jeylan Mortimer, "Family Background and College Influences upon Occupational Value Orientations and the Career Decision" (Ph.D. diss., University of Michigan, 1972); Kohn, *supra* note 39. One might also suspect that the social advantages conferred on those coming from higher status family backgrounds, such as the opportunities to learn social skills of considerable relevance to the successful performance of lawyerly roles, might give them a significant competitive edge over persons from lower socioeconomic backgrounds. This consistent advantage of persons from higher status backgrounds would tend toward the systematic displacement of the less well-endowed competitors.

41. See Blau and Duncan, *supra* note 6, esp. chapter 3; Evans and Laumann, *supra* note 15.

Type of School Attended and Career Placement

The first full-time jobs held by many lawyers after graduation from law school did not require legal training. Some lawyers, for example, found themselves in active military service as officers assigned to nonlegal activities; others worked for banks or real estate offices for a time to support themselves while they prepared for the bar examination that is a precondition of the practice of law in Illinois. To reduce the types of jobs to manageable numbers and to identify homogeneous categories of jobs with relatively well-known content and character, we shall exclude these nonlegal, essentially interim, jobs from further consideration in the following discussion. But we may note in passing that such interim jobs are far more likely to be held by the graduates of local law schools, many of whom worked full time during their law school training. In addition, we do not include in these analyses jobs as clerks for federal judges, even though these are obviously positions requiring legal training. We have two reasons: first, judicial clerkships are usually held for a fixed duration (a year or two); and second, they are explicitly intended as an advanced form of legal apprenticeship. In any event, clerkships are relatively rare and figure more prominently in the career trajectories of law professors than they do for practicing attorneys.

Table 6.4, relating type of law school to practice location of the first major legal job, can be regarded as describing the feeder roles that the different law schools play for different practice settings.[42] It is apparent from the table that the type of law school has a strong tendency to channel graduates to distinct practice contexts. Most striking is the role that elite law schools play in stocking the largest law firms and that the local law schools play in producing solo practitioners. The regional schools have a disproportionate tendency to send their graduates to the offices of corporation house counsel, while government agencies and medium and small firms appear to recruit without partiality from all four types of schools. The sug-

42. We did not include panels for the pre- and post-1960s entering cohorts in table 6.4 because each manifests essentially an identical structure to that observed for the sample as a whole. If anything, there are even signs of a slight accentuation of the feeder pattern of elite law school to large firm and local law school to solo practice in the post-1960 cohort. This would suggest that these supply and demand relations have been quite stable over time and are unlikely to attenuate at least for the forseeable future.

gestion of undifferentiated recruitment by government agencies is quite misleading, however. If we distinguish among the levels of government agencies, we find that local law schools send their graduates primarily to local or state government agencies, such as the office of the state's attorney, while elite and prestige schools are more likely to send their graduates to federal agencies. Thus, the matching of the supply and demand hierarchies by their respective prestige orders is simply masked for government employment taken as a whole and, probably to a lesser extent, for house counsel as well. If we had information sufficient to distinguish the prestige differences among corporations, we would expect to find a similar differentiation in placement in house counsel positions. The principal conclusion to be drawn from table 6.4, therefore, is that there is a rather strict and precise correspondence between the prestige hierarchies of the suppliers of trained personnel (i.e., the law schools) and of the buyers (the employers or employment context).

First Major Legal Job and Current Job

If one's starting position in a legal career had little impact on determining one's ultimate destination, then the sort of law school that

TABLE 6.4

Percentage Distribution of Practitioners from Given Type of Law School by Type of Practice

	Type of Practice						
ype of Law School Attended	Large (30+)	Size of Law Firm Medium (10 to 29)	Small (Less than 10)	Government	House Counsel	Solo	Total
lite	31.4 (+17.2)	9.9 (+1.8)	28.1 (−2.0)	10.7 (−3.3)	12.4 (−2.3)	7.4 (−11.6)	99.9 (n = 121)
restige	21.9 (+7.7)	11.5 (+3.4)	27.1 (−3.0)	14.6 (+0.6)	13.5 (−1.2)	11.5 (−7.5)	100.1 (n = 96)
egional	17.4 (+3.2)	8.1 (0.0)	30.2 (+0.1)	11.6 (−2.4)	19.8 (+5.1)	12.8 (−6.2)	99.9 (n = 75)
ocal	2.0 (−12.2)	5.9 (−2.2)	32.2 (+2.1)	16.1 (+2.1)	14.5 (−0.2)	29.9 (+10.9)	100.6 (n = 255)
Total	14.2	8.1	30.1	14.0	14.7	19.0	100.1 (n = 558)

NOTE: Included in this table are lawyers aged 30 through 75 who were engaged in the practice of law at the me of the survey. Chi-square = 92.9, p < .005, Eta = .353. Numbers in parentheses are the differences between e observed and expected percentages.

one attended would not make such a great difference—the law schools would not be the central allocating institutions for the legal profession as a whole.[43] We therefore turn now to an examination of the degree of persistence of personnel in given starting positions over the course of their careers. Of course, the degree of stability in career trajectories is heavily dependent on how narrowly or broadly the investigator defines the set of status categories across which mobility is to be recognized. Quite obviously, every job switch an individual attorney might make does not denote a major change of social location from the point of view of the profession as a whole. For purposes of describing the general flow of personnel among the various types of practice, therefore, we will not treat a move from associate to partner in the same firm or even from partner in one large firm to another as a significant status move, however important it may be for the individual involved. Thus table 6.5 understates the amount of *job* mobility at the level of individual careers, but it should capture the more substantively significant features of movement among the most important practice settings.

The main diagonal cell entries in Panel A of table 6.5 (demarcated by boxes around them to facilitate their identification) demonstrate quite dramatically the high levels of retention of personnel within each major status category. The fact that the practice settings strikingly differ among themselves with respect to their levels of retention is also obvious, however. By far the most stable practice setting, as measured by this criterion, is large firm practice. Some 78 percent of those who began their careers in a large firm remained in one. At the other extreme, only a third of those who started with government agencies still worked for a government agency at the time of our survey.[44] Overall, 54 percent of the 559 lawyers included in Panel A stayed in the category of practice with which they started (however many job changes may have occurred within the category).

But what can we say about those who do leave their starting status? Are there characteristic two-step moves to be detected in the table? And are there status transitions that are avoided—that is, that

43. See Ivar E. Berg, *Education and Jobs: The Great Training Robbery* (New York: Praeger, 1970); Randall Collins, "Functional and Conflict Theories of Educational Stratification," *American Sociological Review* 36 (1971): 1002–19.

44. Do not forget, of course, that some attorneys who are currently in a given status may have previously entered another status only to return to the category from which they started.

194

TABLE 6.5
Transition Likelihood from Type of Practice of First Major Legal Job to Current Type of Practice

Type of Practice as First Job	Current Type of Practice						
	Large (30+)	Size of Law Firm Medium (10 to 29)	Small (Less than 10)	Government	House Counsel	Solo	Total

Panel A: All Practitioners Between 30 and 75 Years Old

Large firm	77.9	5.2	6.5	0.0	7.8	2.6	100.0
	(+61.4)	(−5.9)	(−20.7)	(−8.6)	(−6.5)	(−19.8)	(n = 77)
Medium firm	6.5	63.0	13.0	0.0	15.2	2.2	99.9
	(−10.0)	(+51.9)	(−14.2)	(−8.6)	(+0.9)	(−20.2)	(n = 46)
Small firm	3.6	5.4	53.3	6.0	8.4	23.4	100.1
	(−12.9)	(−5.7)	(+26.1)	(−2.6)	(−5.9)	(+1.0)	(n = 167)
Government	19.5	6.5	19.5	32.5	6.5	15.6	100.1
	(+3.0)	(−4.6)	(−7.7)	(+23.9)	(−7.8)	(−6.8)	(n = 77)
House counsel	6.1	13.4	19.5	2.4	47.6	11.0	100.0
	(−10.4)	(+2.3)	(−7.7)	(−6.2)	(+33.3)	(−11.4)	(n = 82)
Solo	2.7	3.6	19.1	10.0	8.2	56.4	100.0
	(−13.8)	(−7.5)	(−8.1)	(+1.4)	(−6.1)	(+34.0)	(n = 110)
Total	16.5	11.1	27.2	8.6	14.3	22.4	100.1
							(n = 559)

Chi-square = 632.7, p < .005. Eta = .564.

Panel B: Practitioners Starting Their Practice Before 1960

Large firm	72.0	8.0	4.0	0.0	8.0	8.0	100.0
	(+59.5)	(−3.0)	(−20.2)	(−6.4)	(−7.2)	(−22.7)	(n = 25)
Medium firm	6.3	62.5	6.3	0.0	18.8	6.3	100.2
	(−6.2)	(+51.5)	(−17.9)	(−6.4)	(+3.6)	(−24.4)	(n = 16)
Small firm	4.4	6.7	43.3	5.6	12.2	27.8	100.0
	(−8.1)	(−4.3)	(+19.1)	(−0.8)	(−3.0)	(−2.9)	(n = 90)
Government	20.0	0.0	24.0	32.0	8.0	16.0	100.0
	(+7.5)	(−11.0)	(−0.2)	(+25.6)	(−7.2)	(−14.7)	(n = 25)
House counsel	8.6	20.0	8.6	0.0	45.7	17.1	100.0
	(−3.9)	(+9.0)	(−15.6)	(−6.4)	(+30.5)	(−13.6)	(n = 35)
Solo	2.7	5.5	19.2	5.5	8.2	58.9	100.0
	(−9.8)	(−5.5)	(−5.0)	(−0.9)	(−7.0)	(+28.2)	(n = 73)
Total	12.5	11.0	24.2	6.4	15.2	30.7	100.0
							(n = 264)

Chi-square = 242.1, p < .005. Eta = .481.

Panel C: Practitioners Starting Their Practice in or After 1960

Large firm	80.8	3.8	7.7	0.0	7.7	0.0	100.0
	(+60.8)	(−7.4)	(−22.1)	(−10.5)	(−5.9)	(−14.9)	(n = 52)
Medium firm	6.7	63.3	16.7	0.0	13.3	0.0	100.0
	(−13.3)	(+52.1)	(−13.1)	(−10.5)	(−0.3)	(−14.9)	(n = 30)
Small firm	2.6	3.9	64.9	6.5	3.9	18.2	100.0
	(−17.4)	(−7.3)	(+35.1)	(−4.0)	(−9.7)	(+3.3)	(n = 77)
Government	19.2	9.6	17.3	32.7	5.8	15.4	100.0
	(−0.8)	(−1.6)	(−12.5)	(+22.2)	(−7.8)	(+0.5)	(n = 52)
House counsel	4.3	8.5	27.7	4.3	48.9	6.4	100.1
	(−15.7)	(−2.7)	(−2.1)	(−6.2)	(+35.3)	(−8.5)	(n = 47)
Solo	2.7	0.0	18.9	18.9	8.1	51.4	100.0
	(−17.3)	(−11.2)	(−10.9)	(+8.4)	(−5.5)	(+36.5)	(n = 37)
Total	20.0	11.2	29.8	10.5	13.6	14.9	100.0
							(n = 295)

Chi-square = 391.2, p < .005. Eta = .612.

NOTE: Included in this table are lawyers aged 30 through 75 who were engaged in the practice of law at the time of this survey. Numbers in parentheses are the differences between the observed and expected percentages.

are very unlikely to occur? If characteristic status shifts (or the absence of such shifts) can be identified, one would have a powerful indication of the social organization of legal careers. We may begin the identification of unusually high or low incidences of transition by looking at those off-diagonal entries (in parentheses) that reflect large departures from the expected rates. For example, lawyers starting in medium or large firms appear to have no likelihood of moving to a government agency. Similarly, lawyers beginning in solo practice are unlikely to move to large or medium-size firms, if they move at all.

The longer the interval between one's first and current positions, of course, the greater the opportunities for job movements of any sort. This is reflected in Panels B and C of table 6.5—those who entered practice before 1960 have somewhat lower rates of status retention (see the main diagonal entries) than do the younger lawyers in the post-1960 cohort. What is striking, however, is the consistently high retention rates observed in both panels. More than 57 percent of the lawyers entering practice after 1960 remained in the status category in which they started, and this overall retention rate drops only 6 percentage points for those entering practice before 1960. A number of factors combine to make demonstration of the validity of a particular interpretation of the patterns observed in these two panels difficult, if not impossible. There are simply too many things changing at the same time. First, there is the systematic difference between the two cohorts in the average length of time between first and current (1975) jobs. We thus cannot disentangle the aging effect from the cohort effect. While there are somewhat higher retention effects for the post-1960 cohort, members of this cohort, of course, have had less time to move. The presence of simultaneous changes in the organization of the delivery of legal services, cohort effects, and age effects therefore make the interpretation of relative changes in retention rates highly problematic.

But there may be good reason to believe the story that the comparison of the two panels appear to tell—that the older cohort faced a somewhat less crystallized or stable status structure than the newcomers have faced and will face in the future. Such an interpretation, tempting as it is and though it is consistent with the data, is clearly not the only one possible because of the complete confounding of age and cohort effects. Lending credence to the hypothesis of an increase in the rigidity of lawyers' career lines over time, however, is the well-documented fact of the great growth in demand for legal services by corporate clients (whether governmental or private) relative to the more moderate growth in the demand for legal services by individuals over the past several decades. In response to these changes in the sources of demand, the organization of the delivery of legal services has shifted from the old standby, the solo practitioner, to employment of lawyers in larger and larger law firms, government agencies, and corporate legal offices. These organizational forms for the delivery of legal services more approximate the corporate or bureaucratic mode of organizational structure than do the solo practitioner, small firm, or even medium-sized partnership that once dominated legal practice. We must await data on subsequent cohorts of lawyers to test the hypothesis's implication for the organization of legal careers.

If the hypothesis of increasing rigidity of career lines is provisionally accepted as true, however, it has several important implications for the individual lawyer, the profession as a whole, and the larger society. First, legal careers would be increasingly experienced as orderly and predictable, much as careers in governmental or corporate hierarchies are expected to be. This change would represent a departure from the model of a highly competitive metropolitan bar where individual lawyers were thought more likely to have a variety of experiences during their careers. And not only would there be fewer individuals in the future who had experienced widely divergent practice settings in their personal careers, but those who had such histories would be more likely to be labeled as failures when they were judged against the solidifying standard of an orderly career line. Second, the law schools would play more important roles in allocating individuals to distinctive career trajectories because where you start would increasingly determine where you finish. Competition for the limited pool of places in the elite and prestige institutions would permit them to exercise ever more selectivity in their admission standards and thus serve to reinforce, if not enhance, the significance of graduation from such schools as the certification of exceptional ability for demanding legal work and thus of fitness for admission to the more desirable forms of practice. To the extent that these schools continued their dominant feeder role to the corporate bar, one might anticipate an even greater skewing of the distribution of talent.

More generally, what do our findings tell us about the social organization of the profession as a whole? Suppose we regard the arrangement of the rows and columns in table 6.5 as being ordered so that at each end (that is, the first and last column and top and bottom row) we find the rival *core* practice settings, large firm versus solo practice, forming the central institutional foci of the corporate and private bar, respectively, with the other practice settings located between them, reflecting their intermediary functions. These other types of practice may be either essentially *transit* stations that lead to positions in one or the other bar by affording opportunities for exposure to the relevant clientele or for useful experience (e.g., being a state's attorney is excellent preparation for a solo practice in criminal defense), or they may be *repositories* for those who fail to make it according to the criteria of the rival centers. In short, the polarization of the profession into socially segregated and highly distinctive subsystems of legal effort would become progressively more complete and unequal as the social biographies of the participants in the two sectors themselves became more distinctive.

Conclusion: Survival in First Jobs

Earlier in this chapter we dealt with the general patterns of first job retention by age, but we may conclude and summarize these analyses by giving first jobs more detailed attention. We focus here on the rates of transition out of first jobs within the first five years of practice. Who stays, who leaves, and when? The technique used to address these questions is known as survival, or life table, analysis. Survival analysis takes transition rates or probabilities of events in time and systematically sequences and cumulates them. By so doing, it produces an image of the flows. Because of the small sample size, we are using only a five-year duration, but we hope that future research on larger samples will permit extension of the analysis to longer time spans.

The information we present in the following figures is the cumulative proportion surviving to an exact point in time (known to demographers as the l_x function). The proportion of those starting first jobs is taken to be 1.0, and the transition probabilities systematically reduce the proportion "surviving." The figures below graph the fraction of all starters who are still in their first jobs at the end of the first year, second year, and so on.

We are particularly interested in comparing the effects of certain status attributes of lawyers on the relative rates of exit from first jobs. The underlying assumption is that a person's relative chance of survival in his starting job is positively associated with his competitive advantages for subsequent career advancement. At least short-term stability in a starting position, we argue, should facilitate the acquisition and consolidation of critical practical learning experiences and the development of useful linkages with colleagues and clients. In contrast, too rapid job turnover is usually disruptive and disorienting to the individual both personally and professionally. Insecurities and uncertainties are generally associated with job changes, and these uncertainties may be likely to have particularly adverse impacts at the start of careers. On these grounds, we shall regard a high rate of exit in a given status category as reflecting the relative vulnerability of persons in that status. Statuses characterized by poor survival performances will probably be disvalued by the profession as a whole.

Figure 6.3 presents the five-year survival functions for first major legal jobs in each of five practice contexts. Panel A suggests that large law firms afford the most stable starting positions in the critical first three years; more than 63 percent of those who start in such firms are still there after three years of practice. In contrast, in medium-sized firms only one-quarter of their starters are still there after three years of practice. Solo practice and employment by government or corporations have very similarly shaped curves that are intermediate in stability between these two extremes.

Panel B shows that there has been a historical transformation in the relative stability of individual positions within the two core practice settings, large law firm versus solo. While the post-1960 cohort experienced greatly enhanced stability in large firm positions through the first three years of practice when compared to the pre-1960 cohort, there was a greatly accelerated exit rate in the fourth year so that by the fifth year only 20 percent remained, falling well below the survival rate of the pre-1960 group in their fifth year of practice. On the other hand, solo practice in the post-1960 cohort shows a dramatic general decline after the second year. Panel B thus provides evidence of generally increased instability of first jobs in the post-1960 cohort when compared to the pre-1960 cohort. On its face, this may appear to be inconsistent with the hypothesis of increasing rigidity of career lines among the younger cohort, but when the data presented in figure 6.3 is considered in the light of that in table 6.5, it seems that though the younger cohort may change jobs more often, they do not change status categories. Thus, the younger cohort may be changing only from one large law firm to another.

Figure 6.4 displays the survival functions for first major legal jobs by the four types of law schools. A provocative finding here is that the four types of law schools confer no appreciable differential survival advantage for the first two years of practice, but then begin to diverge. The elite and the local schools provide greater stability than do the prestige and regional law schools in the last three years. These patterns are probably to be explained by the feeder roles that the different sorts of law schools play in placing lawyers in differ-

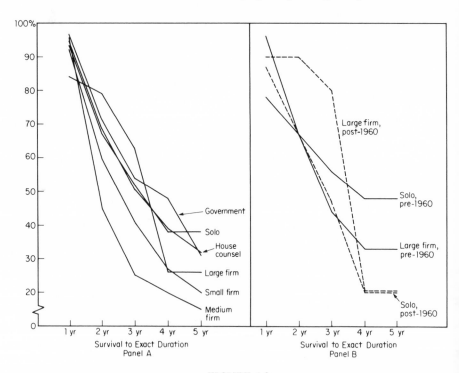

FIGURE 6.3

Five-year Survival Functions for First Major Legal Jobs in Each Practice Context, for Practitioners 30 to 69 Years of Age

ent practice contexts. That is, the elite and local schools are at the respective extremes of the hierarchy, and they are the types that are most clearly differentiated in their roles as suppliers of personnel to the two most extreme core practice settings, large firm and solo practice, respectively. Thus, these two types of schools may be seen as providing the sorts of persons who are "best suited" to the two cores of the bar. Panel B again documents the existence of a cohort effect. The post-1960 cohort experiences greater instability of tenure. But, again, these job changes apparently do not represent transitions across the categories of practice settings but rather are largely movements within the same category.

For one final look at survival in the early years of practice, we shall examine the simultaneous impact of socioeconomic and ethnoreligious group origins on stability in first jobs. Figure 6.5 has two panels, the first of which shows the survival functions for members of the various ethnoreligious groups whose fathers held

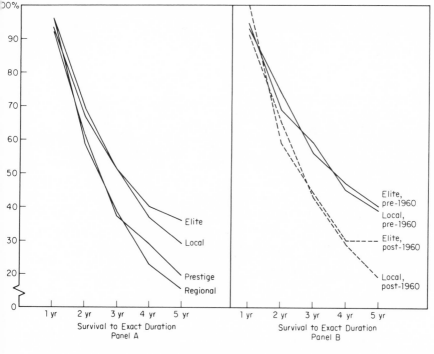

FIGURE 6.4

Five-year Survival Functions for First Major Legal Jobs by Type of Law School Attended, for Practitioners 30 to 69 Years of Age

salaried professional, technical, and managerial positions. The second shows the same thing for the sons and daughters of working-class fathers. In Panel A, one can readily discern the relative advantage of Protestants (Types I and II) and nonidentifiers in stability of first jobs, at least for the first three to four years of practice, when compared to two of the Catholic groups (the numbers of southern and eastern European Catholics in this socioeconomic category are insufficient for analysis) and the two Jewish groups. Orthodox and Conservative Jews from middle-class backgrounds quite obviously fare the worst of the groups represented in the figure. The relatively greater stability of the Protestant groups in first jobs may derive from the fact that they are disproportionately likely to go to the elite law schools and, in turn, to be placed in large law firms, which we already know have higher stability of tenure in the first few years of practice. While it is true that Orthodox and Conservative Jews are somewhat more likely to attend local law schools and

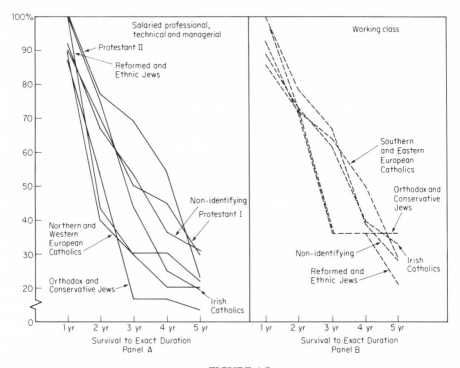

FIGURE 6.5

Five-year Survival Functions for First Major Legal Jobs by Ethnoreligious Group and Socioeconomic Status Origins

much more likely to enter solo practice (which is associated with higher exit rates), we have insufficient evidence in hand (due to insufficient numbers of cases) to say that these two intervening variables wholly explain their survival patterns. In short, their instability in first jobs may be accentuated by the effects of discriminatory hiring and promotion practices, particularly in the large law firms.

We should not assume, however, that differences in Jewish attorneys' participation in different sorts of practice settings is entirely to be explained by discriminatory practices of the employing organizations. Some self-selection may be involved as well. Other than the analysis presented in chapter 5 (see p. 159–60), we have no way of assessing the relative weights of self-selection and discrimination in accounting for the observed results. But we do know that non-Jewish attorneys with self-employed fathers are disproportionately likely to enter solo practice—in this sense, carrying on an entrepreneurial family tradition. There is, thus, reason to think that some practice settings may have particularly positive attractions to prospective entrants because of a personal preference to be one's own boss, a desire to avoid the possibility of being rejected (a form of anticipatory avoidance of possible discrimination), or family pressure to follow in one's father's footsteps.

Have there been changes over time in the distribution of Jewish lawyers across the various practice settings? We pursued several analytic strategies to examine this issue and found convergence around the general proposition that there are some modest differences in the distributions among three birth cohorts. But for each of the three age groups it is readily apparent that Jewish practitioners are overrepresented in solo and small firm practices (see table 6.6, cols. 3, 6, and 9, p. 205) and underrepresented in large firm and corporate house counsel practice settings. In fact, the indexes of dissimilarity between the two percentage distributions in each age cohort indicate that at least one in four Jewish practitioners would have to be redistributed in order to approximate the distribution of the non-Jewish practitioners across the practice settings. The group aged 34 to 45 shows an even more dramatic discrepancy: some 44 percent of the Jewish practitioners would have to be redistributed to approximate the non-Jewish group's distribution. Notice that there is some evidence for a secular decline in the tendency of Jewish attorneys to be in solo practice (a decline from an overrepresentation of 14 percentage points in the "46 years and over" age cohort to an overrepresentation of only 6 percentage points in the youngest group). This decline, however, loses much of its significance when one recalls that there has also been a sharp overall secular decline in the proportion of practitioners in solo practice—that is, the percentage difference cannot be so large in the younger group because the percentage of solo practitioners is, itself, so much smaller in that group. The relative underrepresentation of Jewish lawyers in large firm practice remains remarkably stable across the three age cohorts, and there is some indication of an increase in overrepresentation of Jewish practitioners in small firm practice. We cannot explain the unusually high overrepresentation (34 percentage points) for small firm practice among Jewish lawyers 34 to 45 years of age. Whether this is an idiosyncratic result due in part to sampling error or is a real cohort effect is hard to say. (See chapter 4, note 49.)

Referring back to Panel B of figure 6.5, depicting the survival functions of members of the various ethnoreligious groups who had working-class fathers, we see that the Catholic groups and nonidentifiers have essentially similar curves at approximately the same levels of survival, while the two Jewish groups again reflect greater job instability after the second year of practice. Noteworthy here, however, is the fact that the working-class Catholic groups generally have much *more stable* tenure over the first five years than the middle-class Catholic groups in Panel A. This is also true for the Jewish groups—that is, Jewish attorneys of working-class origin have, overall, greater stability of job tenure than their middle-class coreligionists. How can we account for such counter-intuitive results? One speculation might rest on the notion that the persons of working-class origin who manage to survive all the hurdles and barriers to their entry into a high status profession may have unusually great talent and capabilities, making them especially good at their jobs and thus more likely to succeed than those whose paths to entry into the profession have been smoothed by the social and financial advantages of their families. Alternatively, one might argue that attorneys from working-class backgrounds tend to pick, or are relegated to, the more secure salaried jobs offered by corporations or government agencies or that they are more likely to enter solo practice, where they remain. Despite the romantic appeal of Horatio Alger stories, we suspect that the second explanation is more on target.

TABLE 6.6

Percentage Distributions of Jewish and Non-Jewish Practitioners Across Practice Settings, by Age

Practice Setting	46 and Older			Age 34 to 45			33 and Younger		
	(1) Jewish	(2) Non-Jewish	(3) [(1)–(2)]	(4) Jewish	(5) Non-Jewish	(6) [(4)–(5)]	(7) Jewish	(8) Non-Jewish	(9) [(7)–(8)]
Solo	43	29	+14	26	16	+10	12	6	+ 6
Small firm	29	20	+ 9	53	19	+34	32	19	+13
Medium firm	5	10	– 5	4	13	– 9	13	10	+ 3
Large firm	5	15	–10	9	22	–13	19	31	–12
Government	9	7	+ 2	4	13	– 9	15	19	– 4
House counsel	9	19	–10	4	17	–13	9	16	– 7
Total	100	100		100	100		100	101	
Jews as % of age group	30			33			38		
Index of dissimilarity			.25			.44			.22
Total N of age group	(78)	(182)	—	(74)	(153)	—	(75)	(121)	—

In sum, lawyers' careers appear to follow distinctive, highly interpretable patterns. The two polar or "core" types of careers center, on the one hand, around practice in large firms serving corporate clients and, on the other, around solo practice serving individuals and small businesses. Lawyers in these different sorts of careers are recruited from systematically varying ethnoreligious and socioeconomic origins, and they are trained in different strata of law schools. There is some reason to think that these career patterns may be becoming increasingly rigid, and that there may now be less movement across the status categories than there was formerly, but our evidence on this point is unclear, and we are by no means certain that this is the case. If it were the case, it would mean that the allocation of legal talent to the different sorts of clients in the future would probably come to favor corporations at the expense of individual clients even more than it does at present.

Appendix to Chapter 6:
Retention in Selected Professions

This chapter has examined career patterns of Chicago lawyers based on their reported job histories at all stages of their legal careers. As we noted, the sample necessarily is one of "survivors"—of those who were still in the legal profession at the time the sample was drawn. Interpretation of these career patterns, however, turns on the issue of how many of the young lawyers starting out remain in practice for their entire occupational lives. In another profession, aeronautical engineering, for example, a cross-sectional study of the career patterns of its current practitioners would produce a grossly misleading representation of the careers of all those who enter the profession because the vast majority leave, and leave early. Although, as we shall see, this is not the case for the classical professions, particularly law and medicine, there have been remarkably few quantitative empirical assessments of the strength of the tendency of various professions to retain their members.

Accordingly, in order to put the social biographies portrayed in this chapter in broader context, this brief note presents information about the "holding power" of several professions using data drawn from the 1970 U.S. Census.[1] In order to depict the propensity to stay in the professions over the full course of occupational careers, we present survival functions drawn from period-single decrement life tables which were constructed using the age-specific probabilities derived from the census data. The survival function, l_x, gives the number out of a starting cohort of 100,000 who would still be in the profession at each exact age, x, if the rate drawn from the census were to apply over the course of their occupational lives up to age 60. The survival function can also be thought of as giving the proportion of survivors in the profession at given ages. The data we use to derive the survival functions do not follow any one real cohort throughout its career, but the function can be thought of as either an estimate of real cohort survivorship or as a simulation exercise depicting the implications of the given set of rates.

To put the lawyers' survival function in comparative perspective, we have included comparable data for doctors, clergy, university and college teachers, and chemical engineers. As shown in figure 6.6, lawyers are the most likely of those in any of the professions represented to stay in their profession over the full course of the occupational career. Since the graphs for lawyers and doctors are very similar, we are not inclined to make much of their differences. The relatively steep decline for lawyers between the ages of 40 and 45, however, demands attention in future studies. One speculation worthy of examination is that lawyers between the ages of 40 and 45 are at the peaks of their attractiveness to other career alternatives. They may, for example, be especially tempted at this time in their lives to leave the profession for attractive offers in business or to make a full-time commitment to governmental service or politics.

One might expect that professionals either leave early or remain for the duration of their occupational lives, an expectation which would imply a survival curve shaped like a reverse J. This pattern, however, does not hold for any of the groups shown, except very roughly for the clergy. Indeed, rather than a reverse J, a linear function better describes the patterns both for doctors and for lawyers. The linear pattern suggests that the attractions away from practice

1. For a full description of the data set and the rationale for its selection, and a more complete technical description of its methodology, see Mariah D. Evans and Edward O. Laumann, "Professional Commitment: Myth or Reality?" in Donald Treiman and Robert Robinson, eds., *Research in Stratification and Mobility* (Greenwich: JAI Press, 1983).

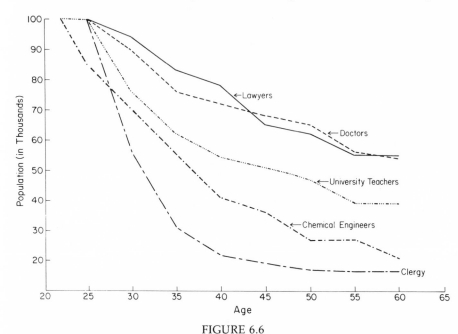

FIGURE 6.6
Survival Functions Depicting Differential Propensity to Remain in Practice for Selected Professions

are fairly uniform over the span of the professional careers of both lawyers and doctors. The nature of these attractions and the kinds of opportunities they represent, however, may well be very different at different ages.

For present purposes, the following observations are probably sufficient: First, lawyers are likely to continue in the practice of law throughout their occupational lives. This means that the cross-sectional sample used to analyze the careers of Chicago lawyers probably produces less biased findings than would be the case for many other professions and semiprofessions. Second, the survival function alerts us to the approximately linear pattern of exits for lawyers and to two potentially important deviations from this pattern: the relatively steep declines between ages 30 and 35 and ages 40 and 45. The first of these steep declines coincides with the "partnership crunch" already discussed and seems likely to be causally related to it, but the causes of the second steep decline are not clear. Compared with some of the other graphs, these declines are relatively modest, but they do suggest the temporal locations of points of special stress in lawyers' careers.

PART IV

Lawyers' Ties: Networks of Association, Organizations, and Political Activities

Chapter 7

NETWORKS OF COLLEGIAL

RELATIONSHIPS

IF THE SOCIAL differences among members of a community are ascribed such salience that they form the basis for a system of stratification, the boundaries among the strata are likely to function as barriers to social mobility. Some mobility across the strata will, of course, occur—sometimes through fortuity, more usually by conspicuous effort or a conspicuous lack of it[1]—but stratification tends to inhibit all varieties of personal relationships among occupants of different strata. The geographical image of the boundary may even be taken literally; members of each stratum will be more likely to live and work in proximity to one another than to residents of other strata. While mere social differentiation need not imply social distance, the very idea of stratification suggests that the strata remain separate and hierarchically ordered. The effects of the stratification system upon patterns of personal interaction within the community thus will have implications for the extent of the community's social solidarity, for the extent to which the various groups will see themselves as sharing a common fate, and for the ease with which they might be mobilized to support common positions on issues that concern the community. Too much differentiation may lead to so-

---

1. Christopher Jencks et al., *Who Gets Ahead? The Determinants of Economic Success in America* (New York: Basic Books, 1979).

cial disintegration and an inability to fashion a base for common action.

But there may be reason to expect that a professional community, such as the Chicago bar, would not experience such social disintegration as a consequence of stratification. To the extent that the professionals share an identity as members of one profession, the profession may display social solidarity in spite of its internal differentiation and perhaps even in spite of substantial internal variation in general social standing. Lawyers may be thought to have undergone a common socialization experience in law school and thus to have developed this sense of common identity at the outset of their careers (the assumption being that the schools follow pretty much a standard model regardless of the prestige of the school); all lawyers in a given jurisdiction are required to pass the same licensing exam, which requires a standard level of competence in a broad range of the fields of law; and nearly the full spectrum of the profession shares membership in the large, general purpose bar associations that purport to speak for and to some extent to regulate the entire profession. All of these—the law schools, the bar exam, and the bar associations—might then serve as mechanisms of social integration tending to unify the profession, to bridge the barriers created by the profession's internal differentiation along lines of tasks, ethnicity, values, prestige, and clients. All lawyers may also be thought to share a common economic interest in restricting entry into the profession, thus controlling the supply of legal services, or at least to share an interest in limiting the "practice of law" to those who have been admitted to the profession.

To assess the extent to which the profession's mechanisms of social integration have managed to overcome any barriers that may have been created by social stratification, we have examined the networks of friendship and professional association of members of the Chicago bar. We asked all of our respondents to identify several characteristics of each of their three closest friends and three closest professional associates. Those characteristics included sex, age, ethnicity, religion, political preference, occupation, type of practice of professional colleagues, frequency of association with colleagues, and length of personal acquaintance. In this chapter, we present our analysis of the patterns of personal interaction among Chicago lawyers, with special attention to the variables that might create social barriers based in stratification. In the following chapters, we exam-

ine the relationships among lawyers in the activities of the organized bar (chap. 8) and the patterns of personal acquaintance with a
selected list of prominent or "notable" Chicago lawyers (chap. 9).

Field Self-Selection

The analysis presented in part II of this book used the field of law
as the unit of analysis. Before analyzing the overall patterns of colleague choice, therefore, we would do well to examine the tendency
to choose as colleagues those who are in one's own field of practice.
The assumption that field self-selection does exist is one of the un-
derpinnings of that earlier analysis.[2] If we were to find no evidence
that lawyers tend to overselect colleagues from their own fields,
that would suggest that the field categories we defined do not organize lawyers' work and are not differentiated by salient social characteristics. Because we know that a field's practitioners tend to work
in the same sorts of practice settings, implying proximity, some bias
toward field self-selection is to be expected. The tendency to select
colleagues in one's own field might reach only a modest level, however, if the practitioners within each field were socially heterogeneous, their conflicting attractions and repulsions thus tending to
offset one another. Low self-selection by field might also occur if
the fields possessed internal social homogeneity but did not create
opportunities or incentives for the formation of social relations
among their practitioners. If we find only random collegial association across the fields, however, such a finding would imply that we
were in error in postulating the fields as mechanisms for the generation of social distance, as bases of structural differentiation within
the legal profession. Consequently, our analyses along these lines
would have been unwarranted. We shall see that this is not the case.

Because of the central position of field self-selection in our argument, we thought it necessary to evaluate the use of several alternative possible measures, none of which was wholly satisfactory. The
problem is that each measure highlights an interesting aspect of
self-selection only at the expense of another of equal interest; no
single indicator is optimal for all purposes that we have in mind. In

2. Edward O. Laumann and Franz U. Pappi, *Networks of Collective Action: A Perspective on Community Influence Systems* (New York: Academic Press, 1976), pp. 39–52.

an appendix to this chapter, we discuss the calculation of each of these various measures in detail and note some of their advantages and disadvantages. But some sense of the degree of field self-selection can be obtained here by inspecting the relative sizes of the numbers in columns 4 through 6 of table 7.1.

All three of the indicators of self-selection presented in the table, whatever their individual strengths and weaknesses, indicate that the fields we identified all manifest some systematic bias toward selecting colleagues from within, but that there is also considerable variability in the strength of this tendency from field to field. In general, the fields showing the strongest tendencies toward self-selection are more specialized in the sense that they command greater proportions of the professional time of their practitioners (see Table 2.3, p. 48) and more homogeneous in the social attributes of their incumbents.[3] In fact, we observe a substantial correlation between the order of the fields with respect to their inbreeding biases and their rank order by the percentages of their practitioners who devote a majority of their time to the fields.[4] Given the relative monopoly of attention that certain fields demand of their practitioners, it should come as no surprise that specialists find their fellow specialists especially attractive for collegial relationships. The very organization of the specialist's work tends to constrain his opportunities for professional contacts. Being more completely and continuously immersed in the field, such a person is likely to formulate his professional identity more self-consciously in terms of his field of practice and is thus likely to find close interaction with like-minded colleagues more rewarding, both instrumentally and subjectively.

Colleague Choice Across Fields

Having established that our fields of practice manifest definite, albeit varying, tendencies toward self-selection and having suggested some reasons why this might be so, we may turn to a consideration

3. See appendix B for a detailed characterization of the social attributes of practitioners in the various fields.
4. The correlation is .58, $P < .01$, excluding the "generalist" field. The percentage of practitioners who give each field a majority of their time can be found in chapter 2, table 2.3.

TABLE 7.1
Percentage Distribution for Fields of Law of Respondents and Their Professional Colleagues, and Measures of Field Self-Selection

Field of Law	No. of Practitioners (1)	Percentage of Respondents[a] (2)	Percentage of Prof. Colleagues[b] (3)	Percentage of Field Self-selection[c] (4)	Index of Association[d] (5)	Inbreeding Bias[e] (6)
Patents	35	5	4	62	15.2	.60
Business litigation	23	3	2	53	32.5	.52
Criminal prosecution	14	2	2	53	24.0	.51
Public utilities	14	2	2	49	24.5	.48
Criminal defense	33	5	6	43	7.5	.40
Antitrust (plaintiffs)	6	1	0.4	39	97.9	.39
Personal tax	36	5	5	37	7.1	.33
Securities	15	2	2	34	16.7	.33
Personal injury (plaintiffs)	28	4	5	35	6.8	.31
Commercial	16	2	2	32	12.8	.30
Labor (union)	11	2	1	30	29.0	.30
Civil rights	7	1	1	30	40.3	.30
Municipal	11	2	1	29	23.4	.28
General litigation	50	7	11	36	3.1	.27
Business tax	12	2	0.4	25	55.9	.25
Labor (management)	14	2	1	24	28.2	.23
Family	13	2	2	23	14.5	.22
Personal injury (defendant)	23	3	4	24	6.6	.21
General corporate	49	7	12	29	2.5	.20
Divorce	23	3	2	21	9.4	.19
Probate	35	5	5	23	4.5	.19
Banking	21	3	1	18	13.4	.17
Business real estate	22	3	1	17	31.0	.17
Antitrust (defense)	12	2	1	13	12.8	.12
General	100	14	10	20	2.0	.11
Personal real estate	52	7	5	14	2.9	.10
Other	24	3	11	17	1.5	.07
Total	699[f]	99	(2,013)[g]	—	—	—

NOTES: For the computations presented in this table, it was necessary to assign the respondents to a mutually exclusive set of fields. That is, there could be no overlap across the categories; no practitioner could be counted in more than one field. Therefore, we adopted the following rules for assigning practitioners to fields: (1) If the respondent was a self-identified specialist (see appendix A, question A2), we assigned him to the field that he indicated as his specialty. Seventy percent of the respondents had self-reported specialties and could thus be assigned in this manner. (2) If the respondent did not have a self-identified specialty, he was assigned to the field in which he works the largest percentage of his time (see appendix A, question A1). (3) If the respondent could not then be assigned because two or more fields were tied in the allocation of his time, he was assigned to the one of his fields that ranked highest in prestige (see chap. 4).

a. Percentage of respondents unweighted = $N_{\underset{N}{i}}(100)$. The weighted percentage of respondents, $A_{\underset{A}{i}}(100)$, is identical for every row except antitrust defense, where the percentage changed from 2 to 1. We, therefore, report here only the unweighted percentages.

b. Percentage of professional colleagues = $\frac{A_{.j}}{A}(100)$.

c. Percentage of self-selection, i = $\frac{A_{ii}}{A_i}(100)$.

d. Index of association = $\frac{i}{(N_i/N)(100)}$.

e. Inbreeding bias, = $\frac{i/100 - A_{.j}/a_{..}}{1 - A_{.j}/A_{..}}$.

f. Excludes 84 colleagues for whom there was no information on field of practice or who presently occupied nonlegal positions, such as executive officers of corporations.

g. This number is smaller than the 2,097 one would expect (699 × 3) because some respondents named fewer than three colleagues.

of whether lawyers, when they do choose lawyers in fields of practice other than their own, follow any principles of systematic selection in making their "out of field" choices. Collegial relations, because they are voluntarily formed and maintained over time and because they represent an important focus of informal social intercourse as well as instrumental exchange (for example, information transfer and client referrals), can be expected to conform to the principles describing the formation of voluntary social ties more generally. There is much sociological literature on interpersonal attraction and friendship formation,[5] and these studies consistently find that the probability of informal social ties between persons increases with the extent to which they share important social attributes. In summarizing these findings, Laumann argued, "Similarities in status, attitudes, and behavior facilitate the formation of intimate (or consensual) relationships among incumbents of social positions."[6] And conversely, "The more dissimilar two positions are in status, attitudes, beliefs, and behavior of their incumbents, the less likely the formation of intimate (or consensual) relationships and, consequently, the 'farther away' they are from one another in the structure."[7]

A very powerful implication may be drawn from these assertions. If these postulates are of general applicability, then we have the basis for the generation of distance among social positions (in our case, fields of law). The relative proximities of positions (based on the likelihood of practitioners in one field of law choosing colleagues in each of the other fields of law) reflect the underlying social similarities and differences among practitioners in the vari-

---

5. E.g., Otis Dudley Duncan and J. W. Artis, "Some Problems of Stratification Research," *Rural Sociology* 16 (1951): 17–29; Henry W. Riecken and George C. Homans, "Psychological Aspects of Social Structure," in G. Lindzey ed., *Handbook of Social Psychology*, vol. 2 (Reading, Mass.: Addison-Wesley, 1954), pp. 786–832; Robert A. Ellis, "Social Stratification and Social Relations: An Empirical Test of the Disjunctiveness of Social Classes," *American Sociological Review* 22 (1957): 570–78; Morton B. King, Jr., "Socioeconomic Status and Sociometric Choice," *Social Forces* 39 (1961): 199–206; Richard Curtis, "Differential Association and the Stratification of the Urban Community," *Social Forces* 42 (1963): 68–77; Theodore Newcomb, *The Acquaintance Process* (New York: Henry Holt, 1961); W. Lloyd Warner et al., *Social Class in America* (New York: Harper Torch Books, 1960); Edward O. Laumann, *Prestige and Association in an Urban Community* (Indianapolis: Bobbs-Merrill, 1966); Edward O. Laumann, *Bonds of Pluralism: The Form and Substance of Urban Social Networks* (New York: John Wiley, 1973); Laumann and Pappi, *supra* note 2; Lois Marie Verbrugge, "Adult Friendship Contact: Time Constraints and Status-Homogeniety Effects, Detroit and Jülich, West Germany" (Ph.D. diss., University of Michigan, 1974).

6. Laumann, 1973, *supra* note 5, p. 5.

7. Ibid.

ous fields. Whatever social grounds are regarded by lawyers as the appropriate ones for attracting or repulsing collegial ties, they constitute the systematic bias rules that organize the patterning of collegial relations in the profession.

As in our earlier analyses dealing with lawyers' values (chap. 5) and their careers (chap. 6), one can distinguish analytically between two broad types of social attributes that are likely to play roles in channeling choices for collegial ties. On the one hand, there are characteristics of practitioners that are "intrinsic" to their professional work, such as the relative frequencies of their state or federal court appearances or the relative amounts of time they spend in different fields of practice. Obviously, if one lawyer chooses another for regular collegial contacts because he shares a field of practice and thus can be expected to encounter similar work problems or because his expertise complements one's own (e.g., a securities specialist picking an antitrust specialist as a colleague), the basis of the interaction rests self-consciously on a community of interest in pursuing work-related professional goals.

Colleagues, on the other hand, may also be chosen because they share with the chooser a social attribute that is "extrinsic" to their professional work—for example, religious preference, ethnic origin, political viewpoint, or even the law school attended. Such social origin characteristics have little, if any, apparent bearing on their work activities. But colleagues selected in this way may be entrusted with professional confidences because the shared extraprofessional social identities are believed to guarantee common points of view and overlapping social interests, some of which are incidentally relevant to their professional identities. Law school classmates, for example, may have shared an intensive social experience during their legal training, creating ties of mutual loyalty, trust, and personal acquaintance that can be reliably activated in their professional work. It is sometimes said that graduates of certain local law schools, such as Loyola and DePaul, help one another in placement in positions of responsibility in the Regular Democratic Organization and, consequently, in Chicago's City Hall.[8] Lawyers who have a strong attachment to their ethnic origins may draw their clients

---

8. Cf. Mike Royko, *Boss: Richard J. Daley of Chicago* (New York: E. P. Dutton, 1971); Len O'Connor, *Clout: Mayor Daley and His City* (Chicago: Henry Regnery, 1975); Milton L. Rakove, *Don't Make No Waves—Don't Back No Losers: An Insider's Analysis of the Daley Machine* (Bloomington: Indiana University Press, 1975).

from their own ethnic groups, which are often concentrated in identifiable neighborhoods.[9] These lawyers may well find collegial ties to others of the same ethnicity to be highly facilitative for client referrals and sharing of work. Clients may prefer to confide their secrets to a lawyer who shares their ethnicity, to "one of their own," and a lawyer tied to an ethnic-based collegium may have an advantage in gathering information about his clients and their social surroundings. In certain ethnic groups, an outsider would simply not be made privy to such matters.

Sorting out the relative importance of intraprofessional characteristics and social origins in channeling collegial ties is an impossible methodological task, given the data available to us, for two reasons. First, we simply did not ask the respondents to tell us the reasons why they selected specific individuals as colleagues. Rather, the respondents merely described some of their colleagues' social attributes. There are, to be sure, reasons to doubt whether the respondents could have been very articulate about the actual grounds for their collegial choices, which are, after all, the result of a very complex set of (often unconscious) social and psychological processes. Second, there is a high degree of covariation among the two sets of characteristics (see Tables 3.1 and 3.2), which we have already discussed as posing in acute form the technical problem of multicollinearity (see p. 69). Multicollinearity among independent variables makes for unstable, unreliable (or artifactual) estimates of parameters in multiple regression analysis and thus precludes inferences about the relative importance of the effects of different independent variables on colleague choice. We would again stress, however, that the multicollinearity itself reflects an important underlying social reality—namely, the "overdetermination" of the social structural features of the system we are studying. That is, conceptually distinct independent variables appear to collude in guaranteeing a particular structural outcome. Whether one argues that lawyers pick others for collegial ties because of their ethnicity (which incidentally links lawyers in the same field of practice because certain ethnic groups are over- or underrepresented in the field) or because of their fields of practice (which incidentally tend to link ethnic compeers), the structural outcome is the same—a highly differentiated

9. Jerome Carlin, *Lawyers on Their Own: A Study of Individual Practitioners in Chicago* (New Brunswick, N. J.: Rutgers University Press, 1962).

structure of collegial ties that segregates the profession into a number of relatively distinct social circles.[10]

In spite of our inability to specify the relative importance of intrinsic and extrinsic attributes in determining the structure of collegial ties among lawyers, we will offer some speculation about how the patterns of colleague choice across fields have come about. There are a number of alternative ways of estimating the fields' profiles of colleague choices, each way possessing some advantages and disadvantages, but our experience to date with many such strategies indicates that they usually yield comparable results.[11] For purposes of this analysis, we will use the index of dissimilarity[12] to estimate the proximity of each pair of fields. The index of dissimilarity (specifically, the sum of the positive percentage differences between two percentage distributions) contrasts the percentage distribution of a given field's colleagues across the set of possible fields with the colleague distribution of another specified field of practice. It tells us the proportion of persons in one group *or* the other that would have to be redistributed to make identical the two percentage distributions that are being compared. Maximum similarity (i.e., an index of "0") between the two fields (and, therefore, the closest proximity) is reached when they recruit their colleagues in exactly the same proportions from among the twenty-seven fields.

The indices of dissimilarity between each pairing of the twenty-seven fields range from .21 to .85. (The actual matrix of indices is omitted for reasons of space.) The largest index, .85, is found between patents and criminal prosecution, and, unsurprisingly, the index between patents and divorce is also extremely high (.76). In contrast, the indices are quite low between such fields as real estate and generalist (.21), real estate and probate (.30), and corporate and real estate (.35), all fields that lack distinctive cores of full-time specialists and thus attract their practitioners from a variety of other fields. We observed in chapter 2 that the overwhelming majority of

10. Charles Kadushin, "The Friends and Supporters of Psychotherapy: On Social Circles in Urban Life," *American Sociological Review* 31 (1966): 786–802.

11. Compare Laumann, 1966, 1973, *supra* note 5: Peter V. Marsden and Edward O. Laumann, "Collective Action in a Community Elite: Exchange, Influence Resources and Issue Resolution," in Roland J. Liebert and Allen W. Imershein, eds., *Power, Paradigms, and Community Research* (Beverly Hills, Cal.: Sage Publications, 1977), pp. 199–250.

12. Otis Dudley Duncan and Beverly Duncan, "A Methodological Analysis of Segregation Indexes," *American Sociological Review* 20 (1955): 210–17.

the practitioners in these fields devote a smaller proportion of their time to them. The average index in the matrix is .60, reflecting the fact that, on the average, over half of the colleague choices made by a given field of practice would have to be redistributed in order to make that field's choice pattern conform to that of another field of practice. To be sure, a substantial portion of this highly segregated pattern of colleague choice is to be attributed to the relatively high rates of field self-selection (see table 7.1) that we have already discussed.

Beyond noting obvious outliers, simple inspection of the matrix of indices of dissimilarity will not suffice to detect its underlying regularities. Smallest space analysis was designed to help the investigator uncover the underlying structure of such a complex matrix as we have here, with its 351 entries and 61,425 possible paired comparisons of these entries. Using the dissimilarity coefficients as our estimates of the proximities of the fields of practice to one another, smallest space analysis computes a representation of the original proximity matrix in a Euclidean space with the smallest possible number of dimensions that is consistent with some limit on the permissible distortion of the original proximities. The "acceptable" degree of distortion is prespecified, according to an objective criterion.[13] What counts in a Euclidean space are the distances between the points and the fact that these distances remain unchanged under rotation of the axes. It is the latter characteristic of Euclidean space that has an important consequence: the coordinates are completely arbitrary and often will have no substantive meaning. When interpreting such structures, we look not only for undimensional arrangements of points along some axis but also for other configurations of points, such as their arrangements into circles, sectors, or clusters.

An acceptable three-dimensional solution, with a Kruskal's stress of .14, is presented in figure 7.1. By now the placement of the fields with respect to one another should be familiar to the reader (see figs. 2.1, 3.1, and 4.1). That three dimensions are necessary to represent the patterns of colleague selection is consistent with the structure of relationships among the fields on quite other variables, especially the multidimensional structure of judgments of the prestige of the fields within the profession (see pp. 118–32 and 311–14).

13. See Joseph B. Kruskal and Myron Wish, *Multidimensional Scaling* (Beverly Hills, Cal.: Sage Publications, 1978). See also explanation of smallest space analysis in chapter 4.

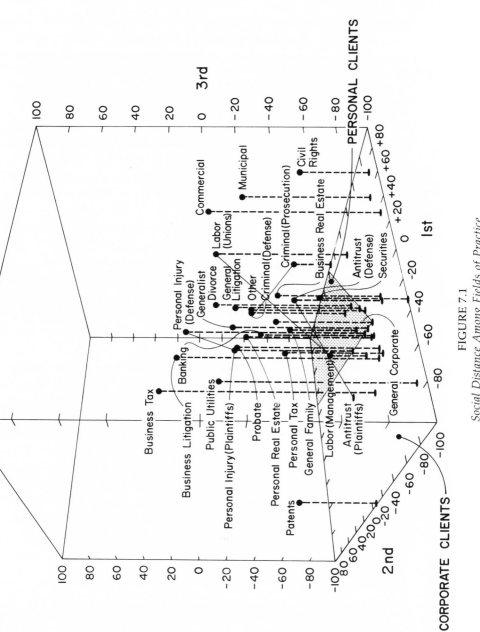

FIGURE 7.1

Social Distance Among Fields of Practice

A useful way to think about the spatial configuration portrayed in figure 7.1 is to visualize a solid V-shaped structure, the inner boundary of which is delineated by the shaded V drawn on the base of the box that encloses the space. The personal client fields tend to be grouped near the point of the V, while the corporate fields are located farther from the V, closer to the "front" of the figure. Fields on the left of the figure generally deal with large business corporations, while those toward the right corner have less prestigious corporate clients, such as small business concerns, labor unions, or state government agencies. Generally, the more highly regarded fields dealing with personal clients, including probate and tax, are located at the intersection of the V. Less highly regarded fields, such as divorce, criminal defense, and personal injury (plaintiff), are toward the back of the space and inside the shaded V.

To facilitate further examination of the picture, we have drawn thin lines between adversarial fields. Note the relatively great social distances between labor unions–labor management and antitrust defendant-plaintiff fields and the relatively closer proximities of personal injury plaintiff-defendant and criminal defendant-prosecution, suggesting that the latter two pairs of adversarial fields have more in common with respect to mutual social attractiveness than do the former two pairs of fields.

Another key feature is its organization into center and peripheral regions.[14] The five fields that fall closest to the centroid of the space[15] are real estate, generalist, general corporate, banking, and "other"—all of which are fields with very low inbreeding biases. In general, the closer the field is to the center, the less specialized its practitioners are in the sense defined in chapter 2—that is, their incumbents spend the major portions of their time in other fields of practice. Conversely, the more peripherally located the field, the more likely are its practitioners to devote the bulk of their professional time to its practice. The degree to which fields have distinctive patterns of colleague choice—that is, the degree to which they associate with or are segregated from other fields—thus corresponds fairly closely to the degree to which the fields demand full-

14. Edward Shils, "Centre and Periphery," in *The Logic of Personal Knowledge: Essays in Honor of Michael Polanyi* (London: Routledge and Kegan Paul, 1961), pp. 117–30.
15. For an explanation of the centroid of the smallest space solution, see chapter 4, note 25.

time commitment from their practitioners. Practitioners in centrally located fields are likely to associate informally with a more heterogeneous set of colleagues (in terms of their fields of practice) and, by inference, are exposed to more diverse opinions about their professional worlds.[16] Studies of the impact on individuals of homogeneously versus heterogeneously constituted informal networks suggest that persons in heterogeneously constituted networks will have far less crystallized and coherent attitudes and beliefs about matters of mutual concern than will persons in homogeneously constituted networks.[17] Moreover, persons active in centrally located fields should be more likely to play integrative or "bridging" roles for the organized bar as a whole because they are much more likely to sustain informal collegial ties with persons in other fields and thus to be known to a wider potential constituency of lawyers.

The Influence of Ethnoreligious and Law School Ties

To round out our picture of the factors involved in channeling lawyers' choices of colleagues, we shall briefly discuss the impact on colleagueship of differences in ethnic and religious background and in the type of law school attended. In the preceding section, we noted that, because of the limitations of the data in hand, we cannot determine the relative effects of these several factors, in conjunction with fields of practice, on colleague choice. We shall thus have to be content with presenting several tables, each reflecting the effect of a factor without regard to the others.

Laumann has demonstrated for a representative cross-sectional sample of native-born white men in Detroit—a city not unlike Chicago in ethnic and religious composition—that ethnicity per se has a substantial impact on friendship choice.[18] This effect, however, is

---

16. Laumann, 1973, *supra* note 5, pp. 83–110.

17. Compare Mark Granovetter, "The Strength of Weak Ties," *American Journal of Sociology* 78 (1973): 1360–80; Mark Granovetter, *Getting a Job: A Study of Contacts and Careers* (Cambridge: Harvard University Press, 1974); Jeremy Boissevain, *Friends of Friends: Networks, Manipulators, and Coalitions* (Oxford: Blackwell, 1974); Carl A. Sheingold, "Social Networks and Voting: The Resurrection of a Research Agenda," *American Sociological Review* 38 (1973): 712–20; Laumann, 1966, 1973, *supra* note 5.

18. Laumann, 1973, *supra* note 5, pp. 42–72, 83–110.

TABLE 7.2
Ethnicity of Respondents, Colleagues, and Friends

Ethnic Groups	% of Respondents	% of Colleagues	% of Friends	Colleagues' Inbreeding Bias	Friends' Inbreeding Bias
Nonwhite	3	3	3	.66	.84
Irish	13	17	16	.30	.39
British (English, Scottish and Welsh)	7	8	8	.12	.13
German	6	7	10	.08	.22
Italian	4	5	5	.15	.33
Polish	2	3	4	.18	.43
Jewish	33	37	34	.56	.70
American	2	10	8	.26	.22
Other western European	1	4	4	.01	.09
Scandinavian	2	3	3	.07	.06
Other eastern and southern European	4	1	2	.05	.11

attenuated for men whose families have been in America for several generations, especially if they are also college graduates. Congruent with Will Herberg's argument about the triple melting pot,[19] Laumann also found that there was continuing, if not enhanced, vitality to the impact of religious differences in channeling friendship choices (when compared to ethnic differences). That is, while people are less inclined than they were formerly to expect their friends to be ethnically akin to themselves, they do appear to require that their friends be drawn from their own broad religious community, be it Protestant, Catholic, or Jewish. Tables 7.2 and 7.3 provide documentation of the operation of these effects among Chicago's lawyers with respect to both friendship selection[20] and colleague choice.

19. Will Herberg, *Protestant, Catholic, Jew,* rev. ed. (Garden City: Doubleday-Anchor, 1955).

20. Respondents were asked the following question (identical in form to the one asked in the Detroit cross-section survey): "Now would you think of the three persons who are your closest friends and whom you see most often. They can be relatives or nonrelatives, as you wish, but excluding a spouse. I'd like to ask you several questions about each, so for convenience could you give me just their first names." We subsequently determined whether any of the friends were also mentioned as one of the three colleagues discussed earlier in the interview. (See appendix A, question A18.) About 36 percent of the sample reported that at least one of their colleagues was regarded as one of their three closest friends. Somewhat less than 3 percent of the sample said that all three of their colleagues were numbered among their three closest friends. Thus the overlap of work and friendship spheres of life occurs only to a moderate extent among lawyers in Chicago.

TABLE 7.3

Religious Preferences of Respondents, Colleagues, and Friends

Religious Groups	% of Respondents	% of Colleagues	% of Friends	Colleagues' Inbreeding Bias	Friends' Inbreeding Bias
Catholic	31	33	33	.42	.57
Jewish	33	37	32	.55	.70
Conservative	13	N.A.	13	N.A.	.76
Liberal	20	N.A.	19	N.A.	.71
Protestant	24	25	26	.35	.46
Congregational	4	2	3	.07	.18
Presbyterian	5	3	3	.08	.21
Episcopal	4	3	2	.12	.16
Methodist	3	1	2	.06	.27
Lutheran	3	2	4	.04	.28
Other Protestant	2	2	3	.16	.32
Protestant, denomination not specified	3	12	9	.20	.19
No religious preference	11	6	8	.09	.19

NOTE: N.A.—Not available.

Two features of the tables are especially noteworthy. First, whether one looks at the individual ethnic groups in table 7.2 or the religious groups in table 7.3, in nearly every instance the inbreeding bias for friends is substantially higher than it is for colleagues. Friendship is a more functionally diffuse relationship than colleagueship, and it typically implies at least on occasion the exchange of intimate information about one's self and one's closest associates. The exchange of such intimacies is facilitated by shared membership in the same ethnic or religious group, which expands and enriches the basis for common normative understandings on matters of personal and social identity—that is, it enhances the ability to anticipate how one's friend is likely to respond to various matters of social and personal behavior. Colleagueship, in contrast, is usually a more mundane, instrumental relationship and thus may not so much require the additional guarantees of a shared normative universe of discourse. To the extent that normative understandings are required for the effective pursuit of professional objectives (as, perhaps, in divorce or criminal defense), however, colleagues may be more likely to be selected with an eye to their cultural origins. Those ethnic and religious groups that are disproportionately represented in fields of practice concerned with personal plight have quite substantial colleagues' inbreeding biases. The inbreeding biases are weakest among the Protestant denominations and the nationalities of northwestern Europe—the so-called WASPs. Since those groups are most overrepresented in the fields of practice that are concerned with big business or corporate clients, our findings may suggest that the legal matters at issue in such a practice less often require supplementary normative understandings.

We thus come to the second feature of interest in these two tables: the extreme variability across the groups with respect to their inbreeding tendencies. Only four ethnic groups manifest strong tendencies toward self-selection: the nonwhites (mostly blacks), the Irish, the Jews, and to a somewhat lesser degree, the Americans (no identified ethnic origin). At the other extreme are the northern European groups, including the British (English, Scots, and Welsh), Germans, and Scandinavians, all of whom have almost no identifiable inbreeding bias regarding either friendships or colleagueship. Italians and Poles have an intermediate level of inbreeding bias— both are groups that are identified in the literature on ethnicity as having retained rather strong cultural identifications.[21] Table 7.3 strongly confirms the Herberg thesis about the triple melting pot— that people tend to associate informally and instrumentally with coreligionists. Observe, for example, how the specific Protestant denominations manifest low inbreeding biases, both for friends and colleagues, but that the inbreeding bias for Protestants as a whole is quite high, though it is still somewhat lower than those for Catholics and Jews.

Two other "extrinsic" attributes expected to play a role in the selection of colleagues and friends are the law school attended and political party affiliation. Law school experience may or may not have lasting impact on the behavior of lawyers,[22] but the relationships formed with classmates during law school and the tendency to favor colleagues from one's own school appear to have remarkable persistence. The top panel of table 7.4 reflects the strength of this impact. Graduates from the highest ranking law schools, as well as graduates from local law schools, seek out "their own kind." If

---

21. Laumann, 1973, *supra* note 5, pp. 42–72, 160–98.
22. Ronald M. Pipkin, "Legal Education: The Consumer's Perspective," 1976 *American Bar Foundation Research Journal* 1161–92, and Frances Zemans and Victor Rosenblum, *The Making of a Public Profession* (Chicago: American Bar Foundation, 1980).

TABLE 7.4

Law School and Political Party Affiliations of Respondents, Colleagues, and Friends

	% of Respondents	% of Colleagues	% of Friends	Colleagues' Inbreeding Bias	Friends' Inbreeding Bias
Law school attended					
Top (including elite and prestige)	40	49	N.A.	.41	N.A.
Regional	16	11	N.A.	.13	N.A.
Local	44	40	N.A.	.33	N.A.
Political party affiliation (national level)					
Republican	26	23	28	.24	.39
Democrat	42	39	37	.21	.27
Independent	32	38	35	.21	.21

NOTE: N.A.—Not applicable.

they cannot find a suitable colleague from their own school, they tend to choose someone from a school of comparable status. The almost negligible inbreeding bias (only .13) of graduates from regional law schools undoubtedly reflects in part the residual character of the category—that is, it includes all the law schools not included in one of the other categories, resulting in a heterogeneous mix of schools. Graduates of Tulane's or Brooklyn's law schools, whatever their predilections to associate with graduates of their own schools, will be hard pressed to find them in the Chicago bar. But the low inbreeding bias of graduates of the regional schools also probably reflects their lack of any distinctive social identity. They do not constitute a community that is based in either geographical proximity or social status; they are more cosmopolitan in their origins than are the graduates of the local schools, but the prestige of their schools is not sufficient to support exclusivity that is based on the old school tie as a badge of honor. They are neither fish nor fowl. The schools at the respective extremes of the prestige hierarchy, however, display inbreeding biases that strongly support our finding, reported in chapter 6, that these categories of schools play distinctive, highly differentiated roles in supplying lawyers for different sectors of the bar.

Turning to the matter of party affiliation, presented in the lower panel of table 7.4, we observe that all three categories—Republicans, Democrats, and Independents—have approximately equal, and generally moderate, tendencies toward self-selection. Especially notable in this connection is the fact that the Independents—frequently accused of being a shapeless residual category, composed of the politically apathetic, ignorant, and tuned out[23]—have as strong an inbreeding bias as do the self-identified Republicans and Democrats in their choices of colleagues, though Republicans have a substantially stronger bias in the selection of friends than do either of the two other political groups. Among lawyers in Chicago, then, "Independent" appears to be a real political group.

The fact that inbreeding biases in colleague choice by political affiliation are nearly as strong as those in the selection of friends suggests that political posture has salience or instrumental utility in professional relationships as well as an expressive utility in the formation of friendship bonds.[24] Politics pervades much that is of concern to lawyers, and the importance of "clout" in the allocation of public goods in Chicago is legendary. There is, then, little wonder that Chicago lawyers are attentive to the political affiliations of their colleagues. A number of lawyers, of course, play public roles; many hold public office, others act as spokesmen for interest groups both within and outside the profession, and still others play the role of broker among competing interest groups.

The remaining chapters of this part of the book explore the political activities of lawyers in the organizations of the bar and in the broader community. We move, then, from this more formal description of the nature of lawyer's networks of friends and colleagues to analyses that seek to relate these networks to the "constituencies" or bases of personal support within the Chicago legal community for the various public roles that lawyers play.

For the present, however, let us stress once again the consistency of the findings reported in this chapter with those noted earlier, particularly those concerning the channeling of lawyers into distinctive, separate career paths. The networks of association among Chicago lawyers, like their employment and their social values, appear to derive in large measure from both their social origins and the sorts of clients that they serve.

23. Norman H. Nie, Sidney Verba, and John R. Petrocik, *The Changing American Voter* (Cambridge: Harvard University Press, 1976); Philip E. Converse, *The Dynamics of Party Support: Cohort-analyzing Party Identification* (Beverly Hills, Cal.: Sage Publications, 1976).
24. See Laumann, 1973, *supra* note 5, pp. 34–39.

Appendix to Chapter 7:
Measures of Field Self-selection

Table 7.1 reports three different measures of the tendency of our respondents to associate with other lawyers who practice in their own fields of law. None of these three measures is wholly satisfactory, however (as we noted above at pp. 213–14), and some comment on their characteristics and limitations is therefore in order.

First, let us take the most straightforward but least satisfactory measure, the proportion of colleagues chosen from one's field (see table 7.1, col. [4]). These percentages, considered by themselves, are unsatisfactory because they are partially determined by the relative sizes of the fields. That is, even under the assumption of random mixing, the larger the number of practitioners in a field, the higher the probability of choosing a member from this field. If half of the lawyers in the sample work in field A, then one would expect 50 percent of the colleagues to be in field A by chance alone. But if, by contrast, a field's practitioners constitute only 5 percent of the total, a self-selection rate of 50 percent would reflect a very strong degree of preference for field mates. Of course, the size effect reflected in this measure is not without substantive interest. To ignore it completely would lead to a serious misrepresentation of the opportunity structure confronting people in finding suitable colleagues.[1]

Our second measure is the index of association—the "Rogoff mobility ratio of observed to chance selection" (see table 7.1, col. [5])—that was originally proposed by students of intergenerational occupational mobility to remedy the drawbacks inherent in simple percentages of occupational inheritance. Values over 1 indicate how much the actual self-selection exceeds that expected by chance, while values under 1 indicate the extent to which people are avoiding the choice of persons in their own group. Unfortunately, as Peter M. Blau and Otis Dudley Duncan have shown,[2] this index still ultimately depends on the row and column marginal distributions

1. David McFarland and Daniel Brown, "Social Distance as a Metric: A Systematic Introduction to Smallest Space Analysis," esp. pp. 238–40, in Edward O. Laumann, ed., *Bonds of Pluralism: The Form and Substance of Urban Social Networks* (New York: John Wiley, 1973); Peter M. Blau, "A Macrosociological Theory of Social Structure," *American Journal of Sociology* 83 (1977): 526–40.

2. Peter M. Blau and Otis Dudley Duncan, *The American Occupational Structure* (New York: John Wiley, 1967).

of respondents and colleagues, respectively, and is thus also affected by the relative sizes of the fields.

Finally, we present the inbreeding bias (see table 7.1, col. [6]), a measure proposed by Thomas J. Fararo and Morris H. Sunshine that goes some way toward eliminating the deficiencies of the other measures at least with respect to depressing the impact of size effects.[3] Our basic table of respondent-colleague choices corresponds to the "who-selected-whom" matrix with which Fararo and Sunshine started when developing their measure. This table can, in turn, be thought to consist of twenty-seven fourfold tables when P_1 stands for a given field of practice and P_2 for all the other fields. If a member of P_1 selects another member of P_1, this is self-selection. The entries for these tables are not respondents, but rather colleague pairs, with the total number of pairs A.. = 2,013. (This does not equal 2,097, the number obtained when one multiplies the number of respondents by the three colleagues we asked about, because some respondents named fewer than three colleagues.) The actual inbreeding proportion is defined as A_{11}/A_1., that is, the number of pairs in which both colleagues are practitioners in the same field P_1 divided by the number of pairs in which only the respondent is a member of P_1. Fararo and Sunshine divide the actual self-selection into two components: the random inbreeding expectation and the inbreeding bias. The random inbreeding expectation corresponds to the proportion of practitioners of a particular field in the entire population—the size effect. This figure is based on individuals and not on pairs (see table 7.1, col. [2]).

There is one precondition of this simple definition of the random inbreeding expectation that is not strictly met in our case—that the colleagues are to be chosen from within a prespecified group. In our case, this would mean that colleague selections should be restricted to the population of lawyers with their offices within the City of Chicago.[4] Our respondents were, in fact, permitted to name colleagues who practice in any locality. We do not know the precise extent to which respondents mentioned colleagues whose offices were outside Chicago's city limits, but it is clear that the vast majority of colleagues were practicing within the city. Because of this

---

3. Thomas J. Fararo and Morris H. Sunshine, *A Study of a Biased Friendship Net* (Syracuse, N.Y.: Syracuse University, Youth Development Center, 1964).
4. See the discussion of the population universe from which we drew our sample, pp. 9–10.

discrepancy in defining the pool of colleagues, however, we decided to take the marginal distribution of the colleagues chosen (table 7.1 col. [3]), A.j A..) as the best estimator of the inbreeding proportion under the assumption of random mixing.

After computing empirical measures of the actual and the random inbreeding proportions, a field-specific bias component in colleague selection can be defined. Fararo and Sunshine give the following rationale for postulating an event on which colleague selection is said to be dependent:

> If the event occurs, then the contact is certain to target on its "own kind." If the event does not occur, then the contact selects its "own kind" in proportion to the existence of this kind in the population, i.e., at random.
> We will not specify what this event is. It remains a hypothetical construction. Instead, we introduce a probability parameter, such that with probability T_i a contact from subpopulation P_1 selects its own kind by virtue of the occurrence of the hypothetical event. Thus, with the complementary probability $1 - T_i$ the event does not occur, so that the contact finds its own kind with probability N_i/N. The first component of inbreeding is here called the biased component of inbreeding—that which is associated with certain selection of the own kind—and the second is called the random component.[5]

Thus, the actual self-selection can be expressed as a sum of two probabilities:

$$S_i = T_i + (1 - T_i) \frac{N_i}{N}.$$

We have used this formula, with the alteration of estimating N_i/N with $A.j/A..$, to compute the inbreeding bias or systematic self-selection. These results are given in the last column of table 7.1. By comparing these numbers with the indices of association, it can be seen that there is some agreement on the relative levels of self-selection of different fields, but the rank-order correlation between the values of these two columns is only .64. Given that these two measures are supposed to be indicators of the same concept, this is a rather low correlation.

---

5. Fararo and Sunshine, *supra* note 3, p. 73.

Chapter 8

THE ORGANIZED BAR*

by John P. Heinz, Edward O. Laumann, Charles L. Cappell,
Terence C. Halliday and Michael Schaalman

THE CHICAGO Bar Association (CBA) is one of the two largest local
bar associations in the United States and, like other major metropolitan bar associations, it has come to reflect the diversity that is now
characteristic of the American legal profession. As we have already
documented, the increasing specialization of law practice—a development that is, in many ways, beneficial—has led to a differentiation of interest that has surely destroyed most of whatever unity the
profession may once have had. Many leaders of the organized bar
now feel a sense of crisis because of deep-seated divisions within

* This chapter is a condensation of an article by John P. Heinz, Edward O. Laumann, Charles L. Cappell, Terence C. Halliday, and Michael H. Schaalman, "Diversity, Representation, and Leadership in An Urban Bar: A First Report on a Survey of
the Chicago Bar," in 1976 *American Bar Foundation Research Journal* 717–85 (summer).

After the publication of the original article, we made corrections in the data tape
with respect to the coding of the respondents' practice characteristics and certain
personal social attributes. Because of the substantial costs in time and data-processing
expenses that would be incurred in redoing the entire analysis with the revised tape,
we have decided to retain the figures used in the published report. For this reason,
there will be minor discrepancies between the marginals reported in this chapter
and those given in the other chapters. (The data reported in all of the other chapters,
except chapter 4, are based on the revised tape and are thus mutually consistent.) We
are confident that the substantive conclusions drawn in this chapter would not be
materially altered by use of the revised data.

the profession over such pressing issues as the certification of specialties, group or prepaid legal services, advertising, fee schedules, judicial selection, and various "no fault" plans. Thus, while the major metropolitan bar associations have sought to expand their memberships so that their positions on the major issues faced by the bar may be perceived as more broadly representative of the totality of the profession, they have at the same time been increasingly riven by the special, often irreconcilable interests of the various sectors of the profession. This chapter documents both the representativeness of the organized bar and the dissension within it.

In the early 1970s, the Chicago Bar Association's Committee on the Development of the Law expressed the concerns that eventually led the Association to invite us to undertake this study:

> Our Association, regarded as one of the outstanding big city bar associations, has been criticized in recent years on a variety of grounds—that it is not responsive to the needs of the public; that the Association has tolerated a mediocre bench and has failed to take effective action to improve the quality of justice in our courts; that the Association is not truly representative of the members of the Bar; that its structure and organization impedes prompt action when needed; and that the association has failed to give leadership in bringing about improvement in the law and in the administration of justice. . . . [T]he persistence of the criticism, coming as it does from many lawyers, and occasionally from the press, justifies a careful evaluation of the role and purpose of the Association.[1]

In attempting to address the several issues raised by these concerns, we gathered a substantial body of information about the CBA, in addition to that concerning the legal profession in Chicago more generally. Three types of information are presented in this chapter in some detail. First, the characteristics of the members of the CBA are compared to those of the bar generally and, to a lesser degree, to those of the members of the American Bar Association, the Illinois State Bar Association, and the Chicago Council of Lawyers (a more liberal "reformist" organization, composed primarily of younger lawyers).[2] The resulting profile gives us a picture of the "constituency" of the CBA or, put another way, of the types of lawyers to

1. Richard Phelan, Alex Elson, and Edgar Vannemann, "The Role and Purpose of the Chicago Bar Association—Project of a Subcommittee of the Committee on the Development of the Law" (Unpublished memorandum, Chicago Bar Association, 1974), p. 2.
2. See Michael Powell, "Anatomy of a Counter-Bar Association: The Chicago Council of Lawyers," 1979 *American Bar Foundation Research Journal* 501–41 (Summer).

which the CBA as presently constituted does and does not appeal. If there are important segments of the bar that the CBA is not presently reaching or recruiting to membership, this analysis should reveal them. Second, we identify the kinds of members who serve on the CBA's committees and who are most likely to hold positions of leadership within the Association. Finally, we analyze the findings of a survey of the opinions of Chicago lawyers about what the purposes of the CBA ought to be and about the effectiveness of the CBA in performing those functions.

Bar Association Membership Rates

Table 8.1 presents rates of membership in four bar associations—the CBA, the American Bar Association (ABA), the Illinois State Bar Association (ISBA), and the Chicago Council of Lawyers (CCL)—for each of the several classifications of lawyers.

Note that none of the demographic variables produces a statistically significant difference in the rates of membership in the CBA, while all of the law-related variables do produce significant differences. In this respect, the CBA differs from the ABA, where the demographic variables are significant. Even in the ABA rates, however, the differences produced by the demographic variables are less highly significant than are those associated with the law-related characteristics. The pattern of membership in the ISBA is quite similar to that in the CBA, with the exception that the age groupings do exhibit significant differences in the ISBA rates (though not in a straight line or consistent direction). The CCL clearly has quite a different membership from that of the other associations. In addition to being much smaller, its membership leans politically toward an Independent Democratic or Independent political preference and is much younger than that of the other bar associations.[3]

Politics and religion produce significant differences in the membership rates of only the ABA and the CCL, but those differences go in opposite directions. Republicans have the highest rate of membership in the ABA, but the lowest rate in the CCL. Protestants and Catholics have higher rates of membership in the ABA than do Jews

3. See also Michael Powell, *supra* note 2.

TABLE 8.1

Percentage of Each Population Subgroup Who Are Members
of Four Bar Associations

Attribute	Chicago Bar Association	American Bar Association	Illinois State Bar Association	Chicago Council of Lawyers
Full sample	64.7	51.4	65.6	7.1
Chicago political preference:	N.S.	*	N.S.	***
Republican	66.7	57.7	70.5	0.0
Regular Democratic	74.2	46.0	71.8	1.6
Independent Democratic	62.7	54.0	62.7	11.9
Independent	59.5	56.5	64.9	9.2
Not applicable	64.6	41.7	64.6	3.1
Ethnicity:	N.S.	*	N.S.	N.S.
Irish	75.5	58.5	72.3	3.2
Black	57.1	47.6	81.0	9.5
Northwestern European	63.9	58.5	61.7	6.0
Southern and eastern				
European	60.3	46.0	63.2	9.8
Other	64.1	47.1	62.8	5.8
Religious preference:	N.S.	**	N.S.	***
Catholic	65.6	51.6	68.8	2.7
Jewish	65.6	42.6	67.9	9.1
Protestant	67.1	60.1	64.2	7.0
None	53.7	47.4	56.8	12.6
Age group:	N.S.	**	**	***
20–34	64.5	60.3	59.1	12.4
35–45	61.5	47.2	74.3	8.7
46–65	66.4	44.8	63.5	2.1
66–90	70.0	57.1	68.6	1.4
Law practice income:	***	***	***	N.S.
Under $15,000	52.5	27.9	59.0	4.9
$15,000–$19,999	56.7	55.0	57.5	11.7
$20,000–$29,999	60.0	42.9	56.5	9.4
$30,000–$39,999	62.5	48.3	72.5	8.3
$40,000–$59,999	73.6	51.2	70.5	3.9
$60,000 and above	78.7	71.3	80.3	4.9
Law school attended:	***	***	***	**
Elite	79.4	67.7	67.1	13.5
Prestige	72.7	51.6	57.8	7.0
Regional	61.8	53.9	71.1	6.6
Local	58.8	43.2	70.1	4.2
Other	47.2	56.6	43.4	9.4
Practice category:	***	***	***	**
Solo	54.1	37.7	68.5	3.4
Firm size:				
Fewer than 10 lawyers	72.5	46.7	77.5	5.5
10 to 30 lawyers	83.3	72.2	65.3	8.3
More than 30 lawyers	76.2	68.9	64.9	16.4
Government	47.9	48.9	52.1	7.4
House counsel	61.6	57.6	63.6	3.0
Nonlegal	54.3	28.3	50.0	2.2

NOTE: The symbols at the beginning of each category indicate the following:
N.S.—Not statistically significant.
*—Significant at the .05 level.
**—Significant at the .01 level.
***—Significant at the .001 level.

and the nonreligious. In the CCL, the opposite is true—the nonreligious and the Jews have higher rates of membership than do the Catholics and the Protestants. For all of the bar associations except the CCL, there is a clear pattern of an increase in the membership rates as law practice income increases. Graduates of "elite" law schools have significantly higher membership rates in the CBA, the ABA, and the CCL, but in the ISBA the "regional" and "local" law school graduates have significantly higher rates. Similarly, lawyers from the larger firms tend to be heavily represented in the CBA, ABA, and CCL, while solos and small firm lawyers are more heavily represented in the ISBA. Later sections of this chapter make use of some of these findings to aid in the explanation of more detailed relationships of these variables to differences in levels of CBA involvement, as well as in attitudes about the goals and effectiveness of the organization.

Patterns Of Participation

In our survey of Chicago lawyers, we heard a wide variety of assertions about which religious or ethnic groups or types of legal specialties or firms dominated the CBA. These ranged from dominance by large firms, to certain named firms, to banks, to newspapers, to the mayor, to corporate, personal injury, divorce, tax, probate, or real estate specialists, to the judiciary! While we cannot offer an assessment of all of these views, we will present an analysis of participation in the CBA by lawyers from the various categories of law schools, types of legal work, income levels, and religious, political, and ethnic groups.

As indicated in table 8.2, about two-thirds of the lawyers in our sample belong to the CBA and, of the CBA members, about two-thirds are on committees and 14 percent have held positions of leadership.[4] The percentages given for each of the characteristics or subgroups indicate the rates of CBA membership, committee mem-

4. For a more extended treatment of the selectivity of recruitment to positions of organizational leadership in the CBA, see Terence C. Halliday and Charles L. Cappell, "Indicators of Democracy in Professional Associations: Elite Recruitment, Turnover, and Decision-Making in a Metropolitan Bar Association," 1979 *American Bar Foundation Research Journal* 697–767 (fall); Charles L. Cappell, "Dynamics of Organizational Decision-Making" (Ph.D. diss., University of Chicago, 1980).

TABLE 8.2

Participation in CBA by Nationality, Religion, and Political Preference

| | Percent of Chicago Lawyers | | | | | |
| | Who Are Members of CBA (65% of Total) | | Having Been on CBA Committees[a] (68% of CBA Members) | | Having Held a CBA Leadership Position[b] (14% of CBA Members) | |
	Percent	(No.)	Percent	(No.)	Percent	(No.)
Ethnicity:						
Irish	76	(71)	61	(43)	17	(12)
Black	57	(12)	75	(9)	0	(0)
Northwestern European	64	(117)	71	(83)	18	(21)
Southern and eastern						
European	60	(105)	69	(72)	10	(10)
Other	64	(143)	69	(99)	16	(22)
Statistical significance	N.S.		N.S.		N.S.	
Religious preference:						
Catholic	66	(145)	66	(96)	13	(18)
Jewish	66	(137)	72	(98)	10	(13)
Protestant	67	(163)	69	(112)	20	(32)
None	54	(51)	63	(32)	14	(7)
Statistical significance	N.S.		N.S.		N.S.	
Chicago political preference:						
Republican	67	(52)	83	(43)	23	(12)
Regular Democratic	74	(92)	54	(50)	9	(8)
Independent Democratic	63	(195)	69	(135)	12	(24)
Independent	60	(78)	68	(53)	18	(14)
Not applicable	65	(82)	71	(58)	15	(12)
Statistical significance	N.S.		**		N.S.	

NOTES: a. Includes respondents who, at the time of our survey or earlier, had been assigned to a CBA committee.

b. Includes respondents who, at the time of our survey or earlier, had been officers of the CBA, members of the Board of Managers, or Chairmen or Vice-Chairmen of committees.

N.S.—Not significant at the .05 level.

**—Significant at the .01 level.

bership, and leadership for lawyers with those characteristics. Thus, the table indicates that 76 percent of the lawyers of Irish extraction are members of the CBA, and 61 percent of the Irish CBA members serve on CBA committees—11 percentage points more and 7 percentage points less, respectively, than the norms for each of those types of participation. Northwestern Europeans and "others" (those who described themselves simply as "Americans" or who expressed no clear ethnic identity) are the most numerous as members, on committees, and as leaders, but the table further indicates that the nationality differences in participation rates are not statistically significant. The three main religious groups are present in almost equal numbers on the committees, though Protestants are somewhat more numerous in positions of leadership. The great number of Independent Democrats in the bar as a whole is reflected in their numerical superiority in CBA membership, committees, and positions of responsibility.

The most important finding presented in table 8.2 is that, in general, participation in the CBA appears to be largely representative of the bar as a whole. Neither nationality nor religion has a statistically significant relationship with any of the types of participation. The only association occurs between politics and participation at the committee membership level, where we find an overrepresentation of Republicans and underrepresentation of Regular Democrats. (Note, however, that each of the other political categories still manages to outnumber the Republicans, and the Independent Democrats outnumber them by far.) The statistical significance of even this relationship disappears, however, when we take account of the effects of law practice income, the category of law school attended, and age. That is, once the effect on committee membership rates of these other characteristics has been taken into account, the effect of political preference is insignificant.[5] Thus, none of the variables

5. Most of the discussion in this chapter is based on an examination of the impact of each of a number of independent variables considered separately. As noted earlier, however, these independent variables are themselves interrelated in important ways. To evaluate the impact of these interrelations on participation in the organized bar, we have submitted the data to multivariate statistical procedures, called covariance analysis and multiple classification analysis (discussed in chapter 5, note 36), that permit us to determine whether a given variable persists in its relation to the dependent variable once the effects of the other independent variables have been "removed" statistically. For example, we find, as indicated in table 8.2, that the association between CBA committee membership and political party preference is statistically significant at the .01 level. The multivariate statistical procedures permit us to determine whether political preference continues to be significantly associated with committee membership once the effects of law school, age, and income differences have been removed. In this case, it does not. The multivariate analyses further reveal, however, that age, income, and law school all remain as significant independent variables. When a multivariate model was used to test the effects of the demographic variables on leadership rates, we also found that nationality and political preference produced a statistically significant "interaction" effect. That is, while these variables acting independently are not useful in understanding leadership rates, when viewed as interacting factors they become useful—i.e., no significant increase in leadership rates accompanies being either a Republican or a northwestern European, but a significant increase does accompany being a Republican and a northwestern European.

We will not report the results of these additional analyses here unless they modify the conclusions drawn from consideration of the variables separately.

presented in table 8.2 has a significant independent effect on these rates of participation in the CBA.

Though ethnicity, religion, and politics seem to have little effect, if any, on the levels of participation, one might expect greater influence from factors more closely related to the practice of law, and table 8.3 gives some support to this thesis. There is a strong relationship between involvement in the CBA and the category of law school attended. Graduates of elite and prestige schools are significantly overrepresented on CBA membership rolls. Elite, prestige, and regional school alumni are found on committees in greater proportions than are those from local and "other" schools. Graduates of prestige, regional, and "other" schools are more or less equally represented in positions of leadership, but graduates of local schools— DePaul, Kent, Loyola, and Marshall—are marginally underrepresented and the alumni of Chicago, Columbia, Harvard, Michigan, Stanford, and Yale are almost twice as likely to be found in leadership positions as are those from any other group. Graduates of elite law schools are, of course, more likely to secure positions in the law firms that offer inducements and support for bar association membership, but multivariate analysis, measuring the effects of the practice and law school categories simultaneously, discloses that each of these variables has an independent effect on the rates of CBA participation.[6]

Table 8.3 indicates that the practice categories produce significant differences in the CBA membership rate but are not significantly associated with committee membership or with leadership. Solo practitioners, government lawyers, and lawyers not presently practicing are underrepresented among CBA members, while law firm attorneys are proportionately and numerically more often found as members. Lawyers from medium-sized and larger firms are more likely to be members than are those from smaller firms. Many large firms pay association dues and make time available for association meetings, while many solo practitioners and small firm lawyers indicated to us that, quite apart from the expense of dues, they could not afford to invest much time in bar associations. Moreover, the offices of many solo practitioners are located outside the downtown

6. Furthermore, the law school and type of practice variables interact statistically to affect CBA participation. That is, the effect on membership produced by working in a particular type of practice is itself affected by the law school attended.

TABLE 8.3

Participation in CBA by Legal Characteristics

	Percent of Chicago Lawyers					
	Who Are Members of CBA (65% of Total)		Having Been on CBA Committees[a] (68% of CBA Members)		Having Held a CBA Leadership Position[b] (14% of CBA Members)	
	Percent	(No.)	Percent	(No.)	Percent	(No.)
Law school attended:						
Elite	79	(123)	78	(96)	25	(31)
Prestige	73	(93)	77	(72)	11	(10)
Regional	62	(47)	79	(37)	13	(6)
Local	59	(208)	58	(120)	9	(19)
Other	47	(25)	44	(11)	12	(3)
Statistical significance	***		***		***	
Law practice income:						
Under $15,000	52	(32)	53	(17)	0	(0)
$15,000–$19,999	57	(68)	59	(40)	0	(0)
$20,000–$29,999	60	(102)	62	(63)	13	(13)
$30,000–$39,999	62	(75)	69	(52)	16	(12)
$40,000–$59,999	74	(95)	74	(70)	14	(13)
$60,000 and above	79	(96)	81	(78)	28	(27)
Statistical significance	***		**		***	
Practice category:						
Solo	54	(79)	70	(55)	11	(9)
Firm size:						
Fewer than 10 lawyers	72	(132)	64	(85)	11	(14)
10 to 30 lawyers	83	(60)	80	(48)	17	(10)
More than 30 lawyers	76	(93)	68	(63)	20	(19)
Government	48	(45)	69	(31)	9	(4)
House counsel	62	(61)	66	(40)	15	(9)
Nonlegal	5	(25)	52	(13)	12	(3)
Statistical significance	***		N.S.		N.S.	

NOTES: a. Includes respondents who, at the time of our survey or earlier, had been assigned to a CBA committee.

b. Includes respondents who, at the time of our survey or earlier, had been officers of the CBA, members of the Board of Managers, or Chairmen or Vice-Chairmen of committees.

N.S.—Not significant at the .05 level.

** —Significant at the .01 level.

*** —Significant at the .001 level.

area, making it difficult for them to reach the CBA's building. The relationship between size of firm and leadership is worth noting even though it is not statistically significant; while only 11 percent of the lawyers in firms with fewer than ten lawyers had been "leaders" of the CBA, 20 percent of those from firms with more than thirty lawyers had held leadership positions.

Many of our respondents suggested that the most salient determinant of ability to become deeply involved in CBA affairs is one's financial position. If CBA involvement takes time, and therefore costs money, the more prosperous practitioner should have an advantage. There is little doubt that he has. There are very strong statistical relationships between income and participation. In short, the higher the lawyer's income, the more likely he is to be a member of the organization, the more likely his name is to appear on committee rosters, and the greater the probability that he will be found in a leadership position. Lawyers with annual incomes from law practice in excess of $40,000 are significantly overrepresented in membership and committee membership; the significant watershed point for those in the leadership positions, however, seems to come at $60,000.[7]

An overview of the variables presented in table 8.3 gives a rather clear picture. Compared to Chicago lawyers as a whole, the CBA has a considerably greater proportion of elite law school, larger firm, higher income lawyers on the membership rolls, on committees, and as leaders. But there is some danger here of overdrawing the case. Note should be taken of the absolute numbers of lawyers in each category. While local law school graduates are underrepresented as committee members on a percentage basis, for example, they remain the most numerous group. Again, though elite law school graduates have a higher probability of holding leadership positions, they are outnumbered by graduates of the other types of schools, and the number of firm lawyers in committee and leadership positions merely reflects, for the most part, their numerical superiority in the bar as a whole.

7. In the correlation between income and leadership, we have no way of knowing which way the causal arrow points—i.e., it may be that higher income makes one more likely to be selected for a CBA leadership position, but it could also be that a leadership position causes higher law practice income.

Keep in mind that we requested current income figures from the respondents, while inquiring whether they had ever held a leadership position. Because of the strong correlation between age and income (see *infra* note 26), part of the correlation between leadership and income may be attributable to the fact that the leadership category includes former leaders, who are likely to be older than the average age of our sample and, consequently, to have higher incomes. Income remained a statistically significant factor in all three levels of CBA participation, however, even after age effects had been taken into account through multivariate analysis.

OLIGARCHICAL CONTROL?

We asked the 777 lawyers in our sample which of the following models of organizational decision making they thought best described the situation in the CBA:

> First, there are those organizations in which vigorous conflicts between the same leaders or groups appear again and again in the handling of issues so that the same persons or groups are always found together in a coalition.
>
> In the second type, there is also controversy about various issues, but there are constantly changing coalitions between various groups or persons so that the coalitions are different depending on the problem being considered.
>
> In the third case there is relatively little argument about organizational measures because there is a relatively high consensus within the organization about what needs to be done.
>
> Fourth, there is a self-perpetuating group of leaders sharing common values and objectives who make most decisions with little or no consultation with the membership. (See appendix A, question A29.)

Nearly half of those responding (48 percent of the 533 lawyers who expressed an opinion) chose the fourth alternative, oligarchical control by a self-perpetuating group of leaders. Another 23.8 percent chose the second alternative, changing coalitions; 21 percent chose the third, consensus; and only 7 percent chose the first, stable coalitions. Further opinion about the extent to which the CBA was thought to be oligarchically governed was solicited in open-ended interviews with selected Chicago lawyers. We found that two rather different stereotypes about the nature of this oligarchy were prevalent. One version had it that the CBA was controlled by a group of the most powerful and prestigious lawyers in town—predominantly Republican, WASP, North Shore,[8] corporate lawyers from big firms. This view is similar to that found by Jerome Carlin in his interviews with Chicago lawyers two decades ago.[9] The other stereotype was that the power and prestige of the CBA were not sufficient to command the time and attention of this top elite of the profession, who concerned themselves instead with the business world or with political or social institutions that they believed to be

8. The "North Shore" is the Chicago term for the wealthiest suburbs, which are located to the north of the city along the shore of Lake Michigan.
9. See Jerome Carlin, *Lawyers on Their Own: A Study of Individual Practitioners in Chicago* (New Brunswick, N.J.: Rutgers University Press, 1962), pp. 175–84.

of greater consequence. According to this version, the oligarchy that governed the CBA was composed of Irish Catholic, Regular Democratic, personal injury lawyers with ties to City Hall.

Neither of these stereotypes gets much support from our data. There is no statistically significant association between leadership in the CBA and political party preference, ethnicity, or religion. Nor does the type of one's law practice correlate significantly with holding a leadership position (see table 8.3). It is true that a larger percentage of Republicans than of those with other political preferences had been CBA leaders, but of the seventy lawyers we interviewed who had held leadership positions in the CBA, only twelve were Republicans. Similarly, of the fifty-two leaders who were in private practice, only nineteen came from the largest firms—more than came from any other category, but not to a statistically significant degree.

Identification of the objective characteristics of the leadership will, however, take one only a part of the way toward determining whether an organization is controlled by an oligarchy. It is possible, for example, that elites might control an organization by installing persons with non-elite characteristics in the positions of power—that is, they might exercise control through agents or "nominees"—but such a hypothesis turns primarily on questions of motivation and, as a practical matter, is virtually untestable. The characteristics of the leadership also do not necessarily determine whose interests will be served by the organization's decisions, actions, or inaction. In addition to the use of nominees, co-optation is at least a hypothetical possibility, as is the manipulation of a balance of power situation to prevent any decisive action, thus favoring those interest groups that will be served by inaction. And, in addition to non-elites exercising power for the benefit of elites, it is also possible that elites might use their power for the benefit of non-elites. We explore these matters a bit further in the final section of this chapter. For now, we will simply reiterate our conclusion that the common view that the CBA is dominated by particular political, religious, or ethnic groups or by a particular type of practice is not demonstrable from our data.

The significant correlations of income level and law school category with leadership roles remain and should not be discounted, but the dominance of social elites in positions of power and influence is, of course, by no means a phenomenon that is peculiar to the

CBA. By comparison, let us consider the United States Congress, a body that is explicitly intended to be representative and that is chosen by a broad electorate. While about 58 percent of the American population is Protestant, in a recent Congress 73 percent of the representatives and 86 percent of the senators were Protestants. Catholics are about 37 percent of the United States population, but they supplied only 23 percent of the representatives and only 12 percent of the senators. One in 9 Americans is black; the proportions of blacks in the Congress were 1 in each 27 representatives and 1 in 100 senators. (Two-thirds of the senators and more than half of the representatives were lawyers.) Of course, at least two possible conclusions may be suggested by these observations: that the CBA leadership is about as representative as might be hoped; or that the American government is not nearly as representative as might be hoped.[10]

From the point of view of the individual aspiring to a position of leadership in the organized bar, the odds of achieving such a position may seem to favor certain types of lawyers and to militate against others. This does not necessarily mean, however, that some lawyers are the beneficiaries and others the victims of invidious discrimination in the recruitment or selection of bar association leaders. Much of the underrepresentation of certain groups in leadership positions is probably the result of self-selection or of factors inherent in the characteristics of the individual quite apart from any actions or motives of other persons in the association. Higher income lawyers, for example, may be better able to donate time to bar association activity than are lawyers who are scrambling to make a living. Thus, a higher income may facilitate involvement in association affairs regardless of anyone else's attitudes toward the member; one of the things that money will buy is the time to pursue the activities of the organized bar. Similarly, one might expect that lawyers from firms who have partners to cover for them and to share the workload would be better able to become deeply involved with CBA affairs than would solo practitioners, who are likely to have less flexibility in arranging their calendars. Moreover, some firms are said to encourage certain of their members to become ac-

10. These figures are cited in support of the latter conclusion in Ira Katznelson and Mark Kessleman, *The Politics of Power* (New York: Harcourt Brace Jovanovich, 1975), p. 295. For other relevant material, see Donald R. Matthews, *The Social Background of Political Decision-Makers* (New York: Doubleday, 1954), and Heinz Eulau and John D. Sprague, *Lawyers in Politics* (Indianapolis: Bobbs-Merrill Co., 1964).

tive in bar associations as a means of maintaining contact with other lawyers and, perhaps, of facilitating the referral of cases to their firms. Finally, given the variety of opportunities for leadership that are open to lawyers, only a limited number may be expected to seek positions of bar association leadership—if, indeed, they choose to pursue any sort of leadership role.

Observations of this sort were summarized by Robert Michels in the hypothesis that he termed "the iron law of oligarchy."[11] Most simply put, this thesis suggests that, even in democratic political systems, only a relatively small number of the potential participants will in fact take part in the decisions—both because the nature of the decisions to be made will usually require information that is so arcane or specialized that most of the population will be unable to master the subtleties of the issue and because most potential participants are likely to be insufficiently concerned with any given issue to expend the time and effort necessary to influence the decision or to gain the requisite expertise. Michels based his generalizations on an intensive analysis of the German Social Democratic party at the turn of the century, but subsequent research on many other types of voluntary associations in America, including labor unions and assorted professional, civic, and welfare organizations, has tended to support his conclusions.[12]

In the case of the legal profession, there are some additional reasons, stemming from the nature of the profession, that might lead one to expect oligarchical control of bar associations. Lawyers— more than most people, even more than most other professionals— are accustomed to dealing with power and influence. One of the features of American government that has been a matter of record since at least the time of Alexis de Tocqueville[13] is the dominance by the legal profession of the public offices of this country, both elected and appointed. Given these characteristics of the American legal profession, one might expect lawyers to seek to use the bar association as a means of organizing and expressing professional support

11. Robert Michels, *Political Parties: A Sociological Study of the Oligarchical Tendencies of Modern Democracy*, trans. Eden and Cedar Paul (New York: Free Press, 1962).

12. See, e.g., Seymour Martin Lipset, Martin A. Trow, and James S. Coleman, *Union Democracy* (Garden City, N.Y.: Doubleday-Anchor, 1962), and Corinne Lathrop Gilb, *Hidden Hierarchies: The Professions and Government* (New York: Harper and Row, 1966), pp. 112–40, 153–56, reprinted and abridged in Sanford A. Lakoff, ed., *Private Government* (Glenview, Ill.: Scott, Foresman, 1973), pp. 144–61.

13. Alexis de Tocqueville, *Democracy in America*, trans. Henry Reeve (New York: Oxford University Press, 1947).

for their own causes. Insofar as the associations might speak for (or be made to appear to speak for) a profession with such strategic access to the levers of power, control of the associations would seem to be a prize worth capturing.[14]

Organizational Objectives and Effectiveness

To ascertain the importance assigned by Chicago lawyers to various objectives that an urban bar association might pursue and to determine their opinions of the CBA's effectiveness in achieving those objectives, our interview schedule listed thirteen possible objectives or purposes. These ranged from purely service functions, such as providing dining or library facilities, through several sorts of reform of the legal profession, to roles dealing with broader social or political issues. The respondents were asked, first, how important it was for the CBA to pursue each of these objectives. Importance was rated on a five-point scale, ranging from "very important" to "not important at all." No constraint was imposed on the number of objectives that the respondent rated in each of the importance categories—that is, the respondent was free to rate all (or none) of the objectives as "very important," "not important," or any of the intermediate values. If, but only if, the respondent rated a particular objective as "important" or "very important," he was asked to rate the CBA's effectiveness in achieving that objective. This rating also used a five-point scale, ranging from "highly effective" to "not effective at all." Again, no limit was imposed on the number of objectives rated in each category.

Table 8.4 gives a condensed version of each objective and the percentage of lawyers who rated it either "important" or "very important." The order in which the objectives are listed in this table may be considered the rank order of importance. The table also indicates the percentage of respondents who rated the CBA's performance on each objective as either "effective" or "highly effective," and ranks the objectives accordingly.

14. See Halliday and Cappell, *supra* note 4, and Cappell, *supra* note 4; Terence C. Halliday, "Parameters of Professional Influence: Policies and Politics of the Chicago Bar Association, 1945–70" (Ph.D. diss., University of Chicago, 1979); and Michael Powell, "Social Change and an Elite Professional Association: The Politics of Incorporation" (Ph.D. diss., University of Chicago, 1982).

TABLE 8.4
CBA Objectives, Ratings of Importance, and Effectiveness

Importance Rank	Objective	Important or Very Important	Effective or Highly Effective	Effectiveness Rank
		Ratings (Percent)		
1	Improve quality of bar	96.2	72.3	2
2	Improve quality of judiciary	93.4	29.5	8.5
3	Improve efficiency of court procedures	92.0	28.8	10
4	Enhance status of profession	87.2	29.5	8.5
5	Initiate legislation	80.5	53.5	3
6	Discipline lawyers	79.9	39.9	6
7	Facilitate referral of cases	71.6	46.7	4
8	Improve police procedures	68.2	13.3	13
9	Library and dining facilities	65.2	93.8	1
10	Prevent unauthorized practice	65.1	40.6	5
11	Improve lot of disadvantaged	50.3	16.6	11
12	Take stands on controversial issues	28.7	15.0	12
13	Facilitate client-getting	24.2	32.6	7

Perhaps the most striking finding is that the CBA is given its highest effectiveness rating by far on the dining and library facilities item, but the importance of this objective is ranked quite low. Almost 38 percent of our respondents rate the CBA's dining and library facilities "highly effective" and another 56 percent rate them "effective." The next highest effectiveness rating is given to "improving the quality of the bar," where a comparatively modest 15 percent rate the CBA "highly effective" and 58 percent give an "effective" rating.

"Improving the quality of the bar" was the only objective of those ranked in the top four in importance on which a majority of our respondents rate the CBA's performance as, at least, "effective." Since the wording of this objective spoke of "keeping lawyers abreast of current developments," it seems probable that the way in which the CBA is thought to be effective in improving the quality of the bar is through the symposia conducted by some of the CBA's committees on recent developments in their areas of the law and perhaps, the articles in the *Bar Record*. Overall, it is important to note that a majority of our respondents rated the CBA's performance as "effective" or better on only three of the thirteen listed objectives.

Because of the great importance given to improving the quality of the judiciary, it is particularly significant to note that the CBA's effectiveness in achieving that objective is so uniformly rated low. More than two-thirds of our respondents give this objective the highest importance rating ("very important"), considerably more respondents than rate any other objective so highly. In the effectiveness ratings, however, only 5 percent of the respondents rate the CBA "highly effective" in improving the quality of the judiciary and only another 25 percent rate the Association "effective."[15]

As might have been anticipated, the importance of "client getting" as an objective of the Association is rated very low, probably because it was perceived as not quite respectable or legitimate. "Facilitating the referral of cases to qualified lawyers," however, is given much greater importance; 22 percent of our respondents rate it "very important" and another 49 percent rate it "important." While there may well be a close relationship between these two objectives, the latter being regarded as a more palatable way of phrasing the point, it is also possible that the responses on the "referral" objective reflect, at least in part, evaluations of the importance and effectiveness of the CBA's Lawyer Reference Plan. (Under the plan, persons seeking legal representation are put in touch with one of the participating lawyers. About 10 percent of the lawyers in our sample participated in this plan.)[16]

It is also interesting to note that the objectives on which the CBA is rated least effective are the three that call for social or political "activism"—improving "the general lot of disadvantaged groups," "taking stands on controversial issues of public policy such as Vietnam, or school busing," and advancing "police procedures that will accord with constitutional standards." On each of these three objectives, the CBA's performance is rated "highly effective" by only about 1 percent of our respondents and "effective" by only an additional 12 to 15 percent. Since only the respondents who rated an objective "important" or "very important" were asked to rate the

15. Our interviews were completed before the CBA received unfavorable publicity in the major Chicago newspapers later in 1975 because the CBA rated both of Mayor Daley's candidates for the Illinois Supreme Court qualified for the office, while finding one of their independent opponents unqualified. The Daley-slated candidates were subsequently defeated in the primary election. See, e.g., Rob Warden and Edmund J. Rooney, "Bar's Court Choice Under Fire," *Chicago Daily News*, March 6–7, 1976, p. 1; *Chicago Sun-Times*, December 5, 1975, p. 3; and *Chicago Sun-Times*, December 6, 1975, p. 16.

16. The lawyers who participate in the plan charge their clients normal fees for this representation. The plan is *not* designed to provide "legal services for the poor," though most of the clients are surely not well-to-do.

CBA's effectiveness on that objective, and since so few of our respondents thought that the "disadvantaged groups" and "public policy" objectives were important, one might well argue that the effectiveness ratings on those objectives represent the views of only a rather small group within the bar. Thus, most Chicago lawyers apparently do not believe that the CBA *should* take stands on public policy issues or seek to improve the lot of the disadvantaged, and only the minority who do were asked to express their views on effectiveness. The relatively few lawyers who see those objectives as important may be considered a "social activist" minority whose low appraisal of the CBA's performance is consistent with their alienation from the mainstream point of view. If the CBA is, in fact, inactive in pursuing such objectives, that would seem to accord with the preferences of most Chicago lawyers rather well. This line of argument does not hold, however, for the objective dealing with police procedures—on which the CBA was rated least effective of all. A substantial 22 percent of our respondents rate that objective "very important" and an additional 47 percent rate it "important." Thus, the respondents who rated the effectiveness of the CBA on this objective cannot be dismissed as a mere "fringe" group. The CBA's leadership had devoted a great amount of time and effort to working with the Chicago Police Department and with other bar and citizen's groups on the issue of civilian review of police misconduct,[17] but in spite of this activity its efforts were widely regarded as inefficacious.

Group Differences

We have also sought to determine whether the opinions expressed regarding these objectives and the CBA's success in pursuing them were influenced by the demographic and law-related variables discussed in the previous sections of this chapter. To this end, we utilized a statistical technique that assesses the extent to which the

17. During the period from 1969 through 1974, several CBA committees devoted major efforts to this issue. James Kissel informed us that, during his presidency of the CBA (1973–74), the police civilian review issue was by far the most time-consuming matter that he had to deal with. See Jeffrey Slovak, "The Chicago Bar Association: The Structure of Organizational Control" (unpublished paper, American Bar Foundation CBA Project, April 1976).

differences of opinion on importance and effectiveness *between* groups (such as Regular Democrats and Republicans or solo practitioners and corporate house counsel) exceed the differences *within* each of those groups on the same issue.[18] The results of this analysis are presented in table 8.5, which summarizes all of the differences between groups that were found to be statistically significant.

MEMBERS VERSUS NONMEMBERS

There are significant differences between members and nonmembers of the CBA in their ratings of the importance of four of the thirteen listed objectives. The first of these is, no doubt, to be expected—members of the CBA rate the importance of library and dining facilities much more highly than do nonmembers. Nonmembers, by contrast, attach significantly more importance than do members to improving police procedures, improving the lot of the disadvantaged, and facilitating client getting. Since the last of these, "client getting," appears to be widely regarded as an illegitimate objective, the nonmembers' higher rating of its importance may reflect a cynical appraisal of the members' motives for joining the CBA. The higher importance rating given by nonmembers to the two "social activism" objectives may suggest that the activist minority of the bar is to be found disproportionately among the one-third of the profession that does not belong to the CBA. It may also suggest one of the reasons *why* they do not belong to the CBA.

In the ratings of the effectiveness of the CBA in achieving the objectives, there are an even larger number of significant differences between members and nonmembers. Such differences occur on eight of the thirteen objectives; in each of these cases, the members rate the effectiveness of the CBA more highly than do nonmembers. The eight objectives on which nonmembers give the CBA lower marks for performance are:

* Improving the quality of the bar
* Enhancing the status of the profession
* Initiating legislation
* Disciplining lawyers

18. This statistical technique is known as "analysis of variance." For an explanation of the technique and the method by which it is computed, see Hubert M. Blalock, Jr., *Social Statistics* (New York: McGraw-Hill, 1960), pp. 242–72.

- Facilitating referral of cases
- Preventing unauthorized practice
- Improving the efficiency of court procedures
- Improving the lot of the disadvantaged

Interestingly, only one of the objectives rated in the top seven in importance—improving the quality of the judiciary, the second ranked objective—produces no significant difference between members' and nonmembers' ratings of the CBA's effectiveness. Neither group rates the performance of the CBA very highly on that objective; it is tied for eighth and ninth in the effectiveness rankings with fewer than 30 percent of the respondents rating the CBA as either "effective" or "highly effective."

POLITICAL PARTY AFFILIATION

The respondents' affiliation in Chicago politics is one of the most significant predictors of their opinions regarding the importance and effectiveness of CBA roles. Table 8.5 indicates that political preference produces statistically significant differences in either the importance or the effectiveness ratings on ten of the thirteen objectives. Moreover, the pattern of these differences is quite clear. Where statistically significant political differences occur, with only one exception, the lawyers who associate themselves with the Republican party or with the Regular Democrats in Chicago politics are more likely than are the Independent Democrats or the Independents to take positions that one might characterize as supporting the status quo or as tending to preserve or to express approval of the established order. The one exception is the position of the Republicans on the importance of improving the quality of the judiciary. In that case, Republicans join with Independents and Independent Democrats in attaching greater importance to seeking an improvement in the quality of judicial candidates and sitting judges. This position might be considered antiestablishment or anti-status quo since it presumably reflects dissatisfaction with the current state of the judiciary and a belief that new, more stringent measures should be used in the selection or evaluation of judicial candidates. When it comes to rating the performance of the CBA on this objective, however, the important difference is between the Regular Democrats, on the one hand, and the Independents and

TABLE 8.5

Differences in Opinion Between Groups of Respondents Concerning Importance and Effectiveness of Bar Association Objectives

Higher Importance	Lower Importance	Significance	Higher Effectiveness	Lower Effectiveness	Significance
Objective 1: Improving the Quality of the Bar by Keeping Lawyers Abreast of Current Developments					
No significant differences			Older age groups	Younger age groups	**
			Republicans & Regular Democrats	Independents & Independent Democrats	***
			Religious	Nonreligious	*
			Blacks & Irish	Southern & eastern Europeans	*
			CBA members	Nonmembers	***
Objective 2: Improving the Quality of the Judiciary					
Republicans, Independent Democrats, & Independents	Regular Democrats	***	Older age groups	Younger age groups	***
			Regular Democrats	Independents & Independent Democrats	***
Nonreligious	Catholic & Jewish	*	Catholic & Protestant	Nonreligious	**
			Blacks & Irish	Southern & eastern Europeans	*
Firm & house counsel	Solos & government	**			
Larger firms	Smaller firms & solos	*			
Regional law schools	Local law schools	**	Lower status law schools	Elite law schools	*
Objective 3: Improving the Efficiency of Court Procedures					
No significant differences			Older age groups	Younger age groups	***
			Regular Democrats	Independents & Independent Democrats	***
			Catholic	Nonreligious	**
			CBA members	Nonmembers	**
			Highest income group	Incomes $15,000–$29,999	*

Higher Importance	Lower Importance	Significance	Higher Effectiveness	Lower Effectiveness	Significance
Objective 4: Enhancing the Status of the Legal Profession in the Eyes of the Public					
Older age groups	Younger age groups	**	Republicans & Regular Democrats	Independents	*
Jewish & Protestant	Nonreligious	*	Catholic & Protestant	Jewish	***
			Blacks & Irish	Southern & eastern Europeans	**
Men	Women	**			
Solos & government	Firm & house counsel	**	CBA members	Nonmembers	***
Solos	Firms with 10–30 lawyers	**			
Incomes $30,000–$39,999	Incomes $40,000–$59,999	*			
Local law schools	Elite law schools	**			
Objective 5: Initiating Legislation in Areas of Interest to Segments of the Bar					
Ages over 35	Ages under 35	*	Older age groups	Younger age groups	*
			Irish	Souther & eastern Europeans	*
			CBA members	Nonmembers	***
			Higher incomes	Lower incomes	*
Objective 6: Disciplining Lawyers According to the Standards of Professional Ethics					
Ages over 45	Ages 45 & under	**	Older age groups	Younger age groups	***
			Regular Democrats	Independents & Independent Democrats	***
			Religious	Nonreligious	***
			Men	Women	*
			CBA members	Nonmembers	**
			Solos	Law professors	*
			Solos	Firms with 10–30 lawyers	**
			Incomes over $60,000	Incomes under $60,000	*
			"Other" & local law schools	Elite law schools	**

TABLE 8.5 (continued)

Differences in Opinion Between Groups of Respondents Concerning Importance and Effectiveness of Bar Association Objectives

Higher Importance	Lower Importance	Signifi-cance	Higher Effectiveness	Lower Effectiveness	Signifi-cance
Objective 7: Facilitating the Referral of Cases to Qualified Lawyers					
Independents	Regular Democrats	**	Older age groups	Younger age groups	***
Nonreligious	Catholic & Jewish	*	Protestant & Jewish	Nonreligious	*
House counsel	Solos	*	CBA members	Nonmembers	***
Objective 8: Promoting the Development of Police Procedures					
Independent Democrats & Independents	Republicans & Regular Democrats	*	Older age groups	Younger age groups	***
			Regular Democrats	Independent Democrats	**
Nonreligious	Catholic	*	Catholic	Nonreligious	*
Nonmembers	CBA members	***	Irish	Blacks	*
Objective 9: Providing Library or Dining Facilities for Members of the Bar					
Protestant & Jewish	Catholic & nonreligious	*	No significant differences		
CBA members	Nonmembers	***			
Firm & house counsel	Government	**			
Small firms	Large firms & solos	*			
Objective 10: Preventing Nonlawyers from Doing Legal Work					
Older age groups	Younger age groups	***	Ages over 65	Ages 45 & under	*
Regular Democrats	Other political groups	*			
Jewish & Catholic	Nonreligious	***			
Blacks	Whites	**			
Men	Women	**	CBA members	Nonmembers	*
Solos	Firms	***			
Small firms & solos	Larger firms	***			
Incomes $30,000–$39,999	Incomes $15,000–$19,999	**			
Local law schools	Elite law schools	***			

Higher Importance	Signifi-cance	Lower Importance	Higher Effectiveness	Lower Effectiveness	Signifi-cance
Objective 11: Exercising Leadership to Improve the General Lot of Disadvantaged Groups					
Ages under 35	***	Ages 35 to 65	Ages over 65	Ages under 35	**
Independents	***	Republicans	Regular Democrats & Republicans	Independents & Independent Democrats	**
				Nonreligious	***
			Catholic		
Blacks	**	Whites	Irish	Blacks	*
Women	*	Men	Men	Women	**
Nonmembers	*	CBA members	CBA members	Nonmembers	
Lowest income groups	***	Highest income groups	Local law schools	Elite law schools	*
Objective 12: Taking Stands on Controversial Issues of Public Policy					
Ages under 35	***	Ages 35 & older	Ages over 65	Ages 35 to 65	*
Independent Democrats	*	Republicans			
Blacks	**	Northwestern Europeans			
Incomes $15,000-$29,999	***	Incomes over $40,000			
Objective 13: Facilitating Client Getting Through Contacts with Other Lawyers					
Younger age groups	***	Older age groups	No significant differences		
Nonmembers	***	CBA members			
Small law firms & solos	**	Largest firms			
Lower income groups	***	Higher income groups			
Local law schools	***	Elite law schools			

NOTE: The symbols indicate the following:
* Statistically significant at .05 level
** Statistically significant at .01 level
*** Statistically significant at .001 level

Independent Democrats, on the other, with Republicans occupying an intermediate position. The Regular Democrats are significantly more likely than other political groupings to attach lower importance to improving the quality of the judiciary and to find the CBA more effective in achieving it. Since the Daley Organization had dominated judicial selection in Chicago for many years, it seems natural that those who were in sympathy with the Daley forces would exhibit a higher degree of satisfaction with the Organization's choices for judgeships.

The Independents (often joined by the Independent Democrats) also give significantly lower ratings to the CBA's effectiveness in improving the quality of the bar, improving the efficiency of court procedures, enhancing the status of the profession, disciplining lawyers, and improving the lot of the disadvantaged. On all of these issues, the Regular Democrats (often joined by the Republicans) take the opposing position.

On the objective concerned with "improving the lot of the disadvantaged," the largest difference was between the Republicans, who rate that objective quite low in importance, and the Independents, who attach significantly greater importance to it. On another of the less popular roles, "taking stands on controversial issues of public policy," the big difference was between the Independent Democrats and the Republicans, the former giving the great importance to that objective.

Regular Democrats and Republicans attach less importance to the objective concerned with police procedures than do Independent Democrats and Independents, while the evaluation of the CBA's performance in this role indicated a significant difference between the two types of Democrats, the Regular Democrats rating the CBA more effective and the Independent Democrats finding it less so.

On a less explicitly political issue, "facilitating the referral of cases to qualified lawyers," there was a significant difference between Regular Democrats, on the one hand, and Independents, on the other, with the Independents attaching greater importance to the role. It is possible that this role may be seen as one of enhancing the availability of legal services to relatively low income persons rather than one of creating a market for the surplus labor of lawyers. If so, a greater commitment to this role would be consistent with the general, more liberal position of the Independents.

The unauthorized practice role, "preventing nonlawyers from doing legal work," is significantly more important to Regular Democrats than to any of the other three political groups. This may well reflect the degree of overlap between Regular Democratic political affiliation and type or kind of practice—that is, we know that higher proportion of the Regular Democrats are solo practitioners. It may be that many of them are engaged in the sort of neighborhood practice where competition from the local real estate agent, accountant, or banker is a matter of more concern than it is to the large firm lawyers and house counsel, who are disproportionately represented among the Republicans, Independents, and Independent Democrats.[19]

SEX

Male lawyers attach significantly more importance than do the women in our sample to "enhancing the status of the profession" and "preventing unauthorized practice." This finding was somewhat of a surprise since we had expected that these objectives would be more important to those whose law practice and professional status was less secure, and we would have thought that the position of women within the legal profession was not as secure, on the average, as that of men. The explanation may lie in other variables that are correlated with the sex of our respondents. The younger age groups, the nonreligious, and the lowest income groups also give lower ratings to the importance of these objectives, and women are overrepresented in each of these categories. It is also possible that women, younger lawyers, and those with lower law practice incomes have weaker ties to the profession—or that they are less dependent on it, personally, professionally, or financially—and that this explains their lower degree of concern with the status of the profession and with the encroachments of nonprofessionals. The other significant difference between the sexes in the importance ratings occurs on "improving the general lot of disadvantaged groups," where the women assign the objective greater importance. This finding is also consistent with the overrepresentation of women in the categories just noted and in the more liberal

19. When we examined the simultaneous impact of age, income, law school attended, and Chicago political preference, the independent effect of political affiliation becomes statistically insignificant.

political groupings. Women may feel they are relatively disadvantaged within the profession or otherwise identify with groups that are discriminated against. In the effectiveness ratings, women give the CBA significantly lower marks on the "disadvantaged groups" and the "lawyer discipline" objectives. The CBA is also given lower effectiveness ratings on the discipline item by the younger age groups, the nonreligious, the more liberal political groups, and the lower income groups, all of which contain disproportionate numbers of women.

AGE AND INCOME

The age and income variables are, of course, highly correlated; older lawyers having significantly higher incomes that younger lawyers.[20] Consequently, it is efficient to consider the two together in summarizing their relationships to the importance and effectiveness ratings.

The pattern in the effectiveness ratings is very clear. There were significant differences between the age groups on ten of the thirteen objectives (for two of the remaining three objectives there were *no* significant differences, on any variable, in the effectiveness ratings). On three of those ten objectives, there were also significant differences between income level groups. In each case in which there was a significant difference, the direction of that difference was the same—older age groups and higher income groups consistently gave the CBA higher effectiveness ratings than did younger or lower income groups. This finding might be interpreted in a number of ways. The younger lawyers' lower ratings might be attributed to a general tendency of the young to take antiestablishment positions. Or the younger lawyers might feel more "alienated" from the CBA, perhaps because they feel excluded from the higher levels of decision making in the Association. In this connec-

20. Thirty-two percent of the lawyers in our sample are under 35 years old, but that age group supplies 74 percent of the lawyers who make from $15,000 to $19,999 a year from the practice of law and only 5 percent of the lawyers who make more than $60,000. The 46 to 65 age group is 31 percent of the sample but supplies 44 percent of those making over $60,000 and only 9 percent of those making $15,000 to $19,999. After age 65, law practice income tends to diminish a bit, but that oldest age group is still substantially overrepresented in the over $60,000 income bracket. In the cross-tabulation of the age and income variables, both chi-square and Kendall's tau are highly significant.

tion, we might note that the Chicago Council of Lawyers attracts a membership that is disproportionately composed of younger lawyers. The Council may, therefore, provide at least some of the discontented younger lawyers with an opportunity to make their voices heard at an earlier age, and the presence of this opportunity in the Council may, in turn serve to emphasize its relative lack in the CBA—so that the CBA suffers by comparison. Similarly, those with lower incomes might have less regard for the effectiveness of the CBA because they may be, or may perceive themselves to be, less able to influence its actions.

The pattern of the importance ratings is much less clear. Older lawyers give higher importance ratings than do younger lawyers to four of the objectives—those dealing with "the status of the profession," "legislation," "disciplining lawyers," and "unauthorized practice." There are also significant income differences on two of these objectives, but one of them is the opposite of what the age difference would lead us to expect. Those in the $30,000 to $39,999 income range rate the importance of "improving the status of the profession" more highly than do those in the $40,000 to $59,999 bracket. This is consistent with a hypothesis that those who make more money will tend to be more secure, and thus less concerned with enhancing the status of their profession. But this line of argument is contradicted by the significantly greater importance given to this objective by older lawyers, whose place in the profession and the world is presumably more established.[21]

Age and income produce three other significant differences in the importance ratings. Younger lawyers and those with lower incomes give significantly higher ratings than do older lawyers and those with higher incomes to the three objectives ranked at the very bottom of the importance ratings—"improving the lot of the disadvantaged," "taking stands on controversial issues," and "facilitating client getting." The greater importance given by younger and lower income lawyers to the first two of these accords with the common view that younger lawyers, like younger persons in general, adhere to a more liberal, activist set of political values than do their older colleagues. A considerable amount of literature in recent years has described the emergence of a breed of "new professionals," particu-

21. When we examined the simultaneous impacts of age, income, law school, and Chicago political preference in a multivariate model, only age and law school remain significant.

larly in the legal profession, as epitomized by the "neighborhood legal services" lawyer.[22] If there is any truth to this literature, we should not be surprised to find that younger lawyers are more likely to espouse "exercising leadership to improve the general lot of disadvantaged groups" and "taking stands on controversial issues of public policy such as Vietnam, or school busing." The remaining objective rated more important by younger and lower income lawyers, however, calls for a different interpretation. "Client getting" appears to be given greater importance by groups that may be characterized as having lower social status within the legal profession—these include solo practitioners, small firm lawyers, and local law school graduates, as well as younger and lower income lawyers. The obvious explanation is that these groups have more need to build up their practices than do the more secure, older, high status lawyers in the larger firms. The ratings of the importance of client getting as a purpose of a bar association may also reflect the different methods by which different sorts of a lawyer get their clients.

ETHNICITY AND RELIGION

Both ethnicity and religion produce several significant differences in these ratings, but most of the ethnic differences appear to be racial differences. Two objectives are given significantly greater importance by blacks than by whites—"preventing unauthorized practice" and "improving the lot of the disadvantaged." Blacks—like solo practitioners and local law school graduates—may assign more importance to the unauthorized practice objective because the types of work in which they are engaged are more likely to be subject to competition from the services of nonlawyers. The obvious interpretation of the other clear racial difference is that black lawyers are specially concerned with the "lot of the disadvantaged" because, among the ethnic groups found in the bar in any number, blacks are the most likely to be considered "disadvantaged." On both of these objectives, the importance ratings of the blacks are

22. See, e.g., "The New Public Interest Lawyers," 79 *Yale Law Journal* 1069 (1970); Ronald Gross and Paul Osterman, eds., *The New Professionals* (New York: Simon and Schuster, 1972); F. Raymond Marks (with Kirk Leswing and Barbara A. Fortinsky), *The Lawyer, the Public, and Professional Responsibility* (Chicago: American Bar Foundation, 1972); Robert L. Rabin, "Lawyers for Social Change: Perspectives on Public Interest Law," 28 *Stanford Law Review* 207 (1976).

significantly higher than those of any of the white ethnic groups, but, among the whites, the northwestern Europeans and the "other" category assign these objectives even less importance than do the Irish and the southern and eastern Europeans. These findings may well reflect general social class differences. On another of the "social activism" objectives, "taking stands on controversial issues of public policy," the clear difference is between the higher importance ratings of the blacks, on the one hand, and the lower ratings of the northwestern Europeans, on the other. Here, blacks may well feel a special stake in some of the controversial issues—particularly the school busing issue that was specifically mentioned in the question. The significantly lower importance assigned by northwestern Europeans may reflect their disproportionate Republican affiliations[23] or a more generally "conservative" political position.

There are significant ethnic differences in the effectiveness ratings of the CBA on six of the objectives. In each case, the Irish give the CBA higher marks. On three of the objectives—"improving the quality of the bar," "improving the quality of the judiciary," and "enhancing the status of the profession"—the blacks join the Irish in giving significantly higher effectiveness ratings to the CBA. On these three objectives, and on a fourth—"initiating legislation"— the ethnic group that has a significantly *lower* opinion of the CBA's effectiveness is the southern and eastern European group. Though the pattern in these ratings appears quite striking, we find it rather difficult to interpret. The finding is generally consistent with the higher membership rate of the Irish in the CBA and the lower membership rate of the southern and eastern Europeans (see table 8.1), but this does not hold for the blacks, who have the lowest CBA membership rate. The position of the blacks on the two remaining significant differences in the effectiveness ratings, however, is consistent with their lower membership rate. The remaining differences occur on two of the "social activism" objectives, where the higher effectiveness ratings of the Irish are opposed by the blacks' significantly lower ratings of the CBA's performance. These two objectives are "improving the lot of disadvantaged groups," discussed above, and "promoting the development of police procedures that will accord with constitutional standards." Given the context of the controversy in recent years over methods of dealing with civilian

23. The percentage of Republicans is about 50 percent higher among respondents of northwestern European origin than it is in the sample as a whole.

complaints of police brutality, given the CBA's extensive involvement in that controversy, and given that a highly disproportionate number of the citizens with such complaints are black, we might have expected a racial difference on this objective. There was one— in the effectiveness rating—though not in the importance rating.

The significant differences between religious groups are quite consistent in the effectiveness ratings. The general pattern is that nonreligious respondents give the CBA lower effectiveness ratings than do respondents who have a religious preference or affiliation. This may reflect a tendency of the nonreligious to be less enthusiastic about organizations in general or to be antiestablishment; thus, their lower ratings of the effectiveness of the CBA may be akin in some way to those of the nonmembers, discussed above. This pattern holds for six of the seven objectives on which there are significant differences among the religious groups. On the seventh—"improving the status of the profession"—Catholics and Protestants give the CBA higher effectiveness ratings than do Jews. This finding is, in turn, consistent with a general tendency of both the Catholics and the Protestants to give the CBA higher marks.

The pattern of the importance ratings is less clear. Insofar as a pattern can be discerned, it is that the significant differences occur between nonreligious respondents, on the one hand, and Catholics and/or Jews, on the other. The nonreligious give significantly greater importance to "improving the quality of the judiciary," "facilitating referral," and "promoting constitutional police procedures," and significantly less importance to "enhancing the status of profession," "providing library and dining facilities," and "preventing unauthorized practice." The explanations of these results seem to lie in the correlations between religion and other characteristics of the respondents, including age and political affiliation.[24]

LAW SCHOOL ATTENDED

In our analysis of patterns of participation in the CBA, we found that the category of law school attended by our respondents was

24. When we used multivariate analysis to control for the effects of age and political preference, religion became insignificant on all of these objectives except "enhancing the status of the profession." There, the independent main effect of religion remained significant at the .04 level.

significantly correlated with several of the participation variables. The law school categories also produce some significant differences in the importance and effectiveness ratings but not so many as several of the other independent variables.

The graduates of elite law schools gave the CBA lower effectiveness ratings than did the graduates of less prestigious schools[25] on the objectives dealing with "improving the quality of the judiciary," "disciplining lawyers," and "improving the lot of the disadvantaged." It may be that the elite law school graduates tend to have higher standards of performance, whether these are inculcated by the schools themselves (we think this unlikely), are related to the types of practice in which the elite law school graduates are engaged, or are a function of the types of personalities who are selected by (and who select themselves for) the elite law schools in the first place.

In the importance ratings, there are significant differences between the law school categories on four objectives. Three of these— "improving the status of the profession," "preventing unauthorized practice," and "facilitating client getting"—are given greater importance by local law school graduates than by those from elite schools. Each of these objectives is quite closely related to the problems of those at the lower end of the status scale in the legal profession. The greater insecurity of such lawyers may lead them to be more concerned about the "status of the profession," the types of work in which they are engaged are more likely to be threatened by competition from the "unauthorized practice of law" by real estate brokers and the like, and they may have more need for "client getting."[26] The fourth objective is quite different in character. It is "improving the quality of the judiciary," which is given significantly less importance by the graduates of local law schools and significantly greater importance by the graduates of regional law schools. The local law school graduates may see improving the quality of the judiciary as a threat to their aspirations for a seat on the bench— thus, they may well see the judicial reform movement as "elitist" and see the existing system of political selection of judges, the tradi-

25. The schools included in the elite category are Chicago, Columbia, Harvard, Michigan, Stanford and Yale; see p. 15.
26. The independent main effect of law school remains significant on each of the objectives when we control for the effects of type of practice and income. This may suggest that the status of law school attended is a better predictor of the generalized status security of lawyers than is their type of practice.

tional target of the reformers, as their most likely avenue into the judiciary. It is more difficult to interpret the finding that regional law school graduates, rather than those from the elite or prestige schools, give the greatest importance to this objective, but it may be that the regional law school graduates feel themselves to be most directly in competition with the graduates of the local schools. That is, if the system were changed in such a way as to give local law school graduates fewer seats on the state bench (and it is the state judgeships that are, no doubt, perceived to be the greater part of the problem), then the beneficiaries of this development might well be the regional law school graduates.

TYPES OF PRACTICE AND SIZE OF FIRM [27]

Four of the significant differences between the "type of practice" categories may be explained by the effects of social and professional status on the structure of law practice. We have just noted the greater importance given by local law school graduates to "improving the status of the profession," "preventing unauthorized practice," and "facilitating client getting." Solo practitioners also attach significantly greater importance than do large firm lawyers to those same three objectives and, if the interpretation offered above was correct, it would seem to be equally applicable here. A disproportionate number of solo practitioners attended the local law schools, and these objectives thus appear to be of unusually great concern to this segment of the bar, whichever characteristics we may use to identify the segment.[28] Similarly, solo practitioners are significantly more likely to rate the CBA as effective on the "lawyer discipline" objective. Carlin has observed that solo practitioners are disciplined (or threatened with discipline) more often than are other lawyers.[29] If this is so, it might explain why solos perceive the system of professional discipline to be more effective.

The significant difference between house counsel and solo practi-

27. In this set of analyses, size of firm was analyzed separately from the type of practice categories—that is, size of firm and type of practice were treated as two variables. In the type of practice analyses here, all firm lawyers were grouped together. A second analysis was then done on all lawyers in private practice, distinguishing among four categories of size of firm—solos, firms with fewer than 10 lawyers, firms with 10 to 30 lawyers, and firms with more than 30 lawyers.
28. See *supra* note 26.
29. Carlin, *supra* note 9.

tioners on "facilitating the referral of cases to qualified lawyers," house counsel giving the objective greater importance and solos giving it less, may be attributable to the relative stakes that the two types of lawyers perceive in CBA referral networks. Many corporate law departments refer out significant portions of the company's legal work—litigation is often handled by outside counsel, as are tax, labor, and antitrust problems—and house counsel may thus value highly the opportunities that the CBA provides for contact with lawyers in these specialties. Solo practitioners, by contrast, have little need to locate qualified lawyers to whom they may refer specialized problems, they receive few of their cases through such referral networks, and, thus, they probably do not see themselves as the beneficiaries of the contacts fostered by the CBA.

Firm lawyers and house counsel give significantly greater importance to the library and dining facilities than do government lawyers. This seems quite understandable, since government agencies are likely to maintain library and dining facilities that are more extensive than those provided by many law firms and businesses, and since government lawyers probably have little professional need for the informal contacts with other lawyers that are facilitated by the CBA's dining rooms. Within the category of those in private practice, lawyers from small firms are more likely to feel that the library and dining facilities are important than are either those from large firms or solo practitioners. Small firms probably do not have law libraries adequate to their needs, while lawyers from larger firms will much less frequently need to use materials that are not available in their own libraries, and the type of practice engaged in by many solo practitioners is less dependent upon library research. Both solo practitioners and big firm lawyers may also have less professional need for the social contacts provided by the CBA dining facilities than do those from smaller firms.

Finally, house counsel and firm lawyers give significantly higher importance ratings to "improving the quality of the judiciary" than do solos and government lawyers. Within the private practice category, large firm lawyers rate this objective as significantly more important than do small firm lawyers and solos. These findings may, again, reflect both the political affiliations of the lawyers in the respective practice categories and their expectations about the most likely paths to the bench for themselves or for their friends who share their characteristics. Regular Democrats are somewhat disproportionately represented among the small firm lawyers, the solos, and, especially, the government lawyers, and these associated groups appear to be more satisfied with the present method of selection of state judges than are, say, the Independent Democrats, who are more heavily represented in the largest firms.[30]

Types of Objectives

To this point, we have been examining how various subgroups within the legal profession evaluate the importance of several objectives that the CBA might pursue. We have noted that lawyers with different social backgrounds, political preferences, and practice characteristics do differ, often in quite profound ways, in their vision of the CBA's mandate to serve the needs of the profession and the larger society. But these results give a somewhat disjointed picture of the more general conceptions of the ideal professional association that might underlie the individual respondents' judgments on specific objectives. If we could somehow identify the nature of the differences among these more general conceptions, we could go some way toward characterizing the various potential and actual constituency groups inside and outside the CBA that have conflicting demands and expectations for the organization.

We have used a statistical technique called factor analysis to determine the presence of common factors that account for similarities and differences in the ways individuals assign relative importance among all the objectives.[31] A person with a high score on a given factor tends to regard the corresponding subset of objectives as being of greater importance than he does certain other objectives. A person with a low score on a factor, of course, tends to reverse this pattern.

We found that four underlying factors accounted for a very substantial part of the common elements in the ways individuals evalu-

30. Multivariate analysis reveals that, when we control for the simultaneous effects of age, income, law school attended, and political preference, the independent main effect of political affiliation is the only one that remains significant.

31. For a brief explanation of factor analysis, see Blalock, *supra* note 18, pp. 383–91. For a more detailed consideration of the subject, see Harry H. Harman, *Modern Factor Analysis* (Chicago: University of Chicago Press, 1960).

ate the possible objectives of the CBA.[32] The nature of the objectives that fall into each of these four categories suggests the following labels for the constituencies that embrace them:

1. Professional reformers
2. Reformers of the profession
3. Enhancers of professional position
4. Enhancers of personal position

The objectives that correspond to each of these four labels are:

1. Take stands on controversial issues
   Improve the lot of the disadvantaged
   Improve police procedures
2. Discipline lawyers
   Improve the quality of the bar
   Improve the quality of the judiciary
   Improve court efficiency
3. Enhance the status of the profession
   Stop unauthorized practice
   Initiate legislation
4. Facilitate client getting
   Facilitate referral of cases
   Provide library and dining facilities

(Keep in mind that we did not assign the objectives to these categories. Rather, this is how factor analysis groups them according to the common tendencies in our respondents' ratings.)

The first of these categories, or factors, would seem to reflect quite clearly what we have already called the "social activist" constituency. The respondents who gave relatively high importance ratings to these objectives appear to favor a broader role for the CBA in the community and in the world of politics, using the influence and authority of the legal profession to foster social goals that they regard as desirable. It is interesting to note that the groups that assign importance to CBA action on these objectives (blacks, Independent Democrats and Independents, young lawyers, and low income lawyers) appear to assume that, were the CBA to take an active role in these matters, it would espouse positions that would accord with their preferences. Given the composition of the CBA, one might well question that implicit assumption. There is, no

32. These four factors cumulatively account for 56 percent of the variance; factor 1 alone accounts for 26 percent of the variance.

doubt, a tendency to believe that one's position on the issues will be shared by all "right-thinking people" or "men of good will," but the social activists should recognize that they are far from a majority of the CBA.

The second factor includes two objectives concerned with making lawyers better—one by weeding out the wicked and the other by enhancing the skills of those who are left. The remaining two objectives are those concerned with improving the judiciary and the courts. Thus, like the first factor, this one has a reformist orientation, but here the focus is on the profession itself rather than on extending the profession's role into the broader society.

The third factor is also oriented toward the profession, but it is less reformist and more "self-interested" in character. Enhancing the status of the profession will, presumably, in turn enhance the status of those in the profession, and stopping unauthorized practice will benefit those members of the profession who are in competition with unauthorized practitioners. The third objective in this factor, "initiating legislation," does not seem to fit our interpretation quite so neatly, but it may be that the role postulated for the CBA is to initiate legislation that would benefit these practitioners by benefiting their clients or by making their practice easier or more comfortable.

The final factor is yet more narrowly oriented. Rather than addressing concerns of the broader society or of the profession as a whole, these objectives have more to do with enhancing the individual's own practice or personal situation. This seems quite clear with the library and dining facilities objectives and with "client getting"—and, as we have previously suggested, "facilitating referral" may simply be "client getting" expressed in more palatable language. The fact that both of these objectives appear in the same factor tends to support this interpretation.

Conclusions

The four categories or "factors" of possible bar association objectives may be thought of as describing four potential constituencies that the CBA might seek to serve. The constituencies are not, of course, mutually exclusive—any lawyer might assign importance to objectives in a number of the categories, and the constituencies thus overlap. Our respondents, however, seem to have assigned a rather clear hierarchy of importance to the four types of objectives. The type that is rated substantially more important than any of the others is the factor that we have characterized as "reform of the profession"—this includes the objectives dealing with improving the quality of the judiciary, improving the efficiency of the courts, improving the quality of the bar, and disciplining lawyers. The percentage of our respondents rating those objectives either "important" or "very important" averages 91 percent for the four objectives in the category. The next most important, in the opinion of our sample, is the "enhancement of professional position" category, where the average is 78 percent. The objectives that are concerned with reform that extends beyond the profession to the broader society are rated least important.[33] Thus, while many of our respondents seem to want the CBA to become engaged in reform, most prefer that these reformist activities be confined within the limits of the profession—that the profession heal itself before attempting to heal the society.

Turning to the effectiveness ratings, we see that the highest levels of satisfaction with the CBA's performance are registered on the objectives dealing with the library and dining facilities (38 percent "highly effective" and 56 percent "effective") and with improving the quality of the bar (15 percent "highly effective" and 58 percent "effective"). We think it significant that these are rather innocuous, noncontroversial roles. The effectiveness ratings of the CBA are lowest, by contrast, on the objectives dealing with improving the lot of the disadvantaged (1 percent "highly effective" and 15 percent "effective"), with stands on controversial issues of public policy (1 percent "highly effective" and 14 percent "effective"), and with reform of police procedures (1 percent "highly effective" and 13 percent "effective"). These objectives are all quite controversial in nature. Our findings concerning the ratings of the CBA's effec-

33. These objectives were rated as either "important" or "very important" by an average of 49 percent of our respondents. There was, however, considerable variation within the category; only 29 percent of the respondents rated "taking stands on controversial issues of public policy" as either important or very important, while 50 percent gave those ratings to "improving the lot of the disadvantaged" and 68 percent thought that the "police procedures" objective was, at least, important. The factor that was rated third in importance deals with enhancing personal interests or position; these objectives were rated important or very important by an average of 60 percent of our respondents.

tiveness might be accounted for in a number of ways, but one good hypothesis is that the CBA finds it very difficult to take effective action if there is any substantial amount of controversy about the issue, though it is capable of doing quite a good job if the goal is almost universally shared. Thus, the members who attach importance to the library and dining facilities are relatively well satisfied, while those who value social activism are frustrated by the CBA's inability to act decisively.

In recent years, the Association has tried to recruit the widest possible segment of the Chicago bar. One past president told us that it was his belief and his goal that "every lawyer in Chicago should belong." As an example of a subgroup in which the CBA might wish to improve its recruiting, let us consider the younger lawyers. It is within this group that the competition from the Chicago Council of Lawyers is felt most keenly (see table 8.1), and there is also the fear that lawyers who are not attracted to membership in the Association while young may learn to get along without it throughout their careers. A CBA leader whom we interviewed was worried that the CBA might "miss out on the next generation of leaders of the bar." We found that younger lawyers attach significantly greater importance to "taking stands on controversial issues of public policy such as Vietnam or school busing." But if the CBA were to attempt to attract new, young members by taking stands on such issues—even assuming that the substance of the stands taken would be sympathetic to the views of these same younger lawyers—the increased attractiveness of the CBA to this constituency would be purchased only at the cost of greatly decreased attractiveness to several other, much larger constituencies. Moreover, if we look more closely at the ratings of the importance of this objective, we find that even for the youngest age group, those under age 35, the mean importance rating was only 2.84 on a five-point scale, slightly below the midpoint of 3.0. That is, even the youngest lawyers rate this objective on the "little importance" side of "undecided." The older age groups were all even more negative about the goal. To purchase some increased attractiveness for the CBA among some younger lawyers, therefore, would almost certainly alienate much larger numbers of lawyers—perhaps even a majority of the youngest age group.[34]

34. Only 37 percent of our respondents in the youngest age group, those under 35, rated this goal as either important or very important.

In analyzing the relationships between, on the one hand, CBA membership, committee membership, and leadership and, on the other, nationality, religion, and political affiliation, we found only one statistically significant correlation—a correlation of moderate strength between political affiliation and committee membership (see table 8.2). Nationality was not systematically related to any of the differences in participation rates; neither was religion. The factors that seem to be much more closely associated with these participation rates are those that have a more direct relationship to the practice of law—that is, law practice income, type of practice, firm size, and law school attended. But when we analyzed the respondents' ratings of the importance of various possible bar association objectives and of the CBA's performance on those objectives, we found that the reverse was true. That is, the law practice variables accounted for much less of the variation in these ratings than did the broader demographic variables, such as religious and political preferences. The priorities given to organizational goals are thus more influenced by the respondents' broader value systems, political or religious, and less influenced by the immediacies of everyday practice situations than are their probabilities of participation in the CBA.

A simple comparison table will quickly indicate the extent to which the CBA membership is representative of the characteristics of the Chicago bar. As table 8.6 makes quite clear, the composition of the membership of the CBA does not look very different from that of the bar as a whole.

But the very diversity of the CBA's membership may be a burden as well as a blessing. Our analysis documents the diversity of opinion within Chicago's bar on major professional and social issues, and the broad-based, representative membership of the CBA, therefore, makes it more difficult to mobilize the organization's resources around specific policy initiatives in controversial areas within the profession or the larger society.[35] Organizations with a narrower

35. When considering the role of a professional association in public affairs, it is important to keep in mind the limits of the influence that any association might reasonably be expected to have on major issues of professional or public concern. Bar associations play minor roles in the professional lives of most lawyers; in competing against the time demands of developing a successful practice and making a living, the associations are at a considerable disadvantage. When an association succeeds in gaining its members' attentions, it is most often as a place to have lunch with a client, to look at a book not available in one's professional library, to get a quick update on recent developments in a legal specialty, or to become known as someone

TABLE 8.6
CBA Members Compared to Full Bar on
Selected Characteristics

Characteristic	Percent of CBA Members	Percent of Total Bar
Irish	16	14
Black	2	3
Southern & eastern European	24	25
Catholic	29	29
Jewish	28	27
Nonreligious	10	12
Independent political affiliation	19	20
Regular Democrats	22	19
Local law-school graduates	42	46
Elite law-school graduates	25	20
Solo practitioners	16	19
House counsel	12	13
Lawyers from firms with more than 30 lawyers	19	16
Law practice incomes over $60,000	21	17

membership, such as the Chicago Council of Lawyers, do not face such serious problems in developing consensus on matters of public policy, but the price they pay is also high. They have a more limited membership appeal, fewer organizational resources and services, and increased vulnerability to charges of special pleading for particular ideological or political interests.

Herein lies the dilemma of every professional association. The more its membership reflects the diversity of the larger society, the more limited and noncontroversial will be the goals that it is able to achieve. Conversely, the more limited or elitist its recruitment, the more it is able to take clear stands on controversial issues, but the less it is able to serve as an effective vehicle for mobilizing both public and professional opinion behind particular courses of action.

The development of the legal profession in Chicago and elsewhere evinces an almost uninterrupted move toward specialization and fragmentation. Not only do these lawyers have specialized knowledge of particular bodies of law but also, as we have argued,

---

(continued)
to whom certain kinds of cases might be referred. The association's official positions on matters of public moment are likely to be only one (and probably not a very important) influence on the thinking of its members.

they come to identify with particular types of corporate or individual clients from diverse parts of the larger society. The clients have competing interests and concerns that are reflected both in the advocacy and in the more subtle value positions of the lawyers representing them. Thus, increasing specialization also produces the rise within the profession of distinctive and often irreconcilable interests and perspectives on legal and social issues. This growing heterogeneity means that a bar association that is broadly representative of the major elements within the profession is less and less likely to be able to satisfy all of its constituencies. Any action of the association that would be likely to be regarded as "decisive" or "progressive" is also likely to offend one or more of these major factions.[36] There are too many groups within the profession that have too many conflicts with too many other groups—conflicts that are deep seated and not subject to compromise.

36. Interests that benefit from the status quo, however, are well served by a standoff among the conflicting veto groups; see p. 243, pp. 326-27, and pp. 346-50.

Chapter 9

THE CONSTITUENCIES

OF "NOTABLE"

CHICAGO LAWYERS

IN THE two previous chapters, we have dealt with the networks of informal association among Chicago lawyers and with the patterns of their more formal joint activity in the principal organization of the city's bar. But there are, of course, important connections among lawyers that are not expressed through the bar associations and that are not directly derived from their work activities and relationships. Many lawyers are involved in politics, for example, and that will certainly bring some of them together. Similarly, some members of the bar will meet and work with other lawyers in community activities such as school boards, hospital boards, or sundry charitable organizations. Some may be active in fraternal lodges or veterans' activities, where they may come into contact with yet other lawyers. Lawyers who have ties to close-knit ethnoreligious communities will form relationships with fellow attorneys who share their membership in those communities. And some lawyers may become acquainted through the industry groups of their client businesses. Thus, a lawyer who serves oil and gas companies may associate with other such lawyers in business conferences or in the activities of the industry's trade associations.

Lawyers—like other citizens, but perhaps more than many—may participate in a variety of public activities, creating overlapping networks of association. These various circles of acquaintance all provide opportunities for lawyers to achieve prominence of one degree of another since the participants in each of these realms of activity will constitute a potential constituency that may provide its leaders with varying amounts of recognition and other resources. The lawyers who are prominent within the profession and outside it thus draw upon several distinct sources of prominence, which may or may not create distinct sets of "leaders of the bar." It is possible that the several sorts of constituencies might give rise to separate "spheres of influence" within the bar or, in the alternative, that the mechanisms and agencies of the profession might serve to integrate some or all of the various bases of leadership, making it possible to mobilize varying constituencies toward common goals. (As we saw in chapter 8, however, the latter does not appear to occur in the Chicago Bar Association, and such political integration probably becomes less likely as lawyers become increasingly specialized by type of client.) The identification of the leaders of the major constituencies—and of the extent of the overlaps among the constituencies and their leaderships—is, then, a preliminary step in charting the distribution of influence within the profession.

Accordingly, one of the principal objectives of our research was to identify and analyze the characteristics of the circles of acquaintanceship of various sorts of "elite" Chicago lawyers. We approached this objective by compiling a list of lawyers who were notable for one or more types of influence.[1] Informants who are knowledgeable about the Chicago bar were consulted during the preparation of the list, and efforts were made to represent several kinds of elites. Some were included because of positions they held. For example, the deans of three law schools and the five most recent presidents of the Chicago Bar Association (CBA) were placed on the list, as were all four of the persons who had, up to that time (1975), served as president of the Chicago Council of Lawyers, a group of younger,

1. The list was not intended to include all of the most noteworthy lawyers in Chicago—and it surely did not. Rather, the list sought to represent notable lawyers with a variety of social and professional backgrounds, as described in the text below, and prominent lawyers of a type that was well represented on the list were, therefore, excluded. It is surely the case that many Chicago lawyers who were not included on our list are more "prominent" or "well known" than some of those who were listed.

reform-oriented lawyers.[2] Chicagoans who had held office in the Illinois State Bar Association were also included. Most of the lawyers chosen were, however, selected reputationally—that is, they were chosen because they were widely reputed to possess the sorts of influence that we wished to represent. Some were selected because they were known to hold power within one of the important political factions in the city, some because they were thought to be "pillars of the establishment" of the profession, and others because they were widely said to be among the best-known and most successful practitioners in particular fields or areas of the law, thus giving them influence based on their prominence, their command of the respect of their professional colleagues.

An effort was made to represent the major ethnoreligious groupings, and the final list was also structured to include solo practitioners and partners in large, medium-sized, and small firms. No special effort was made to include government-employed lawyers or corporate house counsel, and none in fact appear on the list.[3] We deliberately excluded from the list all lawyers who were then in public office, such as judges, prosecutors, and legislators, because we wished to avoid confounding *personal* influence with *governmental* authority.[4] Because our population was deliberately selected to consist of elite, influential lawyers, it substantially overrepresents older persons,[5] graduates of the more prestigious law schools, and senior partners from large firms. Young lawyers, graduates of less prestigious schools, and solo and small firm practitioners are, however, also represented. Few blacks or women had reached positions of great prominence within the bar by 1975 (or even today), and our list includes only three blacks and two women, but in neither case do those numbers underrepresent their proportions of the total bar (see chap. 1).

2. For an extended account of this counter-bar organization, see Michael Powell, "Anatomy of a Counter-Bar Association: The Chicago Council of Lawyers," 1979 *American Bar Foundation Research Journal* 501–41 (summer).

3. See Jeffrey S. Slovak, "Working for Corporate Actors: Social Change and Elite Attorneys in Chicago," 1979 *American Bar Foundation Research Journal* 465–500 (Summer).

4. Some persons included on the list had held public office in the past, and one private practitioner currently held the part-time elective post of trustee of the University of Illinois. We do not believe that that position was likely to be the source of any great power or influence within the profession.

5. Six of the 43 lawyers included on the final list were in their mid-30s (including the 4 presidents of the CCL) and 3 were in their early 70s. The distribution of the remaining 34 lawyers was skewed toward the high end—7 were in their 40s, 11 in their 50s, and 16 in their 60s.

During the interviews with each of our 777 respondents, we handed the respondent a printed card containing the list of "notable" lawyers.[6] (The lawyers on this list are sometimes collectively referred to below as "the notables." This term has the advantage of giving a sociological grouping some of the cachet of a Motown recording group.) The respondent was then asked to go through the list twice. On the first run-through, the respondent was asked to check the names of those lawyers with whom he was "personally acquainted." Then he was asked to select from among the names already checked those notables about whom the respondent could say that, because of their "personal relationship," the notable "would find the time to advise" the respondent. These procedures were intended to get at successively stronger levels of acquaintance. Both the looser, lower standard of acquaintance and the more stringent standard can be used to generate a network structure, and we have analyzed both levels. The two structures are highly similar. The main difference is that the lower standard produces a somewhat weaker, fuzzier solution, presumably because of the chance acquaintanceships or very casual, weak relationships elicited by the less stringent question. We have, therefore, used the results based on the higher standard in the analyses presented here. Since the two questions were both intended to measure acquaintance, of differing levels or strength, we speak below of the stronger level in terms of whether or not the respondents "knew" the notables; this should be read, of course, to mean that they were acquainted with them to the specified degree.

The Likelihood of Knowing Notables

One of the most important things to note about our findings is that fully 38 percent of our random sample of respondents knew *none* of

6. The list of notable lawyers that we used in our interviews included 49 names (see appendix A, question Q19). Six of those have been dropped from the analysis as it is presented here—2 because they were "ringers" in the first place, relatively unknown lawyers included as a validity check and to establish the baseline probability of acquaintance, 1 (a tax lawyer from a small firm) because he died between the printing of the interview instrument and the administration of the survey and we were uncertain about the effect of the development on the results, and 3 because they were elderly and known by relatively few respondents or redundant, given the types of lawyers represented by others on the list.

the forty-three notables. Another 37 percent of the respondents knew from one to three; the remaining 25 percent knew four or more. Only ten individuals claimed to know as many as half of the notables. These findings suggest that only a small minority of the bar is in close or regular contact with any substantial segment of the elites of the profession,[7] even when one considers a broad range of types of elites. Such contacts as occur are, of course, highly differentiated according to the social and practice characteristics of both the respondents and the notables, as we shall see below.[8] For now, however, let us not concern ourselves with the patterns of differential association with varying elites but merely note some of the correlations between the respondents' characteristics and the probability that they will know any of the notables.

The type of law school attended by a respondent significantly affects the likelihood that he will be acquainted with lawyers who are among our forty-three notables.[9] Respondents who attended elite or prestige schools are overrepresented among those who know more notables, while those who attended regional or local law schools are underrepresented among the better acquainted respondents.[10] For example, graduates of elite schools constitute only 14 percent of the respondents who know none of the notables, but they make up 21 percent of the group who know from one to three and 31 percent of those who are acquainted with more than three notables. By contrast, lawyers who went to regional schools make up 25 percent of the group who know no notables, 14 percent of those who know one to three, and only 6 percent of those who know more than three notables. Similarly, respondents who have

---

7. The ringers that we had included among the list of notables (see *supra* note 6) proved to have limited utility for estimation of the baseline probability of acquaintance among any 2 members of the Chicago bar. One of the criteria that we had used for the selection of these ringers was the ethnicity of their names—one was obviously Irish and the other obviously German. The Irishman was a solo practitioner, and the German was a partner in a small firm. We eventually discovered that the German was better known than we had thought, and that he did not, therefore, serve the purpose of indicating the baseline probability of acquaintance. Though he was far less widely known than most of the notable lawyers on our list, he was better known than one of them. The lawyer of Irish descent, however, proved to be genuinely obscure. Only 7 of our respondents claimed to know him. The mean number of respondents knowing each of the 43 notables on the final list is 51.7. The ringer with a German name was known by 26.

8. For the segregation of the notables into distinct networks of elites, see figures 9.1–9.6.

9. Chi square significant at <.01; *r* = .17.

10. See chapter 1, pp. 15–16, for definitions of categories of law schools.

higher incomes are significantly overrepresented among those knowing more notables, while those with lower incomes are underrepresented.[11] The reasons for both of these tendencies are quite obvious.

Age is also correlated with the likelihood of knowing the notables.[12] The mean age of the respondents who do not know any notables is 41.5; the mean age of those who know more than three is 50.6.[13] The interpretation of this finding is, again, quite straightforward—it no doubt reflects both the age of the notables and the tendency to accumulate more acquaintances as one's life goes on. The existence of a correlation between age and the level of acquaintance with notables, however, suggests the desirability of reexamining the correlation between income and acquaintance to determine whether income has an effect that is independent of age or whether the effect is attributable merely to the tendency of income to increase with age. If we correlate income with the number of notables known while controlling for age, we find that the income effect is still significant.[14] Emphasizing the statistical significance of these correlations between income and acquaintance may, however, distort their substantive meaning. Whichever of the correlational methods we use, the relationships between respondents' incomes and the extent of their connections with the notables is not large—income explains only about 10 to 12 percent of the variance in acquaintanceship. Since superior access to notables (often thought of as "contacts") may be of value in increasing one's income over the longer term, this modest correlation between income and notable acquaintanceship is the more surprising. That is, the relationship between the variables may be reciprocal, higher incomes tending to increase access to notables and access to notables tending to increase income. Given the fact that these two tendencies may reinforce one another, the observed correlation is not as high as might have been expected.

Neither the religious affiliations of the respondents nor their political party preferences are significantly correlated with the extent of their acquaintance with notables.[15] Because the list of notables

11. Chi square significant at $<.01$; $r = .34$.
12. The simple Pearson's correlation between age and the number of notables known is .3.
13. F significant at $<.01$; $r = .25$.
14. The partial correlation is .29, significant at $< .01$.
15. That is, the chi squares do not achieve even the .05 level of significance.

was deliberately structured to include a more or less balanced representation of the various religious and political groupings, there would be no reason to expect overall levels of acquaintanceship to be biased by these variables.

There is a significant correlation between the sort of organizational setting in which respondents practice and their levels of acquaintance,[16] but the only strong differences are that respondents from large firms (those with more than thirty lawyers) are overrepresented and house counsel underrepresented among those knowing more than three notables. Both of these tendencies are probably attributable to the composition of the group of notables. Many of the most influential members of the legal profession are partners in the major firms, thus causing them to be substantially overrepresented on the list, and we have already pointed out that the list includes no house counsel.

The Characteristics of the Notables

In analyzing the social networks within the profession, it is necessary to consider a wide range of the notables' characteristics, any one of which might have important impact on the structure of relationships. Because we are dealing with forty-three individuals who occupy a variety of social positions and possess a great many combinations of personal background characteristics, it is not possible to summarize the variables in brief compass and yet do justice to the data. The notables' network structure, as we analyze and present it, includes several broad features that are readily discernible, but other points of interest rest on observations that are more subtle, more fine-grained, and yet distinct.

Therefore, we will set forth the characteristics of each of the forty-three notables in some detail so that the reader may evaluate our interpretation of the features of the structure. In both the biographies of the notables and the presentation of the smallest space analysis that we have used to examine the patterns of relationships (see figure 9.1), each of the notables is given a pseudonym. This has been done to facilitate the depiction of the structure of the relation-

16. Significant at <.01; eta = .20.

ships among broad types of elites within the profession.[17] The initial letters of the pseudonyms indicate the major classifications of the notables.

Categories of Notables	No. in Each Category
B = Leaders of the organized bar	10
D = Law school deans	3
E = Establishment	5
L = Prominent liberals	7
La = Presidents of the Chicago Council of Lawyers	4
M = Miscellaneous	2
R = Regular Democrats	3
T = Trial lawyers	9

Biographical Sketches of Notables

ORGANIZED BAR (B)

Baer. A partner in a small, family firm with her husband and father-in-law, she is in the line of succession to the presidency of the

17. Since many of these notable lawyers will be readily identifiable by persons familiar with the Chicago bar or by others who take the trouble to inquire, the use of pseudonyms will not be adequate to preserve the anonymity of many of the notables. But the real names would mean little or nothing to most of the readers of this book, and for those readers there would thus be no advantage in use of those names. The pseudonyms, however, do provide an advantage—they permit us to use the initial letters of the names to identify the major category of notability that caused the lawyer to be included in the list. This makes figure 9.1 easier to comprehend. When data are as complex as these, a device that organizes the data and aids comprehension is surely welcome.

As to the matter of anonymity, we should note that none of the biographical information presented was obtained from confidential sources. We did not seek to interview the notables. In some instances, however, notables were interviewed as respondents included in one or another of our samples. Two happened to come up in our random sample for the cross-sectional survey. Twelve were included in one or more of the samples of elites, identified positionally, that were used in other surveys conducted by our associates. (See, e.g., Slovak, *supra* note 3.) Even for those notables who were interviewed, however, no use has been made in these biographies of information obtained during the interviews. The information presented here on the subjects' practice and personal characteristics was gathered from published sources or from persons who are well informed about the Chicago bar. Many of the notables are included in standard biographical reference works; newspaper accounts have also been used. In several cases, our biographical sketches do not include information on a notable's political party preference, ethnicity, or religion. These are cases where the

Illinois State Bar Association. She will be the first woman to hold
that post, and she is one of only two women on this list of notable
lawyers. She has been active in organized bar work on civil rights.
There are a great many lawyers in both her family and her husband's, and there are family ties to the Regular Democratic Organization. Age 40; Jewish; graduate of Northwestern Law School.

Baker.   A name partner in a medium-sized firm with a general corporate practice, he specializes in securities work. He is a past president of the Chicago Bar Association. He has also been very active in
the Boy Scouts, serving at the national level, and he is on the boards
of some smaller corporations. Mid-60s; Jewish; Northwestern Law
School.

Barents.   A partner in an old-line firm, specializing in general corporate and probate work, he participated in drafting the Illinois
Probate Court Act. He is a past president of the CBA. In his early
70s, he is one of the oldest persons on this list. Of Dutch ancestry;
educated at Phillips Exeter Academy, Harvard College, and Harvard
Law School.

Beiderbecke.   A partner in one of the largest and most prestigious
Chicago firms, he is the immediate past president of the Chicago
Bar Association. Though his firm is general counsel for several major corporations, his own work is in the the area of personal injury
defense (representing insurance companies). Of German ancestry,
he is 60 and a graduate of John Marshall Law School.

Behan.   Probably the most celebrated personal injury plaintiffs'
lawyer in Chicago. A past president of the CBA, he is an Irish Catholic; went to Loyola for both undergraduate work and law school; a
Regular Democrat; age 51.

Behrman.   A name partner in a medium-sized firm that does general corporate and probate work, he is a past president of the CBA.
He and Behan got more press than other recent presidents of the
CBA; Behrman's press coverage dealt with organized bar affairs,
while Behan's dealt more with his personal injury work. Jewish;
mid-60s; University of Chicago, both undergraduate and law school.

Bigard.   A name partner in a small firm, doing personal injury de-

(continued)
information was not available from published sources nor from persons knowledgeable about the Chicago bar. If these facts were unknown to our informants, it may be
reasonable to assume that the characteristics are not an important part of the roles of
those notables in the profession.

fense and general trial work. Now in the line of succession to the presidency of the CBA, he has long been active in the Association and has held a number of lesser offices. Of northwestern European ancestry, he is in his early 60s and is a graduate of John Marshall Law School.

Blackburn. A senior partner in one of the largest and most prestigious firms, he was president of the CBA several years ago and is now the president-elect of the ABA. His practice is primarily in public utilities and other large corporate work. He has served on many important boards and commissions. He is a registered Republican; WASP; mid-60s; attended Dartmouth College and Columbia Law School.

Brendan. A name partner in a small firm doing general trial work, including some personal injury defense and some probate work, he is the current president of the CBA. Irish Catholic; attended Villanova for undergraduate work and Loyola Law School. He has been described in the Chicago newspapers as a "nominal North Shore Republican but loyal to the Daley Machine." He is in his mid-50s.

Bricker. A name partner in a medium-sized firm, he defends steel companies in environmental pollution actions, but he also does probate work and is a Fellow of the American College of Probate Counsel. He is a past president of the Illinois State Bar Association. He has served on the boards of the Chicago Association of Commerce and Industry and the American Judicature Society and is a member of the Episcopal Diocesan Council. Mid-60s; WASP: graduate of the University of Michigan Law School.

LAW SCHOOL DEANS (D)

Dodds. The dean of the University of Chicago Law School. His specialty is antitrust, and he maintains a consulting relationship with a downtown firm. Before joining the Chicago faculty thirteen years ago, he was on the faculty at Stanford. WASP; mid-50s; graduate of both Harvard College and Harvard Law School.

Dolphy. The dean of the Northwestern Law School. Like Dodds, his specialty is antitrust, and, also like Dodds, he maintained for several years an active relationship with a downtown corporate firm. Protestant of German descent; late 50s; Northwestern both undergraduate and law school; long-time member of the Northwestern law faculty.

Drootin. The dean of the De Paul Law School. He teaches and publishes in the area of property and future interests. He has been a member of the De Paul faculty for ten years, joining it only a year after graduation from Loyola Law School. At 36, he is one of the younger persons on this list.

ESTABLISHMENT (E)

Eldridge. The senior, name partner of one of largest and most prestigious Chicago firms. He is well known as a civil litigator, and he has held numerous important positions. He was a member of the National Commission on the Causes and Prevention of Violence in 1968–69, senior counsel to the Warren Commission, and minority counsel to the House Judiciary Committee during the Nixon impeachment hearings. He has served as president or chairman of the National Conference of Commissioners on Uniform State Laws, the U.S. Supreme Court's Advisory Committee on the Federal Rules of Evidence, the Illinois State Bar Association, the American College of Trial Lawyers, and the American Judicature Society. A Republican, he also has strong ties to some Democratic officeholders in Chicago. His father was a Chicago police lieutenant. He is an Irish Catholic; graduate of the University of Illinois, both undergraduate and law school; age 68.

Eliot. The senior, name partner of a small, family firm specializing in probate and real property work, he is one of the most prominent probate lawyers in Chicago. In addition to his practice, he has for many years held an appointment to the faculty of the Northwestern Law School, where he regularly teaches property and estates (wills and trusts). He has published treatises in those fields. He is a past president of the American College of Probate Counsel. Republican; WASP; graduate of Dartmouth College and Northwestern Law School; mid 60s.

Ellington. A senior partner in one of the most prestigious firms. He is the principal lawyer handling the affairs of Chicago's largest bank, which is also said to be the largest client of the firm, and is the chairman of the board of trustees of Notre Dame University. Catholic; Independent Democrat; Notre Dame undergraduate and Harvard Law School; mid-60s.

Ellsworth. A senior partner in a major, old, established firm (it has been termed the "toniest" in the city, though the point might be disputed), where he represents large corporations and public utilities. He is active and influential in Illinois Republican politics and has served as president of United Charities. Early 60s; of English descent; University of Chicago undergraduate and Harvard Law School.

Elman. The senior partner of one of the largest, most prestigious firms, his speciality is antitrust defense, representing very large corporate clients. He serves on a number of boards and is active in community and cultural affairs, including present service as vice-chairman of the board of the Chicago Symphony. Republican; Jewish; Harvard, both undergraduate and law school; late 60s.

LIBERALS (L)

Presidents of the Chicago Council of Lawyers (La)

Ladinsky. Practices corporate law in a large firm. She is one of two women in this group of notable lawyers and also, at age 33, one of the youngest. She is a member of the U.S. Tax Court bar and has taught real estate finance at De Paul. Jewish; graduate of Northwestern Law School.

Lang. A name partner in a small firm, he specializes in the representation of plaintiffs in employment discrimination cases. His late father was a federal judge. Lang was one of the principal founders and the first president of the CCL. Age 34; Jewish; graduate of the University of Chicago.

Lasser. Does general corporate work, including some real estate and some securities, in a large, traditionally Jewish firm. Counsel to the committee on style and drafting of the 1970 Illinois Constitutional Convention. Age 33; Jewish; graduate of Northwestern Law School; liberal Democrat.

Lawrence. A professor at Northwestern Law School, he was the second president of the CCL. He does some *pro bono* litigation, especially in the fields of broadcasting regulation and welfare reform. Age 34; Jewish; Harvard graduate; liberal Democrat.

Other Liberals (L)

Lewis. He is a name partner in a small firm with a general practice. He does some work in both employment and housing discrimination and represents minority businessmen and entertainers. He is prominent in black liberal political circles, was formerly counsel to Jesse Jackson's Operation PUSH, and was, briefly, a candidate for the Democratic nomination for Mayor of Chicago. A graduate of Northwestern Law School, where he has also done some part-time teaching, he did undergraduate work at Tennessee A & I State. Black; in his mid-40s.

Liebling. Head of a public interest law organization. He has long been prominent in reform litigation, especially in the area of housing discrimination, and he was formerly a partner in a major corporate law firm. Jewish; graduate of Chicago; late 40s.

Lynch. Does corporate litigation for one of the most prestigious firms in Chicago, but has also been active in liberal Democratic politics. He was one of the lawyers for the Singer-Jackson delegation to the 1972 Democratic Convention (the pro-McGovern Illinois delegation that was seated in place of the delegation headed by Mayor Daley) and was a member of the 1970 Illinois Constitutional Convention, where he chaired the committee on style and drafting (see Lasser). He was a law school classmate of Lasser's at Northwestern; mid-30s; Irish Catholic origin.

Leventhal. He is a name partner in a medium-sized firm that represents smaller corporations and does a large amount of "commercial" practice. He has long been prominent in the ACLU and other liberal causes. He is also active in support of the arts and in the American Jewish Congress. Jewish; early 50s; Chicago graduate.

Leonard. He is a name partner in a small firm. Widely known for his labor arbitration work, he also handles general corporate matters. At age 70, he is one of the oldest of the notables. He has been very active for many years in liberal and reform-oriented associations. He also has strong ties to the academic community, having been a lecturer or visiting professor at the law schools at Yale, Northwestern, and Arizona State. Jewish; University of Chicago graduate.

Lonsdale. He is a partner in an old-line firm, where he does corporate litigation. Characterized by associates as a "liberal gadfly," he has undertaken *pro bono* work in environmental pollution, voting rights, and housing cases. He has been active in the organized bar, formerly serving as secretary of the board of the Chicago Bar Association, and he was also a member of the first board of directors of the Chicago Council of Lawyers. He sits on boards of several civic and cultural organizations, including the board of the Chicago

Symphony. A graduate of Harvard Law, he has done some teaching at Chicago. Mid-50s; English ancestry; politically independent.

Locke. Does corporate litigation and securities work as a partner of a large firm, and is influential in Independent Democratic politics. Headed the state's ethics board under Governor Daniel Walker. A graduate of Harvard College and Northwestern Law School; early 50s; WASP.

MISCELLANEOUS (M)

McShann. A name partner in one of the largest firms specializing in labor law, he is perhaps Chicago's most prominent labor lawyer on the management side. As might be expected due to his role with corporate management, he is a Republican, and he serves on the board of the United Republican Fund. In his early 60s; University of Chicago, both undergraduate and law school.

Mingus. A name partner in a small to medium-sized firm, he specializes in state and local tax matters, especially property taxes. Prior generations of his family provided Chicago with lawyers who were among the first Jews to attain prominence in the bar, and his late father's name still has pride of place in the firm name of one of the city's largest traditionally Jewish firms. He married into another prominent, wealthy Jewish family. He is a patron of the arts and serves on the boards of literary and cultural associations and institutions, including the board of trustees of Lake Forest College. He attended Lake Forest College and the University of Virginia Law School; late 50s.

Regular Democrats (R)

Robinson. A solo practitioner, he is a trial lawyer who is often called upon to represent, as a special counsel, the City of Chicago, other Cook County governmental bodies, and the Democratic Party Organization. He is a trustee of the University of Illinois (an elective office) and was recently chosen by the board to serve as its chairman. His career was advanced by Mayor Daley, who took a liking to him. His father was judge who was close to Congressman William Dawson, long the most powerful black in Chicago's Democratic Organization. Black; late 40s; University of Illinois undergraduate and University of Michigan Law School.

Rosenbloom. A name partner in a small firm, he does general trial work. He is well connected in Regular Democractic circles, earning substantial fees as a special counsel to the Chicago Sanitary District. Jewish; mid-40s; Northwestern undergraduate and Harvard Law School.

Ryan. A name partner in a small firm, his specialty is eminent domain work, where his political connections are thought to be useful in negotiating compensation for the land condemned. He is a former United States Attorney and serves as counsel to the Cook County elections board. He has talked of running for governor. Irish Catholic; Regular Democrat; Loyola undergraduate and University of Detroit Law School; early 50s.

TRIAL LAWYERS (T)

Taft. A partner in a medium- to large-sized firm, where he specializes in civil litigation, especially personal injury defense work. He has represented several insurance companies and Phillips Petroleum. Republican administrations have appointed him to various positions of public service. WASP; Republican; University of Nebraska undergraduate and Nebraska and University of Chicago law schools; mid-50s.

Takas. Among the most highly regarded criminal defense specialists practicing in Chicago. He is now in partnership with one other lawyer. Though he formerly did a great deal of work in the state criminal courts, he now devotes more of his efforts to the federal courts, representing more affluent clients accused of financial crimes. Twenty-five years ago, he was an assistant state's attorney. Greek Orthodox; University of Chicago, both undergraduate and law school; mid-50s.

Tendler. A partner in one of the largest and most prestigious corporate firms, he specializes in libel law and represents several of the news media. He also does general corporate work and litigation. He is well connected in both Republican and Regular Democratic circles and is called on to represent politicians who find themselves in legal difficulties. Of Jewish origin, he is now a Presbyterian, and he married into a socially prominent family. He is a graduate of Northwestern, both the college and the law school, and is a member of Northwestern's board of trustees. He is in his late 40s.

Tristano. The senior, name partner in a small, family firm specializing in divorce. Five of the nine lawyers in the firm are Tristanos. He is one of the best-known divorce lawyers in Chicago. Italian Catholic; De Paul University, both undergraduate and law school; late 60s.

Tolman. The senior, name partner in a small firm specializing in antitrust plaintiffs' work. He is probably the most prominent antitrust plaintiffs' specialist in Chicago. Very active in support of the arts, particularly music, he is a member of the board of and counsel to the Lyric Opera of Chicago. He has commissioned new musical compositions and operatic productions. Jewish; undergraduate work at Syracuse, graduate of Northwestern Law school; mid-60s.

Tower. A name partner in a medium-sized firm with a general commercial practice, he is a prominent trial lawyer. Known for his work as a courtroom advocate, he has served as a "special prosecutor" of prosecutorial officials accused of crimes. He has long been active in the ABA, serving as chairman and a long-time member of the House of Delegates. He has also been president of the Illinois State Bar Association and of the American College of Trial Lawyers. He is a graduate of Georgetown Law School and did his undergraduate work at St. Thomas College in Minnesota. Catholic. At age 73, he is the oldest person on this list of notable lawyers.

Trumbauer. A name partner in a medium-sized firm specializing in personal injury defense work. He represents insurance companies, particularly in the defense of product liability claims. He was long active in the Chicago Bar Association and served as a member of its Board of Managers. Of German descent; he is a graduate of Chicago Kent Law School; late 60s.

Turpin. A solo practitioner, he specializes in criminal defense work. He served as president of the Cook County Bar Association, the black lawyers' association. Black; undergraduate work at University of Illinois, law at the University of Chicago; mid-40s.

Tyrone. The senior, name partner of a small firm, he is one of the best-known personal injury plaintiffs' lawyers in Chicago. He has held the presidencies of four associations of trial and personal injury lawyers. He also gained some celebrity through his representation of Dick Butkus, the Chicago Bears' football star, in contract negotiations. Irish Catholic; undergraduate and law school at Loyola; early 60s.

Smallest Space Analysis of Notables' Networks

To determine whether these notable lawyers have distinct, regularly structured networks of association with other Chicago lawyers, we have used smallest space analysis to summarize the patterns of our respondents' reports of their acquaintances with the notables.[18] Each of the forty-three notables is represented as a point in space (see fig. 9.1), and the relative proximities of the points reflect the degree of similarity of their patterns of association within the profession. That is, notables who were known by many of the same respondents will be located close together in the space; notables who shared few acquaintances will be far apart. The solution is computed to optimize the simultaneous representation of the relationships among all pairs of points. Notables will tend to be near the center of the space if they are known by large numbers of respondents who are drawn from varying circles of acquaintance. It is also possible, though less likely, for a notable to be centrally located even though relatively few respondents know him—if the few who do know him are approximately equally likely to know the notables who are located at the respective extremes of the space, this will tend to place him equidistant from those extremes, or at the center. A notable will be located in the margins or periphery of the space if the respondents who know him are highly homogeneous in key social characteristics that set them apart from the notables on the other side of the space. Since homogeneity is more likely among limited subsets of respondents, the notables in the periphery are also likely to be known by fewer respondents.

An accurate depiction of the relationship between notables X and Y that simultaneously represents the relationship of each of those points to that of notable Z—together with the exact relationships of those three points to and among each of the other forty—is highly unlikely in a space with only two or three dimensions. Unless the structure of the data is quite simple, a perfect depiction of the relationships among all of the pairs of points may well require a solution with only one less dimension than there are points (i.e., $N-1$). It is difficult to think in terms of a forty-two–dimensional space, and it would not even be particularly helpful if one could. To develop theory about the nature of a system, we need to seek a more

18. The reader will, by now, be familiar with the essentials of smallest space technique and with the general mode of its interpretation (see chap. 4).

"parsimonious" account of its properties. But because solutions with only two or three dimensions will be less than perfect, statistical tests have been developed to assess the extent to which the representation accurately portrays, or "fits," the actual data. One such measure is Kruskal's stress. Using that measure, we determined that a two-dimensional representation of the notables' networks does not depict the relationships among the points with sufficient precision to satisfy the usual criterion, but that the use of three dimensions produces a more satisfactory fit with the data.[19] We have already presented two three-dimensional diagrams in this book (see chaps. 4 and 7), and we are not eager to burden the reader with another. As it happens, that may be avoided in this case without sacrificing substance. The third dimension of the solution does not contribute much additional differentiation to the space. Ninety percent of the notables are located within only 42 percent of the range on that dimension, and they are rather evenly distributed around the most central actor's position on the dimension. Only four of the notables fall outside this restricted range; they appear to be providing most of the additional variance that is represented by the third dimension. All four of those points are located toward the negative end of the dimension, and they are separated from the other points by a relatively substantial gap. In the figure presenting the smallest space analysis, therefore, we are using the three-dimensional solution, but we represent the third dimension only by placing downward arrows next to these four points. Looking at figure 9.1, we see the arrows next to the points representing the positions of Ladinsky, Drootin, Mingus, and McShann—two being at the top and two near the bottom of the space, forming a rough square. These four persons were less widely known than most of the other notables and that probably accounts for their low position on the third dimension.[20]

19. In two dimensions, Kruskal's stress was .19; in the three-dimensional solution it declines to .148. An alternative measure of fit, the Guttman-Lingoes coefficient of alienation, produces similar results—for the two-dimensional solution it was .21; using three dimensions, it declines to .162. Both of these measures indicate that the representation of the relationships among the points includes a good deal of stress, even in three dimensions, but it is minimally satisfactory. See J. B. Kruskal, "Multidimensional Sealing by Optimizing Goodness of Fit to a Nonmetric Hypothesis," *Psychometrika* 29 (March 1964): 3; and Louis Guttman, "A General Nonmetric Technique for Finding the Smallest Coordinate Space for a Configuration of Points," *Psychometrika* 33 (December 1968): 486.

20. The average number of respondents knowing each of these 4 persons is 27.5, compared to an average of 51.7 for the 43 notables overall.

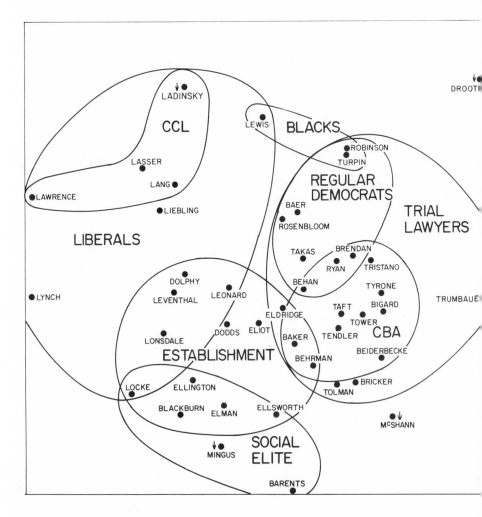

FIGURE 9.1

Patterns of Acquaintance with 43 Notable Chicago Lawyers (Three-dimensional Smallest Space Solution)

To aid the reader in using the figure, we have drawn rough ovals around some of the regions of the space that we believe can be identified with reasonable certainty. These boundaries are *not* determined empirically. Rather, they represent our interpretations of the nature of the primary affinity of the notables who occupy those regions. We have made those interpretations by observing whether notables who are proximate appear to share characteristics that might plausibly account for their proximity. That is, using the known characteristics of the notables, we have induced a proposition about the nature of the bond that ties these sets of notables. A particularly clear example is the four presidents of the Chicago Council of Lawyers, who are relatively close together at the upper left of the space (in the area labeled "CCL").[21] Because each notable occupies multiple role positions, a given notable may well have a characteristic that fits the region where he is located and yet have another characteristic that matches the label that we have given to some other region of the space. Lynch, for example, is a litigator. In that respect, he is like Taft, Tendler, and Tolman, who are all located within the region labeled "Trial Lawyers." (But the sorts of litigation that all of those lawyers do is quite unlike that handled by Turpin, Takas, Tristano and Tyrone; see pp. 288–89.) The fact that Lynch is not located in close proximity to the Trial Lawyers, however, and that he is more proximate to other lawyers who are engaged in liberal political activities, suggests that his liberal affiliations are more salient than is his role as a litigator in structuring his relationships with other lawyers.

The fit of the notables with the labels given their regions is generally quite good, but it is not always exact. Tendler, for example, has never been closely identified with the CBA, but he does clearly belong within the broader Trial Lawyers region. Cases that do not fit are rare, and there is *no* such problem within the precisely defined regions such as those labeled "Blacks" and "CCL." Even when his region's characteristic is not the one that caused a particular notable to be chosen for inclusion on the list, his characteristics almost always fit the region within which he is located. For example, Baer was included primarily because she was in the line of succession to the presidency of the Illinois State Bar Association. But she is found in the Regular Democrats area of the space (not far from some other bar leaders), which is consistent with her ties to the Regular Demo-

---

21. Their age also sets these 4 apart from most of the other notables, but we doubt that youth is their most salient common characteristic. Drootin, the dean of the De Paul Law School, is the same age, for example, but he is found on the opposite side of the top of the space, at the far upper right. One of the distinctive characteristics of the CCL is the relative youth of its members and leaders, however, and age may well be a part of the ties that unite the CCL constituency. The age and CCL variables are, thus, confounded in a manner that has substantive significance. This illustrates the point that, because each notable has multiple characteristics, they can be "put together" in a number of alternative ways, and we certainly make no claim that the interpretations that we have made are the only possible ones.

cratic Organization through family members. When a notable's point falls near the boundary of one of the regions, it might often have been plausible to draw the line either to include or to exclude that notable from the category. In such cases, we have used our judgment, which is certainly open to question.[22] But these close cases should not cause us great concern. The purpose of labeling the regions is only to suggest broad properties of the space. Two notables, Drootin and McShann, did not seem to us to be clearly assignable to any of these regions. We have, therefore, left them in limbo; these two persons—like others who are found in the outer ring or periphery of the space—are significantly less widely known than most of the other notables.

With these explanations and caveats in mind, we may now turn to our interpretation of the substantive significance of the results of the analysis. Some of the properties of the smallest space solution are readily apparent. Noting the general categories of the notables and their location in the figure, we find that the liberals (L) (including the presidents of the Chicago Council of Lawyers, as a subset of liberals) are located exclusively on the left, particularly at the upper left. The leaders of the organized bar (B), rather thoroughly mixed in with the trial lawyers (T), tend to be located on the right, particularly at right center; the trial lawyers tend to be higher in the space and a bit further right than the leaders of the organized bar. The establishment is found relatively low in the space, most of them just left of center. But that should not be taken as a political statement; these dimensions (the vertical and horizontal axes) have no substantive meaning in themselves. If one wished to draw a line through the space that would separate the political right from the political left, that line should depart from the vertical, slanting from the upper right to the lower left and dividing the establishment area about in half (see fig. 9.6). This would still place some of the Regular Democrats on the right side of the line (though not so far right as it appears on the horizontal axis of figure 9.1), and that is probably correct in political terms.

The locations of those groupings of the notables labeled "Blacks" and "Social Elite" are illustrative of a general property of the structure of the circles of acquaintance of the profession's elites: social opposites—whether the source of the opposition is politics, social

22. It is more important to note that, in any event, the less clear cases of classification occur near the margins of the categories that are in question.

class, or law practice characteristics—tend to be found on opposite sides of the space. Thus, the location of the black notables is diametrically opposed to that of the social elite (i.e., those notables who have the closest ties to high society, to the world of private clubs and newspaper society pages). Similarly, the presidents of the Chicago Council of Lawyers are located about as far as is possible from the leaders of the Chicago Bar Association, the established, conservative organized bar that it was created to oppose. (While Bricker was president of the Illinois State Bar Association, he strongly resisted the seating of a representative of the CCL in the ABA's House of Delegates. This occurred during Lawrence's term as president of the CCL. The two are located opposite one another, Lawrence at the upper left and Bricker at the lower right.) And the criminal, divorce, and personal injury plaintiffs' lawyers among the notables tend to be found opposite those who do antitrust defense and the other sorts of work that serve the large corporations; the personal plight lawyers are located toward the upper right and the large corporate practitioners toward the lower left. As we have already observed, these represent the extremes of the two broad sectors of the profession (see chap. 3). In a sense, our findings confirm that these types are in fact social opposites—that they are separated by substantial "social distance," as measured by their circles of acquaintance (see chap. 7). The smallest space solution, reflecting this social distance, assigns them to opposite sides of the space.[23]

One of the most striking findings is the proximity of the blacks to one another in spite of their quite different characteristics. Robinson is a fixture of the Daley Organization (he is *the* black who was most relied on by Daley for legal work, and he was reported to be personally close to the mayor), while Turpin is a criminal defense lawyer who had been active in the black lawyers' association. These two are so close in the figure as to be virtually on top of one another. The third black, Lewis, is about as different from Robinson as it is possible to be in Chicago political terms—Lewis is a liberal Independent Democrat who is affiliated with Jesse Jackson's sociopoliti-

23. It is quite unlikely that a given respondent will know both of 2 notables who are located on opposite sides of the space. Thus, of 70 respondents who know either Lynch or Trumbauer, for example, only 1 knows both of them. This is the case in spite of the systematic bias in the set of respondents who are likely to know any of the notables (see pp. 277–80) and in spite of the fact that both Lynch and Trumbauer are litigators who represent major corporations. Their other characteristics obviously serve to assign them to two, separate, largely segregated circles of acquaintance.

cal activities. (In Chicago, such Republicans as existed in 1975 were probably closer to the Regular Democrats, in most ways, than were the Independent Democrats.) Yet Lewis is located quite near to Robinson and Turpin in the figure, just to their left—toward the liberals. Given the extreme political differences among them, particularly between Robinson on the one hand and Lewis on the other, the fact that the blacks end up so close together strongly suggests that blacks move within quite narrowly restricted circles within the bar. But we should note that these three notables also share some practice characteristics. They all do some sort of litigation, and they are all either solo practitioners or in small, rather informal partnerships. These characteristics alone, however, would not seem to account for their close proximity. Most of the litigators from small firms are located somewhat lower on the right side of the space (the vicinity of Takas, Brendan, Behan, Ryan, Tristano, and Tyrone). The most plausible interpretation of these findings is surely that race has a strong effect on lawyers' circles of acquaintance within the profession.

Lewis is located about halfway between the other two blacks and the most proximate of the young liberals who had served as president of the Chicago Council of Lawyers. The four CCL presidents—Ladinsky, Lasser, Lang and Lawrence—are also clustered within a relatively restricted region of the space, indicating that many of their acquaintances overlap or that the people who know them have very similar patterns of contact with the other notables, located in other regions of the space. There is a substantial gap between the CCL presidents and most of the other notables; only Liebling, the public interest lawyer, is very near them. Lewis, Lynch, a young liberal political activist, and Dolphy, the dean of the Northwestern Law School, are next closest. The relative segregation of the CCL leadership is probably explained by their youth and by the tendency for reformers, like other out-groups, to have a limited, homogeneous circle of acquaintances.[24] Persons opposing established interests or challenging conventional roles may well find that association with the like-minded is reassuring. It reduces dissonance.

Note that, though the liberals' region of the space is large, it is

24. See Howard S. Becker, *Outsiders: Studies in the Sociology of Deviance* (New York: Free Press, 1973). The youth of the CCL presidents probably largely accounts for the fact that they were less widely known than most of the notables (see *supra* note 21). The careers of these persons have progressed since the time our data was gathered, and they would probably be substantially better known today.

rather lightly populated. The dispersion of the liberals indicates that they are of varying types and perhaps that they tend to operate as free agents—that socially, as in the figure, they are not tightly clustered. Moreover, there appear to be distinct wings of the liberals. At the far upper left of the space is a group of liberals who tend to be younger, affiliated with the CCL, and probably more left in political terms as well. The four CCL presidents and Liebling are all Jewish; Lewis is black; Lynch is Irish. Lower and closer to the center of the space is the "liberal establishment." Though two of these liberals are also Jewish, the only WASPs in the liberal group are found here.

If the establishment region of the space has a liberal wing, the separation of that wing from the balance of the establishment notables is less clearly demarcated by any natural boundaries. But the establishment does include a group that is more certainly a part of the social elite. (In fact, the only notables in our social elite region of the space who are not also included within the establishment region are Mingus and Barents.[25]) Similarly, yet another wing of the establishment can be identified. Toward the upper right of the establishment region is a group of notables who derive some of their authority from the organized bar. Eldridge, Baker, and Behrman have all served as presidents of bar associations—Eldridge, of both the Illinois State Bar Association and the American College of Trial Lawyers, and the latter two, of the CBA.

These overlaps among the regions also suggest that individuals who are located within the areas of overlap or at the points of intersection of the various regions are well situated to serve as mediators among those spheres of influence. And a person who bridges two constituencies may not only act as a messenger between them but may also be able to mobilize the resources of both. Eldridge, again, is a prime example. He is a member in excellent standing of both the establishment and the litigators' elite (the trial lawyers' region), and is located in their area of overlap. He is also situated in close proximity to both the Regular Democrats and the CBA leadership.

25. Mingus is a member of a socially elite Jewish family and is a patron of the arts; Barents, a past president of the CBA, is a partner in an old, conservative firm. Though both surely qualify as notable lawyers, neither is so close to the power centers of the profession (quite apart from his position in the figure) as to be generally thought of as a member of the profession's establishment. Neither represents major corporations in his law practice or is an influential figure in the world of business and finance.

Eldridge is thus in a fine position to serve as a go-between for these groups, to confer legitimacy on the proposals of each in dealing with the other, and to gain recognition and power by mobilizing these multiple sources of influence. If the reader refers to our simple biographical sketch, he will see that Eldridge has made good use of these opportunities. One of the statistics used in interpreting smallest space analysis is a measure of "centrality." If all of the points in the space were equal weights resting on a weightless plane, the centroid would be the balance point.[26] By this measure, Eldridge is the most central of the notables.

The opposite of this phenomenon is illustrated by the two notables that we have not included within any of the regions bounded by ovals—Drootin and McShann seem unlikely to be able to mobilize any of those constituencies. Recall that Drootin is the dean of the De Paul Law School and McShann is a labor specialist who represents management. Both are low on the third dimension, indicating that they are not widely known. Fewer of our respondents know McShann than know any other of the forty-three notables. His specialty, labor law, probably does not bring him into regular contact with a wide range of other lawyers. We do not have a patents specialist among our notables, but if we did we would expect to find him similarly isolated. Drootin is also far less widely known than most of the other notables. His location in the space is in the direction of the Regular Democrats, the trial lawyers, solo and small-firm practitioners, notables who practice in the personal plight fields, Catholics, and notables from ethnic groups with lower socioeconomic status—the social types found in disproportionate numbers among the graduates of De Paul Law School—but he is in the periphery, beyond the cluster of the other notables with those characteristics. The deans of Chicago and Northwestern, by contrast, are located far closer to the center of the space.[27] The deanship of De Paul probably does not provide the entree to the councils of the profession's establishment that comes with the position of dean at the University of Chicago or at Northwestern, but Drootin's relative youth surely also contributes to his lack of connections.

26. See chap. 4 at note 25.
27. We have included both of them in the establishment area. Northwestern's dean, Dolphy, is clearly on the liberal side of that region. Dolphy and Dodds, Chicago's dean, are located quite close together, near a number of the notables who have strong relationships with one or the other of their law schools. Leonard, who has ties with both schools, is about equidistant between Dolphy and Dodds.

Most of the notables who represent the largest corporations are not located at the very center of the space. The corporate establishment is only one of the profession's power centers. Others are the Regular Democratic Organization (which controls City Hall and has the allegiance of most of the judges of the local courts), the organized bar (particularly, the Chicago Bar Association), and the independent liberal political forces (which have access to influence through state and national politics, particularly through the governor and through Illinois' United States senators, who of course control appointments to federal judgeships). Each of these constituencies or spheres of influence occupies an identifiable region of the profession's network structure, and these regions overlap to form a generally circular structure. The elites who are found closer to the centroid of the space either lead multiple constituencies or play mediating roles (sometimes, of course, they can do both); those who are located farther from the center tend to be more closely identified with one or another of the distinct constituencies. Elites located in the periphery may be "pure types," each commanding the attention of his own constituency, but only his. In the alternative, they may be notables who derive their influence primarily from relationships *outside* the profession, or their notability may be largely personal or symbolic, leaving them unable to mobilize any substantial constituency within the profession.

These social networks within the legal profession are not, then, linear or bipolar. Though the structure is oppositional in nature— social opposites are found on opposite sides of the space—other constituencies or groups within the profession mediate between the opposites, and these mediating groups are not necessarily located more centrally in the space but may themselves be peripheral, being located at other points around the rim of the structure.

The proposition that the notables' network structure has distinct regions—separate "spheres of influence"—may be examined through the use of another type of analysis, to which we now turn.

The Notables' Space as Defined by Respondent Characteristics

Rather than focusing on the characteristics of the notables in identifying the regions of the space, we may use the characteristics of the respondents who claim acquaintance with each of the notables to define the nature of the notables' overlapping circles of acquaintance. That is, if we continue to treat each notable as a point in space, as presented in figure 9.1, and then assign to each point the characteristics of the respondents who know that notable, we may observe the patterns of relationship among the points on those characteristics. To the extent that the notables' associations within the profession are random, we will see no clear patterns; to the extent that the notables' acquaintances are differentiated by these variables, we should be able to observe distinct patterns, distinct regions of the space. If a characteristic of the respondents varies systematically as we move along any vector that can be drawn through the points—that is, if the values of the points on that variable change in a consistent direction along that dimension—it will suggest that the variable organizes that portion of the network structure, that it explains that dimension of lawyers' relationships with the notables. But a straight-line dimensionality is only one possibility. If, for example, the fields of practice of the acquaintances should change in an orderly fashion as we move around the circle from one region of the space to another, it also would suggest that the notables' networks of association are influenced by that variable.

To present these data, we have prepared a number of additional figures, all of which duplicate the social space presented in figure 9.1. In figures 9.2 through 9.5, each notable's point in that space is labeled with a number that indicates the extent to which the respondents who are acquainted with the notable differ from the norm of all of our respondents on the variable in question.

For example, figure 9.2 analyzes the extent to which respondents who were acquainted with each of the notables varied from our respondents overall in holding positions of leadership in the established organized bar.[28] That is, the variable is whether or not the respondent himself had held a leadership position in the Chicago Bar Association or the Illinois State Bar Association. Only 10 percent of our respondents had played such a role. The numbers by the notables' points in figure 9.2 state the extent to which the respon-

28. All 777 respondents were asked whether they had held office in a bar association. The variable used here includes the respondents who reported that they had served as a committee chairman, as a member of the board, or as an officer (president, secretary, etc.) of either the Chicago Bar Association or the Illinois State Bar Association.

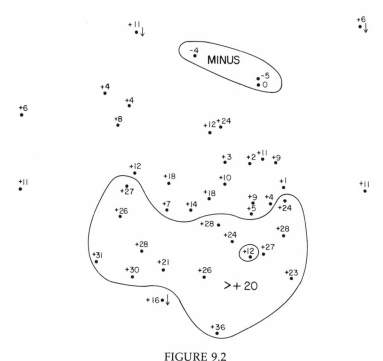

FIGURE 9.2

Characteristics of Respondents Acquainted with Each of 43 Notables: Percentage Difference from Total Percentage in Leadership Role

dents who know each notable depart from that norm—that is, + 5 indicates that 15 percent of the respondents who knew that notable had, themselves, held positions of leadership in the organized bar.

The most obvious lesson of figure 9.2 is that the lawyers who know the notables are disproportionately likely to have held leadership roles. Leaders are more likely to know other leaders. Almost all of the numbers in figure 9.2 are positive, indicating that the acquaintances of almost all of the notables were more likely than were average respondents to have held bar leadership positions. Recall that only 62 percent of our respondents knew any of the notables and only 25 percent knew more than three of them (see pp. 277–78). One of the factors that appears to influence likelihood of acquaintance with the notables is, then, the respondent's occupancy of a leadership role. In a sense, this finding is probably a validation of the selections that we made for our list of notables. We appear to have succeeded (in some measure, at least) in selecting leaders who are likely to have come into contact with other leaders in the course of organizing support for their causes or of basking in the same limelight.

But an equally striking—and far more interesting—feature of figure 9.2 is that the *only* points where leaders are not overrepresented are those of the black notables. (The three points, toward the upper right, are labeled "minus," though only two are actually negative. One is a zero, indicating no difference from the norm.) The obvious hypothesis as to why this should be the case is that blacks move within separate circles of acquaintance that do not include the sorts of lawyers who are likely to be active in the Chicago or Illinois State Bar Associations. That the circles of acquaintance of black lawyers tend to be separate from the balance of the profession has already been suggested by the fact that the three quite different black notables are grouped so closely in the smallest space solution (see pp. 295–96). The Chicago Bar Association was closed to blacks until 1945,[29] and black lawyers consequently formed their own organization, the Cook County Bar Association. Though a few blacks have more recently held office in the CBA, many no doubt continue to pursue alternative opportunities for professional recognition. Moreover, most black lawyers work in small firms or as solo practitioners, often doing "personal plight" work, and lawyers in these sorts of practice are, regardless of race, among the least likely to be active in the organized bar (see table 8.3).

Following the general tendency for opposites to be located on opposite sides of the space, we also find that the notables with the largest proportions of bar leaders among their acquaintances occupy a region that is directly across the space from that of the black notables. These are in the area labeled "> + 20"; that is, over 30 percent of the acquaintances of each of the notables within the area have held bar leadership positions, more than three times the proportion of all respondents. (One notable found within the area, Tolman, does not fit that criterion. His acquaintances are only 12 percentage points higher on this variable. As with any point that does not fit the label given its area in figures 9.2 through 9.6, his point is circled.) This area overlaps the establishment and the CBA regions of figure 9.1. Since the types of leadership roles that were used in defining the variable were positions in the establishment bar associa-

29. Herman Kogan, *The First Century: The Chicago Bar Association 1874–1974* (Chicago: Rand McNally, 1974), pp. 202–4.

tions (i.e., not in the Chicago Council of Lawyers, the Cook County Bar Association, or the American Trial Lawyers Association),[30] this pattern is easy to understand.

Figure 9.3 is a bit less clear-cut, but it is no more difficult to interpret. The variable analyzed is the percentage of law practice income that the lawyers receive from "major corporate clients." The mean of all respondents is 34 percent, and the figure again indicates the extent to which each notable's acquaintances depart from that mean. As in figure 9.2, this variable organizes the space in a generally vertical direction, somewhat tilted from the upper right to the lower left. The blacks and the trial lawyers who are in fields like criminal defense, divorce, and personal injury plaintiffs' work are found in the area where the acquaintance's percentages of income from major corporate clients are more than 10 percentage points lower than the average of all respondents. (That is, the mean percentage for the acquaintances of each of the notables in that area is 24 percent or less.) The area with the highest percentages of income from major corporate clients (labeled "> + 10") includes only one of the CBA leaders—Beiderbecke, a personal injury defense lawyer who is a partner in one of Chicago's largest firms. The only notables in that area who are not partners in large firms are the deans of the two prestigious law schools. The high degree of interaction between the establishment of the profession and the lawyers who represent the largest corporations is well documented by figure 9.3.

The variables dealt with in figures 9.2 and 9.3 are of quite different types, being organizational roles and client differences, respectively, and in figure 9.4 we analyze a variable that reflects yet another type of differentiation of lawyers, the differences in the tasks that they perform (see pp. 61–62). The task type variable that we have selected for analysis here is the frequency of litigation in state courts. We have found this to be a highly useful diagnostic variable, one that distinguishes among the fields of practice rather clearly (see tables 3.1 and 3.2). Here, again, the pattern is sharply defined. The notables who have acquaintances with above average rates of appearance in the state courts can, with only one exception, be separated from those with below average rates by a line drawn with a

30. The Chicago Council of Lawyers is an organization of younger, reform-oriented lawyers; see Powell, *supra* note 2. The Cook County Bar Association is the black lawyers' organization, and the American Trial Lawyers Association includes primarily personal injury lawyers and criminal defense lawyers.

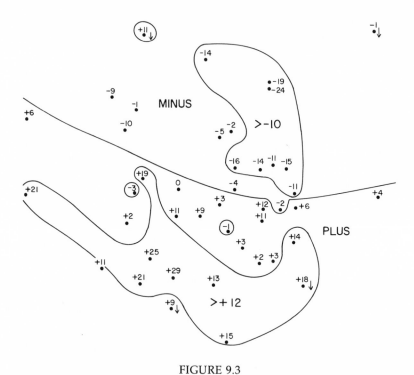

FIGURE 9.3

Characteristics of Respondents Acquainted with Each of 43 Notables: Percentage Difference from Total Percentage of Income from Major Corporate Clients

ruler. Of course, it matters little whether that line of separation is exactly straight or a bit irregular, but given that we are dealing with friendships among real people, who might be expected to behave idiosyncratically at times and who surely do not form even their professional relationships for instrumental reasons alone, the orderliness of these data is rather remarkable.

There is a general relationship between the pattern of the rates of state court appearances and that of the income derived from major corporate clients (see fig. 9.3), but the state litigation rate vector appears to be more sharply tilted than is the major corporate client vector. (The litigation vector would run at approximately a right angle to the line that separates the "plus" from the "minus" side of figure 9.4. That is, the vector would run from the lower left to the upper right, at about a 45-degree angle.) The area of the space with the higher rates of state court appearances among the acquaintances

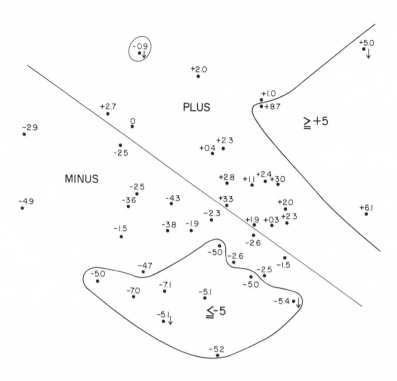

FIGURE 9.4

Characteristics of Respondents Acquainted with Each of 43 Notables: Difference from Total for Mean State Court Appearances per Month

of the notables is, again, the area where we find the notables who are criminal defense lawyers and personal injury lawyers, conforming once again to the principle of homogeneous choice of associates. The area with the lowest state litigation rates includes notables who practice antitrust, securities, public utilities, labor law, and probate—fields that either consist primarily of office practice or deal with federal rather than state courts.

Figure 9.5 is, if possible, even more sharply defined. It presents the findings for yet another basis of differentiation among lawyers, ethnoreligious differences. As figure 9.5 indicates, the notables who have the highest percentages of Roman Catholics among their acquaintances are concentrated at the right of the space. The degree of segregation of the above average percentages from those that are below average is, again, quite remarkable. Moreover, the percentages of Catholic acquaintances decrease in a generally orderly fash-

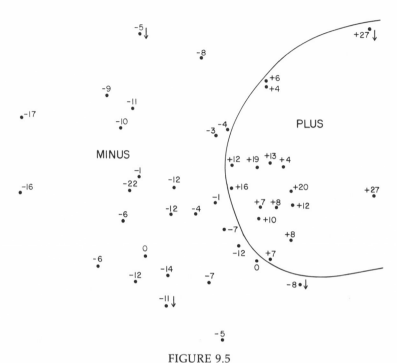

FIGURE 9.5

Characteristics of Respondents Acquainted with Each of 43 Notables: Percentage Difference from Total Percentage of Catholics

ion as we move from right to left in the space. The vector, here, is much more nearly horizontal than that in figure 9.4—the Catholic acquaintance vector appears to tilt only slightly from the lower left toward the upper right.

In progressing through figures 9.2 to 9.5, then, we have seen the directions of the vectors of each variable shift from nearly vertical in figures 9.2 and 9.3, to a 45-degree angle in figure 9.4, and to near horizontal in figure 9.5. The degree of the angles at the intersections of these vectors reflects the degree of the intercorrelations of the variables.

In figure 9.6, we present the analyses of six more variables in a simplified form. The space is the same, of course, but the scores that are given next to each point in figures 9.2 through 9.5 have been eliminated here. The reader has, by now, been exposed to four sets of such scores and is thus familiar with the meaning of the figures; the individual scores are not necessary to an appreciation of these general patterns of acquaintance.

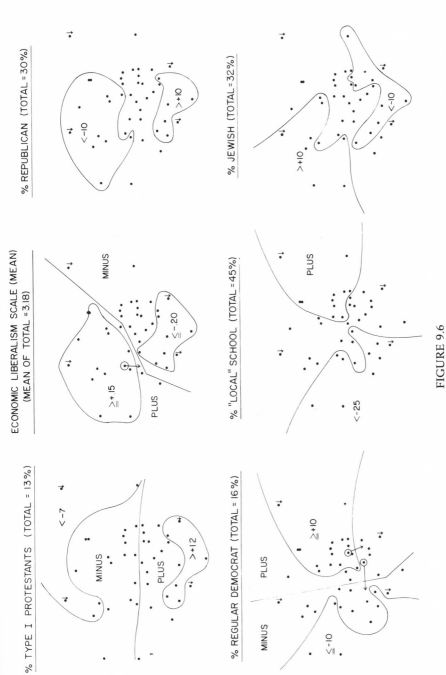

FIGURE 9.6

Characteristics of Respondents Acquainted with Each of 43 Notables: Summary Representation of Differences on Six Related Variables

Three of the variables presented here display, for the first time, vectors that are tilted in the other direction—that is, from the lower right to the upper left. These variables are the percentages of Republicans and of Jews among the notables' acquaintances and the extent to which the notables' acquaintances have high or low scores on the economic liberalism scale discussed in chapter 5. The Republican vector is the most nearly vertical of the three, while the Jewish vector runs at approximately a 45-degree angle (about perpendicular to the state court appearance vector). These three variables are obviously correlated. There is a strong negative association between the percentage of Republicans and the percentage of Jews or of economic liberals among a notable's acquaintances.[31]

Turning now to the other variables presented in figure 9.6, we see a clear relationship between the extent to which a notable's acquaintances are Regular Democrats and the extent to which they are likely to have attended one of the four "local" law schools. Both of these variables are, in turn, also positively correlated with the percentages of Catholics among the notables' acquaintances[32] (see figure 9.5) and with the acquaintances' rates of state court appearances (see figure 9.4). The area at the right center of the space on both the local school variable and the Regular Democrat variable corresponds rather closely to the "Plus" area, in the shape of a half-circle, that we see on the Catholic variable (fig. 9.5).

The final variable presented in figure 9.6 is the percentage of Type I Protestants among the notables' acquaintances.[33] The regions with the lowest percentages on this variable, understandably enough, are those with the highest percentage of Catholics (at the upper right) or of Jews (at the upper left). The area with the highest concentration of Type I Protestants is at the bottom of the space, overlapping the establishment and social elite regions. This variable is obviously correlated with the tendency to represent major corporate clients (see figure 9.3), where the vector is also almost vertical (perhaps with a slight tilt toward the right, just as here) and where there is a clear separation between the top and the bottom of the space.

The multicollinearity of these variables once again makes it very

31. The correlations among these three variables all range between .75 and .78, ignoring the signs; p = < .0001 (see pp. 111-12).
32. Catholics are, of course, disproportionately represented among the graduates of Loyola and De Paul law schools.
33. These are Protestants of generally higher social status (see chap. 1).

difficult to determine whether one or another of them is "causal"—
here, whether the patterns of acquaintance that we observe are to
be attributed to one of these variables rather than another. It is likely that the variables reinforce one another. That is, multiple bases of
similarity may be expected to enhance the likelihood of cohesion
among the lawyers (see pp. 216–18), and this no doubt helps to account for the quite orderly structure that we have observed in the
notables' patterns of acquaintance. The clarity of the organization of
the space by the variables presented confirms the major findings of
our other analyses. It indicates that, in yet another respect, the legal
profession is a highly differentiated, quite stratified social system.
The precision of the patterns of association, with so few of the notables failing to conform to the characteristics of their regions of the
space, suggests that lawyers know their place—that they associate
largely with those whose positions within the profession are similar
to their own or with others whose roles are related to theirs in ways
that are clearly defined, usually hierarchically ordered, and presumably functional.

The Spheres of Influence

One of the most important tenets of a pluralist view of politics is
that not only will a large number and variety of different political
interests have access to the locus of decisions but the demands made
by each group will be constrained by the representation within that
group of persons who have a wide variety of other interests, other
social identities.[34] Each group will be likely to include a membership that cuts across some or all of the social distinctions created by
differences in occupation, religion, ethnicity, class, values, or personal circumstances, and the overlap among the memberships of
the various interest groups will thus serve to moderate the positions
adopted by each group and to give the polity cohesion, to bind it
together.

In his major synthetic work, *The Governmental Process*, David Truman stresses the importance of overlapping group membership as

34. Mancur Olson refers to the modern proponents of this view as "analytical
pluralists"; see Mancur Olson, Jr., *The Logic of Collective Action* (Cambridge: Harvard
University Press, 1965), p. 118.

one of two crucial elements in his conception of the political process:

> The idea of overlapping memberships stems from the conception of a group as a standardized pattern of interactions rather than as a collection of human units. Although the former may appear to be a rather misty abstraction, it is actually far closer to complex reality than the latter notion. The view of a group as an aggregation of individuals abstracts from the observable fact that in any society, and especially a complex one, no single group affiliation accounts for all of the attitudes or interests of any individual except a fanatic or a compulsive neurotic. No tolerably normal person is totally absorbed in any group in which he participates. The diversity of an individual's activities and his attendant interests involve him in a variety of actual and potential groups. . . . Such heterogeneity may be of little significance until such time as these multiple memberships conflict. Then the cohesion and influence of the affected group depend upon the incorporation or accommodation of the conflicting loyalties of any significant segment of the group, an accommodation that may result in altering the original claims. Thus the leaders of a Parent-Teacher Association must take some account of the fact that their proposals must be acceptable to members who also belong to the local taxpayers' league, to the local chamber of commerce, and to the Catholic Church.[35]

The separation that we have observed among the varying constituencies within the Chicago bar suggests, however, that this tendency toward the moderation of demands may not obtain there. There are, of course, some prominent lawyers who serve as intermediaries among several of the different interest groupings, but these tend to be exceptions. If there is little movement of either leaders or followers across the boundaries of the major constellations of interests within the bar, then the expression of narrow interests will be less constrained and the politics of the bar will be more likely to be characterized by divisive conflict, perhaps creating further barriers to the integration of the professional community. But it is difficult to be certain that our findings concerning these separate interest groupings are not, in part, an artifact of our research design. The nature of the patterns of acquaintance, after all, reflects categories that were used in the selection of our list of notables. Would liberals have emerged as a separate group if we had not consciously included a set of liberals among the notables? Even with our pro-

35. David B. Truman, *The Governmental Process* (New York: Alfred Knopf, 1951), pp. 508–09. The other conceptual element that he views as "of crucial significance" is "the function of unorganized interests, or potential interest groups" (p. 508).

cedure, we might have found that the liberals were spread through-out the space. But they were not. A selection criterion might, then, prove to be irrelevant. But this one did not.

It would be very difficult to construct a list of influential lawyers that did not rest upon some preconceptions about the kinds of con-stituencies that might exist within the profession or the types of power that might be useful in mobilizing corresponding types of lawyers, and we do not believe that the mix of positional and repu-tational methods used to select our list was likely to distort any important reality of the relationships among lawyers. Assuming, therefore, that we are entitled to place some confidence in our find-ings, three principal spheres of influence appear to exist in the Chi-cago bar.[36]

The first of these is based in liberal politics. This sphere, which includes the leaders of the Chicago Council of Lawyers, is engaged in explicit political activity both inside the profession and in the broader polity. To the extent that partisan political activity is in-volved, these elites largely work through the independent wing of the Democractic Party in Chicago (i.e., *not* the Regular Democratic Organization) and, more occasionally, through moderate to liberal Republicans (e.g., Senator Charles Percy). Issues on which this sphere was active include "merit" selection of judges (i.e., selection by appointment rather than election and, more generally, selection in ways that would minimize the influence of the Regular Demo-crats), open housing, welfare reform, and abortion.

The second of the major spheres of influence is the corporate es-tablishment. It includes the lawyers for the largest corporations, the deans of the prestigious law schools (both of whom, here, happen to be antitrust lawyers, which may enhance their inclusion in this group), and some, but a distinct minority, of the leaders of the orga-nized bar. The principal basis of the influence of this sphere is its connections to the business and financial community. Though it is probably less directly involved in political activity, the party of choice for such activity is most often the Republican party. (If the Republican party had been healthier in Chicago, this sphere might

36. The earlier chapters of this book argued that the principal division within the bar is that between lawyers who represent corporations or large organizations and those who represent individuals or small businesses, while in this portion of our analysis we find the bar to be divided not into two principal parts, but three. This is not really an inconsistency but rather a consequence of the difference in the subjects of the analyses. See pp. 353–55 and 379–82.

perhaps have been more active in partisan politics.) The public issues that concern it usually involve governmental regulation of business.

The third and last of these major spheres is a bit more amorphous but still clearly discernible. Its core is the trial lawyers who practice in fields such as personal injury and criminal law, and it includes many of the leaders of the Chicago and Illinois State Bar associations. Many Chicago lawyers believe that the personal injury bar has made a concerted effort over the past several years to capture the leadership of the local bar associations. If the personal injury lawyers have done so, their purpose may have been to enhance their prestige or to gain greater influence over such issues as "no fault" compensation in automobile accident cases. The elites in this sphere concern themselves with a relatively broad range of public and professional matters, specifically including "no fault" and judicial selection. When they engage in partisan political activity, they usually work with the Regular Democrats.

In attempting to explain the patterns of acquaintance with the notables and, thus, the bases of these spheres of influence, we are faced with the fact that ethnoreligious differences among the acquaintances correspond to these spheres or regions of the space, thus rendering interpretation more difficult. The trial lawyers sphere is dominated by Catholics, Jews are overrepresented in the liberal region, and the corporate establishment sphere tends to overrepresent high status Protestants. The problem, then, is to determine, if we can, whether the patterns of association among lawyers are attributable to the political, professional, and ideological affinities just described or, instead, to selection of associates on the basis of ethnic homogeneity. It is unlikely, of course, that either factor operates without the influence of the other—it is almost certainly the case that ideological and ethnic affinities go hand in hand (see chap. 5, table 5.3).

In previous chapters, we have emphasized the part that client interests play in determining the structure of the profession, though we have also noted substantial, systematic ethnoreligious differentiation among lawyers. If ethnicity plays an important part in defining this social space, then, that should come as no surprise, and it certainly requires no further qualification of the thesis that client interests have important influence on the definition of lawyers' professional roles. The distinguishing characteristic of these notable lawyers is their public role. It therefore makes good sense that, while lawyers' professional roles may be circumscribed by the interests of the clients that they serve, the *public* roles of lawyers should be determined more by their social background characteristics, including ethnicity and religion. Ethnicity and social class of origin are often salient to one's position on public issues;[37] they may sometimes also be important, though probably less often so, to the lawyer-client relationship.

By saying all of this, however, we do not mean to imply that client type variables have no relationship to the data on the notables' circles of acquaintance. The fit of client variables with the notables' smallest space solution is, in fact, at least as neat as that of the ethnoreligious variables (see, e.g., fig. 9.3). (Two of the notables in the region with the lowest percentages of Jewish acquaintances, for example, are themselves of Jewish origin.) The daily legal work of the notables will, of course, tend to bring them into contact with other practitioners in their own fields. But the roles of these notables as leaders or even just as notables might be expected to give them a broader, more cosmopolitan range of acquaintances with whom they might confer on issues concerning the course of the organized bar or on extra-professional matters, including partisan political activity, issues of public policy, and their personal investments and business ventures. Given that the notables' networks of association are subject to these important determinants that are largely unrelated to their clients' interests, it is striking to note the extent to which acquaintance with the notables corresponds to the fields or sectors of law practice.

Because of the tendency for Catholics to be disproportionately represented among Regular Democrats in Chicago, Jews to be overrepresented among independent liberals, and WASPs among Republicans and the corporate elite, political and client affinities will loosely correspond to religious ones.[38] But whether client interests,

---

37. See generally chap. 5. See also Clyde Nunn, Harry Crockett, and Allen Williams, *Tolerance and Nonconformity* (San Francisco: Jossey-Bass, 1978).

38. The correlation between religion and Chicago political preference is very strong; $\chi^2 = 125.9$, $p = < .00001$. While 32 percent of the Type I Protestants in our total sample express a preference for the Republicans, only 6 percent of the Catholics and 3 percent of the Jews share that preference. Forty-eight percent of the Jews call themselves Independent Democrats, while 34 percent of the Catholics and 27 percent of the Type I Protestants choose the label. Though Regular Democrats are only 16 percent of our total sample, 26 percent of the Catholics express that preference, compared to 16 percent of the Jews and only 6 percent of the Type I Protestants.

political allegiances, or social background characteristics (or, as is almost certainly the case, some combination of all of these) is thought to determine lawyers' patterns of acquaintance and networks of influence, the important point to note is that none of these organizing factors is rooted in the norms, doctrines, or organizational rules of the law or the legal profession. Instead, the spheres of influence within the legal profession draw upon sources of power that are located outside the profession. The liberal sphere quite clearly has its origins in liberal politics. It has explicit ties to liberal candidates for public office and to ideologically based voluntary associations that are extra-professional or far broader than the profession, organizations such as the American Civil Liberties Union. The trial lawyers/CBA sphere has clear political ties to the Regular Democrats. It is probable that one of the principal sources of the influence of this sphere within the profession is its ability to mobilize the resources of the city and county governments, to secure the benefits that it is within the power of City Hall to confer. This sphere is also associated with particular types of clients; its lawyers tend to represent individuals and smaller, family-owned businesses. The corporate establishment sphere is even more clearly identified with a particular type of client and less tied, perhaps, to public politics. The source of its power within the profession is its access to (and its presumed influence upon) the business and financial community.

Arthur Bentley, the father of the interest group approach to political science, contended that "The great task in the study of any form of social life is the analysis of [interest] groups. . . . When the groups are adequately stated, everything is stated. When I say everything, I mean everything."[39] Refreshing as this dose of certitude may be in a work of social science, one need not be so unequivocal as Bentley to recognize that identification of the affinities that organize lawyers into varying social groupings is a useful step in an analysis of the constituencies of the leaders of the profession. The nature of the interests that unite and divide groups of lawyers sets limits on the freedom of action of the leaders both in their activities within the bar and in their roles in the broader community; the leaders overstep the bounds of their constituencies' interests only at the peril of weakening their own positions as leaders. Our findings concerning

39. Arthur F. Bentley, *The Process of Government* (1908; reprint Evanston, Ill.: Principia Press, 1949), pp. 208–9.

the patterns of relationships between Chicago lawyers and the elites of the profession thus suggest two principal conclusions. First, the rigidity of the structure of relationships indicates that, though the three major spheres of influence have some areas of overlap, for the most part their differing constituencies inhabit separate social worlds. The relative lack of shared members and of leaders whose influence extends across the boundaries of the major interest groupings suggests that tendencies toward conflict among the interests are unlikely to be moderated, as might be the case if there were a greater community of concern and more multiple memberships among the groups. Second, the sources of the interests that appear to organize the principal constituencies of the profession's elite lie outside the profession. The conflicts that occur between the major groups within the bar will thus reflect the agendas of the broader community rather than a set of issues that arise only in the professional context or that are peculiar to the norms or concerns of the profession. The bar, then, is likely to function less as a guild than as a sort of guildhall—that is, as a forum within which the various external interests will press their cases and contend for advantage.

PART V

Conclusion

Chapter 10

THE HEMISPHERES OF THE LEGAL PROFESSION: SUMMARY AND SPECULATION

AS WE NOTED at the outset of this book, it comes as no surprise to find that Chicago lawyers are not a solid phalanx, marching ahead in lock step. The bar's variety and dissension have been made public with enthusiasm. But perhaps the types of lawyers are not quite so various as we might have supposed. As the analysis presented in this book has unfolded, we have advanced the thesis that much of the differentiation within the legal profession is secondary to one fundamental distinction—the distinction between lawyers who represent large organizations (corporations, labor unions, or government) and those who represent individuals. The two kinds of law practice are the two hemispheres of the profession. Most lawyers reside exclusively in one hemisphere or the other and seldom, if ever, cross the equator.

Lawyers who serve major corporations and other large organizations differ systematically from those who work for individuals and small businesses whether we look at the social origins of the lawyers, the prestige of the law schools they attended, their career histories and mobility, their social or political values, their networks of friends and professional associates, or several other social variables. Though there certainly are distinctions among lawyers that cut across the line between the two broad classes of clients, this fundamental difference in the nature of the client served appears to be the principal factor that structures the social differentiation of the profession.

One might argue, however, that it is not the form of organization of the client that matters but rather the wealth of the client.[1] That is, one might contend that the fundamental distinction is that between rich clients and poor clients (or, because few of the poor ever get to be lawyers' clients, perhaps we should say "less wealthy clients"). Surely the representation of an individual Rockefeller must be fully as remunerative and prestigious as is legal work for a state government, a labor union, or even most corporations.[2] Rich people do, after all, tend to pay their bills, and mingling with the Social Register elite, at their hunt balls and polo clubs, will carry with it as much cachet as does association with the sorts of persons who are now likely to become the chief executive officers of American corporations.[3]

1. See Dietrich Rueschemeyer, *Lawyers and Their Society: A Comparative Study of the Legal Profession in Germany and the United States* (Cambridge: Harvard University Press, 1973), pp. 13–30; Erwin O. Smigel, *The Wall Street Lawyer: Professional Organization Man?* 2d ed. (Bloomington: Indiana University Press, 1969), pp. 171–204.

2. One might even wonder whether these two categories of clients are really served by different lawyers. That is, will not the same law firms who handle the legal work of corporations owned or controlled by wealthy individuals also look after the personal legal affairs of those individuals? Perhaps, and perhaps not, but even if the same *firm* handles both sorts of work we find that the two are unlikely to be done by the same *lawyers* within the firm. A few large law firms have added divorce lawyers to their staffs to help the corporate executives disentangle their marital difficulties, several large corporate firms have probate departments, and many of the firms will accommodate corporate executives by handling the purchase or sale of their residences. But the lawyers who do the corporate work within the firm may have little in common with, and relatively little contact with, their partners or associates who do the divorce work and who draft the wills or do the estate tax planning. And if the residential real estate closing or title search is handled by the same real estate department within the firm that does real estate development work, syndications, and acquisitions of real estate for the corporate clients, the residential work is likely to be done by the most junior members of that department. See Robert L. Nelson, "Practice and Privilege: Social Change and the Structure of Large Law Firms," 1981 *American Bar Foundation Research Journal* 112–17. See also *infra* note 9.

3. See E. Digby Baltzell, "The Protestant Establishment Revisited," *The American Scholar* 45 (1976): 499–518; idem., *Philadelphia Gentlemen: The Making of a National Upper Class* (New York: Free Press, 1966); idem., *The Protestant Establishment: Aristocracy and Caste in America* (New York: Random House, 1964).

But our attempts at generalization here are just that; we do not mean to assert that there are no exceptions to the rule. And it would, of course, be a mistake to overdraw the precision of the cleavage between the corporate and personal client hemispheres of the Chicago bar. The client type distinction is too crude and too simple to account for the full complexity of the social structure of the profession. Any scholar who had the temerity to suggest that such a large bundle of social phenomena was anything less than polycrystalline and polymorphic would very likely be sent to stand in the corner with the journalists. One who wishes to look for variability, imprecision, or ambiguity in the structure of the legal profession would surely find it. It is there. There are, in some respects, larger differences within the hemispheres than between them. The greatest difference in the social values of lawyers in different fields is, for example, not that between the corporate and personal client hemispheres but the difference between lawyers who practice in the personal plight fields and those in the business or wealth-oriented fields of the personal client sector. And, as we argue below (see pp. 378-79), the different roles of litigators and office lawyers may create a systematic difference in the distribution of power between lawyer and client that cuts across the distinction between types of clients. Nonetheless, the distinction between corporate and individual clients is a very important one, and that distinction is probably key to an understanding of the social structure of the legal profession and of that structure's consequences for the distribution of power and influence.

Because an ever increasing amount of social power has come to be concentrated in corporations, the lawyers who are in a position to influence the affairs of corporations are now likely to have the most impact on the transactions that are of greatest consequence for our society. James S. Coleman has summarized the historical growth of the power of corporations.

> [I]ndividuals in society, natural persons, show a general and continual loss of power to corporate actors. . . .

> [L]ooking back at the thirteenth through the seventeenth centuries, [we can see that this was a period] when the feudal structure was breaking up, when natural persons were coming to have rights, that is, powers, before the law, and when the early corporations were conceived in the form of boroughs and churches. At that time, the corporation and the trust were outgrowths of the newly born "natural rights" of persons,

extending their powers vis-à-vis the power of the state or the king. In effect, the law's recognition of boroughs as legal persons, the extension of this recognition to non-landed corporations, and the endowing of trusts with the powers of persons, legitimated the idea that an individual could extend his powers through combination. The increase in power by coalition-formation was brought about through this recognition. The nineteenth and twentieth centuries have witnessed a vast extension of these possibilities. Today we find ourselves confronted by a world of corporate actors to whom much of our sovereignty has gone.[4]

Thus, lawyers who represent corporations have access to the decisions that are most likely to have important effects on the allocation of scarce goods and resources, on the manner of development and use of both public and private property, and on the course of governments. This greater power of the corporate lawyer to determine social outcomes may be one of the reasons why corporate practice differs so fundamentally from that serving individuals.[5]

Our thesis that the profession is divided into two quite distinct, largely separate hemispheres therefore rests on the proposition that the principal independent variable is not a continuum, like wealth, but a dichotomy, the difference between corporate and personal clients.

In addition to the difference in social power associated with these two types of clients, the nature of the interaction between lawyer and client may also differ systematically with client type. Most individuals, even the wealthiest persons, will not devote any substantial portion of their time and energy to direct supervision of their lawyers' work. Persons who are not wealthy will usually be too busy earning a living to use their time for this purpose, and wealthy individuals will usually have better things to do. Organizations,

4. James S. Coleman, "Loss of Power," *American Sociological Review* 38 (1973): 1–17.
5. The greater financial resources of corporations also permit their lawyers to go into their legal problems in greater depth, exploring the full complexity of the issues. Indeed, the more complex the issues can be made, the better the corporation often likes it. The complexity prolongs the litigation and thus puts off the day of reckoning, which is often to the advantage of the corporation. Until the issue is resolved, the corporation has the use of its money, and the deep pocket has the advantage in the war of attrition. The delay in collecting the claim and the mounting legal costs of the protracted litigation may force the corporation's adversary to settle cheap, or even to fold.
But the greater depth and complexity of analysis that the corporate assets make possible may enhance the sense of professional accomplishment of corporate lawyers. It is not so necessary for them to deal "superficially" with a high volume of cases, and they may, therefore, in fact as well as in perception, more commonly deal with challenging intellectual problems (see pp. 128–29). This may tend to increase their self-esteem and their degree of satisfaction with the practice.

however, will assign to an employee the responsibility for looking after the organization's legal affairs. Thus, lawyers are likely to have greater freedom of action, greater control over how they practice law, if their clients are individuals rather than corporations or other large organizations (see pp. 108-9).

The professional's freedom from client control is often cited as one of the most fundamental of the characteristics that distinguish the professions from other occupations.[6] But our argument suggests, quite ironically, that the lawyers who serve the more powerful, corporate clients are likely to be less "professional" in this respect than are those who serve the less powerful clients, individuals. This inference needs to be examined further, and we will therefore return to this important issue, treating it in more detail.[7]

Size, Separation, and Specialization of the Two Hemispheres

Though the two principal parts of the Chicago bar are not exactly equal in size, the total amounts of effort devoted to each and the total numbers of lawyers practicing in them are roughly comparable.[8] The corporate sector is somewhat larger, but not so much so as to overwhelm the personal client practice or to render it insignificant. More than three-quarters of the practicing lawyers devoted at least some of their time to fields in the corporate client sector, while more than three-fifths of them devoted time to personal client fields. There is, then, substantial overlap in these categories—that is, a number of lawyers practiced in both hemispheres—but a solid majority of the practicing lawyers worked exclusively in one hemisphere or the other. Only about two-fifths of them reported devoting any time to work in both hemispheres. And if we look not merely at whether they spent any time at all in fields in both sectors, but if we take the devotion of at least 25 percent of their time to a field as a measure of greater commitment to that area of practice, we find that only 101 of our respondents (i.e., only about a

6. See, e.g., Wilbert E. Moore, *The Professions: Roles and Rules* (New York: Russell Sage, 1970), pp. 15-16. See also Ernest Greenwood, "Attributes of a Profession," *Social Work* 2 (1957): 45-55.

7. See pp. 365-73.

8. See chapter 2 at table 2.1.

seventh of the 699 practicing lawyers) devoted that much time to fields in both of the hemispheres. The two hemispheres thus tend to be largely separate, to be populated by different lawyers. Relatively few lawyers do substantial amounts of work in both.

Because he perceives client demand for full service (see pp. 54–55), a lawyer often spreads his work across a range of fields, encompassing various doctrinal areas, but this demand will be limited by the range of needs of the lawyer's particular type of clients, and the doctrines dealt with will therefore be confined within client type boundaries. Corporations seldom worry that their refrigerators will be repossessed.[9] The neighborhood lawyer may be called upon to do individual income tax returns, real estate transactions of modest size, wills, divorces, accident cases, debt collections, and perhaps some criminal defense work. The lawyer who practices in the corporate hemisphere is likely to work in a narrower range of fields, but the large firms in which most such lawyers practice will also feel some pressure to serve a broad range of the demands of the firm's clients. Thus, the large law firm that looks after a corporation's tax problems will also be likely to handle its securities issues, antitrust problems, and real estate development or zoning matters. The firm will often be reluctant to refer a portion of the client's business to a specialist in another firm, fearing that the client may develop too permanent or extensive a relationship with the specialist's firm and, perhaps, may then take more of its business to that firm or to another where it will receive full service.[10] There are, of course, a few true specialties among the fields of law, but we found that the only fields to which a majority of the field's practitioners devote as much as half of their time are criminal prosecution, patents, and labor law work for unions. While labor law practiced on

9. On the other hand, corporate officers do get divorced with some regularity, and a few of the large, corporate law firms have therefore added small divorce departments as an accommodation to these clients. The more usual pattern, however, is to refer the divorce cases of corporate officers to small firms specializing in divorce work, who present no threat of taking over any portion of the corporation's legal work. In such referrals, the divorce specialist handles the divorce itself and related questions of child custody or visitation rights, but the large firm may often retain control of the financial settlement.

10. For this reason, we have in recent years begun to see the emergence of some quite small, very highly specialized firms that are self-consciously organized to handle only a clearly restricted range of corporate law problems so that they may more "safely" be referred the specialized work, the specialty firms being unlikely to pose a competitive threat to the large firms that practice corporate law generally. Those new firms, which have been called "boutique specialty firms," deal with areas such as bankruptcy and corporate takeover bids. See Nelson, *supra* note 2.

the union side is included in this exclusive list of true specialties, it is instructive to note that lawyers who practice labor law on the management side are substantially more likely to spread their time across a range of fields. We suggest that the explanation for this difference may be that the legal problems confronted by management (that is, corporations) are more varied than are those faced by labor unions, and the organization of the lawyers' work responds to the demands of their clients.

The very meaning of the term "specialization" among lawyers is also worth examination. What is the nature or kind of specialization that lawyers have in mind when they say that they are "specialists"? Seventy percent of our sample of Chicago lawyers told us that they regarded themselves as specialists, but their self-labeling may be biased by the prestige that attaches to the term. It connotes expertise and special skill. One may, therefore, prefer to think of himself in such terms. But it is also possible that lawyers may regard themselves as specialists if they concentrate on service to a particular type of client. That is the sort of specialization that we observe in the Chicago bar, and it may be that the lawyers' perceptions of themselves as specialists are based on client type. Our respondents were significantly more likely to regard themselves as specialists if they practiced exclusively in either the corporate or the personal client sector, even though they might work in a variety of fields within their respective sectors.

Unlike the task specialization that Durkheim associates with mutual interdependence, the division of labor along client lines may mean that lawyers become devoted to such a narrow range of interests that they have little stake in or dependence on lawyers who serve other sorts of clients.[11] No less than task specialization (and

11. Durkheim, among others, has noted that specialization creates interdependence among the specialized parts and thus a pressure toward coordinating or integrating the parts so that they are in some sort of adjustment. Emile Durkheim, *The Division of Labor in Society*, trans. George Simpson (New York: Free Press, 1964), pp. 62, 200, 301–2, 353, 364, 406 passim. But the simultaneous existence of substantial numbers of both specialists and generalists may lead to conflict. Inherent antagonisms arise between the interests of specialists and the interests of part-timers or dilettantes. Because the specialists are wholly devoted to a narrowly circumscribed field of activity, their standing among their peers rests on their unremitting service to their chosen field. They tend to be acutely aware of the variable levels of competence, performance, and knowledgeability of practitioners, and they have a strong interest in raising standards of performance by eliminating the "unqualified" who grab the occasional case and bungle it, thus threatening the reputation of the field. The part-timer, by contrast, has an interest in maintaining ease of entry into a field of practice; he will thus oppose formal certification procedures and other barriers to

perhaps more), client specialization thus may have consequences for the integration and coherence of the profession. If specialization has not only disaggregated lawyers' interests but created conflicts among them, we would expect these conflicts to emerge in disputes over "territory," over the monopolization or control of types of work or clients.

Fifty years ago, for example, the organized bar might readily reach a consensus that lawyers were the proper persons to search real estate titles and to handle the closings of home sales. Performance of these functions by anyone else would have been said to constitute "the unauthorized practice of law." Today, the bar is sharply divided on this issue. There is now a substantial interest group within the profession consisting of lawyers who regularly represent real estate brokers and title companies. It is, of course, these clients who would engage in that "unauthorized practice." Rather than retain lawyers to perform these routine tasks, the title companies would prefer to use their own, less well-paid employees to do these jobs, keeping for themselves any profit that is to be made on the services. The paradigm of the general practitioner—

(continued)

entry, such as specialized referral schemes. The specialist's interest in standardizing entry and practitioner performance will be viewed by the part-timer (and perhaps others) as a tactic for securing a monopoly position; see, generally, Jerold S. Auerbach, *Unequal Justice: Lawyers and Social Change in Modern America* (New York: Oxford University Press, 1976); Eliot Freidson, *Profession of Medicine: A Study of the Sociology of Applied Knowledge* (New York: Dodd, Mead, 1970); idem., *Professional Dominance: The Social Structure of Medical Care* (New York: Atherton Press, 1970); Magali Sarfatti Larson, *The Rise of Professionalism. A Sociological Analysis* (Berkeley: University of California Press, 1977).

The history of the emergence of medical specialty boards is replete with examples of these confrontations between specialists and generalists (see Glenn Greenwood and Robert F. Frederickson, *Specialization in the Medical and Legal Professions* [Chicago: Callaghan, 1964], pp. 15–24; Rosemary Stevens, *American Medicine and the Public Interest* [New Haven: Yale University Press, 1971]), and history appears to be repeating itself in the more recent controversies in the legal profession over specialty certification (see Barlow F. Christensen, *Specialization* [Chicago: American Bar Foundation, 1967]; Richard Zehnle, "Specialization in the Legal Profession," in *Legal Specialization*, American Bar Association, Specialization Monograph no. 2 (Chicago, 1976); Jerome A. Hochberg, "The Drive to Specialization," in Ralph Nader and Mark Green, eds., *Verdicts on Lawyers* [New York: Thomas Y. Crowell, 1977], p. 118). Our findings suggest that the balance of power among lawyers on the issue of specialization is now heavily weighted in favor of the generalists in most fields of practice, but the increasingly successful prosecution of malpractice suits against lawyers could, of course, produce growing pressures toward certification of specialties. (Insurance companies already require specialty certification as a prerequisite to the issuance of certain kinds of medical malpractice policies.) Note, however, that such pressure for change would not be endogenously generated but rather would be a lagged response to extra-professional demands for accountability.

the nineteenth-century lawyer or perhaps the present day small town lawyer—would represent home buyers or sellers one day and the local real estate agent the next. But specialization within the profession has now created, in addition to the group of lawyers who represent the brokers, a second distinct faction: neighborhood lawyers who almost never represent large real estate brokers or title companies but have many middle-class clients who buy and sell their homes and small businesses. For this second interest group, real estate closings are bread and butter. The two groups have reason to conflict. And they do.

The conflicts need not be motivated exclusively (or even primarily) by self-interest or client interest. Like other persons, lawyers have private causes. They may act as "moral entrepreneurs,"[12] and this may bring them into conflict with other lawyers who have opposing moral principles. But their principles may also be influenced by their areas of practice. The corporate lawyers who dominate the Association of the Bar of the City of New York advocate "no fault" systems of automobile accident compensation. They never touch a personal injury case. And they are vigorously opposed by the personal injury plaintiffs' lawyers, whose voice is the American Trial Lawyers Association. The personal injury lawyers complain that the corporate lawyers "don't understand our problems."[13] It is certainly true that one of the consequences of specialization is that the different roles may come to exist in separate social worlds and that, as they lose contact with one another, the lawyers may also lose their sensitivity to one another's problems, thus diminishing consensus on the profession's goals.

Max Weber wrote extensively on the important role of specialists in rationalizing, systematizing, and codifying cultural belief systems and practical knowledge,[14] and he noted that it will usually be specialists rather than generalists who will have the impulse to reform. Generalists have relatively little investment or stake in each of the fields in which they practice and they will therefore be relatively indifferent to improving the quality of practice in any field.

12. Howard S. Becker, *Outsiders: Studies in the Sociology of Deviance* (New York: Free Press, 1973), pp. 147–63.

13. Jerome E. Carlin, *Lawyers on Their Own: A Study of Individual Practitioners in Chicago* (New Brunswick, N.J.: Rutgers University Press, 1962), pp. 175–84.

14. Max Weber, *Economy and Sociology: An Outline of Interpretive Sociology*, ed. Guenther Roth and Claus Wittich (Berkeley: University of California Press, 1978), pp. 775–76.

This means that generalists will be unlikely to devote uncompensated time to the bar activities directed toward improvement or reform of any particular area of practice, and the fields that have few specialists will therefore tend to lack advocates for rationalization of the field—that is, for bringing order to its conceptual framework.[15] But lawyers may well seek changes in the law—if they perceive that their regular clients have an important stake in such changes. It may not be necessary for the client to tell them or hire them to do this if the lawyer has a large enough investment in the client. The lawyer's role in securing such changes may well earn the gratitude of the client but changes in the law that make things easier for the client will also often make things easier for his lawyer. To the extent that lawyers are specialized by client type, therefore, we may expect them to be organizationally or politically active, if at all, in areas that are defined by client interests.

The degree and kind of specialization within the profession is also likely to influence the nature and extent of the profession's internal social differentation. If the division of lawyers' labor occurs along lines defined by social types of clients, the impulse toward social homogeneity between lawyer and client may tend to produce social differences among lawyers that correspond, to a greater or lesser degree, to those among the client types.

SOCIAL DIFFERENTIATION OF LAWYERS AND CLIENTS

There are, of course, subdivisions within the two hemispheres of the profession. The most important of these is the distinction between litigation and office practice. In the figure below, the "corporate hemisphere" is at the right and the "personal hemisphere" is at the left, the circle being further subdivided into quadrants that engage in, respectively, corporate litigation, office practice for corporate clients, office practice for personal clients, and litigation for persons.

In our data, however, we find an exception to this generally circular structure. The two sorts of litigation fields—those representing corporate clients and those representing persons—are separated by a considerable social distance. A closer rendering of the arrange-

15. For a discussion of law's "cognitive base," see pp. 341–42.

FIGURE 10.1
General Structure of Law Practice

ment of the fields in social space, therefore, more nearly resembles a U than an O. At the bottom of the U—that is, in the office practice fields—the difference between the hemispheres in wealth of clients, the nature of their legal work, and the character of the relationships among lawyers and clients is probably less pronounced than it is in the litigation fields at the top of the U. The great bulk of the office practice done for persons is no doubt work done for relatively wealthy individuals on such matters as estate planning, personal income tax avoidance, and real estate deals. There is also a considerable volume of commercial law work (debtor- creditor, contracts, Uniform Commercial Code matters) done for businesses owned or controlled by individuals. This work is probably much more like the office practice of law for corporate clients than is corporate litigation like personal litigation. Corporate litigators are as likely to represent the largest corporations as are the office lawyers in the corporate hemisphere, but personal client litigation is more likely to involve the poor to moderate income end of the personal client spectrum.[16] Thus, defendants in criminal cases, evictions and

16. Within the corporate hemisphere, we find no significant differences between litigators and office lawyers in the percentages of their practice income that they receive from major corporations and from smaller businesses. In the personal client hemisphere, however, the litigators receive far more of their income from blue-collar workers than do the office lawyers (17 percent for the office lawyers and 30 percent for the litigators; this difference is significant at the .001 level). Personal client litigators also receive significantly more of their income from unemployed persons and from sales and clerical workers than do office lawyers practicing in the personal client hemisphere.

repossessions, and plaintiffs in personal injury and civil rights claims are likely to have below average incomes. Parties to divorce cases that consume any substantial amount of litigation time almost surely have above average incomes, but they need not be wealthy. It is therefore likely that social distinctions will be greater between lawyers engaged in litigation for the two, broad sorts of clients than between practitioners in the two types of office practice.

The existence of this U-shaped social structure was first suggested by a multidimensional scalogram analysis that permitted us to examine the relationships among the fields on several variables considered simultaneously (see p. 75). In the resulting figure, which depicts the fields as points in a two-dimensional space, we found the points arranged in a rough U, with a cluster of corporate litigation fields at the upper right, a cluster of "personal plight" litigation fields at the upper left, and the office practice fields at the bottom, less widely separated but with corporate practice generally toward the right and personal matters toward the left.

We also found that the allocation of prestige to these fields of law, determined by an entirely separate set of questions asked of our respondents, was very highly correlated with the same U structure. The rank order of the fields along the U substantially reproduced the rank order of the prestige scores assigned to the fields by our respondents (see chaps. 3 and 4). Thus, the kinds of variables that were used in the multidimensional scalogram analysis—the types of clients represented, the mechanisms by which lawyers obtain business, the sorts of tasks performed, the organizational setting of the practice, the type of law school attended, and the religion of the practitioners[17]—appear to create an overall structure that is strongly associated with the extent to which Chicago lawyers perceive that each of the fields has a claim to deference within the profession. Further analysis persuaded us that the nature of prestige within the profession largely reflected the types of clients served by the fields. An alternative hypothesis that we considered is that prestige might be determined by the extent to which the field presents intellectual challenge—that the profession might value intelligence, high levels of professional skill in legal research, and creativity in devising original arguments or theories, and might therefore accord prestige to fields that present greater opportunity for the display of

17. For a more complete description of these variables, see pp. 75–76.

such talents. Because there will be fewer such opportunities in the sort of law practice that processes a large volume of cases for relatively impecunious clients than in the practice of law for clients who are able to pay for the hours consumed in creativity and introspection, prestige accorded to creative, intellectually satisfying work will *ipso facto* be accorded to work done for clients with deep pockets. The wealth and intellectual challenge variables are, thus, closely interrelated, and it is therefore difficult to determine whether the prestige of the fields is to be attributed more to client type or to the differential opportunities that the fields present for the exercise of intellectual skills. But comparison of the prestige of the two sides of doctrinal areas of the law that the adversary system divides into opposing fields—criminal prosecution versus criminal defense, labor law work for unions versus labor work for management, personal injury plaintiffs' work versus personal injury defense, environmental plaintiffs versus environmental defense, antitrust plaintiffs versus antitrust defense, and consumer law work for debtors versus consumer work for creditors—discloses that the side of the case that characteristically represents corporate clients is consistently assigned higher prestige than is the side that more often represents individuals (see pp. 127–28). It may be that the greater wealth of the corporate clients means that their lawyers are regularly able to devote greater resources to the issues and thus that the opportunities for creativity are consistently higher in the corporate fields even when the general doctrinal area of the law is held constant. We believe, however, that our findings provide strong support for the inference that the prestige accorded by the legal profession to the fields of law, constituting a set of distinct lawyers' roles, is determined in large measure by the types of clients served by the fields. Fields that serve corporate, wealthier, more "establishment" clients are accorded more deference within the profession than are those that serve individual, poorer clients. This suggests the thesis that prestige within law is acquired by association, that it is "reflected glory" derived from the power possessed by the lawyers' clients.

We also found a strong relationship between the types of work that lawyers do and their social background characteristics, including ethnoreligious origins (see chaps. 3 and 6). Lawyers from less prestigious social origins were overrepresented among those practicing in the less prestigious fields. A Catholic respondent was three times more likely than either a Protestant or a Jew to be working as a prosecutor. A respondent who was affiliated with a high status Protestant denomination (that is, a Type I Protestant—Episcopalian, Presbyterian, Congregationalist, etc.) was five times more likely than either a Catholic or a Jewish respondent to be found doing securities or antitrust defense work. Jews were more than twice as likely as were Catholics to do divorce work, and they were incalculably more likely to do so than were Type I Protestants—in our sample, we found no one of high status Protestant origin who did a substantial amount of divorce work. Other fields with particularly high concentrations of Type I Protestants were banking, patents, municipal, and personal tax; Jews were disproportionately represented in labor law, both on the union and on the management side, in business tax, commercial work, criminal defense, and personal injury plaintiffs' work; and Catholics were greatly overrepresented in personal injury work, on both the plaintiffs' and the defendants' sides, and in both business litigation and general litigation. Generally, WASPs were more likely to be found in the corporate hemisphere, Jews in the personal client hemisphere, and Catholics in the litigation fields. Thus, the kinds of tasks that a lawyer performs and the kinds of clients for whom he does those tasks are strongly associated with the lawyer's social origins.

As a "learned profession," avowedly devoted to high ideals, the bar professes the principle that attainment within the profession should be determined by merit. Talcott Parsons argued that the professions are a "sector of the cultural system where the primacy of the values of cognitive rationality is presumed,"[18] and Terence Johnson has observed that it is a part of the ideology of professionalism that "prestige within the occupation is dependent upon colleague evaluation and, as a result, technical competence is a significant criterion of individual worth."[19] Thus, the professional's proficiency in the lawyerly skills should determine professional success if this ideal-typical model of the profession prevails. The Chicago bar does not appear to conform closely to the model. To illuminate some of the reasons why, it may be instructive to compare the law with medicine and to note how the two differ in re-

18. Talcott Parsons, "Professions" in David L. Sills, ed., *International Encyclopedia of the Social Sciences* (New York: Free Press, 1968), p. 539; Talcott Parsons, "The Professions and Social Structure," in *Essays in Sociological Theory* rev. ed. (Glencoe, Ill.: Free Press, 1954), pp. 34–49.

19. Terence Johnson, *Professions and Power* (London: Macmillan, 1972), pp. 56–57.

spects that might influence their degree of conformity to the meritocratic model.

THE LEGAL AND MEDICAL PROFESSIONS COMPARED

Like the medical specialties, most fields of law are characterized either by a substantive concentration (nephrology and cardiology, antitrust and tax) or by a common technology or skill (radiology or surgery, drafting or litigation). The legal system's adversary mode frequently bifurcates areas of the law, however, causing lawyers to specialize according to the type of client or side of the case—this is a part of the more general tendency for legal specialties to be organized around the needs of clients who are distinguishable by social type, a pattern that is not so characteristic of medicine. A patient may be classified as a "kidney problem" without any reference to his wealth or social position, but only a wealthy client of a lawyer is likely to have antitrust or securities law problems. It is true that certain diseases disproportionately afflict the rich, and many others are more likely to be diagnosed in rich than in poor patients, but social implications seem likely to flow more naturally from the organization of legal specialities than from medical specialization. Certain types of legal problems can, by definition, afflict only corporations. Thus, lawyers who specialize in those fields of law will have a clientele with a disproportionate amount of economic power and, perhaps, of social and political power as well. Beyond this necessary correspondence between some doctrinal areas of the law and particular social types of clients, however, the structure of the demand for legal services induces most lawyers to handle a variety of problems, a variety that cuts across doctrinal areas and that reflects the perceived legal needs of the lawyer's set of clients, which usually includes only a narrow range of social types (see chap. 2). Substantive specialization in law has therefore lagged well behind that in medicine. Demand for medical services is not usually tied to the patients' social type; some doctors specialize in serving the poor, the rich, old people, young people, or one sex, and some diseases of genetic origin disproportionately afflict persons of distinct racial or ethnic heritage, but most illnesses are shared broadly throughout the population, providing a considerable range of social types of patients even if the doctor specializes in a particular malady.

333

Apart from the economic pressure to make efficient use of scarce technology or technology that requires a distinct skill, the lines of specialization within medicine have largely been dictated by scientific theory. Medicine, engineering, and other professions in the sciences are structured around their conceptual bases, as developed by autonomous scholars in universities and scientific research institutions, and innovations in the knowledge bases of these professions usually account for changes in the organization of practice over time. This is not the case in law. We do not say that the law lacks theory but rather that its theory does not appear to organize the profession. The issue (for present purposes, at least) is not whether the law boasts some systematic body of knowledge or concepts corresponding to the scientific base of medicine but whether such systematic knowledge as exists structures the delivery of legal services. We are aware that concepts of "disease" may be defined, in part, by social variables.[20] Our contention, nonetheless, is that the structure of the delivery of medical services is organized in large measure by a body of scientific theory and empirical knowledge, while such division of labor as occurs in law tends to follow the boundaries between identifiable social groups of clients who share distinct sets of legal needs.

This identification of lawyer with client may reflect the process and criteria by which clients select lawyers. The intimate nature of many medical problems notwithstanding, personal intimacy perhaps more often characterizes the relationship between lawyer and client than that between doctor and patient. Our relations with doctors tend to become routinized. In our early years, we submit to preschool physical exams; later, as the indignities of age afflict us, we are told to have routine annual physicals. Though these occasions involve some procedures that are, in a sense, intimate, the interactions usually follow a standard format and become familiar. Doctors tend to adopt a matter-of-fact, somewhat laconic manner, perhaps designed to reassure the patient that his case is not exceptional and perhaps to speed case processing.[21] Even when we are ill,

20. See Freidson, *supra* note 11, *Profession of Medicine,* pp. 203–331; idem., *Professional Dominance,* p. 6; Barbara Wootton, *Social Science and Social Pathology* (London: Allen and Unwin, 1959); and Kingsley Davis, "Mental Hygiene and the Class Structure," *Psychiatry* 1 (1938): 55–65.

21. Talcott Parsons observed that the professional role emphasizes "affective neutrality"; see his *The Social System* (Glencoe, Ill.: Free Press, 1951), chap. 10.

the doctor's questions are often standard: "Any nausea?" "Any abdominal cramps or pains?" Most of us see our lawyers, however, only when "ill"; we do not get routine annual legal examinations. When lawyers perform strictly legal functions, as opposed to general business or tax planning, the client has usually determined in advance that he has a problem and often that he faces some particular sort of "trouble."

It is important that the lawyer, in discussing a client's problems, speak the client's language, both literally and symbolically. The legal profession's greater reliance on extensive conversation between lawyer and client, rather than on a checklist of symptoms, may require that the lawyer and client share a range of discourse. But beyond this, the patient with nephritis probably cares less that his doctor share an outlook on life than that the doctor be well informed about kidneys. The client, of course, also wants his lawyer to be technically competent, but the matters that law addresses often require a trust that goes beyond confidence in professional skill. The client must trust the lawyer's discretion and may even feel a need to have the lawyer sympathize with his position. A client may, therefore, prefer a lawyer who shares his social characteristics. It is probably more often important to clients than to patients that their professionals are of their own ethnic group, went to the same sort of school, or belong to the same clubs. This, then, is another reason why social types of clients tend to produce corresponding groupings of lawyers.

DEFINING THE WORK IN LAW AND IN MEDICINE

Sociological thought concerning the professions has largely been shaped by the model of the medical profession[22] and has consequently identified freedom of occupational activity as one of the

22. In addition to the works of Eliot Freidson, *supra* note 11, see, e.g., Jeffrey L. Berlant, *Profession and Monopoly: A Study of Medicine in the United States and Great Britain* (Berkeley: University of California Press, 1975); Larson, *supra* note 11, Robert Stevens and Rosemary Stevens, *Welfare Medicine in America* (New York: Free Press, 1974); Rosemary Stevens, *supra* note 11. Dietrich Rueschemeyer has explicitly compared the legal and medical professions; see his "Doctors and Lawyers: A Comment on the Theory of the Professions," *Canadian Review of Sociology and Anthropology* 1 (1964): 17. His perspective differs from ours, but he covers some of the same points and we have benefited from his analysis.

principal characteristics of a profession.[23] This autonomy is said to result, at least in part, from the professionals' possession of arcane knowledge that their patients or clients lack.[24] Since, by hypothesis, the client does not know the essentials of the professional's work and cannot evaluate it, the professional acts with a freer hand than do members of occupations whose customers have a broad understanding of the occupation's work. A professional's client will, of course, usually know whether his lawsuit has been won, or whether his illness has been cured, but he may not know whether another result should have been expected. The law may differ from medicine, however, in the extent to which the problems it addresses are defined by clients rather than by the professionals. Physicians use professionally defined standards to discriminate between cases that need attention and those that do not. The lawyer's client, by contrast, plays a larger role in defining legal problems, in deciding whether and when he needs help. Indeed, there may be a distinction between the role of "client," a person who employs an expert to perform more or less well-defined services, and the role of "patient," a person whom the physician treats. It is only a bit too glib to put the point this way: the doctor decides when the patient needs an appendectomy, but the client decides when the client needs a divorce.

Within the legal profession, the extent to which the client defines the problem may well vary with the type of law and the nature of the client. Securities lawyers or corporate tax experts serve sophisticated business enterprises that can recognize and define their legal problems in considerable degree, while the generally less sophisticated clients of family lawyers are much less aware of their legal needs. Thus, the corporation planning a securities issue, an acquisition, or a merger will present a relatively specific set of issues to the lawyer, while the blue-collar worker may not recognize that he has entered into a contract or may not see the need for a formal divorce. This suggests somewhat ironically that lawyers doing high prestige work are less likely to define their clients' problems than are lawyers doing lower status work (see pp. 103-9). On the other hand, in the legal work that enjoys high professional prestige, those who

23. See Greenwood, *supra* note 6; Douglas Rosenthal, *Lawyer and Client: Who's in Charge?* (New York: Russell Sage, 1976).
24. Other factors possibly contributing to this autonomy are, e.g., social class differences between professional and client, or mystification that sets apart the role of the professional regardless of any real difference in knowledge.

bring cases to lawyers will often be other lawyers. Large corporations that have significant securities and antitrust problems will also have corporate house counsel who will identify and analyze the businesses' legal problems and will select specialized outside counsel to whom the work may be referred. Thus, though the client identifies the problem in such high status work, a professional is still in control—it is a lawyer, not someone outside the profession, who defines the need for legal work. But these lawyers are, after all, full-time employees of the client corporations, answerable to corporate management and, no doubt, generally responsive to the management's wishes.

This observation suggests another important difference between the legal and medical professions—both the buyers and the sellers of legal services are much more likely to be organizations than are the actors in the medical market. This difference has several implications for the structure of the market. It affects the means used by professionals and consumers to locate or select one another, and it influences the nature of the referral systems among professionals. Because the large law firm can handle a wide variety of the problems that confront businesses and because small law firms and solo practitioners usually feel no need to refer out the typical legal problems of individuals, lawyers are probably more likely than are physicians to refer cases to professionals who rank below them in the prestige hierarchy. In medicine, the general tendency is that the less specialized practitioners, with lower prestige, refer difficult or exotic cases to more highly specialized, higher prestige physicians. The typical referral is from the "family doctor" to a "specialist." In law, the cases flow in the opposite direction—higher prestige lawyers more commonly refer work to lower prestige practitioners. As we noted above, a large firm will usually refer out the divorce case of a corporate executive. The size of large law firms and the volume of business handled by them permits specialization within the firm, and the prominent specialists in corporate law fields such as tax, antitrust, securities, and real estate development will usually be found within such firms. Competition among these firms ordinarily induces each of them to provide a broad range of the services demanded by their clientele and, concomitantly, discourages them from referring cases to specialists in other large firms (see pp. 44–45). When doctors practice in groups (or share a suite of offices), the groups are usually rather small and the practice is often limited to one specialty. A typical arrangement would consist of from three to five urologists, sharing a suite, consulting with one another, substituting for a colleague who is ill or on vacation, and referring cases to one another (usually from seniors to juniors) to even out the workload, but without a formal group practice or the sort of team work that characterizes the large law firms.[25] The most prestigious doctors, as well as the family practitioner, are therefore likely to refer patients to specialists in other fields who are housed in other offices. That this sort of referral occurs far less often among lawyers deprives the legal profession of an important incentive for the maintenance of contacts among professionals and thus deprives it of one of the significant mechanisms for the enhancement of the profession's social solidarity.

But the differences in organizational character between doctors' patients and lawyers' clients are probably even more consequential than are the differences in organization of the firms that deliver services in the two professions. In the corporate client hemisphere, the clients are likely to be large organizations with substantial market power, and a law firm may depend heavily on the business of one large client. The consumers of medical services are, by contrast, individuals who are relatively seldom organized into groups or into the corporate form.[26] Thus, clients of the legal profession's corporate hemisphere will usually enjoy greater power vis-à-vis their lawyers than will patients vis-à-vis their doctors, while the autonomy of lawyers who practice in the personal client hemisphere may more closely approximate the doctor's degree of independence from client control. This is a view from another perspective, then, of the

25. Hospitals are, of course, large organizations, and they do exercise several forms of control over both physicians and patients (see p. 347). But it is important to note here that hospitals of any size or consequence are not owned by individual doctors, nor even by groups of doctors, but are responsible in form at least to boards of trustees, usually composed in substantial part of laymen representing interests external to the profession. In terms of their regulatory effects upon the structure of the profession—as institutions that touch and in part control the profession, institutions that are partly within the profession but also partly controlled from outside—hospitals are probably more closely analogous to the courts than they are to the large law firms. See Charles Perrow, "Hospitals: Technology, Structure and Goals," in James G. March, ed., *Handbook of Organizations* (Chicago: Rand McNally, 1965), pp. 910–971.

26. We are, of course, aware of the growth in recent years of HMOs and other group health plans. Even by the most optimistic of estimates, however, these plans serve no more than 5 percent of the nation's population, and most HMOs are operated by insurance companies or by Independent Physicians Associations (IPAs), not by consumers. See *Group Health News*, 22 (May 1981): 2. See also Jeffrey C. Goldsmith, *Can Hospitals Survive?* (Homewood, Ill.: Dow Jones–Irwin, 1981), pp. 93–95, esp. at fig. 4-2, p. 94.

same irony that we have noted before—that lawyers doing less prestigious sorts of work for personal clients have greater "professional autonomy" than do lawyers performing more prestigious work for corporate clients.[27]

There is at least one other reason, however, why clients may enjoy more control over their lawyers, in either hemisphere, than do patients over doctors. A primary method of control in any producer-consumer relationship is, of course, control of the purse strings, and clients seem likely to exercise more of that sort of control than do patients. It is common for clients to instruct their lawyers,

> "Look into this estate for me, but don't run the bill up over $500 without first informing me about how much I may expect to inherit,"

Or,

> "Let me know when your total billings to my company for the current fiscal year have reached $10,000, and we will then review our situation and decide how we wish to proceed."

By contrast, it is probably the rare patient who tells his doctor, "I am willing to spend $1,000 to have you take care of my heart and attempt to prevent another coronary." Most legal matters are primarily concerned with money, and it is possible to make a more or less rational calculation of the amount that it is prudent to spend in order to protect the amount at risk, given the probabilities. In medical cases, the costs of the exposure to risk are more difficult to calculate. The greater uncertainty will enhance the professional's power.[28]

We should note at this point an important distinction between two quite different sorts of control that clients might exercise over lawyers. The first and more obvious of these is direct impact on decisions made about the nature of the lawyers' work, including positions taken and the extent to which particular problems are explored in depth. We have already argued that this sort of client influence is likely to occur more often in the corporate hemisphere where the clients are both more sophisticated and more powerful.[29]

27. See pp. 322–23 and 336–37.
28. The greater availability of insurance for medical expenses may also serve to enhance the patient's relative lack of concern with the cost of the doctor's services. Though Blue Cross/Blue Shield and the Medicare/Medicaid programs have announced intentions to give closer scrutiny to medical charges in the future, both will use physicians to provide that scrutiny and the control will, thus, be intraprofessional.
29. See pp. 320–23.

The second, and perhaps even more important, sort of client influence on the profession is impact on the profession's social structure, on the patterns of differentiation of its component parts and thus on the form of organization of the delivery of legal services. We have much better evidence of the latter influence than of the former. Our survey of the Chicago bar was not designed to collect direct data on the substance of the relationships between individual lawyers and individual clients—that is, on the decision process through which various strategic judgments are made concerning the manner in which the clients' cases will be handled.[30] But we do have data on the relationship between client type and the profession's social structure. Though we will continue in the frankly speculative manner of this concluding essay, we might then return now to a system-wide analysis—more at the macro than at the micro level—focusing not on the dyadic relationship between lawyer and client but on more general characteristics of the social structure of the legal profession, still using medicine as a point of comparison.

THE CONCEPTUAL FRAMEWORKS OF LAW AND MEDICINE

Dietrich Rueschemeyer has observed that there is far greater societal dissensus about the "central value" of the law—justice—than about that of medicine—health:

> Apart from borderline cases there exists a near-universal *consensus about the central value* toward which the medical profession is oriented. Physician and patient, the doctor's colleague group and the patient's family, his friends, and his role partners in other contexts, as well as the larger community and its various agencies, agree essentially on the substantive definition of health and on its importance compared with other values.

> The situation is far more complex for the legal profession. Justice, like health, ranks high in the societal value hierarchy. In the substantive definition of justice, however, there are considerable ambiguities and wide discrepancies, . . . the notion of unjust law is by no means uncommon.[31]

The division of labor in the law will, then, tend to have consequences for the structure and legitimacy of the legal profession that are quite different from the consequences of specialization in medi-

---

30. For a study that did deal with the individual lawyer-client relationship, see Rosenthal, *supra* note 23.
31. Dietrich Rueschemeyer, "Doctors and Lawyers," *supra* note 22, pp. 17, 19.

cine. The interests of a dermatologist and a cardiologist seldom conflict. But the distinct social types of clients served by most lawyers—even those who work in a number of fields—will often have conflicting economic and political interests. To the extent that the interests of lawyers' clients conflict,[32] the interests of the lawyers will also conflict and the social integration of the profession will suffer.

The conceptual framework of the law does little to bridge these gulfs. Just as a lawyer's clients tend to be limited to particular social types, the applicability of many legal doctrines is restricted to narrowly delimited social types[33]—broadcasters, landlords, securities brokers, or those who would limit the use of an invention, for example. Because the law has no overarching conceptual framework that is broad enough or strong enough to encompass all of these discrete doctrinal areas, scholarly contributions to legal theory and practice tend not to be cumulative. Even the broadest of the law's concepts—abstractions like the right to privacy—take on different colorations in different factual contexts, meanings that often differ systematically with the type of client.[34] Although the boundaries between many areas of the law are undoubtedly indistinct, this is less often due to the presence of a common core of theory than to the absence of any theory that might clearly define boundaries. In

32. The adversary nature of the litigation process, as well as the clients' differing social types, make that conflict inevitable—e.g., labor unions versus management, criminal defendants versus prosecutors, taxpayers versus tax consumers.

33. The fact that both the doctrines and the lawyers' practices tend to be bounded by clients' social types is surely not coincidental but a result of interrelated, mutually dependent processes. That is, the doctrinal limits may be defined in part by client type (perhaps through client influence on the curricula of law schools), and the boundaries between doctrines may in turn define the literature that a given practitioner will read, the literature in which he will attempt to "keep up with developments."

34. Dean William Prosser argued that the right to privacy, the creation of which owed much to the noted article by Samuel Warren and Louis D. Brandeis, "The Right to Privacy" (4 *Harvard Law Review* 193 [1890]) referred to "not one tort, but a complex of four." Prosser continued, "The law of privacy comprises four distinct kinds of invasion of four different interests of the plaintiff, which are tied together by the common name, but otherwise have almost nothing in common except that each represents an interference with the right of the plaintiff, in the phrase coined by Judge Cooley, 'to be let alone.'" William Prosser, "Privacy," 48 *California Law Review* 383, 389 (1960). For a historical account of the Warren and Brandeis collaboration and contribution, see Dorothy Glancy, "The Invention of the Right to Privacy," 21 *Arizona Law Review* 1 (1979); for the view that Prosser's own influence on the law of privacy rivals that of Warren and Brandeis, see Edward Bloustein, "Privacy as an Aspect of Human Dignity: An Answer to Dean Prosser," 39 *NYU Law Review* 962, 964 (1964). Leon Green wrote often on the limits of doctrine and on the extent to which the

spite of plentiful ambiguity, the law is decidedly *not* a seamless web.[35] It has not only seams but darts, tucks, pleats, gaps, and open zippers. Is this as true of medicine? Some medical specialities are, of course, quite distinct from some others, and doctors certainly regard much of the literature that is produced in remote specialities as irrelevant to their own work, but all of medicine deals with a human body that is conceived of as a set of interdependent systems, subject to a relatively rigidly classified set of diseases, and studied by one set of general principles, "the scientific method." The procedures dictated by scientific method, whatever the ambiguities, are more clearly defined than those dictated by "due process." Because the elements of legal theory and knowledge are less clearly interrelated, the effects of the innovations of legal scholars are often felt only within separate, delimited doctrinal spheres, and law professors therefore play a lesser role than do academic scientists in determining the structures of their respective professions. We have already noted the existence of dissensus about the nature of justice. This dissensus may lead legal scholarship to be directed toward differing—perhaps conflicting—goals, thus contributing further to the lack of conceptual integration.

We will return briefly below to a further comparison of the legal and medical professions, assessing the extent to which some of their key institutions serve to promote social integration of the two professions. For now, however, let us close this catalog of the professions' differences and turn to a further analysis of the degree of autonomy or independence of the legal profession.

(continued)
content of doctrine is determined by the contexts of the cases; see his *Judge and Jury* (Kansas City: Vernon Law Book Co., 1930), pp. 2–3, 16, and 19–20; idem., "The Study and Teaching of Tort Law," 34 *Texas Law Review* 1, 18 (1955); idem., "Tort Law: Public Law in Disguise (pt. 2)," 38 *Texas Law Review* 257, 266 (1960); idem., "Protection of Trade Relations Under Tort Law," 47 *Virginia Law Review* 559, 560 (1961). See also Clarence Morris, *How Lawyers Think* (Cambridge: Harvard University Press, 1937).

35. Maitland's famous metaphor, commenting on history rather than law, was first published in his "Prologue to a History of English Law," 14 *Law Quarterly Review* 13 (1898). It is also found in the first sentence of the second and subsequent editions of Frederick Pollock and Frederic William Maitland, *The History of English Law*, Vol. 1, 2d ed.; reissue (Cambridge: At the University Press, 1968).

Interests from Within and Without

A critical issue in the study of any profession is this: to what extent does the profession manifest client interests (or, perhaps, the interests of others outside the profession) and to what extent does it reflect its own concerns, interests, or values? Common lore says that lawyers are "hired guns," that within the vague limits of "professional responsibility" they do their clients' bidding. But the lore also holds that some forces or agencies within the legal profession serve to unify it, to give it a sense of identity or coherence. Thus, the bar associations, the law schools, or the court-appointed boards that control lawyer discipline and admission to the bar may be thought to create or enforce norms and values that originate within the profession. How accurate is the lore?

As our statement of the question implies, the issue is one of degree. Every profession reflects to some extent the economic, social, and ideological interests of its clients. All the professions also reflect norms and values of the professionals qua professionals—tenets that spring from the profession's own interests, ideology, and socialization processes. To varying degrees and in varying ways in the different professions, the professionals sometimes speak for themselves and at other times advocate the interests of outsiders. Beyond their "hired gun" role (but by no means unrelated to it), lawyers and other professionals may adopt their clients' views and, thus, advocate client interests because they have accepted them as their own. A cancer specialist may campaign for the control of environmental carcinogens even though a successful campaign might reduce the number of his patients. A tax lawyer may seek to simplify the tax code even though simplicity would reduce the demand for his professional advice. If we are correct, however, a lawyer is not likely to advocate the abolition of a tax shelter if that would conflict with his client's interests.[36]

Professions may also reflect client interests in a more subtle, but perhaps more fundamental, manner. The interests may affect the social structure of the profession itself—they will influence the or-

---

36. Though we did not attempt it, one approach toward assessing the relative importance to a profession of internal and external interests might be to examine the frequency with which the professionals advocate each sort of interest, but this assumes that these interests could be clearly distinguished. They may, in fact, often be inseparable.

ganization of the bar into groups or fields, the distribution of lawyers from different social origins among those groups, and the patterns of relationships among the lawyers. External influences that may shape the legal profession's social structure include the interests of clients and the baggage that the professionals bring with them into the profession. The attitudes and behavior of professionals as professionals are, no doubt, affected by their other roles—as spouses, parents, churchmen, Daughters of the American Revolution, or Sons of Italy. The early socialization of professionals may also be relevant to their professions, as may their commitments to religious, political, or social values.

But what is the relevance of our findings to these issues, and what are their implications for the profession? One conclusion suggested by our findings is that the bar associations, law schools, and court agencies accomplish little social integration of the profession. While our research documents the divisions within the legal profession, however, it does not provide direct evidence about the internal processes of these institutions. A fair inference from our data is that client interests play, at the least, an important role in the failure of these institutions to achieve integration of the profession, but we have examined the functioning of the bar associations, the law schools, and the agencies that regulate the profession only in an exploratory, impressionistic fashion.[37] With this caveat in mind, let us proceed to speculate a bit about some of the reasons why these institutions might have failed as integrative mechanisms, using the medical profession again as a basis for comparison.

The principal integrative institutions of the medical profession are the medical societies, the major hospitals, and the medical schools.[38] These may be thought of as roughly analogous to the bar

37. Some of our colleagues, however, have examined the bar associations in detail; see Terence C. Halliday and Charles L. Cappell, "Indicators of Democracy in Professional Associations: Elite Recruitment, Turnover, and Decision-Making in a Metropolitan Bar Association," 1979 *American Bar Foundation Research Journal* 697–767 (fall); Michael Powell, "Anatomy of a Counter-Bar Association: The Chicago Council of Lawyers," 1979 *American Bar Foundation Research Journal* 501–41 (fall); Charles L. Cappell, "A Legal Elite: Investigations into the Structure of Decision-Making and the Production of Law" (Ph.D. diss., University of Chicago, 1982); Terence C. Halliday, "Parameters of Professional Influence: Policies and Politics of the Chicago Bar Association, 1945–70" (Ph.D. diss., University of Chicago, 1979); Michael Powell, "The Politics, Policies and Influence of a Legal Elite: The Association of the Bar of the City of New York" (Ph.D. diss., University of Chicago, 1982).

38. These institutions are either within the profession or ancillary to it, depending upon how one defines the scope of the profession, an issue that does not concern us here.

associations, the courts, and the law schools, respectively, but there are important differences. The medical societies appear to be much more effective as regulatory mechanisms than are the bar associations. Bar associations have, in fact, been losing their regulatory powers over the profession in recent years. In 1973, the Chicago Bar Association (CBA) voluntarily ceded its power to discipline lawyers to an agency of the Illinois Supreme Court, known as the Attorney Registration and Disciplinary Commission. The leadership of the CBA had concluded that the association had been generally ineffective in carrying out the disciplinary function, and the CBA had also found the process expensive to administer. The cost of retaining the disciplinary power outweighed the perceived benefits to the organized bar.[39] In 1980, the Association of the Bar of the City of New York also yielded its disciplinary authority to the courts, not so voluntarily.[40] In our survey of Chicago lawyers, we asked our respondents whether they thought that the investigation of unethical conduct by attorneys should be carried out by the professional associations or by a governmental body under the supervision of the courts. Only 29 percent of our respondents favored control by the professional associations. Thus, the profession's power of self-regulation—a power that is usually included among the most important of the characteristics that are thought to distinguish the professions from other occupations—was supported by only a minority of Chicago lawyers.[41]

39. Michael Powell, "Professional Self-Regulation: The Transfer of Control from a Professional Association to an Independent Commission" (Paper read at the American Sociological Association's Annual Meeting, New York, 1976).

40. Michael Powell, "Developments in the Regulation of Lawyers: Intra- and Extra-Professional Controls" (Paper read at the American Sociological Association's Annual Meeting, Toronto, 1981).

41. Albert P. Blaustein and Charles O. Porter, *The American Lawyer* (Chicago: University of Chicago Press, 1954), p. 253, assert that "the power of the courts to investigate and to control the membership of the bar through disciplinary proceedings is as old as the profession itself."

The courts might be thought of as merely a part of the legal profession and, if so, the transfer of power from the bar associations to the courts might be seen not as taking the control away from the profession but merely as transferring it from one of the profession's institutions to another. Note that the law is the only profession about which such a contention might plausibly be made—the transfer of any part of another profession's governance from an association of the professionals to a governmental agency would constitute a clear loss of power by the profession. But, because the courts and the agencies under their control are staffed largely by a "special sort of lawyer," it can be argued that court control of the profession is *intra*-professional control. (And lawyers are, of course, said to be "officers of the court.") The courts are, however, just as clearly also agencies of government, and it is not at all clear that the primary loyalty of judges is to the profession from which they came to the bench.

In his classic work, *The Governmental Process*, David Truman remarked:

In striking contrast to medicine, the legal profession in the United States has been notably lacking in cohesion. . . .

[T]he centrifugal effects of specialized practice and wide income differentials have placed limits on the effectiveness with which bar associations stabilize the relationships of their potential membership and upon the completeness of association among lawyers.[42]

We find ourselves in accord with Truman's observations. The organized bar appears to us to function less as an interest group than as a forum within which interest groups compete for power. Unless some coalition within the bar can mobilize powerful constituencies, often from outside the bar, and can thus impose its will on the profession as a whole, the profession is unlikely to take a definite stand on a consequential issue. The legal profession can and does take definite stands, however, on issues that lack moment for most of the profession and most of its clients, and the organized bar often delegates such decisions to the concerned subgroup within the profession.[43] In sum, the profession is so riven by the conflicting interests of its clients that the bar can reach consensus only on inconsequential or symbolic issues that permit the profession's differences to be papered over (see pp. 249–73).

Unlike the bar associations, the medical societies and related organizations (such as certifying boards) retain tight control over the standards of medical competence, over admission to practice, over the certification of specialists, and over ethical standards of conduct. David Truman also noted that "in a closely knit profession like medicine, where reputation is crucial to a successful practice and where access to hospitals and other medical institutions is essential,

(continued)
Judges may well feel bound by standards and principles that are independent of the profession and that may conflict with those of the profession. There is certainly no guarantee, nor perhaps even a likelihood, that the judges' decisions on these matters will be representative of the collective views of the bar.

42. David B. Truman, *The Governmental Process* (New York: Alfred Knopf, 1951), pp. 202 and 96. See also, Rue Bucher and Anselm Strauss, "Professions in Process," *American Journal of Sociology* 66 (1961): 325–34.

43. That occurred in the Chicago Bar Association, for example, when it delegated the drafting of a new criminal code to a committee composed almost exclusively of criminal lawyers. See John P. Heinz, Robert W. Gettleman, and Morris A. Seeskin, "Legislative Politics and the Criminal Law," 64 *Northwestern University Law Review* 277, 317–25 (1969).

sanctions can be effective. . . . "[44] This points to the second of the medical institutions—hospitals—that we wish to examine and to compare to the integrative institutions of the legal profession. The law does not have any institution quite like the hospital. An affiliation with a hospital is an essential precondition of most sorts of medical practice.[45] A doctor will be unable to hospitalize his patients or to treat them while they are in the hospital unless he has a staff appointment or some sort of "hospital privileges." This gives the hospitals a significant form of control over individual physicians and standards of medical practice. Large law firms are important concentrations or assemblages of practitioners and in that sense may be analogous to hospital staffs, but the law firms lack this sort of control. The lawyer can pursue a great many alternative arrangements that will permit him to practice, often quite successfully, even though he may be denied access to a large firm. Moreover, as we have seen, the large law firms are quite specialized institutions, serving only a narrow range of clientele, and they thus do not perform the integrative role that makes hospitals so important to the social solidarity of the medical profession. Large hospitals typically treat a wide range of ailments, they usually serve patients from a variety of social classes, and they thus bring together physicians from virtually the full spectrum of specialities who then make collective decisions about the management of the hospitals and the allocation of resources, as well as about the treatment of patients. Because of their regulatory functions—their *de facto* control over entry into the practice of medicine and their role in setting and enforcing standards—the hospitals are probably more closely analogous to the courts than to the large law firms.

The large, corporate law firms do little to bridge the two hemispheres of the legal profession. They have little occasion to come in contact with either the clients or the lawyers of the personal client hemisphere. The growth of the large firms over the past few decades, the increase in salaried lawyers who are full-time employees of corporations and governments, and the simultaneous decline in the numbers of solo practitioners do represent a consolidation of a sort in the structure of law practice. But, because of the gulfs that

44. David B. Truman, *The Governmental Process*, 2d ed. (New York: Alfred Knopf, 1971), p. 200.
45. It may be unnecessary in some forms of public health medicine, but it is essential even for those doing most forms of medical research.

separate lawyers who serve different types of clients, these trends have not enhanced the social integration of the profession. Indeed, the distinctions and divisions may be becoming even sharper (see pp. 195–197 and 206).

What, then, of the courts? Whether conceived of as institutions that are internal or external to the profession, why do they not succeed in giving the profession coherence, in creating social solidarity or integration among lawyers, in assuring that the lawyer will come closer to being a "standard model"? Unlike the English bar, which has always been self-governing,[46] the American legal profession is subject to the supervisory authority of the courts,[47] but the courts have seldom used their licensing and disciplinary powers to exact conformity to any one, clear vision of the "proper lawyer." Administration of the courts' rules governing bar admission and attorney discipline is sometimes delegated to bar associations or to other groups of practitioners, and the courts for the most part have been content to impose rather minimal, rather laxly administered requirements for admission to practice—requirements that applicants

46. See Brian Abel-Smith and Robert B. Stevens, *Lawyers and the Courts: A Sociological Study of the English Legal System, 1750–1965* (Cambridge: Harvard University Press, 1967); Michael Zander, *Lawyers and the Public Interest: A Study in Restrictive Practices* (London: Weidenfeld and Nicolson, 1968), p. 2, observes:

> The regulation of the Bar, its practices, and rules has never yet been the subject of legislative interference. Every barrister has to belong to one of the four ancient Inns of Court which, since their foundation, probably in the fourteenth century, have had control over the admission of students, the examination required before Call to the Bar, and the discipline of students and barristers. The government of the Inns, and thus of the profession, was in the hands of the Benchers of the Inns, a self-perpetuating body of elders including, since 1875, judges. Many of the powers of the Inns, including examinations and discipline, have recently been delegated to the Senate of the Four Inns of Court established in 1966, two-thirds of whose members are practising barristers, the remainder being judges. The General Council of the Bar, or Bar Council, by contrast, is a voluntary association, founded as late as 1895, whose function it is to look after and promote the interests of practitioners. It is the Bar Council, rather than the Inns, which has promulgated the Bar's rules of etiquette and practice. . . . About ninety percent of the 2,200 or so practising barristers subscribe to the Bar Council.

Unlike barristers, however, solicitors are regulated by the English courts.

47. See Alfred Z. Reed, *Training for the Public Profession of the Law* (New York: Carnegie Foundation for the Advancement of Teaching, 1921), pp. 35–40. See also Martin Garbus and Joel Seligman, "Sanctions and Disbarment: They Sit in Judgment," in Ralph Nader and Mark Green, eds., *Verdicts on Lawyers* (New York: Thomas Y. Crowell, 1976), pp. 47–60; Ronald L. Akers, "The Professional Association and the Legal Regulation of Practice," 2 *Law and Society Review* 463–82 (May 1968); "Disbarment in the Federal Courts," 85 *Yale Law Journal* 975–89 (June 1976); Comment "Controlling Lawyers by Bar Associations and Courts," 5 *Harvard Civil Rights–Civil Liberties Law Review* 301–92 (April 1970).

must be of suitable character, must have completed a specified number of years of professional education, with very few required courses,[48] and must have passed a comprehensive bar examination that varies from jurisdiction to jurisdiction and from time to time in coverage and in degree of difficulty. Recently, however, we have seen initiatives by some judges to exert a greater degree of control over the content of legal education. Reflecting the view that many advocates are incompetent (a view expressed by Chief Justice Burger, among others),[49] committees of both federal and state judges have recommended and adopted requirements for admission to practice that demand the completion of a more extensive list of substantive law school courses, thus establishing required law school curricula.[50] These requirements usually include a prescribed amount of "clinical" legal education (supervised work in a legal clinic), and some would make experience in a certain number of trials (sometimes distinguishing further between jury trials and bench trials) a precondition of full admission to the bar.[51]

For the most part, however, the courts have not attempted to set

48. In most jurisdictions, the only required course has been "professional ethics." The limited number of courses available in the curricula of many law schools may also result in de facto course requirements, however—that is, the students may not have a wide range of choice. Because the bar exams cover specified lists of subjects, students may also feel pressure to take courses in those areas.

49. See Warren Burger, "The Special Skills of Advocacy: Are Specialized Training and Certification of Advocates Essential to Our System of Justice?," 42 *Fordham Law Review* 227–242 (December 1973). See also Judge Irving Kaufman, "The Court Needs a Friend in Court," 60 *American Bar Association Journal* 175–178 (February 1974). While Burger and Kaufman have argued that as many as one-half of trial attorneys are "incompetent," research on the subject has indicated that the majority of federal judges view the figure as much lower; see Dorothy Maddi, "Trial Advocacy Competence: The Judicial Perspective," 1978 *American Bar Foundation Research Journal* 105–51 (winter); Roger C. Cramton and Erik M. Jensen, "The State of Trial Advocacy and Legal Education: Three New Studies," 30 *Journal of Legal Education* 253–69 (November 1979).

50. In 1973, for example, the Indiana Supreme Court adopted Admission and Discipline Rule 13, which mandated certain law school courses as a prerequisite to taking the bar examination. See Frances X. Beytagh, "Prescribed Courses as Prerequisites for Taking Bar Examinations: Indiana's Experiment in Controlling Legal Education," 26 *Journal of Legal Education* 449–66 (November 1974). At least one state supreme court has followed Indiana's example (see the Rules of Admission to the Bar of South Carolina, 5A, 5B, 16). For background, see Bruce Littlejohn, "Ensuring Lawyer Competency: The South Carolina Approach," *Judicature*, 64 (1980): 109–13.

51. The primary impetus for such requirements was the "Devitt Report," the result of a commission chaired by Federal District Judge Edward J. Devitt; see Final Report to the Judicial Conference of the United States of the Committee to Consider Standards for Admission to Practice in the Federal Courts (September 19–20, 1979). See also Edward J. Devitt, "The Search for Improved Advocacy in the Federal Courts," 13 *Gonzaga Law Review* 897–933 (November 1978).

rigid or rigorous standards for the profession nor to determine the characteristics that lawyers must possess. Note that the training and experience requirements just discussed deal only with litigation skills—the judges' expressions of concern about lawyer competence have largely been limited to competence as an advocate. Similarly, in the area of lawyer discipline, judges will punish lawyers who disrupt sessions of court or who are insulting or insubordinate in direct dealings with the bench, but the courts seldom concern themselves with the far greater volume of legal business that takes place outside the courtroom. The investigation and setting of punishment for lawyers' ethical infractions that do not involve behavior in court and the screening of bar candidates for qualities and skills that are not of direct and immediate relevance to performance in court are likely to be left to the organizations of the profession.[52] Because most lawyers appear in court seldom or not at all, most of the profession is thus little subject to supervision by the judiciary. And because the organized bar is largely ineffectual, decisive action being blocked by the diversity of the bar and the resulting "veto groups," the authority delegated by the courts to the bar to control both discipline and admission to practice is little used to give the profession coherence or a distinctive character.

The remaining institution that might serve to enhance the social integration of the profession is the law school. The schools might inculcate norms that would endure through all or much of the professional's career, influencing the way he does his work and sees his role, or might train the lawyer in habits of mind that would shape his definition of the nature of legal work, his relations with clients, or even his perceptions of social reality.[53] Legal education is widely reputed to be an intensive, demanding, emotionally

52. See Rueschemeyer, *supra* note 1, p. 62. That lawyers and their organizations play a part in choosing judges may help to explain why the courts defer to the bar associations in these matters. The candidates who wish to be chosen (including sitting judges with further aspirations) may prefer to avoid giving offense to any important segment of the organized bar, and the ones eventually chosen may be those who are least likely to give offense in the future. In states that elect judges (as does Illinois), the bar associations customarily rate the candidates for judicial office and publish their recommendations; in appointive jurisdictions, including the federal system, the bar associations usually screen the judicial candidates and make recommendations to the appointing body.

53. See Frances Kahn Zemans and Victor G. Rosenblum, *The Making of a Public Profession* (Chicago: American Bar Foundation, 1981).

charged, anxiety-producing experience. It is replete with rites of passage and status degradation ceremonies. The traditional, though now seldom practiced, classroom style—the "Socratic method" as employed by mythological monsters like Professor Kingsfield—is portrayed as intimidating and authoritarian, calculated to exact conformity to the professor's (and the profession's?) values, or *else*.[54] Moreover, and probably more important, American law schools are said to adhere closely to a standard model created by Dean Langdell at Harvard in the 1870s. Thus, almost all of the schools use appellate court opinions in actual cases rather than treatises or textbooks as the basic teaching materials, certain best-selling collections of these appellate opinions (assembled in edited versions in casebooks, bearing the names of professors at the better schools) are widely used across the full spectrum of law schools, from the most to the least prestigious, and the curricula of almost all of the schools include highly similar lists of standard courses in basic areas of the common law, taxation, and economic regulatory law.[55]

But there is little evidence that American legal education produces a standard product. As we have seen, Chicago lawyers differ substantially in their views on social and economic issues, and they do work that varies greatly in character, in the service of clients of a variety of social types. Assuming that certain habits of mind may be particularly useful in or well adapted to the performance of certain types of work, we might nonetheless expect to find little in common among the modes of problem solving used in the characteristic tasks of the litigator who tries personal injury cases, the business advisor who gives tax counsel along with investment advice, the scientist who drafts patent applications, the artist who drafts indenture instruments,[56] and the public relations lawyer who handles a corporation's dealings with government. Law schools may prepare lawyers for only a narrow range of lawyers' roles, but the variety of

54. See Duncan Kennedy, "How the Law School Fails: A Polemic," 1 *Yale Review of Law and Social Action* 71 (1970).

55. On the development and structure of legal education in the United States, see two works by Robert B. Stevens, "Two Cheers for 1870: The American Law School," in Donald Fleming and Bernard Bailyn, eds., *Perspective in American History* (Cambridge: Harvard University Press, 1971), vol. 5, *Law in American History* pp. 405–58; and "Law Schools and Legal Education, 1879–1979," in 14 *Valparaiso University Law Review* 179–259 (winter 1980).

56. Professor William Carey, a former chairman of the S.E.C., said of Francis T. P. Plimpton that he "can write an indenture in iambic pentameter"; see Geoffrey Helman, "Period Piece Fellow," *The New Yorker*, December 4, 1971, p. 103.

jobs that lawyers are called upon to do in urban America guarantees that, as a practical matter, the notion of "thinking like a lawyer" will be largely meaningless.[57]

In the first decades of the twentieth century, the Carnegie Foundation sponsored studies of both medical and legal education in the United States with a view toward improving quality. The report on the medical schools, known as the Flexner Report, succeeded in stimulating the profession and the political process to abolish the marginal schools and to subsidize the remaining ones.[58] By contrast, the analogous report on the law schools by Alfred Z. Reed failed to achieve any such objective. Reed may have erred in being too permissive, too democratic. The report called for a two-tiered system of legal education, one track (and perhaps one set of schools) designed to prepare students for membership in what he called the "Inner Bar," practicing largely corporate law, and another, less demanding track preparing other students to join the "General Body of Practitioners,"[59] practicing "conveyancing, probate . . . , criminal law, and trial work."[60] Though Reed's prescription sounds elitist enough today, it was regarded by the bar establishment at the time as a threat to the exclusivity of the profession. The defect in Reed's position was that it would not close the proprietary law schools and the night schools, and thus would not cut off the access to the profession of the new immigrants who had arrived in the United States in such large numbers in the late nineteenth and early twentieth centuries.[61] The statement of Professor Arthur L. Corbin of Yale that is quoted in the epigraph at the front of this book was one of the pieces of rhetoric brought forth by the controversy—he argued that the democratic tendency "to open wide the gates of a profession to 'the average man'" insured the "utter mediocrity of judges and lawyers" and rendered a part of the profession "incompetent and dan-

57. See pp. 340–42.
58. Abraham Flexner, *Medical Education in the United States and Canada. A Report by the Carnegie Foundation for the Advancement of Teaching* (New York, 1910). For a discussion of the effects of the Flexner report, see Rosemary Stevens, *supra* note 11, pp. 66–73.
59. Reed, *supra* note 47, pp. 237–39.
60. Ibid., p. 419. Our notion that the legal profession might be separated into hemispheres, one corporate and one personal, thus has a precursor that is sixty years old. (The old ideas are always best.) The unpalatability of Reed's observation helps to account for the hostile reception given his report. We are resigned.
61. Jerold S. Auerbach, *Unequal Justice: Lawyers and Social Change in Modern America* (New York: Oxford University Press, 1976), pp. 98–100, 106–9.

gerous to the public welfare."[62] Though the Association of American Law Schools sought to achieve educational hegemony, forcing the marginal schools out of business, it did not succeed. A number of proprietary schools, night law schools, and other opportunities for part-time law study persist to this day.[63] Thus, legal education never became as highly standardized as did medical education in the United States; a greater variety of institutions continued to train candidates for the bar, the number of seats available in law schools was far less limited than in the medical schools, and the law schools thus have produced a considerable volume and variety of graduates. As law schools have conformed less to a standard model than have medical schools, so too, very likely, have their graduates.[64]

Sources of the Profession's Social Organization

If the formal institutions of the legal profession—the bar associations, the courts, the law schools, and the large law firms—do not determine its social organization, what then is the source of its structure? It is surely not random; the data are far too clearly organized for that to be the case. We have argued that the primary determinant of the social structure of the profession is the interests and demands of the lawyers' clients, but we have also pointed repeatedly to the role played by social origins—particularly ethnoreligious identification—in structuring the allocation of lawyers to varying professional roles.

62. Arthur L. Corbin, "Democracy and Education for the Bar," 4 *The American Law School Review* 731 (1922).

63. See Donna Fossum, "Law School Accreditation Standards and the Structure of American Legal Education," 1978 *American Bar Foundation Research Journal* 515–43 (summer 1978).

64. The medical schools may have overdone their exclusivity; the restrictions on the number of places available in American medical schools resulted in increased pressure to supply the domestic market with physicians trained abroad. Recently, the medical profession has begun to sound the alarm once again, claiming that the United States now has an oversupply of doctors. The Graduate Medical Education National Advisory Committee of the U.S. Department of Health and Human Services, chaired by Dr. Alvin R. Tarlov of the University of Chicago, predicted in 1980 that there will be a "surplus" of 70,000 doctors by 1990, and the Committee's report recommended reductions in medical school enrollments. (U.S., Department of Health and Human Services, Report of the Graduate Medical Education National Advisory Committee to the Secretary, 7 vols. [Washington D.C.: Government Printing Office, 1980] vol. 1, pp. 3, 21–22.)

The patterns of interaction among lawyers are influenced in significant degree both by the lawyers' fields of practice, a variable that is closely associated with the types of clients served, and by the ethnoreligious affiliations of the lawyers (see chap. 7). Moreover, the ethnoreligious and client type variables overlap—lawyers' ethnicities vary systematically by the type of client served (i.e., lawyers of particular ethnicities tend to serve particular kinds of clients). This overlap of two variables does not exist only in the allocation of lawyers to types of work; we also saw it in our analysis of the patterns of acquaintance with a list of selected "notable" Chicago lawyers, a set of the profession's elites. The patterns were divided into readily identifiable regions or networks, one area being composed disproportionately of WASPs who serve the largest corporate clients and another having a great preponderance of Catholics who do trial work for individuals and smaller businesses (see pp. 292–314). We found that acquaintance with notable Jewish lawyers did not correspond quite so neatly to client type, however. The Jewish notables tended to be spread somewhat more evenly across the types of practice—some located in the corporate area with the WASPs and some with the Catholics in the region characterized by trial work for individual clients and general commercial work for smaller businesses. The variable that appeared to organize the patterns of acquaintance of Jewish lawyers was, rather, the lawyers' positions in the political spectrum. Jews were much more likely to be acquainted with leaders of liberal political view—with liberal Democrats rather than with Republicans or those of conservative persuasion. Indeed, one quite separate, readily identifiable network of acquaintances where Jews clearly predominated was the network of lawyers active in liberal causes such as the ACLU and other reform-oriented organizations (see pp. 307–308).

The most remarkable thing about all of this is that *intra*-professional concerns, motivations, and interests appear to count for so little in the social structure of the profession. All of the organizing principles that appear to have the greatest influence—client demand, ethnoreligious origin, and politics—arise outside the profession. Talcott Parsons contended that one of the identifying characteristics of the professions is that they are not "self-regarding" but externally oriented.[65] The sort of external orientation that Parsons had in mind is rather different, however, from the one that we ob-

65. Talcott Parsons, *The Social System* (Glencoe, Ill.: Free Press, 1951) pp. 434–73.

serve. He argued that the professions display a "collectivity orientation," that they are devoted to the commonweal. We find that Chicago lawyers are devoted to the interests of their clients, to
ethnoreligious loyalties, and to political causes. There may be a substantial tendency for the advocate to equate client interests with
"the general interest," but the adversary nature of the legal process
prevents any professionwide consensus about the validity of such
equations. Lawyers who represent Citizens for a Better Environment may differ from those who represent Commonwealth Edison
in their view of the national interest concerning the development
of atomic power, those who work for the Internal Revenue Service
may not share corporate tax counsel's view that the general welfare
will be served by a tax avoidance scheme, and those who represent
insurance companies may not see the justice of the position, taken
by personal injury plaintiffs' lawyers, that accident victims should
be fully compensated for pain and suffering. But in spite of their
differing views, it is important to note—as Parsons might have—
that lawyers on both sides of all of those disputes and many others
seek to harmonize the commonweal with their clients' interests.[66]
And the other sources of differentiation and conflict within the bar,
ethnic and political loyalties, can no doubt be harmonized with a
particular view of the general interest at least as readily as may client interests. But because the ethnic and political identities are associated with service to particular types of clients, such loyalties may
serve to reinforce the homogeneity of outlook of the lawyers serving those clients, to enhance their adherence to a shared conception
of the commonweal. Thus, the reinforcement of client interests by
ethnic and political networks may strengthen the devotion of lawyers to their clients' causes.

Many scholars who have written about the legal profession, however, have argued that the lawyer is the dominant party in the
lawyer-client relationship.[67] Lawyers are said to use various sorts of
powers—intellectual powers, mastery of legal learning, silver
tongues, the monopoly of the license to practice, the formality and

66. Doctors probably feel even more confident about assuming that the health of
their individual patients is entirely consistent with the general interest; there are
few institutional mechanisms that confront them with the proposition that the common interest might be anything other than the sum of the individual interests of
each patient. See Rene Dubos, *The Mirage of Health: Utopias, Progress, and Biological
Change* (New York: Harper and Row, 1959).
67. See, e.g., *Time*, April 10, 1978, pp. 56, 66.

mystification of legal procedures (silk ribbons and sealing wax, black robes and, in England, wigs), impenetrable jargon (Latin, "law French," and polysyllabic neologisms), and general bluster and chicanery—to manipulate and control their clients. But these writers have usually had in mind the part of the profession that we have referred to as the personal plight practice, the representation of individuals with legal difficulties that are (at least in large part) personal rather than economic in nature—fields such as divorce, personal injury, and criminal law. In his widely cited article, "The Practice of Law as a Confidence Game," Abraham Blumberg argued that lawyers manipulate their clients, but he was considering there the practice of criminal law, where the clients are particularly vulnerable, usually impecunious, sometimes dependent on the state for the provision of counsel, and often not in a position to take their business elsewhere.[68] Douglas Rosenthal's pioneering and suggestive empirical study, *Lawyer and Client: Who's in Charge?* was done within the context of personal injury cases.[69] Though Rosenthal found that plaintiffs who took an active role in the supervision of their cases were likely to obtain better results than those who did not, the plaintiffs in such cases are nonetheless seldom the wealthiest and most powerful clients. Those who lack the resources to pay their lawyers in advance and, therefore, must find lawyers who are willing to take their cases on a contingent fee basis[70] will usually be in a subservient or dependent relationship to their lawyers. Pursuing Blumberg's theme, James Eisenstein and Herbert Jacob have observed that defense counsel who are regulars in felony courts may be less concerned with pleasing their clients than with accommodating the other regulars in those courts, the judges, clerks, and state's attorneys with whom they deal on a continuing basis.[71] Though the clients who appear in felony court may be awesome in some ways, they usually do not have the sort of power that counts with their lawyers.

A lawyer who represents a lower class person charged with a

68. Abraham S. Blumberg, "The Practice of Law as a Confidence Game: Organizational Cooptation of a Profession," 1 *Law and Society Review* 15–39 (June 1967).
69. New York: Russell Sage, 1976.
70. That is, the lawyer will be paid from the client's award of damages only if the lawyer wins the case. The fee is usually a percentage of the award or settlement—typically, as much as a third.
71. James S. Eisenstein and Herbert Jacob, *Felony Justice: An Organizational Analysis of Criminal Courts* (Boston: Little, Brown, 1977), p. 50; Blumberg, *supra* note 68; idem., *Criminal Justice* (Chicago: Quadrangle, 1967), p. 47.

crime (and most criminal defendants are, indeed, lower class) will usually be able to prevail if a direct conflict arises between the lawyer's interest and the client's interest. A common situation regards the payment of the lawyer's fee. Many, perhaps most, private criminal defense lawyers insist upon payment in advance because they have found that most defendants who are convicted (even if to a lesser charge, by plea bargain) will not pay later, particularly if they go to prison, and because the lawyers know that most defendants are, in fact, convicted. Even if the defendant should be acquitted, it is notoriously difficult to collect fees from clients who are as mobile, unreliable and, some might even say, untrustworthy as are criminal defendants as a class. Paid *in advance* means that the fee must be paid before the lawyer will try the case. The practical effect of this for the defendant who lacks sufficient money for release on bail (perhaps because funds that might have been used for bail are needed to pay the lawyer) is that he must remain in jail until his family or friends have managed to pay the full amount of the lawyer's fee, often on the installment plan. This may take many months. Pending full payment, the lawyer will seek continuances of the defendant's trial on one pretext or another. Despite the obvious ethical problems raised by such a practice, it is said to be widespread.

But when a similar conflict arises between the interests of a corporate lawyer and his client's interests, what does that lawyer do? Let us consider another example. Lawyers who specialized in the representation of airlines in route and rate regulation cases were recently confronted with a proposal that federal law be changed to remove or greatly lessen regulation of airline competition. What position would such a lawyer take on the proposal? Would he lobby against it? Because most airlines favored deregulation, open opposition to their interests might well have offended the clients. Would the lawyer, therefore, perhaps seek to work quietly behind the scenes to oppose deregulation? Apart from any political activity, what would he *think* about it? Would he identify with the interests of his clients, or would he worry about the effect of deregulation on his practice?

After deregulation had occurred, we asked these questions of a lawyer who had devoted most of his career, nearly thirty years of practice, to airline regulation work. The lawyer had been extremely successful and had regularly represented one of the major carriers, but after deregulation his practice had fallen off drastically. In mid-career and middle age, he was thus confronted with the need to develop a new, entirely different specialty. Had he seen this coming, we asked? Well, he said, he had of course known that deregulation was being proposed and debated. Had he taken any part in that debate? No. We knew that he had held responsible positions in the federal government and was well-acquainted in the Executive Branch—had he, therefore, attempted to use his contacts to express doubts about deregulation? No. What had he thought about the proposed deregulation? Not much; he had been too busy with his practice at the time. Did he anticipate or worry about the decline in demand for his services that deregulation might bring? No; he had assumed that it "would turn out all right." He had believed the old lawyers' adage that whatever the government does creates work for lawyers—airline regulation had created work, and deregulation, if it occurred, would also create work. It did not. We are confident that the lawyer's responses were truthful, and we believe that he is not atypical.

Corporate lawyers are accustomed to talk as if they have more business than they can handle, as if there is an inexhaustible reservoir of clients demanding their services. It is certainly true that the large law firms serving corporate clients have expanded greatly in recent years, and most forecasters believe that corporate law continues to be a healthy "growth industry" (given reasonable stability in the economy generally). It may also be the case that the expansion of the firms has made them less dependent upon any one client or, perhaps, even upon any one type of work (though this is not necessarily true).[72] But the firms do need to maintain their volume of business in order to support the investment that they have made in plant and staff—in word-processing equipment, computers, copiers,

72. One of the major forms of expansion in large law firms has been the growth of "specialty firms," which formerly had relatively few lawyers, into organizations that rival in size the largest of the general corporate law firms. An example in Chicago is the firm of Seyfarth, Shaw, Fairweather and Geraldson, a firm specializing in labor law work on the management side. Other specialties where such growth has occurred are litigation and tax, specialties for which there is an especially broad market. Because the flow of work to these firms is less dependent upon a few large clients than upon their reputation for their specialty, they may enjoy greater autonomy. Another type of firm that has grown substantially in recent years is the "boutique specialty firms"—firms with an even more intense specialization in an even narrower area of corporate law, such as takeover bids or bankruptcies. These firms are usually still relatively small (though a few of them are now quite large) and most of them are new firms, having been organized within the last two decades. See *supra* note 10.

and walnut paneling; in secretaries, technicians, paralegals, and lawyers—and the firm as a whole is no doubt less dependent upon the continued flow of any particular kind of legal business than is the partner, team, or department within the firm who handles that kind of business. Lawyers who work in large firms are compensated in accordance with their productivity (at least, the more senior ones are). If they are not very busy or are not bringing many clients into the firm, their compensation and their power and prestige within the firm will eventually suffer.[73] The individual lawyers who handle the work for major corporate clients are therefore usually wary of offending such clients.

Corporate lawyers seldom perceive any conflict between their interests and those of their clients.[74] In most cases, there probably is none—events that make the clients stronger will usually make their lawyers stronger in the long run as well. Or so goes the faith. The corporate lawyer may thus come to regard his own interests as inseparable from those of his clients. After a lawyer has advocated his client's position for several years—after he has, time and again, been called upon to think of and express all of the strongest arguments for his client—it may well be impossible for him to step out of that role and to consider and assert his own interests apart from those of his clients. Corporate lawyers may thus behave like the managers of boxers; A. J. Liebling, the Max Weber of the prize ring, observed that managers habitually use the first person singular in describing what their boxers will do to opponents—as in "I am going to jab him silly."[75]

But the criminal defense lawyers, in our first example, appear to have no difficulty in discerning where their interests lie, even when their interests rather clearly conflict with those of clients. What is the source of the difference in the nature of the relationships between lawyers and clients in these two situations? The answer seems rather clearly to lie in the differing distributions of power among the lawyers and their clients. The criminal defense lawyer deals with clients who, typically, lack wealth, political pow-

73. For a thoughtful and systematic consideration of the sociology of the large law firm, see Robert Nelson, *supra* note 2.

74. In his survey of practitioners in large Chicago law firms, Robert Nelson asked, "Have you ever refused an assignment or potential work because it was contrary to your personal values?" Of 222 respondents, only 36 had ever done so and only 12 of these had done so as often as twice. Robert Nelson, American Bar Foundation Project on Large Law Firms, 1980-82 (research in progress).

75. A. J. Liebling, *The Sweet Science* (New York: Viking Press, 1956), pp. 68–71.

er, prestige, rectitude, and other deference entitlements,[76] while the lawyer is, himself, a member of a high status profession, middle class, and relatively well connected. The criminal defense lawyer represents a large volume of clients with quite rapid turnover, and he is therefore not much dependent upon any one client for his livelihood. The corporate lawyer deals, by contrast, with the most powerful class of client, the major corporation that has considerable economic and political resources and a voice that may make or break reputations. These lawyers are, themselves, usually of the highest standing, the cleverest, the best educated, the most prestigious, the wealthiest, and the best connected, but their power is modest compared to that of their clients and their continued success is highly dependent upon the maintenance of their client base.

TERENCE JOHNSON'S TYPOLOGY

In his seminal essay, *Professions and Power*, the British sociologist Terence Johnson distinguishes between "collegiate" and "patronage" occupations. In Johnson's typology, a collegiate occupation is one in which "the producer defines the needs of the consumer and the manner in which these needs are catered for," while a patronage occupation is one in which "the consumer defines his own needs and the manner in which they are to be met."[77] The ordinary notion would be that, in these terms, the classic professions should be "collegiate" since the arcane knowledge of the professionals will give them autonomy in their work, permitting them to define "the needs of the client and the manner in which these needs are catered for." But some of the professions clearly fit this better than others. That was Johnson's point.

The profession that probably is most often collegiate is medicine. Even doctors do not always prevail over their patients and would not if they could, but they come closer to the pure collegiate type than does any other profession. Engineering, by contrast, is pretty clearly of the patronage type. Most engineers are full-time employees of a corporation; there are relatively few independent consulting engineers. As employees, answerable to one employer, most en-

76. Harold D. Lasswell and Abraham Kaplan, *Power and Society* (New Haven: Yale University Press, 1950).
77. Johnson, *supra* note 19, pp. 45–46.

gineers probably have less control over defining the scope and strategy of their work. Architects and accountants fall somewhere between these two. Their roles are even more variable. Accounting has, perhaps, changed from being more of the patronage type to being more collegiate. Historically, the evolution of the bookkeeper employed by a business firm into the chartered public accountant was designed to reassure investors in stock companies, thus enhancing the growth of capitalism. That rationale required that the accountants possess at least the appearance of independence from the management of the companies, but a very large proportion of the accounting profession always consisted of full-time employees of businesses and even the independent accountants typically served a few large clients, upon whom they were highly dependent.[78] The consolidation of the accounting profession in the United States into the "Big Eight" accounting firms may, however, have moved it into a more collegiate posture.[79]

But what of the law? Where does the profession of the bar fall along this spectrum? When we apply Johnson's distinction to our analysis of the Chicago bar, we find that the profession again splits along its major divide. Of the two great parts, the personal client hemisphere more nearly approximates the collegiate type—the ideal of a profession—while the corporate client hemisphere comes closer to fitting the definition of patronage. That is, in the personal client hemisphere, the lawyers largely define the needs of the client and the manner in which they will be met, but the corporate client has a much larger role in defining its own legal needs and the strategy that will be used in pursuing them. Thus, the personal client hemisphere is, in an important sense, "more professional." This contradicts the common assumption that the attributes of professionalism inevitably enhance social status. It is demonstrable that corporate lawyers enjoy greater prestige than do those who serve persons (see chap. 4), but professional autonomy from client control is greater in the personal sector. Thus, the "less professional" hemisphere is the more prestigious one, an observation that lends further support to the hypothesis that the principal source of the prestige of lawyers is their clients—that the status they enjoy or suffer is

78. Ibid., p. 66.
79. See U.S., Congress, Senate, Committee on Government Operations, staff study prepared by the Subcommittee on Reports, Accounting, and Management, "The Accounting Establishment," Doc. 95–34, March 31, 1977. 95th Cong., 1st sess.

acquired by association, that what enhances the status of a lawyer is not his autonomy as a professional but his access to centers of influence and his avoidance of service to the powerless and despised (see pp. 118–32).

But while the characterization of the corporate client as the patron of its lawyer may be a suggestive way of thinking about that relationship, it does not quite ring true to describe the personal client hemisphere as collegiate. There is relatively little collegiality among the practitioners in that sector, relatively little collective decision making or social intercourse among the lawyers who handle divorces, personal injury claims, criminal charges, wills, taxes, repossessions, and sales of property. The social and professional relations of those lawyers are, to be sure, disproportionately likely to take place with others who are in similar lines of work (see pp. 213–23), but that fact does not suggest that these relations need be frequent or intense. The lawyer in the personal client sector probably has fewer and less regular occasions to interact with other lawyers, particularly with opponents or those from other firms, than does the lawyer who serves corporations. Collegiality in this sense, however, is not at all implied by Johnson's definition of a collegiate occupation. The essential element is that the decisions about the work are controlled by the members of the profession—by the professional colleagues—rather than by the clients. The lawyers might well dominate their individual clients without any necessary collegial interaction among the lawyers.

Nonetheless, we may want to consider another possibility. In addition to the collegiate and patronage types, Johnson proposes a third category of occupations. He calls this type "mediative," and he places in it occupations in which "a third party mediates in the relationship between producer and consumer, defining both the needs and the manner in which the needs are met."[80] Principal mediating institutions have, historically, included the state and the church. As we have already noted, the state regulates the legal profession in certain respects, chiefly in licensing (admission to practice) and in the discipline of lawyers for ethical lapses, though both of these sorts of regulation may be in large part delegated by the state to elements of the profession itself. To the extent that regulation of the bar is effective at all, the main impact of it falls upon the

80. Johnson, *supra* note 19, p. 46.

362

personal client sector. Few candidates for the bar who have only marginal qualifications for admission to practice or who have much to fear from the bar examiners manage to find employment in the large corporate law firms. The corporations and the corporate law firms are capable of protecting their own interests, and they have far more elaborate systems of gate keeping that do so. Official screening of potential lawyers to eliminate the incompetent or unusually venal is in effect, then, directed at protecting the interests not of corporate clients but of persons as clients, in relatively small cases. Similarly, the disciplinary system of the profession is also mainly brought to bear on the personal client sector, as Jerome Carlin, Jerold Auerbach,[81] and others have observed. The Code of Professional Responsibility (formerly the Canons of Ethics) deals for the most part with ethical issues at the level of ambulance chasing, not with issues that may arise in the practice of corporate law.[82] Critics of the code have observed that it covers handing out business cards in the hospital's emergency room but does not address the solicitation of business on the golf course at the country club.[83]

If the degree of regulation of the personal client sector makes it substantially mediative in character, that raises another interesting possibility. Carlin and Auerbach have argued that the power of the state to regulate the bar is delegated to high status, corporate lawyers, who then use the power to control the lawyers who serve persons. If this is true, we have a patronage type occupation—the corporate bar—serving as a mediating institution that intervenes in the relationship between lawyer and client in the personal client sector. Thus, a part of the bar that is lacking in autonomy, being itself subject to the influence of patrons outside the profession, regulates a subordinate part of the profession. The entire profession is there-

81. Jerome E. Carlin, *Lawyers' Ethics: A Survey of the New York City Bar* (New York: Russell Sage, 1966), pp. 176–82; Auerbach, *supra* note 61, pp. 4–7.

82. American Bar Association, Special Committee on Evaluation of Ethical Standards, *Code of Professional Responsibility*, Final Draft, July 1, 1969. Thus, Disciplinary Rule 2-104(A) forbids in-person solicitation of clients who have not requested legal advice. This "ambulance chasing" restriction was upheld against a First Amendment challenge by the United States Supreme Court in Ohralik v. Ohio State Bar Association, 436 U.S. 447 (1978). See Andrew Kaufman, *Problems in Professional Responsibility* (Boston: Little, Brown, 1976), pp. 445–463.

83. Carlin, *Lawyers' Ethics, supra* note 81, pp. 66–83. It may be, of course, that the potential consumers of legal services who are solicited at the country club are, as a class, more sophisticated than are those solicited in the emergency room, and that only the latter are in need of protection by the machinery of the bar.

fore subject, directly or indirectly, to control by extra-professional sources of power.

But there is a good case for the proposition that the formal regulatory mechanisms of the profession—the control of admission to practice and of disciplinary proceedings—are so little used and so generally ineffectual that their impact on the character of the profession may safely be discounted.[84] Even if this is so, however, the personal client sector might still be mediative rather than collegiate in nature.

Some third parties other than the profession's regulatory authorities may well intervene in the relationships between personal sector lawyers and their clients. In many cases, those lawyers may be answerable not to their clients but to bailiffs, court clerks, insurance claims adjustors, real estate brokers, title insurers, and so on. The lawyers will often be dependent upon these third parties for the continued flow of business; they are principal sources of client referral. The third parties may also control the lawyer's practice environment in ways that can make his work easy, difficult, or impossible. It may be within the power of these persons to expedite the settlement of cases, to move the lawyer's file to the top or the bottom of the pile, and thus to determine the volume of business that the lawyer can handle. Because the profitability of the work of these lawyers depends upon their ability to process large numbers of cases, the lawyer may be more concerned with cultivating and accommodating an insurance claims adjustor than with obtaining the maximum possible settlement for a client. The lawyer is likely to deal with that claims adjustor again soon; he may never see the client again. Though word-of-mouth among clients may be an important source of business for some lawyers, even those lawyers may well feel that they need the continuing good will of the adjustor if they are to make clients happy in the future. The fact that personal sector lawyers regularly exercise control of their clients does not, therefore, imply that they enjoy complete professional autonomy. They will often be dependent upon and constrained by other actors with whom they deal in the course of their practice.

Thus, the personal client hemisphere might plausibly be classi-

84. Carlin, *supra* note 81, pp. 160–61; American Bar Association Special Committee on Evaluation of Disciplinary Enforcement, *Problems and Recommendations in Disciplinary Enforcement* (Chicago: American Bar Association, 1970), pp. 1–9; F. Raymond Marks and Darlene Cathcart, "Discipline Within the Legal Profession: Is It Self-Regulation?," 1974 *University of Illinois Law Forum* 193–236.

fied, in the alternative, as a mediative occupation. The corporate hemisphere could not be. The control of the corporate patrons is sufficient that the state, the professionals who act for the state, and other third parties are unlikely to interfere significantly. Though there is little point in manipulating definitional categories, this characterization of the set of interrelationships among lawyers and clients seems to us to be useful and not unrealistic.

The most problematic and the most controversial portion of this analysis, however, will no doubt be our suggestion that corporate clients often dominate their lawyers. We may, therefore, want to give that point a bit more attention.

Corporate Lawyers and Their Clients: Further Thoughts on the Allocation of Autonomy

To what extent are the needs of corporations for legal services and the strategies to be used in pursuit of those needs determined by the corporations rather than by their lawyers? One of the problems in addressing that question is the difficulty of deciding how to treat corporate house counsel. Who is the corporation and who are its lawyers? Are officials of the corporation who are themselves lawyers to be counted as part of the corporation or as part of the bar? They might, of course, plausibly be regarded as either or both. Whichever they are, they are a factor of great and increasing weight, and that is the most important thing to note here.

According to a study by a management consulting firm, the legions of corporate house counsel quadrupled between 1950 and 1978, in the latter year numbering about 50,000 of a total United States lawyer population then estimated at 450,000.[85]

Terence Johnson would expect this development:

Patronage, where it is the rule, creates the "housed" practitioner. The aristocratic patron "keeps" his artist, architect, doctor and priest; he maintains them on his estates or in some location socially or politically

85. The study was conducted by Daniel Cantor and Co., Inc., of Philadelphia; see Doug Lavine, "Corporate Legal Units Moving Up," *The National Law Journal*, October 9, 1978, pp. 1, 11. The same article also notes that 60 corporations responding to a survey by the *New York Law Journal* reported that their in-house legal staffs had grown by an average of 62.5 percent in the preceding five years (i.e., 1973 to 1978); nearly a quarter of the respondents said that their staffs had doubled during that period.

controlled by him. The practitioner is a courtier and must share the social manners and social graces of the courtier. Similarly, corporate patronage gives rise to the "house" man, either directly as an employee or within the organizational context of a professional bureaucracy.[86]

Corporate executives explain the growth of their legal departments somewhat more prosaically. They point to very substantial increases in fees paid to law firms over the past decade or two and note that it appeared rational to attempt to cut (or, in any case, to slow the increase in) those costs by doing more of their legal work within the corporation, thus retaining for the corporation the profit that would otherwise have been made on the work by the outside firms.[87]

A certain amount of the legal work that arises in the course of any corporation's business is quite routine—documents to be prepared following standard forms, recurring personnel matters, or routine reports that must be filed with the government periodically. Rather than pay the high hourly rates charged by large law firms, corporations increasingly use their own staffs to handle these matters. Beyond this routine work, however, corporate house counsel often perform tasks for their corporations that are more subtle and more consequential for the structure of the corporate sector of the legal profession. One of those is the identification of legal issues that might not have been noticed if a lawyer were not present in the organization, scrutinizing the daily operations. Thus, house counsel may see potential tax or antitrust consequences in a proposed business transaction, consequences that would not have been identified by a corporate officer who lacked legal training. This is said to enable the corporation to anticipate legal problems before they become acute. But there will also be cases where the problem, though it exists, would never have become acute—that is, if it were left untreated, it would go away. And there will be times when the potential problem that house counsel thinks he sees turns out, upon further examination, not to be a real problem at all. It is probable, therefore, that a net effect of the growth of corporate house counsel is to define more of the corporation's problems as legal problems, thus increasing the amount and expanding the range of the work done in the corporate sector of the bar.[88]

86. Johnson, *supra* note 19, p. 68.
87. Such reasoning assumes, of course, that the corporation will be able to do the work as efficiently and competently as would the law firm.
88. In relatively rare cases, house counsel may even induce a dispute where none existed before. By noting the existence of a potential legal claim that its corporation

Another important function of corporate house counsel is to select, or at least to participate in the selection of, outside counsel to handle the complex legal work that calls for a specialist. Traditionally, before the recent increase in numbers of house counsel, corporations maintained long-standing relationships with large law firms. One law firm often did all or most of the corporation's legal work, and a close working relationship was established over the years between the corporation's executives and the lawyers in the firm. In some cases, the lawyers came to serve not only as lawyers but as general business advisers. This is probably less often true today. With the greater mobility of corporate executives, increasing specialization of lawyers, and growth of house counsel, law firms are less likely to maintain such close ties with their corporate clients.

It is particularly important to note that house counsel have reason to discourage these established connections between their corporations and outside law firms. Inside and outside lawyers compete for the blessings that their patrons can bestow. If a corporate executive does not have a close, personal relationship with an outside lawyer, he is more likely to turn to the inside man for advice, thus increasing the dependence of corporate management on house counsel and, consequently, enhancing the power of the inside lawyer. If access to centers of influence is the principal source of the prestige of the corporate sector, then the lawyer who has the ear of the corporate officer has a superior claim to that prestige. And access to the powerful is, of course, itself a kind of power.[89] The role of corporate house counsel in distributing to outside firms the legal work that will not be done by the corporation's own legal staff places them in a good position to see to it that no one firm is able to establish close and continuing ties with the corporation's management.[90] It is prob-

---

might make against another business enterprise, counsel may create litigation that otherwise would not have been brought. As we argue below, however, this is unlikely to occur unless it is consistent with business purposes; see pp. 376–77.

89. The status of house counsel appears to have improved recently, consistent with this speculation; see Morris I. Leibman, "The Change in Client Relationships—The Interface with General Counsel," *The Business Lawyer* 34 (1979): 957–62.

90. One of the troubling issues that we raised at the beginning of this consideration of the roles of lawyers and clients in the corporate sector was the ambiguity concerning whether house counsel were to be regarded as lawyers or clients, as a part of their corporations or a part of the bar. When the house counsel is not engaged in servicing the legal problems that are handled inside the corporation but is choosing outside counsel and negotiating with them the fees that they will be paid by the corporation, it seems to us that he is essentially performing the role of the client—

able, then, that the increase in numbers of house counsel preceded rather than followed the weakening of the established relationships between corporations and outside law firms. Whichever is cause and which effect, however, the corporation that once regarded a single, large firm as outside general counsel, to which it returned again and again with a wide variety of its legal problems, now often articulates a policy of selecting the "best qualified lawyer" (whether qualified by special expertise or by being well situated or well connected) to represent the corporation with respect to each discrete legal problem.

This greater tendency to distribute corporate legal work among a number of firms makes the firms a bit more insecure. While the large firms could formerly count on receiving a continuing, steady volume of business from each of their major corporate clients, the flow of work may now be less certain. As a result, the power relationships between lawyer and client—the claims that each can make upon the other—are altered somewhat. The older pattern of close, continuing ties between the corporate clients and their law firms more nearly resembled a traditional system of patronage. The law firms were, to some degree, sheltered by their clients; when the firms could depend on their patrons, it was natural for them to do so, to become dependent on their continuing patronage. While the present situation bears less resemblance to the patron-servant model, the lawyers do not enjoy the sort of liberation that might be characterized as capturing the manor house. The corporate lawyer is no longer, so much, the loyal retainer, but his role as entrepreneur is probably more precarious.[91]

(continued)

acting for the client as its agent, not as its counsel. (To make a legal distinction, the house counsel is then acting more as an "attorney-in-fact" than as an "attorney-at-law.") Though house counsel may use different criteria of judgment or different types of expertise than would other corporate officers in making these decisions about the use of outside counsel, the role would nonetheless be the same. Someone would still need to select the lawyers and to scrutinize the fees. House counsel are, in a very real sense, the *consumers* of the services of the corporate law firms.

One part of the legal profession thus regularly performs the role of client of another part of the profession. To what extent does this occur in other professions? Employed engineers probably play a similar role with respect to independent, consulting engineers, but to what extent are consulting engineers regularly or often retained by corporations that already have engineers as employees? The referral from one doctor to another is not analogous—just as referrals among lawyers are not—because in that situation the referring professional is not in any sense the consumer of the services.

91. Most large law firms are, by the way, notoriously undercapitalized enterprises.

If large law firms are, in fact, unsure of their clients' commitment to them, we would expect to observe some behavior manifesting that insecurity, to see some demonstration of their need to go out of their way to curry favor with their clients. Are there any such signs?

One manifestation might be found in the fact that so many firms have, quite literally, gone out of their way for their clients by opening branch offices. The increase in the numbers of branch offices of large law firms is one of the most notable recent developments in the corporate sector of the bar. We examined the branching histories of the dozen largest Chicago law firms—that is, the twelve firms that had the largest numbers of lawyers in 1979. The total number of branch offices of those twelve firms in 1960 was two. By 1970, they had four. In 1980, the dozen firms had a total of twenty branch offices. In 1960, only two of the twelve firms had branches; by 1980, only three did not.[92] If these branch offices were always profitable and caused no great problems for the firms, then this expansion would prove little about the sensitivity of the firms to their clients' wishes. But they are not always profitable and they do give rise to other problems in the management of the firm. The mere fact that one or more major clients of a Chicago law firm would find it convenient if the firm had an office in Los Angeles or in London does not assure that there will be sufficient demand for the firm's services there to make the branch office profitable. Some firms have opened branch offices as an accommodation to a few major clients without much knowledge of the demand that might be expected, though no doubt hoping that it would prove to be adequate, and they have in some cases been disappointed to find those branches unprofitable.[93] Moreover, the branch offices often pose serious prob-

92. The source of this information for 1960 and 1970 is *Martindale-Hubbell Lawyer's Directory;* the 1980 information is from the "national law firm survey" of the *National Law Journal,* October 6, 1980, pp. 32–37, and October 13, 1980, pp. 34–39. For the purposes of this analysis, we excluded the firm of Baker and McKenzie, which is conceived as a multicity and, indeed, multinational enterprise.

Much of the growth has occurred in branches in Washington, D.C., which firms have used to serve their clients' "federal" business. A survey in 1980 found that 178 out-of-town firms had branches in Washington, D.C., employing nearly 1,800 attorneys; of the 25 largest Washington firms, 7 were branches. In contrast, there were virtually no branches in the early 1970s. "Out-of-Towners Muscle In," *Legal Times of Washington,* June 9, 1980, pp. 26–29, 32.

93. We have interviewed several lawyers, both in Chicago and in Washington, D.C., who have acknowledged that many branch offices do not cover their own costs. (They were understandably reluctant to discuss their own firms' finances on the record, however, and we are therefore not at liberty to cite examples.) See also Orville

lems of management control. If the Washington branch of a Chicago firm is successful and attracts new clients, it may begin to develop a life of its own, independent of the parent. That is, it may become more difficult to run the Washington operation from Chicago, to set policy in Chicago that will govern the Washington office's decisions about the types of clients and work that will be accepted, the fees to be charged, the hiring of personnel, the handling of ethical issues, and so on. In at least one or two well-publicized cases, a successful branch has seceded from the parent firm, taking clients with it.[94] The problems of managing and controlling a branch office mean, then, that it is rational to open one only if the firm is quite sure that the branch will be profitable or if the need to satisfy particular clients is compelling. Because branches have been opened when profitability was not assured, client considerations appear to loom large. Indeed, when partners in large firms are asked why they decided to open branches, their usual answer attributes the decision to pressure from clients.[95]

Another manifestation of the insecurity that large law firms may feel about their relationships with their major clients is the firms' avoidance of certain types of work and certain smaller clients. That is, an important factor influencing the firms' decisions concerning

---

(continued)

N. Schell, "The Development of National Law Firms," *The Business Lawyer* 34 (1979): 963–68.

94. See "Crowell & Moring Debuts Friday," *Legal Times of Washington*, May 28, 1979, p. 7. In addition to these management problems, branch offices also increase the likelihood that the firm will become involved in formal conflicts of interest. It constitutes a conflict of interest if lawyers from the same firm represent opposing parties or parties whose interests are likely to be in conflict. Given the number of corporations that come and go as clients and the number of potential relationships and transactions among these corporations, it is quite difficult to monitor the firm's work for the existence of possible conflicts. That difficulty is compounded by branch offices, where supervision is more difficult. See Westinghouse Electric Corp. v. Kerr-McGee Corp., 580 F. 2d 1311 (7th Cir. 1978), cert. denied, 439 U.S. 955 (1978).

Branch offices also raise issues about the manner in which the income of the firm will be divided. Will income from the main office and all of the branches be pooled, the less profitable branches sharing in the income produced by the more profitable ones, or will the partners who work in a particular branch share only in the revenue generated locally? Put another way, what portion of the profit of a successful branch will be taken by the main office? Such issues can be quite divisive.

95. A senior partner of a major, highly prestigious Chicago law firm told us that one of the firm's most important clients had said to the firm, "Do you want to go to New York with us, or don't you?" He also told us, "Another client took the position that it wasn't a first rate law firm if it wasn't in Washington." The firm went both places. See also Schell, *supra* note 93.

the types of work and clients that they will take on is their expectation about how such work or clients would be regarded by their important, major clients. Many large firms perceive that criminal law work, for example, would be regarded by their corporate clients as unseemly, and that corporate management would not wish to be associated with the sort of person who is charged with a crime. (This was especially the case before criminal antitrust and securities prosecutions became more common.) Divorce work has traditionally been regarded in the same way,[96] as has much work that might have been done *pro bono publico.* A principal reason large firms have given for their reluctance to represent the poor, downtrodden, friendless, and despised, or to take on various public interest causes, is that this sort of thing would give offense to their regular clientele. The defining characteristics of the friendless and despised are, after all, that they lack important friends and that many persons find them distasteful, and the difficulty with reformist causes is that they may well be controversial. This is, of course, closely akin to the rationale used by large firms for many years (less so now) to explain their failure to hire women lawyers or those from certain ethnic groups. "The clients wouldn't stand for it!" "The clients would not want to deal with them." The preference ascribed to clients probably corresponded quite closely to those of the lawyers themselves, but there is also little doubt that the lawyers correctly perceived their clients' preferences and that those preferences were, in fact, given weight by the law firms.

This avoidance of work that might be offensive to major clients is not merely an excuse for declining to take cases that would not pay. If the new client or the work is likely to alienate a corporation that is important to the firm as a source of income, influence, or prestige, the firm will often refuse the work even if the potential client could well afford to pay the firm's bills. Certain criminal defendants are obvious examples, but there are also more subtle ones. Thus, for many years most of the law firms that regularly defended

96. As divorce has become more common in polite society, however, matrimonial work has become more acceptable in the large firms, and more now do some of it as an accommodation to the personal needs of corporate executives. But the increasing use of criminal charges in antitrust cases does not yet seem to have resulted in much increase in the criminal work done by large, corporate law firms, apart from those large firms that began as litigation specialty firms. The defense of corporate executives charged with price-fixing is still usually referred to trial lawyers experienced in "white-collar crime" cases.

antitrust claims refused to accept antitrust plaintiffs' work.[97] As very large corporations have begun to use antitrust claims as weapons against one another, especially in takeover situations, this old taboo has been eroded, but the defense firms used to worry that their regular corporate clients, corporations that found themselves defending antitrust claims, would see the firm's representation of an antitrust plaintiff as trading with the enemy. The defendant corporations objected to the use of the law firm's knowledge and resources in aid of a litigant that threatened the general legal stance and the public policy positions of the defendant corporations. This was almost a matter of ideology. For the law firm to align itself with a party that attacks the defendant corporations' brethren—corporations situated similarly to themselves—may therefore be perceived as a symbolic defection, as an act of apostasy.

A Chicago lawyer recounted to us an example of this thinking that is, perhaps, somewhat ludicrous in its extremity but that illustrates the point very clearly. Following the reformist ferment of the late 1960s and early 1970s, when law students and young lawyers increasingly expressed a desire to devote a portion of their effort to public service, a large, prestigious Chicago firm adopted a policy permitting its lawyers to spend some of their time on *pro bono* work, including the defense of criminal cases. All went well until a young lawyer reported to the firm that he had been assigned to defend a man accused of bank robbery. It happened that one of the principal clients of the firm was a major bank. The bank that was the firm's client had no connection with the bank that had been robbed (the two were widely separated both in space and in kind), but the firm

---

97. Some litigation specialty firms represented both plaintiffs and defendants in antitrust cases, but those firms were the exception. Litigation specialty firms do most of their work on referral. They thus have few regular clients to whom loyalty might be expected and by whom it might be demanded.

The reason that was often given by the defense firms for avoiding plaintiffs' work was that they did not wish to be in the position of "making law against themselves"—that is, they expressed concern that their work on behalf of an antitrust plaintiff might create a legal precedent that they would then, later, have to overcome in their role as defense counsel in another case. Though this could happen, it is not really very likely. The rationale assumes, first, that the firm's work for the plaintiff would be so ingenious that it would create a legal theory that would not be constructed by other counsel who might represent the plaintiff nor by those who will represent other plaintiffs in similar cases, and thus the law on the subject would in fact be appreciably different than it would have been but for their participation; and, second, that some lawyer from the firm will then have a subsequent case that raises, from the opposing side, exactly that same point of law. The latter of the two necessary assumptions is much more plausible than the former—which is not very plausible at all.

nonetheless ordered the young lawyer to withdraw from the representation of the defendant. It was inconceivable that the case would make new law on bank robbery that would then permit other felons to steal from the client bank with less fear of retribution. As in most cases of bank robbery, the only issues were questions of fact. The reason for the firm's order to withdraw, apparently, was that bank robbers are the enemies of banks, and for the firm to permit one of its lawyers to represent a bank robber might therefore be seen as disloyalty to a major client.

That law firms are so cautious about giving offense to their major clients suggests that they are in a rather vulnerable, subordinate position. If the firm's expertise were of special value to the corporate client and not easily replaced by that of other firms, it might feel more confident that the client would continue to need and use its services, regardless of its representation of the occasional bank robber or labor union. The firm might then feel free to discharge its professional responsibilities as it saw fit, resting its decisions solely on its own criteria, whether those were professional norms or the profit motive. But that is not usually the case. Our data indicate that fewer than 5 percent of the lawyers who devote a quarter or more of their time to the defense of criminal cases work in firms with ten or more lawyers, and only 15 percent of the lawyers who devote as much as a quarter of their time to work for labor unions work in firms of ten or more, none of them in firms with thirty or more lawyers. One of the effects of the firms' reluctance to take on clients who might be regarded with distaste by their regular clientele is to limit the large firms to a very narrow range of potential clients, thus further heightening both specialization by client type and the firms' anxiety about continuation of the demand for its services. An end product of all of these tendencies is, then, to enhance the power of the patron and to reduce the power of the professional in the lawyer-client relationship in the corporate sector.

Increasing Rigidity of the Lines of Stratification

The most rapidly growing parts of the legal profession are clear cases of patronage—corporate house counsel and their government counterparts, the lawyers who are full-time employees of federal, state, or municipal agencies. Together, these constitute a quarter of the entire profession or about a third of the corporate hemisphere. Whatever ambiguity may remain about the power of big firm lawyers in their relationships with clients, therefore, there can be no doubt that the large share of the corporate sector that is made up of full-time employees works in a sheltered, dependent relationship to a single client, their practice being carried on within their patron's organizations. The anxiety that lawyers in large firms feel about their supplies of clients may help to explain why so many lawyers are entering full-time employment. As compared to the entrepreneurial role in which the partners of the big law firms increasingly find themselves, positions as house counsel will usually provide a much greater degree of personal security. Lawyers who wish to reduce uncertainty in their careers might, then, prefer a job in a corporation or a government agency to a junior position in a large law firm. But the number of lawyers in the largest law firms is also growing quite rapidly, and we think it likely that lawyers' choices of career are more determined by the opportunities open to them than by considerations of job security or the lack of it.

The predictability of the career paths of lawyers employed by corporations and by governments is, however, an important factor to be noted in assessing the changing structure of the legal profession. Lawyers who pursue those careers will tend to have a narrower range of experience. Not only will their range of clients be narrow, of course, but the scope of the legal doctrines that they deal with will also be more limited, and they will tend to perform a more predictable set of tasks and to have a more limited variety of ultimate career destinations (see chap. 6). This means that, with the growth in the proportion of lawyers who are employed as house counsel, there will be a consequent increase in the rigidity of lawyers' careers.

We found that Chicago lawyers who entered practice after 1960 had somewhat less career mobility, within comparable stages of their careers, than did those who entered before 1960 (see pp. 195–97). The position in which a lawyer begins the practice of law appears to be more than ever likely to determine the position in which he will end his career, and the position where a lawyer starts is, as much as before, determined by his social origins. Thus, the social hierarchy within the legal profession may be becoming more fixed, more rigid, more difficult to surmount.

374

Functional and Conflict Perspectives Reexamined

This discussion of the nature of the relationships between lawyers and clients has emphasized the distribution of power among the parties and has not given much notice to the system maintenance functions of the bar's social stratification. At the beginning of this book, we noted that both the "power" or "conflict" school of thought on social inequality and the "functionalist" school have distinct and appreciable contributions to make to our understanding (see pp. 6–7 and 21–24). We have focused in this concluding essay, however, more upon the perspective of the conflict school than upon the functionalist school. Let us try to restore some balance between the two approaches, drawing upon themes already stated.

The greater recent role of corporate house counsel as the purchasers of services of lawyers in large firms suggests further rationalization of the market for legal services in the corporate sector. Corporate house counsel probably behave as better informed, more rational consumers of those services than did the corporate executives who previously purchased them. The greater tendency to pick and choose among lawyers and firms for the handling of particular pieces of work, rather than using the same outside counsel for all of the corporation's legal problems, suggests that more discriminating judgments are being made. To the extent that decisions about the allocation of work among practitioners of corporate law are made by "professional" criteria—by criteria based in knowledge of law and in expert judgment concerning the competence of the lawyer or firm to handle the matter—the distribution of legal work within the corporate sector and the resulting social structure of lawyers and clients will be less subject to idiosyncratic variation produced by personal caprice or by random events. Though stable and predictable outcomes may also be produced by a system that is dominated by traditionalism, by close adherence to traditional norms and the maintenance of established relationships, or by an autocratic system of authority based in great concentrations of power, the outcomes produced by an economic calculus that is based in the nature of the work itself will be more "functional." Because the logic of the allocative decision proceeds from the work that is to be done and the skills or competence of those who are to do it, productive efficiency should be increased. Though functional interdependencies also exist under a traditional system, those of a more eco-

375

nomically rational division of labor will enhance what Durkheim called "organic solidarity,"[98] and the maintenance of the system should be enhanced.

The dominance of corporate lawyers by their clients may also facilitate the formation of new business relationships. For a business firm to enter into a transaction with another organization that is not well known to it or with whom it does not have a history of dealings may entail substantial risk. It will help to bring such transactions about, therefore, if the lawyers who are acting for the companies are in a position to be able to reassure them that the risk is within acceptable limits. If the lawyer is thought by the client to be acting independently, then the client may well feel that the lawyer's advice should be given less weight because the lawyer may have an interest in seeing the transaction go ahead. It will create work for the lawyer. On the other hand, if the client knows that the lawyer is highly dependent upon the client's favor and would be vulnerable if the client should be injured or displeased, then the client may have greater trust in the lawyer's assurances. The dependence of the lawyer on the corporate client may thus serve the function of enhancing the likelihood of transactions in a large, mobile, national, and multinational business environment, where the transactions cannot be based upon personal ties.

Though concepts drawn from both functionalist and power theorists contribute to an understanding of the social structure of the legal profession, then, the power perspective may be peculiarly appropriate to the case of the bar. Lawyers are accustomed to deal in the allocation of power. They are regularly confronted in their work with situations of conflict, and the relative power of the competing parties is relevant to their strategic decisions. Lawyers may, therefore, be predisposed to think about social relations in power terms and to react to social stimuli in ways that reflect their assessments of power differentials. If this is true, as seems to us likely, then social relations within the legal profession may be unusually sensitive to the differential distribution of power and the structure may be especially likely to evolve in ways that manifest power relations.

A conflict model of sorts is, after all, built into the adversary process. The American notion of due process of law specifically in-

98. See Durkheim, *supra* note 11, chap. 3.

cludes, for example, such elements as the right of confrontation of your accuser and the right to cross-examination. The research of Thibaut and Walker and their associates[99] suggests the existence of a general preference for adversarial modes of legal procedure rather than for an "inquisitorial" system—that is, for the decision of contested legal issues through the clash of competing parties rather than through an impartial inquiry by a detached fact finder. But the right to confront your accuser, Thibaut and Walker's research, and much of the general public's thinking about the legal process all take place within the context of the personal client hemisphere of the legal profession, and particularly in what we have called the personal plight cluster of fields. Conflict is, indeed, the preferred mode for the handling of many criminal, divorce, and personal injury cases, though even in those fields the greater share of the cases are disposed of by negotiated settlements.

The adversarial, conflict model is probably an especially inappropriate way of characterizing the actual process of the practice of law in the corporate hemisphere, however. The practice of corporate law far more often deals with negotiation, with drafting, with office practice that is directed not toward prevailing in conflict but toward the avoidance of conflict. Corporate lawyers often serve a mediative or facilitative function—they bring corporate organizations together to form relationships among them. Though there is, of course, an area of conflict in the negotiation of a contract, it is important to note that that conflict takes place within the context of a larger, shared interest of the parties, the interest in consummating a productive business transaction. The advice lawyers give to corporations that are merging is intended not only to secure advantage for their own clients, though it surely is often intended to do just that, but also to minimize conflict between the parties in the longer run, to avoid disputes with the government over antitrust, tax, or securities matters, and to reduce the likelihood of litigation with investors or customers of the merging companies.

Much of the work of the personal client hemisphere also has a similar goal, of course. Wills and trusts, real estate closings, and commercial transactions between individuals and small businesses

99. John Thibaut and Laurens Walker, *Procedural Justice* (New York: Halsted Press, 1975), chaps. 8 and 12, esp. pp. 78–80, table 8.5; see also Steven LaTour, Pauline Houlden, Laurens Walker, and John Thibaut, "Procedure: Transnational Perspectives and Preferences," 86 *Yale Law Journal* 258 (1976).

are all areas where the principal concern is with the avoidance of conflict. But the personal plight area is much more characterized by litigation and other forms of disputes, and such cases—particularly, criminal and personal injury matters—dominate much of both academic and popular thought about the work of the legal profession.[100] Litigation is, of course, also an important part of the corporate sector of law practice and is probably becoming more so, but it does not yet preoccupy corporate practitioners and has not come to dominate the ethos of the sector.

If the corporate sector is, at least in large part, concerned with a facilitative rather than an adversarial role, with negotiation, persuasion, and putting deals together rather than with formal disputes, does that fact carry implications for the relations between lawyers and clients? Will the distribution of power or advantage between lawyer and client in a predominantly adversarial setting characteristically differ from that in a predominantly facilitative one? It may. Most clients will probably feel more competent to deal with the issues that arise in office practice than with the conduct of litigation. There is less lay understanding of procedures in the courtroom and in other formal hearings, of the rules of evidence, and of whether it is better to challenge or not to challenge a potential juror than there is of the terms that should be insisted upon in a contract negotiation. The conduct of the contract negotiation is more likely to involve matters of business judgment and hunches about which tactic is likely to be most successful, and laymen may well feel comfortable challenging their lawyers' judgments on these matters. (Litigation may, in fact, involve similar hunches about tactics, but it will often be less clear that that is what they are.) Even on matters as technical as tax law, laymen and corporate house counsel may feel better informed and thus more competent to question their lawyers' judgments than they would on a matter of litigation procedure—on whether it is or is not advisable to take the deposition of a particular potential witness, for example. If we are right about this, clients in the adversarial, litigation setting will perceive a greater disparity between their knowledge and that of their lawyers than will be the case in the facilitative, office practice setting, and the portion of the lawyer's power vis-à-vis his clients that is derived from the lawyer's possession of special expertise will therefore be

100. See chap. 1, at notes 1–4.

less in the office practice areas. This is, then, yet another reason why the relation between client and lawyer in the corporate sector might often resemble that between patron and servant, while the relation in personal plight work does not.

Conclusion

Any profession will surely include disparate parts, but we doubt that any other is so sharply bifurcated as the bar. Only, perhaps, in architecture is there a similar fundamental division between types of clients that has such inevitable consequences for the nature of the work and for the relative power positions of professional and client—and in architecture the number of individual clients is trivial. The difference between serving corporations and serving individuals is, for a lawyer's work and career, a difference that has important, highly predictable implications, several of which have been explored in this book. That there is a fundamental split of some sort within the American legal profession has been recognized at least since the Reed report of the early 1920s distinguished between the "inner bar" and the "general body of practitioners."[101] The difference between litigators and office lawyers has, of course, also been widely noticed for a long time; it has for centuries been formalized in England in the distinction between barristers and solicitors. But that is a task or skill difference, analogous to that between physicians and surgeons. The distinction within the American bar that is based in service to corporations, on the one hand, and to individuals and their small businesses, on the other, is quite another sort of phenomenon with quite different consequences.

It would clearly be mistaken to assert that these two sectors of the legal profession are entirely separate, but the extent to which the complexity of the social structure of the Chicago bar may be sorted out by the fundamental difference between the two types of clients is nonetheless remarkable. In devising a summary measure of the extent of the differences between lawyers practicing in the two hemispheres, we first assigned all of our respondents to one hemisphere or the other depending upon the fields to which the lawyers

101. See *supra* notes 59–60.

devoted the majority of their time. We then tested for differences between these two, mutually exclusive categories of practitioners on sixteen variables of different sorts—including where the lawyers went to law school, their age, their religious identities, their political affiliations, their incomes, their practice settings (whether in large firm or in solo practice), the extent of their appearances in state courts, and their economic liberalism and civil libertarian values scores. We found statistically significant differences between the two hemispheres on twelve of the sixteen variables tested. The only variables where the differences were not significant were the percentages of Catholics, the income variable, and the two values scores.

Other important differences between the hemispheres have been noted in preceding chapters. These include very substantial differences in the prestige of the two sectors, lawyers serving corporate clients being much more likely to be accorded deference within the profession. We have also noted that lawyers who work in one hemisphere relatively seldom form friendships or close professional relationships with those who practice in the other. This, in turn, corresponds to the differential connections of the two hemispheres to the several spheres of influence in Chicago politics, community affairs, and the organized bar. The probability that a Chicago lawyer will know other lawyers who are influential in each of these realms differs systematically with the fields in which he practices and the nature of his clients. The client-based structure of the profession is, then, directly related to the structure of various sorts of power in the broader community.

In sum, the Chicago bar consists, to an extent that is quite striking, of two separate professions, quite different in type and content and both of substantial size. The more prestigious is, ironically, the less independent. It is a patronage type occupation, in Terence Johnson's terms, where corporate clients to a large degree dictate the nature of the work done. The other profession, serving individuals and small businesses, is either a collegiate occupation by Johnson's definition, because the lawyers dominate their clients in the decisions that are made about the work, or mediative in type because governmental authorities and other, third parties mediate the relationship between lawyer and client, intervening in or regulating some aspects of that relationship.

The claims to professionalism of the lawyers in the two sectors

380

are thus based in fundamentally different sorts of social power. Lawyers who practice in the personal client sector usually have the greater degree of authority vis-à-vis their clients because the wealth and social standing of the lawyers more often exceeds that of the clients and because the clients are ordinarily more dependent upon the lawyers than are the lawyers upon any one client. But what is it, precisely, that these personal sector lawyers have that their clients need so badly? The lawyers' knowledge and skills are not widely shared by the public at large, perhaps, but the skills required for many of the tasks performed by personal sector lawyers are not really all that abstruse, surely a good deal less so than those regularly needed by lawyers in the corporate sector, and the requisite knowledge could often be mastered by reasonably diligent non-professionals who had a sufficient incentive to do so. Obviously, what the client often needs, at least in part, is the license to practice law. The officially sanctioned monopoly that is granted to licensed lawyers limits the entry of unlicensed persons into this market—it excludes nonlawyers from the performance of some, but only some, of the tasks regularly done by the personal client sector of the bar. Plea bargaining on behalf of defendants in criminal cases is, for example, effectively restricted to lawyers, even though nonlawyers might conduct the bargaining equally well, but searches of real estate titles are often now done by employees of real estate brokers, title insurance companies, and the like, who may or may not be lawyers.

In other portions of their market, personal sector lawyers may compete with marriage counselors or women's centers that provide assistance in divorce cases, with freelance accountants or franchised tax return preparers, or with do-it-yourself probate kits. In these latter situations, the lawyers' monopoly of the relevant services is imperfect, at most. To the extent that clients choose to employ lawyers in such matters, therefore, they may have some affirmative reason to do so.

The reason for that preference is probably often the belief—one that sometimes, at least, has a sound basis in fact—that the lawyer will have superior access to networks of authoritative decision makers, networks that include the persons who have the power to solve the client's problem, to confer upon him the benefit he seeks or to relieve him of the burden he seeks to avoid. This belief is commonly expressed as some variant of a statement that the lawyer knows the ropes at the criminal courts building or has friends at City Hall or has clout in the zoning board. Scholarly researchers on the criminal courts have confirmed the existence of "courtroom work groups" that consist of the judge, the lawyers who regularly appear in that court, whether for the prosecution or the defense, the bailiff, and the court clerk.[102] In such circumstances, it can, indeed, be advantageous to be a member of the work group and disadvantageous to be an outsider. The stock in trade of the lawyer in the personal client sector may therefore often be perceived, by both the client and the lawyer, to be his "connectedness." His access to the relevant networks may be improved by his license to practice law; it may enhance his acceptance as a member of the club. Ethnicity or political affiliation, however, may also be important criteria for membership in such networks, and this fact helps to account for the salience of ethnic and political group memberships in the social organization of the profession.

The types of social power that can be mobilized by lawyers in the corporate sector are quite different. Connectedness is probably less highly valued by them and by their clients, though their contacts will surely sometimes be useful. The corporations that are the clients of this sector of the bar more often maintain their own networks of relationships with the authoritative decision makers whose actions are most often relevant to the conduct of their operations. Corporate officers are themselves often persons of considerable influence, political and otherwise. Thus, what corporations need and expect from their lawyers is in large measure the lawyers' special skills and arcane knowledge. The skills and knowledge that are valued are not, of course, always *legal* skills or knowledge of legal doctrine narrowly defined. Rather, knowledge of business circumstances or of the cast of characters participating in a particular matter, skill as an advocate or a negotiator, or simply good judgment may recommend the lawyer to the corporate client. Such power as corporate lawyers have over their clients is power of the sort that derives from the clients' belief in the lawyers' skills and from the correlative need of the clients to have some external expert to believe in. Corporate executives often operate in conditions of great uncertainty. One of the classic impulses of persons in precarious positions is to seek to reduce the uncertainty, to gain control over it,

102. See Eisenstein and Jacob, *supra* note 71, pp. 19–39.

through the assistance of a sage or a conjurer.[103] In such situations, faith in the powers of the savant or shaman is crucial to his utility.

Similarly, the power of lawyers may be based largely in their repute. (This may be true of both corporate and personal sector lawyers, though the types of repute that will be important to them will be quite different.) To nurture the appropriate sort of repute and to conserve it once it has been attained, corporate lawyers engage in various kinds of status display. Their furniture is often upholstered in leather and their walls are lined with books whether those books are often consulted or not; where the walls are not covered with books, they are often covered with hardwood paneling or with sophisticated paintings; the lawyers dress conservatively and they behave with circumspection[104] (much like bankers, though perhaps not carrying this to quite such an extreme); and a certain type of prestigious corporate lawyer tries hard to keep his name out of the newspapers, knowing that some of his clients retain him in the belief that he has the ability to keep their names out. The style of the corporate bar is, thus, designed to reassure its clientele, the power of that sector of the bar being highly dependent on the clients' confidence in the sagacity, discretion, and stability of the corporate lawyer.

Assuming that the corporate lawyer succeeds in gaining the confidence of his client, however, what sort of power has he then? As Edward Shils points out, persons are accorded deference corresponding to the degree to which they serve the central value system of the society.[105] Because corporate lawyers advise persons who hold authority to make the most consequential decisions regarding the allocation of economic resources and because modern, industrial societies attach great importance to economic values, we might expect corporate lawyers to be accorded deference to the extent that they are perceived to influence these allocative decisions.

The social power of the corporate sector of the bar is, then, based in its perceived influence on the distribution of the wealth of the society, influence that is derived from the belief of corporate officers in the wisdom and arcane skill of these lawyers, while the

103. See Moore, *supra* note 6, pp. 28–36; Bronislaw Malinowski, "Magic, Science and Religion," in Malinowski, ed., *Magic, Science and Religion, and Other Essays* (New York: Free Press, 1948), pp. 17–92.
104. Smigel, *supra* note 1, p. 314.
105. Edward Shils, *Center and Periphery* (Chicago: University of Chicago Press, 1975), pp. 4–6, 267–71, 279.

claim to professionalism of lawyers working in the personal sector is based less in special skills and more in their superior access to networks of relatively minor, relatively low visibility decision makers, such as insurance claims adjusters, police, state judges, court clerks, building inspectors, zoning commissions, and aldermen. The social origins of the practitioners in the two sectors are, as Shils predicts, consonant with the degree to which they are perceived to be entitled to deference on other grounds.[106] That is, Shils observes that the deference to which one is thought to be entitled on the basis of one's social origins is not likely to be greatly inconsistent with the deference that one's occupation is thought to warrant. Our data support this generalization.

The two sectors of the legal profession thus include different lawyers, with different social origins, who were trained at different law schools, serve different sorts of clients, practice in different office environments, are differentially likely to engage in litigation, litigate (when and if they litigate) in different forums, have somewhat different values, associate with different circles of acquaintances, and rest their claims to professionalism on different sorts of social power. For the most part, these lawyers find themselves unable to cooperate in the formal organizations of the bar. Only in the most formal of senses, then, do the two types of lawyers constitute one profession.

Why should the degree of cohesion among lawyers be of concern? Some reasons will already be apparent. The social structure of any occupation that places so many of its members in positions where they can influence the allocation of scarce resources is of interest because the nature of the bonds and the divisions among the occupation's membership may have consequences for who gets what—in the case of lawyers, consequences for the distribution of legal services and for values that may be affected by the distribution of legal services. If the members of an occupation are so influentially placed, the ability to mobilize them toward a common purpose will carry the potential for great political and societal power. If, on the other hand, the social composition of the occupation suggests that it will be able to unite on common goals only rarely or only within a narrow range of issues, then the relative impotence of the occupation *qua* occupation is also of interest. But there may be an-

106. Ibid., pp. 301–3.

other, less obvious consequence of the lack of social integration of the legal profession. To the extent that the public perceives the separation of lawyers into two hemispheres or two occupations, the symbolic unity of the law, and thus its legitimacy, will be weakened. The efficacy of law depends, in very large measure, on voluntary compliance with its requirements, and the disposition to comply depends, in turn, on the existence of a consensus that the legal system is legitimate. To secure this public support, a legal system will need to honor the society's central ideals, including those concerning equality of treatment that are manifested in such legal standards as "equal protection of the laws." The perception of equality (and the reality of at least one type of it) is served by the symbolism of a unitary legal system—that there is only one law, one set of rules and procedures that determines justice for all. If lawyers of distinct social types work in distinct realms of law, serve separate sorts of clients, and deal with separate systems of courts and government agencies, symbolic unity can be maintained only with mirrors and smoke, and then unreliably. Ethnic diversity within the bar, reflecting the pluralism of the broader society, might enhance the legitimacy of the system if lawyers from the full range of social backgrounds were well-represented and if they were all participating in the same system. But if the reality is that large cities like Chicago have two legal professions, one recruited from more privileged social origins and the other from less prestigious backgrounds, while yet other social groups are almost entirely excluded, and if the first kind of lawyer serves corporate clients that are quite wealthy and powerful, and the other serves individuals and small businesses that are far less powerful, then the hierarchy of lawyers suggests a corresponding stratification of law into two systems of justice, separate and unequal.

Appendixes

Appendix A

THE CHICAGO BAR

PROJECT

Interview Schedule

Sampling # (ID)

Time Began: 1–4

I. ORGANIZATION OF WORK   DECK   01
These initial questions concern the organization of your   5–6
professional activities.

A1. While a lawyer's time is often spread over many different areas of the law, we wish, for comparative purposes,
to characterize those areas in which you spent the major
part of your time ... CARD A ... during the last 12
months ...
In which of the listed areas have you spent:
   a. more than 50% of your time?
   b. between 25% and 50% of your time?
   c. between 5% and 25% of your time?

HAND
CARD
A

	50% or more	25–50%	5–25%	
Admiralty	3	2	1	7
Anti-trust–plaintiffs	3	2	1	8
Anti-trust–defendants	3	2	1	9
Banking	3	2	1	10
Civil Litigation	3	2	1	11
Civil Rights/Liberties	3	2	1	12

Commercial Law (Uniform Commercial Code)	3	2	1	13
Condemnations	3	2	1	14
Consumer Law and Debtor/Creditor– Consumer/Debtor	3	2	1	15
Consumer Law and Debtor/Creditor– Seller/Bank/Creditor	3	2	1	16
Criminal Law–Prosecution	3	2	1	17
Criminal Law–Defense	3	2	1	18
Divorce (including family law, adoption, etc.)	3	2	1	19
Environmental Law–Plaintiffs	3	2	1	20
Environmental Law–Defendants	3	2	1	21
General Corporate	3	2	1	22
General Family Practice–Poverty Level Clients	3	2	1	23
General Family Practice–Paying Clients	3	2	1	24
Labor Law–Unions	3	2	1	25
Labor Law–Management	3	2	1	26
Landlord–Tenant	3	2	1	27
Municipal Law (including bond issues)	3	2	1	28
Patent, Trademarks and Copyright	3	2	1	29
Personal Injury–Plaintiffs	3	2	1	30
Personal Injury–Defense	3	2	1	31
Probate (Wills and Trusts)	3	2	1	32
Public Utilities, Administrative Law, and Regulated Industries	3	2	1	33
Real Estate	3	2	1	34
Securities (Mergers, etc.)	3	2	1	35
Tax	3	2	1	36
Other (specify) _____	3	2	1	37

_____ 38–39

_____ 40–41

A2. Do you regard yourself as a specialist?
Yes (ASK [A])   1
No   2   42
A. What specialty is that?

_____ 43–44

A3. Current Occupation
A. In what year did you begin your current job?

19___ 45–46

HAND CARD B

B. Which category of CARD B best describes that job? Please give me the name and the number on the card.

_____

_____

CARD B

TYPE OF PRACTICE

Solo	01
Firm	02
Government (1) Federal	03
(2) State	04
(3) Municipal/County Government	05
(4) Military Legal Service	06
House Counsel (1) Corporate	07
(2) Insurance	08
(3) Banking	09
(4) Railroad	10
Other	11

IF OTHER, SKIP TO F.   47–48
IF SOLO, GO TO Q.A4.

C. How many lawyers are in your firm/office now?

                                              49–51

Don't know.   .998

D. (1) What was the title of your job when you first started?

_____   52–53

(2) What is your present job title?

_____   54–55

E. What is the present name of your firm/office/department?

_____   56–58

SKIP TO A4

F. OTHER:
   IF LAW CLERK:
   (1) Is that on the state or federal bench?
      State   1
      Federal 2   59
   (2) Is that the trial or the appellate court?
      Trial   1
      Appellate 2   60
   (3) What is the location of the clerkship?

_____   61–63

GO TO Q.A8.

   IF MILITARY SERVICE:
   What is the nature of this job?
   (RECORD VERBATIM)

_____

_____

GO TO Q.A8. |___ 64-65

   IF NON-LEGAL JOB:
   What is the title of this job?
   (PROBE IF NECESSARY)

   _____

   _____

GO TO Q.A8. |___ 66-68

   SOLO AND FIRM LAWYERS ONLY

A4. During the past 12 months, approximately how many
    clients have you done some work for—more than just
    going through a file, or turning over a file to another
    lawyer?

                       _____   69-71

A5. During the past 12 months, what proportion of your in-
    come was derived from work on personal matters, and
    what proportion was derived from representing busi-
    ness clients?
       Work on personal matters (such as divorce,
       wills, residential real estate)   _____%   72-74

       Work representing business clients   _____%   75-77

    IF WORK ON *BUSINESS* REPRESENTS *10% OR MORE*   END OF
    OF INCOME, ASK (A) AND (B)   DECK 01

    IF WORK ON *BUSINESS* EQUALS *LESS THAN 10%* OF
    INCOME, GO TO (C)

    A. With what kinds of businesses do you mostly have
       to deal with? (e.g., insurance companies, retailers,
       clothing, steel, etc.)
                              (ID)   ___
       (RECORD VERBATIM)   1-4

       _____ DECK   02
                                            5-6

       _____

       _____ |___   7-8

    B. What proportion of your business income would
       come from the following size business clients?

> HAND
> CARD
> C

       Major Corporations   (Overall DK) |___   9
       (e.g., Standard Oil, American National
       Bank, Abbott Laboratories, Playboy Enter-
       prises, Pepper Construction—i.e. over $10
       million sales per year)   _____%   10-12

       Medium sized firms   _____%   13-15

       Small businesses (e.g., neighborhood stores,
       local restaurants, local real estate brokers,
       etc.—less than $250,000 sales per year) _____%   16-18

IF RESPONDENT DOES 10% OR MORE WORK ON PERSON-
AL MATTERS, GO TO (C). OTHERWISE, SKIP TO A6.

   C. Would you now think about the clients for whom
you have handled personal matters in the last 12
months.

OVERALL DK

What proportion of your clients fall into the occupational categories listed on CARD D?   19

HAND CARD D		

Professional, Technical, Managerial   ____%   20–22

Sales and Clerical   ____%   23–25

Blue Collar Workers   ____%   26–28

Unemployed   ____%   29–31

Retired, In-School, Keeping house   ____%   32–34

   D. Does a substantial proportion of your clientele come
from a particular ethnic or racial background?

Yes (ASK [A] and [B])	1
No	2
Don't Know	8

   35

   (A) Which ethnic groups?

   (B) What percentage for (NAME GROUP)?

GROUPS	CODE	PERCENT
_____	36–37	38–40
_____	41–42	43–45
_____	46–47	48–50

   E. What proportion of your clientele come from your
residential neighborhood, from other parts of the
metropolitan area, and from outside the Chicago
metropolitan area?

(OVERALL DK) ___   51

Residential neighborhood   ____%   52–54

Other parts of the metropolitan area   ____%   55–57

Outside Chicago metropolitan area   ____%   58–60

HAND CARD 1	A6. Could you now indicate what percentage of your new clients you get by each of the means listed on CARD 1?

D.K. ___

Through the Chicago Bar Association
Reference Plan   ____%   ____

Through other attorneys met at the
Chicago Bar Association ____% ____

Referred by other lawyers not met
through the CBA ____% ____

Referred by past or present clients ____% ____

Direct contacts with the new clients,
whether persons or businesses ____% ____

Other (specify) _____ ____% ____

_____ ____% ____

_____ ____% ____

____

____

____

A7. What proportion of all your clients have you represented for 3 years or more?

____% 61–63

A8. A. In the course of your practice, during the last 12
months, how many times *per month* have you appeared in:

Times per month

State Trial Courts _____ 64–66

State Appellate Courts _____ 67–69

B. In the course of your practice in the last 12 months,
how many times have you apeared in:

Federal Trial Courts _____ 70–72

Federal Appellate Courts _____ 73–75

C. Have you appeared before any other courts in the
last 12 months?

Yes (ASK [1]) 1 76

No 2 END OF
DECK 02

(1) Please specify the court and the number of times
you have appeared before it.

(ID)

Name	*Code*	*Times*
	7–8	9–11
	12–13	14–16
	17–18	19–21

1–4
DECK 03
5–6

22–26
BLANK

HAND
CARD
2

A9. Different kinds of law require different kinds of professional activities. CARD 2 contains a series of paired
statements which describe such different demands
made on the lawyer. Each pair represents polar opposites. Please circle the number which best represents
your position in relation to the two opposites. If the situation in your practice is midway between poles, circle
code 3; if your situation is at one or other extreme, circle 1 or 5; if your position leans somewhat to either
pole, circle 2 or 4.

A		B
1. My area requires a great deal of reading legal material in order to keep abreast of new developments.	1 2 3 4 5	Things don't change too rapidly in my area of the law, so there is little need for constant revision of my knowledge and activities.
2. The area of law in which I work is so highly specialized that it demands I concentrate in just this one area.	1 2 3 4 5	The nature of my legal practice is such that I can handle a range of problems covering quite a number of different areas of legal practice.
3. The nature of my practice is such that it is often necessary to accept clients whom I would prefer not to have.	1 2 3 4 5	In the course of my practice I have rather wide latitude in selecting which clients I will represent.
4. One of the things that I like about my area of practice is that I can do largely whatever I like without		In my practice of the law I work closely with more senior lawyers who provide relatively close guidance

395

having someone looking over my shoulder and directing my work.   1 2 3 4 5   in the nature of my work.

5. The type and content of my practice is such that even an educated layman couldn't really understand or prepare the documents.   1 2 3 4 5   A para-professional could be trained to handle many of the procedures and documents in my area of the law.

6. There are aspects of my professional work which are being encroached upon by other occupations.   1 2 3 4 5   No other occupation is engaging in the kinds of legal matters with which I am primarily concerned.

7. My specialty and type of practice requires skills in negotiating and advising clients, rather than detailed concern with technical rules.   1 2 3 4 5   My area demands skills in handling highly technical procedures rather than skills in negotiation and advising clients.

A10. Now I would like to ask you a few questions about your occupational history. Other than your current position, have you held *any* other jobs (including non-legal positions) since becoming an attorney?

Yes (ASK A-F)   1
No (GO TO Q.A11)   2   27

Let's begin with the first job you held after you qualified as an attorney? CODE EACH RESPONSE ON THE OCCUPATIONAL CHART

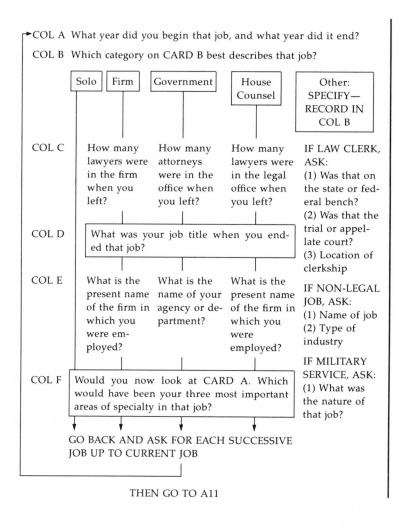

COL A What year did you begin that job, and what year did it end?

COL B Which category on CARD B best describes that job?

Solo	Firm	Government	House Counsel	Other: SPECIFY— RECORD IN COL B

COL C How many lawyers were in the firm when you left? | How many attorneys were in the office when you left? | How many lawyers were in the legal office when you left? | IF LAW CLERK, ASK: (1) Was that on the state or federal bench? (2) Was that the trial or appellate court? (3) Location of clerkship

COL D What was your job title when you ended that job?

COL E What is the present name of the firm in which you were employed? | What is the name of your agency or department? | What is the present name of the firm in which you were employed? | IF NON-LEGAL JOB, ASK: (1) Name of job (2) Type of industry

IF MILITARY SERVICE, ASK: (1) What was the nature of that job?

COL F Would you now look at CARD A. Which would have been your three most important areas of specialty in that job?

GO BACK AND ASK FOR EACH SUCCESSIVE JOB UP TO CURRENT JOB

THEN GO TO A11

397

OCCUPATIONAL CHART (JOB HISTORY)   OMIT

	COL A (Dates)	COL B (Practice)	COL C (Size)	COL D (Title)	COL E (Name)	COL F (Specialty)
1st job	Began: _____ Ended: _____	# _____ _____				1st _____ 2nd _____ 3rd _____
2nd job	Began: _____ Ended: _____	# _____ _____				1st _____ 2nd _____ 3rd _____
3rd job	Began: _____ Ended: _____	# _____ _____				1st _____ 2nd _____ 3rd _____
4th job	Began: _____ Ended: _____	# _____ _____				1st _____ 2nd _____ 3rd _____
5th job	Began: _____ Ended: _____	# _____ _____				1st _____ 2nd _____ 3rd _____
6th job	Began: _____ Ended: _____	# _____ _____				1st _____ 2nd _____ 3rd _____
7th job	Began: _____ Ended: _____	# _____ _____				1st _____ 2nd _____ 3rd _____

II. LEGAL ISSUES

The following questions concern various issues on which members of the bar in Chicago have taken different positions.

A11. (DISCIPLINE) Would you please read through the issue on CARD E and give me your position on that issue. RECORD COMMENTS VERBATIM.

HAND
CARD
E

CARD E

As you probably know, complaints charging lawyers with ethical misconduct are now dealt with by the "Attorney Registration Commission," a procedure that was recently adopted after many years of controversy. Previously, the Chicago and Illinois State Bar Associations performed these functions. Many lawyers still feel that it would be more appropriate for attorney discipline to be handled by the bar associations, which are more representative of the profession than is an administrative agency like the Attorney Registration Commission.

Which would you prefer: placing this responsibility for the enforcement of professional ethics in the hands of bar associations, in the hands of an administrative body like the Attorney Registration Commission, or do you have no opinion on this issue?

A. In the hands of the Bar Association   1
   In the hands of the Administrative body 2   28
   No Opinion (GO TO C)   7
   Neither   8

B. Have you participated in any way in the debate over this issue? By participation, in this and other questions, we mean calling your views on the issue to the attention of someone who is in a position to influence the outcome of the controversy—as contrasted, for example, to casual conversation with a colleague who is not involved in the controversy, or cocktail party conversations with friends or relatives.

   Yes (ASK [1])   1
   No   2   29

   (1) In what way did you participate? RECORD VERBATIM.

C. How important is this issue to you?
   Of great importance, some importance, little importance, or no importance?

   Great Importance   1
   Some Importance   2   30
   Little Importance   3
   No Importance   4

A12. (POLICE REVIEW) Would you not turn to the next issue on CARD F and indicate your position on that issue?

```
┌──────────┐
│  HAND    │
│  CARD    │     CARD F
│    F     │
└──────────┘
```

The local bar associations have been involved for the past few years in the question of who should investigate and review complaints by citizens against the police—that is, charges of police brutality and the like. One of the proposals was that the Chicago Bar Association and the Cook County Bar Association should jointly appoint a committee of lawyers to "monitor and audit" complaints against policemen and then to make periodic reports to the general public. An alternative proposal called for a "Civilian Review Board" composed of citizens generally (not necessarily lawyers), with specific provision for representation of various ethnic and racial minorities, and would vest this Board with the power to investigate complaints against police and to impose discipline on police found guilty of misconduct.

Which of the two alternatives would you prefer—having a Bar Associations committee, or a Civilian Review Board, or do you not have an opinion on this matter?

A. Handled by Bar Associations committee   1
    Handled by a Civilian Review Board   2   31
    No Opinion (GO TO C)   7
    Neither   8

B. Have you participated, in any way, in the debate?

    Yes (ASK [1])   1
    No   2   32

    (1) In what way did you participate? RECORD VERBATIM.

C. How important is the issue to you?
    Is it of great importance, some importance, little importance, or no importance?

    Great Importance   1
    Some Importance   2
    Little Importance   3   33
    No Importance   4

A13. (PRE-PAID LEGAL SERVICES)
    Could we now go on to CARD G. What position would you take on this issue?

<table>
<tr><td>

HAND
CARD
G

</td></tr>
</table>

CARD G

The organized bar has debated for some time the propriety of several alternative plans of "group legal services" or "pre-paid legal services," intended to increase the availability of legal advice and representation to the middle class (particularly, to lower middle class persons). One of the issues in this debate has been the relative merits of "closed panel programs," whereby the client's choice of a lawyer is limited to a specific group of lawyers hired or retained by the plan, *versus* an "open plan," whereby the client may use the monetary "insurance-type" benefits provided by the plan to hire any lawyer of his choice.

Would you prefer a "closed-panel" type plan of group legal services, or an "open plan," or do you have no opinion on this issue?

A. "Closed panel"   1
   "Open plan"   2   34
   No Opinion (GO TO C)   7
   Neither   8

B. Have you participated, in any way, in the debate?

   Yes (ASK [1])   1
   No   2   35

   (1) In what way did you participate? RECORD VERBATIM.

C. How important is the issue to you?
   Is it of great importance, some importance, little importance, or no importance?

   Great Importance   1
   Some Importance   2   36
   Little Importance   3
   No Importance   4

A14. (JUDICIARY) CARD H looks at another matter—that of the bar and the judiciary. Please read this through.

<table>
<tr><td>

HAND
CARD
H

</td></tr>
</table>

CARD H

Some groups of lawyers feel that the maintenance of a high quality, professional judiciary requires that the bar associations use rigorous standards of professional competence and conduct in evaluating judicial candidates and sitting judges, and that failure to meet these standards should be publicized to the profession and to the general public in candid, explicit terms. Other groups of lawyers feel that it is inappropriate for the

organized bar to arrogate to itself the function of passing judgment on the quality of the judiciary, that it de-
means the standing of the judiciary in the eyes of the
general public, and is thus destructive of public respect
for the rule of law generally for the bar to publish
harsh, explicit criticism of sitting judges.

Which of these two views is closer to your own position—the former, calling for the candid evaluation of
judges by the bar, or the latter, calling for restraint by
the bar in such matters, or do you have no opinion on
this matter?

A. Candid evaluation   1
   Restraint in evaluation   2   37
   No Opinion (GO TO C)   7
   Neither   8

B. Have you participated in this debate?

   Yes (ASK [1])   1
   No   2   38

   (1) In what way did you participate? RECORD
   VERBATIM.

C. How important is the issue to you?
   Is it of great importance, some importance, little importance, or no importance?

   Great Importance   1
   Some Importance   2
   Little Importance   3   39
   No Importance   4

A15. (CLASS ACTION SUITS) Would you now turn to the
next matter—CARD I.

> HAND
> CARD
> I

CARD I

In the past few years there has been a great increase
in the number of class actions filed, especially in the
federal courts, many of them dealing with environmental pollution or with consumer claims, such as "truth-
in-lending" cases. Some lawyers argue that the doctrines and rules pertaining to class actions should be
interpreted to permit liberal use of the class action technique, thus affording a means of relief to groups of
plaintiffs whose individual claims would be too small to
make it practicable for each of them to bring his own
suit. In opposition to this view, other segments of the
bar argue that class actions should be strictly limited because they impose a great burden on an already over-
crowded court system and because permitting the aggregation of small claims provides a bonanza to certain

plaintiffs' lawyers at the expense of unfairly large, financially ruinous burdens to the defendant businesses.

Which of these two views comes closer to approximating your own—liberal use of class action suits, limited use of such suits, or do you not have any opinion on this issue?

A. Liberal use of class action suits   1
    Limited use of class action suits   2   40
    No Opinion (GO TO C)   7
    Neither   8

B. Have you participated in any way in this debate?

    Yes (ASK [1])   1
    No   2   41

    (1) In what way have you participated? RECORD VERBATIM.

C. How important is the issue to you?
    Is it of great importance, some importance, little importance, or no importance?

    Great Importance   1
    Some Importance   2   42
    Little Importance   3
    No Importance   4

A16. The final issue is on CARD J. What is your position?

HAND
CARD   CARD J
   J

One of the issues that has generated so much controversy about the various versions of "no-fault" automobile plans concerns the extent to which victims would continue to be able to recover compensation for "pain and suffering." Which of the following two views would be closer to your own:

(1) That automobile accident victims should have an unrestricted right to sue for compensation for pain and suffering, in any amount, just as for any other sort of damage; or

(2) That the right of recovery for pain and suffering should be limited to cases in which the amount of the "actual" medical damages exceeds a minimum or "threshold" figure such as $10,000?

Or, do you not have an opinion on this issue?

A. Unrestricted right to sue   1
Limiting right of recovery   2
No Opinion (GO TO C)   7   43
Neither   8

B. Have you participated in any way in this debate?

Yes (ASK [1])   1
No   2   44

(1) In what way have you participated? RECORD VERBATIM.

C. How important is this issue to you?
Is it of great importance, some importance, little importance, or no importance?

Great Importance   1
Some Importance   2
Little Importance   3   45
No Importance   4

III. SOCIAL ACTIVITIES

The following set of questions is concerned with the relations of different segments of the bar to each other. They enable us, by using statistical analyses, to describe accurately the social structure of the bar in Chicago.

A17. Would you think of three persons in the legal profession with whom you most enjoy discussing law related matters? I don't need to know who they are, but as I'd like to ask you several questions about each, for convenience could I have just their *first names* or an *initial*.

	1. _____	2. _____	3. _____
A. To what specialty does _____ devote most of his time? PROBE FOR SPECIFIC.	_____ 46–47	_____ 56–57	_____ 66–67
B. What kind of practice does _____ engage in?	Solo 1 Govt. 3 Firm 2 H.C. 4 Other _____ _____ 5 48	_____ 1 2 3 4 5 58	_____ 1 2 3 4 5 68
C. (EXCEPT SOLO) What (firm, government agency, corporation) does _____ work for?	Same as resp. 001 Other (specify) _____ _____ 49–51	_____ _____ 59–61	_____ _____ 69–71

404

D. What law school did _____ graduate from? Chicago 01 Marshall 08 Columbia 02 Michigan 09 De Paul 03 North- Harvard 04 western 10 Illinois 05 Yale 11 Kent 06 Other Loyola 07 (SPECIFY) None 96 D.K. 98	ENTER CODE $\overline{52}$-$\overline{53}$ Other _____	ENTER CODE $\overline{62}$-$\overline{63}$ _____	ENTER CODE $\overline{72}$-$\overline{73}$ _____
E. Do you know what _____'s religious preference is? (IF PROTESTANT): What denomination is that?	Catholic 01 Jewish 02 Protestant _____, 03 None 96 D.K. 98 54-55	$\overline{64}$-$\overline{65}$	$\overline{74}$-$\overline{75}$

END OF CARD 03

BEGIN CARD 04 _____
1-4

DECK 04
5-6

	1. _____	2. _____	3. _____
F. Do you happen to know the ethnicity of _____ ? Irish 01 German 06 Polish 02 Spanish 07 Italian 03 American 08 Black 04 British 09 Jewish 05 Other _____ 10 D.K. 98	$\overline{7}$-$\overline{8}$ $\overline{9}$-$\overline{10}$ Other _____	$\overline{16}$-$\overline{17}$ $\overline{18}$-$\overline{19}$ Other _____	$\overline{25}$-$\overline{26}$ $\overline{27}$-$\overline{28}$ Other _____
G. Is _____ generally a Republican or a Democrat, Independent, or what?	Republican 1 Democrat 2 Independent 3 Other 4 D.K. 8 11	1 2 3 4 8 20	1 2 3 4 8 29

405

Question	Response	1		2		3	
(1) IF REPUBLICAN/ DEMOCRAT, Would he be a strong or not strong Republican/ Democrat?	Strong 1 Not strong 2 D.K. 8	1 2 8 12		1 2 8 21		1 2 8 30	
(2) IF INDEPENDENT, Would he be closer to the Democratic or Republican party?	Republican 1 Democrat 2 Neither 3 D.K. 8 	1 2 3 8 13		1 2 3 8 22		1 2 3 8 31	
(3) IF DEMOCRAT, Locally, is he Regular Democrat or Independent Democrat?	Regular Democrat 1 Indep. Dem. 2 D.K. 8 	1 2 8 14		1 2 8 23		1 2 8 32	

H. All in all, how often do you get together with _____ ?	More than once
	  per week 1
	Once per week 2
	2–3 times per
	  month 3
	Less 4
	
		1
		2
		
		3
		4
		
		15
				1
				2
				
				3
				4
				
				24
						1
						2
						
						3
						4
						
						33	

	1. _____		2. _____		3. _____	
I. Where do you usually meet?	Work 1 C.B.A. 1 Private Club (SPECIFY) _____ 1 Restaurant or bar 1 Home 1 Other _____ 1	34 35 36 37 38 39	1 1 1 1 1 1	48 49 50 51 52 53	1 1 1 1 1 1	62 63 64 65 66 67
J. (i) What bar associations does _____ belong to? (ii) FOR EACH ASSOCIATION ASK IF HE HAS A POSITION, IS HE ACTIVE OR INACTIVE. CIRCLE POSITION (3), ACTIVE (2), INACTIVE (1)	D.K. __ CBA 3 2 1 ISBA 3 2 1 ABA 3 2 1 CCL 3 2 1 __ 3 2 1 __ 3 2 1	40 41 42 43 44 45 46	D.K. __ CBA 3 2 1 ISBA 3 2 1 ABA 3 2 1 CCL 3 2 1 __ 3 2 1 __ 3 2 1	54 55 56 57 58 59 60	D.K. __ CBA 3 2 1 ISBA 3 2 1 ABA 3 2 1 CCL 3 2 1 __ 3 2 1 __ 3 2 1	68 69 70 71 72 73 74
K. Colleague's sex?	Male 1 Female 2	47	1 2	61	1 2	75

L. Of these three friends, how many of them enjoy discussing law-related matters with one another?

All three of them	1	
Two of them (GO TO A)	2	
None of them	3	76

A. Which two friends discuss with one another?

_____

_____ _____ 77

END OF CARD 04

BEGIN DECK 05   ID # _____
1-4

DECK   05
5-6

A18. Now would you think of the three persons who are your closest friends and whom you see most often. They can be relatives or non-relatives, as you wish, but excluding a spouse. I'd like to ask you several questions about each, so for convenience could you give me just their first names.

	1. _____	2. _____	3. _____
CODE SEX OF FRIEND	Male 1 Female 2 7	Male 1 Female 2 16	Male 1 Female 2 25
A. Is _____ a relative?	Yes (ASK 1) 1 No 2 8	Yes (ASK 1) 1 No 2 17	Yes (ASK 1) 1 No 2 26
(1) IF YES: What relationship is he/she to you?	_____ ____ 9-10	_____ ____18-19	_____ ____27-28
B. Would you say _____ is a very close friend, a good friend, or more an acquaintance?	Very close 1 Good 2 Acquaintance 3 11	1 2 3 20	1 2 3 29
C. How many years have you known _____ ?	_____ years 12-13	_____ years 21-22	_____ years 30-31
D. Approximately how old is _____ ?	_____ years 14-15	_____ years 23-24	_____ years 32-33

	1. _____	2. _____	3. _____
E. Could you please give _____'s religious preference? IF PROTESTANT: What denomination is that?	Catholic 01 Jewish 02 Protestant 03 None 96 D.K. 98 34–35	01 02 03 96 98 D.K. 48–49	01 02 03 96 98 D.K. 62–63
F. Is _____ generally a Republican, a Democrat, or an Independent?	Republican 1 Democrat 2 Independent 3 Other 4 D.K. 8 36	1 2 3 4 8 50	1 2 3 4 8 64
IF DEMOCRAT: Locally is _____ a Regular Democrat or Independent Democrat?	Regular 1 Independent 2 D.K. 8 37	1 2 8 51	1 2 8 65
G. Do you happen to know the ethnicity of _____? Irish 01 German 06 Polish 02 Spanish 07 Italian 03 American 08 Black 04 British 09 Jewish 05 Other _____ 10 D.K. 98	ENTER CODE 38–39 40–41	ENTER CODE 52–53 54–55	ENTER CODE 66–67 68–69
H. All in all, how often do you get together with _____?	Every other day 1 More than once per week 2 Once per week 3 2–3 times per month 4 Less often 5 42	1 2 4 5 56	1 2 3 4 5 70
I. Does _____ live in your neighborhood, in another part of the Chicago metropolitan area, or outside the Chicago area?	Neighborhood 1 Chicago area 2 Outside Chicago area 3 43	1 2 3 57	1 2 3 71

J. What is the main oc-
cupation of _____ ?
What is his job called?

	44–46	58–60	72–74

K. CODE   WHETHER
FRIEND   SAME   AS
COLLEAGUE

Not same	4	4	4
Same as #	1	1	1
	2	2	2
	3	3	3
	47	61	75

END OF CARD 05

A19. Would you now turn to CARD 3.

OMIT

HAND
CARD
3

	Column A	Column B		Column A	Column B
47	Agate*	7	32	Lawrence	56
48	Agee	8	33	Leonard	57
49	Agnew	9	34	Leventhal	58
50	Baer	10	35	Lewis	59
51	Baker	11	36	Liebling	60
52	Barents	12	37	Locke	61
53	Beiderbecke	13	38	Lonsdale	62
54	Behan	14	39	Lynch	63
55	Behrman	15	40	McShann	64
56	Bigard	16	41	Mingus	65
57	Blackburn	17	42	Phelps	66
58	Brendan	18	43	Phillips	67
59	Bricker	19	44	Robinson	68
60	Dodds	20	45	Rosenblum	69
61	Dolphy	21	46	Ryan	70

*These are not the actual names used in the inter-
views but rather the pseudonyms used throughout the
book.

409

	Drootin				Taft	
62		22	47			71
	Eldridge				Takas	
63		23	48			72
	Eliot				Tendler	
64		24	49			73
	Ellington				Tolman	
65		25	50			74
	Ellsworth				Tower	
66		26	51			75
	Elman				Tristano	
67		27	52			76
	Gonnigan				Trumbauer	
68		28	53			77
	Ladinsky				Turpin	
69		29	54			78
	Lang				Tyrone	
70		30	55			79
	Lasser			END OF DECK 11		
71		31				

END OF DECK 10

A. This is a selected list of some lawyers in Chicago. Would you go through this list, and in Column A check the names of those you are personally acquainted with?

B. AFTER COMPLETING LIST ASK: Of the people you identified in this list, whom can you be reasonably assured that, because of your personal relationship, he would find the time to advise you? Check in Column B.

The following questions are about your position on certain legal and social matters on which many people have different points of view.

A20. Would you please answer the question on CARD 4 by circling the appropriate response code for each statement?

HAND
CARD
4

	Strongly Agree	Agree	Unde- cided	Dis- agree	Strongly Disagree
a. The protection of consumer interests is best insured by a vigorous competition among sellers rather than by federal government intervention and regulation on behalf of consumers	5	4	3	2	1

b. To cope effectively with the problems facing our society, what is needed is a general strengthening and reliance on lo-

cal government institutions, rather than the federal government in finding solutions to these problems	5	4	3	2	1
c. To lead a good life it is necessary for a person to be guided by the teachings and beliefs of an established religious group	5	4	3	2	1
d. A man ought to be guided by what his experience tells him is right rather than by what any institution, such as church or government, tells him to do	5	4	3	2	1
e. Labor unions have become too big for the good of the country	5	4	3	2	1
f. The right to associate with whom one pleases is being endangered by the excesses of civil rights legislation	5	4	3	2	1
g. Differences in income among occupations should be reduced	5	4	3	2	1
h. So far as possible, a father should share equally with the mother in taking care of the needs of infants and very young children	5	4	3	2	1
i. There is too much power concentrated in the hands of a few large companies for the good of the country	5	4	3	2	1
j. One of the most important roles of government is to help those who cannot help themselves, such as the poor, the disadvantaged, and the unemployed	5	4	3	2	1
k. All Americans should have equal access to quality medical care regardless of ability to pay	5	4	3	2	1
l. Churches are necessary to establish and preserve concepts of right and wrong	5	4	3	2	1
m. Economic profits are by and large justly distributed in the U.S. today	5	4	3	2	1
n. The gains that labor unions make for their members help make the country more prosperous	5	4	3	2	1

411

o. It is who you know that counts in
getting ahead in life and not
what you know   5   4   3   2   1

A21. The statements on CARD 5 concern matters on which
lawyers have different opinions. The statements are not
drawn from real cases, nor are we concerned with
knowledge or precedent, but rather with your personal
opinion on these matters. Please check whether you
strongly agree through *strongly disagree*, for each item.

> HAND
> CARD
> 5

	Strongly Agree	Agree	Unde-cided	Dis-agree	Strongly Disagree
1. The decisions of our appellate courts should reflect "general neutral principles" that prevail for generations, rather than being like railroad tickets "good for this day and train only"	5	4	3	2	1
2. Preservation of the traditional moral values of the community in such areas as prostitution, gambling, and homosexuality is a perfectly legitimate objective of the criminal law	5	4	3	2	1
3. The provisions of the U.S. Constitution should be construed strictly so as to implement the intent of the framers	5	4	3	2	1
4. A group of feminists remove all their clothing in public at the site of a Hugh Hefner speech in order to protest *Playboy*'s treatment of women as "sex objects." To punish them for indecent exposure would abridge their right to political expression	5	4	3	2	1
5. Plea bargaining is a useful and legitimate tool in facilitating the administration of criminal justice	5	4	3	2	1
6. Prosecutorial discretion should be an important part of our criminal justice system because it is impossible to draft statutes with precision in areas such as obscenity, disorderly conduct, and disturbing the peace	5	4	3	2	1
7. Publishing a directory of homosexuals, describing the acts that					

they are willing and available to perform, should be punishable as a conspiracy to corrupt public morals   5   4   3   2   1

8. Broadcasting court proceedings would demean them   5   4   3   2   1

9. The Chicago Bar Association's review of judicial candidates has generally been characterized by a lack of candor and, consequently, has made little contribution to improving the state of the judiciary   5   4   3   2   1

10. Access to the court should be carefully limited—through strict application of such requirements as "standing," "economic interest," and "exhaustion of remedies," and through dismissal of all cases that are "moot" or not "ripe" for decision—because it is more important to preserve the *quality* of justice than it is to increase the *quantity* of cases dealt with by our courts   5   4   3   2   1

11. It would be better to select our state judges through appointment by an independent, bipartisan commission rather than through election by the public at large   5   4   3   2   1

A22. Here is a list of the kinds of organizations that many people belong to. Please look over this list (HAND CARD K) and for each heading *give the names* of the organizations you belong to. READ EACH HEADING.

OMIT

> HAND CARD K

B. (ASK FOR EACH ORGANIZATION LISTED:) How actively involved are you in (NAME OF ORGANIZATION)? Have you held a leadership position in the organization, are you actively involved, or are you inactive?

A.	B. Involvement		
	Leader	Active	Inactive
a. Religious Connected Groups			
1. _____	3	2	1

2. _____	3	2	1
b. Business Groups			
1. _____	3	2	1
2. _____	3	2	1
3. _____	3	2	1
c. Political Groups or Organizations			
1. _____	3	2	1
2. _____	3	2	1
3. _____	3	2	1
d. Country Clubs (and other clubs with dining or athletic facilities)			
1. _____	3	2	1
2. _____	3	2	1
3. _____	3	2	1
e. Legal Clubs (*not* Bar Associations)			
1. _____	3	2	1
2. _____	3	2	1
f. Veterans Organizations			
1. _____	3	2	1
2. _____	3	2	1
g. Fraternal Organizations or Lodges			
1. _____	3	2	1
2. _____	3	2	1
h. Civic, Charity or Welfare Organizations			

	3	2	1
1. _____	3	2	1
2. _____	3	2	1

i. Organizations of People of the Same Nationality

	3	2	1
1. _____	3	2	1
2. _____	3	2	1

j. Other Organizations

	3	2	1
1. _____	3	2	1
2. _____	3	2	1

k. On Boards of Directors, Boards of Trustees, etc.

	3	2	1
1. _____	3	2	1
2. _____	3	2	1

l. Other

ID   1–4

DECK   06 / 5–6

IV. PROFESSIONAL ACTIVITIES

The following questions concern your involvement in the activities of Bar Associations.

A23. A. Please list, in order of importance to you—though not necessarily measured by time—the Bar Associations in which you presently hold membership.

	None	1	7
1st most important _____		___	8–9
2nd most important _____		___	10–11
3rd most important _____		___	12–13
4th most important _____		___	14–15
Others _____		___	16–17

415

	18–19
———————— —	20–21

IF MEMBER OF CBA GO TO Q24.

B. Have you *ever* been a member of the Chicago Bar
   Association?

Yes (ASK Q24, 25 & GO TO Q28)	1	22
No (GO TO Q28)	2	

A24. Let's now think about your membership in the CBA.

A. What years have you belonged to the CBA?

From _____ To _____
         23–24   25–26

From _____ To _____
         27–28   29–30

B. To which committees have you ever been appointed? RECORD IN CHART

None	1	31

Committee Name	Code	From	To	All	Most	Some	None	
1. _____	____ 32–34	____ 35–36	____ 37–38	4	3	2	1	39
2. _____	____ 40–42	____ 43–44	____ 45–46	4	3	2	1	47
3. _____	____ 48–50	____ 51–52	____ 53–54	4	3	2	1	55
4. _____	____ 56–58	____ 59–60	____ 61–62	4	3	2	1	63
5. _____	____ 64–66	____ 67–68	____ 69–70	4	3	2	1	71
6. _____	____ 72–74	____ 75–76	____ 77–78	4	3	2	1	79

The "Attendance" label spans the All/Most/Some/None columns.

END OF DECK 06
BEGIN CARD 07 ID#

	1–4
DECK	07
	5–6

7. _____ | _____ | _____ _____   4   3   2   1   14
             7-9 | 10-11 12-13

8. _____ | _____ | _____ _____   4   3   2   1   22
            15-17 | 18-19 20-21

C. Please give the years in which you were a member
   of _____ committee. RECORD IN CHART

D. Now taking each committee of which you are *presently* a member: For the (NAME COMMITTEE) do
   you attend all meetings, most meetings, some meetings, or none? REPEAT FOR EACH CURRENT
   COMMITTEE
   RECORD IN CHART

E. Have you held any offices in the CBA?
   Yes (ASK [1])   1   23
   No (GO TO Q25)   2

   (1) What offices have you held and in what years
   did you hold them? Please give me up to *five* of the
   most important offices you have held, or hold.

   RECORD IN CHART

COMMITTEE WHERE RELEVANT	Code	Office	Code	From	To
1. _____	_____ 24-26	_____	_____ 27-28	_____ 29-30	_____ 31-32
2. _____	_____ 33-35	_____	_____ 36-37	_____ 38-39	_____ 40-41
3. _____	_____ 42-44	_____	_____ 45-46	_____ 47-48	_____ 49-50
4. _____	_____ 51-53	_____	_____ 54-55	_____ 56-57	_____ 58-59
5. _____	_____ 60-62	_____	_____ 63-64	_____ 65-66	_____ 67-68

417

A25. Could we turn now to other CBA activities which do not involve committee memberships or officerships.

A. RESIGNERS EXCLUDED
   Over the past *five years,* how many times have you:
   a. Attended the annual meeting of the CBA? _____   69
   b. Voted for CBA officers?   _____   70
   c. Attended the Christmas Spirits show? _____   71

B. How often do you eat in a CBA restaurant?
   More than once per week (ASK 1 & 2)   1
   Once per week (ASK 1 & 2)   2
   2-3 times per month (ASK 1 & 2)   3
   Less   4   72

   IF THE ANSWER IS 2-3 TIMES PER MONTH OR MORE:

   (1) What percentage of these occasions are principally for meeting with clients?   _____ %   73-75

   (2) What percentage of these occasions are meetings with colleagues?   _____ %   76-78

C. How often do you use the CBA Library?
   More than once per week   1
   Once per week   2
   2-3 times per month   3
   Less   4   79

D. How often would you say you discuss Chicago Bar Association activities, matters of controversy, etc., with friends and colleagues?
   More than once per week   1
   Once per week   2
   2-3 times per month   3
   Less   4   80
                                   END OF
                                   DECK
                                   07

                            ID   —
                                  1-4

                          DECK   08
E. Are you a member of the Lawyer's Reference Panel?   5-6
   Yes (ASK [1])   1
   No   2   7

   (1) IF YES: How often do you get clients referred from the panel?

   Once a month   1

Once every two months	2	
Twice a year	3	8
Once a year	4	
Less	5	

F. Would you say that you usually read the *Communica-tor* pretty thoroughly, casually, or scarcely at all?

Thoroughly	1	
Casually	2	9
Scarcely at all	3	

G. Are there other important aspects of your involve-ment in the CBA, or use of CBA facilities, that we have not mentioned?

Yes (ASK [1])	1	
No	2	10

   (1) Please specify these activities. RECORD VERBATIM.

11-12

A26. Within the past couple of years, the Chicago Bar Associ-ation has considered moving out of its present, leased quarters and building a new building of its own.

A. Were you aware that this step was being considered?

Yes	1	
No	2	13

B. Would you favor or oppose the CBA acquiring a building of its own tailored to its own specifications?

Favor	1	
Not favor	2	14
Neither	3	
No opinion	4	

C. Did you participate in any way in the debate over whether or not to move to a new building?

Yes	1	15
No	2	

OMIT

A27. A. What are the reasons that you belong to the Chicago Bar Association? RECORD VERBATIM. PROBE IF NECESSARY.

419

B. Would you now turn to CARD 6.

Here is a list of some of the personal reasons some lawyers give for belonging to the CBA. Please go through this list and indicate how important each reason is for *your* membership in the Chicago Bar Association.

	Very Impor- tant	Impor- tant	Not Impor- tant
a. To help solve certain problems facing the profession at large	3	2	1
b. Because of good dining and library facilities	3	2	1
c. Because of the feeling that lawyers have a moral obligation to participate in community and civic affairs	3	2	1
d. Because the Association gives opportunities for leadership within the bar	3	2	1
e. Educational activities are useful in your practice	3	2	1
f. As a good place to meet other lawyers socially	3	2	1
g. A chance to influence the direction of legislation which affects the practice of law in your area	3	2	1
h. Gives the little man in the profession an opportunity to make a wider contribution	3	2	1
i. Enables you to fulfill legal interests other than those which are part of your legal practice	3	2	1
j. Provides good experience for possible future opportunities for service in state or federal government	3	2	1
k. Is strongly encouraged by your firm or employer	3	2	1
l. Enables you to have some impact on the local or national level	3	2	1
m. Provides an opportunity to meet colleagues who can be of assistance in your practice	3	2	1

A28. Here is a list of objectives which the Chicago Bar Association could pursue. HAND CARD 7.

> HAND
> CARD
> 7

OBJECTIVES OF A BAR ASSOCIATION

	COLUMN I						COLUMN II				
	Very Important	*Important*	*Undecided*	*Little Importance*	*Not Important at All*		*Highly Effective*	*Effective*	*Undecided*	*Little Effect*	*Not Effective at All*
a. To facilitate client-getting through contacts with other lawyers	5	4	3	2	1	46	5	4	3	2	1
b. Taking stands on controversial issues of public policy such as Vietnam or school busing	5	4	3	2	1	47	5	4	3	2	1
c. To discipline lawyers according to standards of professional ethics	5	4	3	2	1	48	5	4	3	2	1
d. Improving the quality of the bar by keeping lawyers abreast of current developments	5	4	3	2	1	49	5	4	3	2	1
e. Improving the quality of the judiciary	5	4	3	2	1	50	5	4	3	2	1
f. Exercising leadership to improve the general lot of disadvantaged groups	5	4	3	2	1	51	5	4	3	2	1
g. Providing library or dining facilities for members of the bar	5	4	3	2	1	52	5	4	3	2	1
h. Promoting the development of police procedures that will accord with constitutional standards	5	4	3	2	1	53	5	4	3	2	1
i. To enhance the status of the legal profession in the eyes of the public	5	4	3	2	1	54	5	4	3	2	1
j. Facilitating the referral of cases to qualified lawyers	5	4	3	2	1	55	5	4	3	2	1
k. Improving efficiency of court procedures	5	4	3	2	1	56	5	4	3	2	1
l. Preventing non-lawyers from doing legal work	5	4	3	2	1	57	5	4	3	2	1
m. Initiating legislation or quasi-legislative proposals in areas of interest to segments of the bar	5	4	3	2	1	58	5	4	3	2	1

A. ASK EVERYONE:
   In your opinion, how important is it that the CBA pursue these objectives? Circle your answer in COLUMN I.

B. ASK *CBA MEMBERS:* For each objective you have circled as important or very important, in your opinion how effective has it been in meeting that objective. Circle the appropriate number in Column II.

   ASK *NON-CBA MEMBERS:* For each objective you have circled as important or very important, *from your general knowledge* how would you rate the performance of the CBA? Circle the appropriate number in Column II.

A29. Would you now give me your impression about the issue mentioned in CARD 8?

> HAND
> CARD
> 8

The following is a typology describing four different ways in which bar associations make decisions. Which of the following most accurately describes the Chicago Bar Association?

First, there are those organizations in which *vigorous conflicts between the same leaders or groups* appear again and again in the handling of issues so that the same persons or groups are always found together in a coalition.

In the *second* type, there is also controversy about various issues, but there are *constantly changing coalitions* between various groups or persons so that the coalitions are different depending on the problem being considered.

In the *third* case there is relatively little argument about organizational measures because there is a *relatively high consensus* within the organization about what needs to be done.

Fourth, there is a *self-perpetuating group of leaders* sharing common values and objectives who make most decisions with little or no consultation with the membership.

D.K. _____

First description	1
Second description	2
Third description	3
Fourth description	4

A30. In your opinion, are there any individuals, law firms, groups, or specialties who exert great influence on CBA organizational affairs or policies?

Yes (ASK [1])	1	
No	2	16
Don't Know	8	

(1) Who are these groups?

1. _____ ____ | 17–19

2. _____ ____ | 20–22

3. _____ ____ | 23–25

4. _____ ____ | 26–28

CBA MEMBERS, SKIP TO QUESTION 32

A31. IF RESPONDENT HAS *NEVER BEEN A MEMBER OF THE CBA,* ASK (A)
IF RESPONDENT IS A *RESIGNEE FROM THE CBA,* ASK (B)

A. What are the primary reasons *you do not belong* to the CBA? RECORD VERBATIM.

B. What are the primary reasons you resigned from the CBA? RECORD VERBATIM.

(CHECK: DID YOU ASK QA24 & A25?)

A32. INTERVIEWER QUESTION ONLY:

LOOKING AT THE LIST OF BAR ASSOCIATIONS IN QUESTION 23, *CIRCLE BELOW* THE MOST IMPOR-TANT BAR ASSOCIATION OTHER THAN THE CHI-CAGO BAR ASSOCIATION:

Chicago Council of Lawyers (GO TO #33)	1	
Illinois State Bar Association (GO TO #33)	2	
Others (GO TO #34)	3	29
No other Bar Associations (GO TO #35)	4	

A33. A. What years have you belonged to (Chicago Council of Lawyers/Illinois State Bar Association)? CIRCLE NAME.

From _____ to _____
     30–31   32–33

From _____ to _____
     34–35   36–37

B. Of which committees are you *now* a member?

None (GO TO D)   1   38

Committee Name	CODE	All	Most	Some	None	
1. _____	_____ 39–41	4	3	2	1	42
2. _____	_____ 43–45	4	3	2	1	46
3. _____	_____ 47–49	4	3	2	1	50
4. _____	_____ 51–53	4	3	2	1	54
5. _____	_____ 55–57	4	3	2	1	58

C. TAKING EACH COMMITTEE IN TURN:

Do you attend all meetings of (NAME COMMITTEE), most meetings, some meetings, or none?

D. Here is a list of objectives that the (Chicago Council of Lawyers/Illinois State Bar Association) could pursue. HAND CARD 9.

HAND
CARD
9

(1) In your opinion, *how important* is it that it pursue each objective? Circle the appropriate response on Column I.

(2) For each objective you have rated as important or very important, in your opinion *how effective* has it been in meeting this objective? Circle the appropriate response in Column II.

424

	COLUMN I						COLUMN II				
	Very Important	*Important*	*Undecided*	*Little Importance*	*Not Important at All*		*Highly Effective*	*Effective*	*Undecided*	*Little Effect*	*Not Effective at All*
a. To facilitate client-getting through contacts with other lawyers	5	4	3	2	1	12	5	4	3	2	1
b. Taking stands on controversial issues of public policy such as Vietnam or school busing	5	4	3	2	1	13	5	4	3	2	1
c. To discipline lawyers according to standards of professional ethics	5	4	3	2	1	14	5	4	3	2	1
d. Improving the quality of the bar by keeping lawyers abreast of current developments	5	4	3	2	1	15	5	4	3	2	1
e. Improving the quality of the judiciary	5	4	3	2	1	16	5	4	3	2	1
f. Exercising leadership to improve the general lot of disadvantaged groups	5	4	3	2	1	17	5	4	3	2	1
g. Providing library or dining facilities for members of the bar	5	4	3	2	1	18	5	4	3	2	1
h. Promoting the development of police procedures that will accord with constitutional standards	5	4	3	2	1	19	5	4	3	2	1
i. To enhance the status of the legal profession in the eyes of the public	5	4	3	2	1	20	5	4	3	2	1
j. Facilitating the referral of cases to qualified lawyers	5	4	3	2	1	21	5	4	3	2	1
k. Improving efficiency of court procedures	5	4	3	2	1	22	5	4	3	2	1
l. Preventing non-lawyers from doing legal work	5	4	3	2	1	23	5	4	3	2	1
m. Initiating legislation or quasi-legislative proposals in areas of interest to segments of the bar	5	4	3	2	1	24	5	4	3	2	1

425

E. What offices have you held in the (NAME OF ASSOCIATION)?

None (GO TO A35)　　　　　　　　　　1　　　59

Office

_____ ____　60–61

_____ ____　62–63

_____ ____　64–65

SKIP TO QUESTION A35　　　　END OF DECK 08

A34. TAKING *MOST IMPORTANT* BAR ASSOCIATION OTHER THAN *CBA, CCL, ISBA*:

A. What are the major differences between (WRITE NAME OF ASSOCIATION _____) and the Chicago Bar Association? RECORD VERBATIM. PROBE IF NECESSARY.

B. What are the reasons you belong to (NAME ASSOCIATION)? RECORD VERBATIM. PROBE IF NECESSARY.

ID　　1–4

DECK　09 / 5–6

A35. Finally, in this section, would you circle the appropriate responses on CARD 10.

HAND CARD 10

Different sectors of the legal profession have a variety of goals for professional advancement. How accurately do each of the following realistically describe your anticipated future interests and activities? Would they be very important, important, or not important in your plans?

	Very Important	Important	Not Important
1. A position of leadership in the Chicago Bar Association as a whole	3	2	1
2. A position of leadership in a section or committee of the CBA	3	2	1
3. A position of leadership in another Bar Association (specify)	3	2	1

4. A position of seniority in a law firm	3	2	1
5. A position of seniority in a corporate legal department	3	2	1
6. A strong solo practice	3	2	1
7. A seat on the state or federal bench	3	2	1
8. A position of leadership in local, state, or federal agencies concerned with the administration of justice	3	2	1
9. A position of leadership in other government agencies	3	2	1
10. A position of leadership in local, state, or federal politics	3	2	1
11. A position of leadership in various community institutions	3	2	1
12. A position of leadership in a corporation	3	2	1
13. Other (specify) _____	3	2	1

V. BACKGROUND CHARACTERISTICS

The final set of questions are about the background characteristics of the Chicago bar. Although they ask about you, please keep in mind that they are to be used in a statistical form only, much like the U.S. Census.

A36. Was your father a lawyer?

Yes (ASK 1)	1	
No (ASK A37)	2	7

(1) What law school did he graduate from?

Chicago	01	Loyola	07	
Columbia	02	Marshall	08	
De Paul	03	Michigan	09	
Harvard	04	Northwestern	10	
Illinois	05	Yale	11	
Kent	06	Other (specify)		
		_____	12	8-9
		None	96	

SKIP TO A38

A37. Turning to CARD L, which of these categories best describes the kind of work your (father/father substitute) usually did while you were growing up.

HAND CARD L

U.S. CENSUS OCCUPATIONAL CODE

A. *Professional and Technical*
(ex: accountants, engineers, physicians, nurses, social workers, teachers, draftsmen, actors, computer programmers)

B. *Managers and Administrators*
(ex: treasurers, buyers, office managers, government officials, sales managers, restaurant managers)
C. *Sales Workers*
(ex: newsboys, real estate agents, retail sales clerks, manufacturers sales representatives)
D. *Clerical Workers*
(ex: bank tellers, file clerks, mail carriers, dispatchers, office machine operators, secretaries)
E. *Craftsmen*
(ex: bakers, floor layers, foremen, machinists, mechanics and repairmen, sheet metal workers, tailors)
F. *Operatives*
(ex: assemblers, clothing pressers, produce graders, machine operators, sailors, textile operatives, bus drivers, taxicab drivers, deliverymen)
G. *Laborers*
(ex: fishermen and oystermen, garbage collectors, warehousemen, laborers, lumbermen and woodchoppers)
H. *Farmers and Farm Managers*
I. *Farm Laborers*
J. *Service Workers*
(ex: janitors, waiters, nursing aides, airline stewardesses, elevator operators, hairdressers, barbers, cooks, maids)
K. *Unemployed*
L. *Retired, in school, keeping house*

Please give me the letter code: _____ ____ | 10

A. Was he self-employed, or did he work for someone else?

Self-employed	1
Someone else	2
Don't Know	8

11

A38. Which of the categories on this card comes closest to the type of place you were living in during most of the time you were at high school?

HAND CARD M

In open country or on a farm	1
In a small city or town (under 50,000)	2
In a medium-sized city (50,000–250,000)	3
In a suburb near a large city	4
In a large city (over 250,000)	5
Don't know	8

12

A39. In what state or foreign country were you living during most of the time you were at high school?

REFER TO STATE CODES BELOW AND ENTER CODE NUMBER IN BOX ⊔⊔ 13–14

428

IF STATE NAMED IS ILLINOIS, ASK:

Was this in the Chicago metropolitan area or
elsewhere?

Chicago metropolitan area	1	15
Elsewhere	2	

Alabama	63	Louisiana	73	Oklahoma	72
Alaska	94	Maine	11	Oregon	92
Arizona	87	Maryland	52	Pennsylvania	23
Arkansas	71	Massachusetts	14	Rhode Island	16
California	93	Michigan	34	South Carolina	57
Colorado	86	Minnesota	41	South Dakota	45
Connecticut	15	Mississippi	64	Tennessee	62
Delaware	51	Missouri	43	Texas	74
Washington, D.C.	55	Montana	81	Utah	85
Florida	59	Nebraska	46	Vermont	12
Georgia	58	Nevada	84	Virginia	54
Hawaii	95	New Hampshire	13	Washington	91
Idaho	82	New Jersey	22	West Virginia	53
Illinois	32	New Mexico	88	Wisconsin	31
Indiana	33	New York	21	Wyoming	83
Iowa	42	North Carolina	56		
Kansas	47	North Dakota	44	Foreign country	97
				(specify)	

A40. A. Are you a college graduate?

Yes (ASK B)	1	
No (ASK C)	2	16

   B. From what college or university did you receive
   your undergraduate degree?

   _____ _____ 17–19

   SKIP TO D

   C. Did you spend any years at college?

Yes (ASK [1])	1	20
No	2	
(1) How many years was that?	_____	21

   D. Do you have a law degree?

Yes (ASK E)	1	
No (GO TO Q41)	2	22

E. From what university or law school did you receive your law degree?

Chicago	01	Michigan	09
Columbia	02	Northwestern	10
De Paul	03	Yale	11
Harvard	04	Other (specify)	
Illinois	05		
Kent	06	_____ 12	
Loyola	07		
Marshall	08		

23–24

F. Which section of your graduating class would most accurately reflect your standing?

Law Review or top 10%	1
Top 10% to 25%	2
Second 25% of class	3
Third quarter of class	4
Lowest quarter of class	5
Don't know	8

25

A41. With respect to national politics, do you usually think of yourself as a Republican, Democrat, Independent or what?

Republican (ASK A)	1
Democrat (ASK A)	2
Independent (ASK B)	3
Other (GO TO Q42)	4

26

(specify) _____

A. IF REPUBLICAN OR DEMOCRAT: Would you call yourself a strong (Republican/Democrat) or not a strong (Republican/Democrat)?

Strong	1
Not strong	2

27

B. IF INDEPENDENT: Do you think of yourself as closer to the Republican or Democratic party?

Republican	1
Democratic	2
Neither	3

28

A42. With respect to Chicago politics, do you think of yourself as Republican, Regular Democrat, Independent Democrat or what?

Republican	1
Regular Democrat	2
Independent Democrat	3
Other	4
Not applicable	5

29

A43. Do you have a religious preference? That is, are you either Protestant, Roman Catholic, Jewish or something else?

Roman Catholic	01
Protestant (specify)	
_____	02
Jewish (Would that be):	
Orthodox	70
Conservative	71
Reform	72
Other	73
Other _____	80
None	96

30-31

A44. How often do you attend religious services? USE CATEGORIES AS PROBES, IF NECESSARY.

Never	0
Less than once a year	1
About once or twice a year	2
Several times a year	3
About once a month	4
2-3 times a month	5
Nearly every week	6
Every week	7
Several times a week	8

32

A45. Are you currently married, widowed, divorced, separated, or have you never been married?

Married	1
Widowed	2
Divorced	3
Separated	4
Never married	5

33

A46. A. What nationality background do you think of yourself as having—that is, besides being American? (RECORD EXACT ANSWER)

_____ .

REFER TO NATIONAL CODES BELOW
AND ENTER NUMBER IN BOX

34-35

B. IF MARRIED:
What nationality background does your spouse think of (herself/himself) as having—that is, besides being American? (RECORD EXACT ANSWER)

_____ .

REFER TO NATIONAL CODES BELOW
AND ENTER NUMBER IN BOX

36-37

431

NATIONAL CODES

American Indian	30	Mexico	17
Africa	01	Netherlands (Dutch,	
Austria	02	Holland)	18
Canada (French)	03	Norway	19
Canada (Other)	04	Philippines	20
China	05	Poland	21
Czechoslovakia	06	Puerto Rico	22
Denmark	07	Russia (USSR)	23
England and Wales	08	Scotland	24
Finland	09	Spain	25
France	10	Sweden	26
Germany	11	Switzerland	27
Greece	12	West Indies	28
Hungary	13	Other (SPECIFY)	29
Ireland	14		
Italy	15	More than one country/	
Japan	16	can't decide on one	88
Don't know			98

A47. In what year were you born? _____ 38–39

A48. CODE RESPONDENT'S SEX:

Male   1

Female   2   40

A49. In which of these groups did your earnings *from the practice of law,* for last year—1974—fall? That is, *before taxes* and other deductions. Just tell me the letter.

HAND CARD N

A. Under $10,000   01
B. $10,000 to 14,999   02
C. $15,000 to 19,999   03
D. $20,000 to 29,999   04
E. $30,000 to 39,999   05
F. $40,000 to 49,999   06
G. $50,000 to 59,999   07
H. $60,000 to 69,999   08
I. $70,000 to 79,999   09
J. $80,000 to 89,999   10
K. $90,000 to 99,999   11
L. $100,000 to 499,999   12
M. Over $500,000   13

Refused   14   41–42
Don't know   98

A. What percentage would that represent of your personal total income?

_____ %   43–45

A50. CODE WITHOUT ASKING ONLY IF THERE IS *NO* DOUBT IN YOUR MIND.

What race do you consider yourself?

White	1
Black	2
Other (specify)	3

46

RECORD VERBATIM *AND* CODE

NOTE: IF YOU ASKED R'S RACE, NOTE:

Asked	1
Not asked	2

47

A51. Could you now tell us your residential zip code?

_____   48–52

┌─────────────────┐
│ Time Ended   │
└─────────────────┘

INTERVIEWER REMARKS

(TO BE FILLED OUT *AS SOON AS POSSIBLE* AFTER LEAVING RESPONDENT)

A52. Length of Interview   _____ minutes   53–55

A53. Date of Interview   _____ _____   56–59
                                  Month   Day

A54. In general, what was the respondent's attitude during the interview?

Friendly and interested	1
Co-operative but not particularly interested	2
Impatient and restless	3
Hostile	4

60

A55. INTERVIEWER NUMBER _____   61–62

433

Appendix B

SELECTED CHARACTERISTICS OF LAWYERS BY FIELD OF LAW PRACTICED

TABLE B.1
Differentiation of Fields of Law by Client Characteristics

	Number of Practitioner Respondents (1)	Mean % of Business Income from Business Clients (2)	Mean % of Business Income from Major Corp. Clients (3)	Mean % Stable Clients (4)	Median Number of Clients per Year (5)	Mean % Blue-collar Clients (6)	Mean % Clients from Neighborhood (7)	Mean % Clients from Outside Chicago (8)	Mean % Clients Referred by Lawyers (9)	Mean % Clients Referred by Clients (10)	Mean % Direct Contact Clients (11)
A. Corporate Sector											
Large Corporate Cluster											
Antitrust (defense)	20	93**	77**	55	18	1*	1	4	13	28	7
Business litigation	31	95**	57**	59	26	3*	0*	2	21	32	14
Business real estate	41	94**	53**	75	24	2**	4	7	17	28	16
Business tax	30	95**	62**	76	26	2	1	2	24	22*	10
Labor (management)	22	80**	66**	70	20	0*	1	3	14	32	14
Securities	22	93**	61**	60	26	0**	0	2	10	37	19
Cluster score	151	92**	62**	69	25	2**	2**	4	17	29**	14
Regulatory Cluster											
Labor (unions)	13	59	32	82	23	12	1	4	9	36	13
Patents	34	95**	62**	77	22	6**	1	4	32**	35	15
Public utilities	29	62	46	92**	2	3**	4	2	26	18*	8
Cluster score	77	75**	50**	83**	20	6**	2*	3	26**	28*	12
General Corporate Cluster											
Antitrust (plaintiffs)	10	60	22	54	18	0	1	13	34*	37	10
Banking	33	87**	58**	76	25	3*	5	3	16	34	14
Commercial	38	74**	41	75	31	5**	3	3	16	37	15
General corporate	135	76**	39	72	35	6**	7	5	14	37	18*
Personal injury (defense)	42	71*	60**	69	30	8	6	2	13	30	18
Cluster score	226	74**	43**	71*	33	6**	6	5	15	35	16
Political Cluster											
Criminal (prosecution)	15	Government is the only client									
Municipal	18	53	19	70	22	6	8	1	14	26	22
Cluster score	32	30**	11**	84**	3	3*	4	0*	13	14**	12

TABLE B.1—Continued

	Number of Practitioner Respondents (1)	Mean % of Income from Business Clients (2)	Mean % of Income from Major Corp. Clients (3)	Mean % Stable Clients (4)	Median Number of Clients per Year (5)	Mean % Blue-collar Clients (6)	Mean % Clients from Neighborhood (7)	Mean % Clients from Outside Chicago (8)	Mean % Clients Referred by Lawyers (9)	Mean % Clients Referred by Clients (10)	Mean % Direct Contact Clients (11)
B. Personal Sector											
Personal Business Cluster											
General litigation	24	44	17*	59	86	17	6	15**	16	50	24*
Personal real estate	62	37**	8**	60	99	29**	20**	5	7**	67**	19*
Personal tax	32	42*	16*	61	50	9	18**	9	12	54**	20
Probate	100	48**	22**	70	60	14	16**	8	9**	54**	19*
Cluster score	165	46**	18**	64	75	18**	15**	8**	11**	54**	20**
Personal Plight Cluster											
Civil rights	14	41	25	83	3†	11	0	4	16	23	8
Criminal (defense)	44	10**	5**	41**	100†	31**	11	7	24*	40	14
Divorce	57	23**	4**	42**	102†	38**	13**	7	15	59**	19
Family	27	28**	7**	64	78	38**	7	3	11	49	15
Personal injury (plaintiffs)	62	24**	14**	42**	149†	43**	11	8	26**	48*	14
Cluster score	171	23**	10**	49**	100†	34**	9*	6	20*	46**	15
Other Specialties	36	18	14**	83**	3	4*	0*	1	14	14*	4**
Generalists	86	61	41	71	50	15	6	9	18	38	12
Total sample	699	58	35	67	35	13	7	5	17	37	14

NOTE: The asterisks and the daggers that appear next to the numbers in the tables of Appendix B refer to tests of statistical significance. Single asterisks or daggers indicate that the difference between respondents who are included within the field or other category and those who are not in that category is significant at the .05 level. Double asterisks or daggers indicate that the difference is significant at the .01 level or better. Asterisks are used for variables that were tested by standard analysis of variance procedures. Because such procedures are not appropriate for variables that consist of median scores, another procedure was used to test for differences in the medians, and the results of these tests are indicated by daggers.

Medians were assessed using the nonparametric median test developed by Alexander Mood, as described in Sidney Siegel, *Nonparametric Statistics for the Behavioral Sciences* (New York: McGraw-Hill Book Co., 1956) at pages 111–16. This procedure creates a 2 by 2 table—those in the field or other category being compared to those not in the category, and those above the median score being compared to those below or equal to the median. A chi-square test with one degree of freedom is then applied to this 2 by 2 table.

Because each respondent may be included in more than one field and/or cluster, the numbers of practitioners in the fields and clusters will total more than the number of respondents.

The following notes explain each of the column headings in Table B.1:

(1) *Number of Practitioner Respondents.* This is the number of respondents who devoted 25 percent or more of their time to the field of law or area of practice. All other entries in the row are computed on this sample base but are reduced by the number of respondents who did not provide the information reported.

We used the following question to determine the lawyer's distribution of time in different areas of law: "While a lawyer's time is often spread over many different areas of the law, we wish, for comparative purposes, to characterize those areas in which you spent the major part of your time during the last twelve months. [The respondent was handed a card listing 30 areas of law practice.] In which of the listed areas have you spent more than 50 percent of your time, between 25 percent and 50 percent of your time, between 5 percent and 25 percent of your time?" For purposes of analysis, the thirty areas of law were reduced to twenty-five as follows: four fields of law (admiralty, environmental defense, environmental plaintiff, and condemnations) were excluded because of insufficient numbers of practitioners. Three areas of law were redefined to include fields that, by themselves, had insufficient cases. (Family law was redefined to include general family practice–paying clients, general family practice–poverty levels clients, and consumer–buyer. Commercial law was redefined to include consumer–seller. Personal real estate was redefined to include landlord–tenant.) Lawyers who spent time on tax, real estate, and civil litigation were classified as follows: if 80 percent or more of their income was derived from business clients, they were classified as business real estate, business tax, and business litigation; if less than 80 percent of their income was derived from business clients, or if this information was missing, they were included in personal real estate, personal tax, and general litigation.

(2) *Mean Percentage of Income from Business Clients.* This is the average of the percentages reported in response to the following question: "During the past twelve months, what proportion of your income was derived from . . . representing business clients?" Corporate house counsel were not asked this question and are here assigned a value of 100 percent; government lawyers were also not asked, and are here assigned a value of 0.

(3) *Mean Percentage of Business Income from Major Corporate Clients.* This is the average percentage reported by respondents who had indicated that they received 10 percent or more of their income from work for businesses, and who then answered the following question: "What proportion of your business income would come from the following size business clients?" The categories included major corporations (e.g., Standard Oil, American National Bank, Abbott Laboratories, Playboy Enterprises, Pepper Construction,—i.e., those with over $10 million in sales per year), medium-sized firms, or small businesses (e.g., neighborhood stores, local restaurants, local real estate brokers, etc.—i.e., those with less than $250,000 income per year). Practitioners who were employed as corporate house counsel were not asked this question, and are here treated as deriving 100 percent of their income from major corporate clients. Government lawyers were also not asked, and are here treated as deriving no income from major corporate clients.

(4) *Mean Percentage of Stable Clients.* This is the average of the estimates given by respondents in answer to the following question: "What proportion of all your clients have you represented for three years or more?" Corporate house counsel and government lawyers were not asked this question and were assigned a value of 100 percent on this variable.

(5) *Median Number of Clients per Year.* This is the median of the responses to the following question: "During the past twelve months, approximately how many clients have you done some work for— more than just going through a file, or turning over a file to another lawyer?" Corporate house counsel and government lawyers were not asked this question and were assigned a value of 1.

(6) *Mean Percentage of Blue-Collar Clients.* This is the average of the estimates given by respondents in answer to the following question: "Would you now think about the clients for whom you have handled personal matters in the last twelve months. [The respondent was handed a card listing five

occupational categories.] What proportion of your clients fall into these occupational categories . . . ? Professional, Technical, Managerial; Sales and Clerical; Blue-Collar Workers; Unemployed; Retired, In-School, Keeping House." Column (6) is the average estimate of the percentage of blue-collar clients. Corporate house counsel, government lawyers, and lawyers who devoted less than 10 percent of their work to personal matters were not asked this question and were here assigned a value of 0.

(7) and (8) refer to the average proportions reported in response to the following question: "What proportion of your clientele come from your residential neighborhood, from other parts of the metropolitan area, and from outside the Chicago area?"

(7) *Mean Percentage of Clients from Neighborhood.* This is the average percentage of clients who were reported to come from the respondents' residential neighborhoods.

(8) *Mean Percentage of Clients from Outside Chicago.* This is the average percentage of the respondents' clients who were reported to come from outside the Chicago metropolitan area.

(9)–(11) refer to the average percentages reported in response to the following question: "Could you now indicate what percentage of your new clients you get by each of the means listed?" [The respondent was then handed a card listing five different means of acquiring clientele.]

(9) *Mean Percentage of Clients Referred by Lawyers.* This is the average percentage of clients obtained through referrals from other attorneys, as reported by respondents.

(10) *Mean Percentage of Clients Referred by Clients.* This is the average percentage of clients referred by other clients, as reported by respondents.

(11) *Mean Percentage of Direct Contact Clients.* This is the average percentage of clients obtained through direct contacts with the lawyer, as reported by respondents.

TABLE B.2
Differentiation of Fields of Law by Practice Characteristics

	Number of Practitioner Respondents (1)	% High Negotiation and Advising (2)	% High on Technical Expertise (3)	% High of Work Specialization (4)	% High Change in Law (5)	% High Client Choice (6)	% High Autonomy in Work (7)	% High Encroachment on Practice (8)	Median State Court Appearances per Month (9)	Median Federal Court Appearances per Year (10)	% Appearing Before Regulatory Agencies (11)	% with Law Income $40,000 or More (12)
A. Corporate Sector												
Large Corporate Cluster												
Antitrust (defense)	20	55	45	45	75*	35	30*	20	1	12	45	39
Business litigation	31	16**	57	32	55	44	48	23	5	25†	29	32
Business real estate	41	43	46	45	38	67	64	29	1	0	12*	39
Business tax	30	7**	77**	73**	87**	65	25**	40	0	0	13*	39
Labor (management)	22	59	68	59	68	56	59	23	1	6	64**	32
Securities	22	23	86**	72**	59	61	14**	36	0	1	23	45
Cluster score	151	33	62**	53*	60**	56	44**	30	1	2	25	39
Regulatory Cluster												
Labor (unions)	13	31	54	77**	77**	64	46	54	1	18†	77**	42
Patents	34	30	65	76**	47	72*	55	9**	0	12	41	58*
Public utilities	29	54	55	72**	38	75	46	36	0	0	45	33
Cluster score	77	40	60	75**	49	72**	51	26	0	5	49**	37
General Corporate Cluster												
Antitrust (plaintiffs)	10	10	40	50	70	75	40	0*	0	6	20	30
Banking	33	20*	55	43	58	50	43	32	1	0	18	50
Commercial	38	40	61	26*	43	55	49	21	2	6	26	32
General corporate	135	37	62**	30**	49	70*	53	35	14†	0	20*	48**
Personal injury (defense)	42	36	44	43	52	37*	52	31	2	12	36	35
Cluster score	226	35	57	35**	50	60	50	31	2	3	24**	41
Political Cluster												
Criminal (prosecution)	15	18	50	53	87**	29	33	20	19	0	0**	0**
Municipal	18	31	59	28	44	64	39	17	8	2	22	29
Cluster score	32	26	55	38	66	52	34	19	9	1	12*	16*

TABLE B.2—Continued

Differentiation of Fields of Law by Practice Characteristics

	Number of Practitioner Respondents (1)	% High Negotiation and Advising (2)	% High on Technical Expertise (3)	% High Specialization of Work (4)	% High Change in Law (5)	% High Client Choice (6)	% High Autonomy in Work (7)	% High Encroachment on Practice (8)	Median State Court Appearances per Month (9)	Median Federal Court Appearances per Year (10)	% Appearing Before Regulatory Agencies (11)	% with Law Income $40,000 or More (12)
B. Personal Sector												
Personal Business Cluster												
General litigation	24	35	21**	29	26*	61	52	33	15†	10	29	38
Personal real estate	62	53*	40	18**	26**	61	67	48**	7	0	24	23*
Personal tax	32	35	55	52	69*	58	50	38	2	0	38	42
Probate	100	44	49	26**	52	65*	53	37	5	0	30	34
Cluster score	165	42	43*	30**	43*	62*	56	38**	6	1	31	33
Personal Plight Cluster												
Civil rights	14	36	64	43	64	45	36	7	2	71†	57*	29
Criminal (defense)	44	44	44	48	59	36**	77**	21	20†	5	32	33
Divorce	57	57**	36*	23**	34*	52	67*	52**	15†	2	30	33
Family	27	68**	31*	11**	30*	46	67	56**	10	0	44	38
Personal injury (plaintiffs)	62	53*	42	38	40	39*	64	33	16†	5	44*	34
Cluster score	171	52**	42**	36*	45	45*	65**	34	15†	4	39*	32
Other Specialties	36	26	60	42	50	48	46	26	1	0	39	19*
Generalists	86	41	49	33*	45	56	62	25	5	2	31	37
Total sample	699	40	52	45	50	55	54	30	3	2	31	37

NOTE: For an explanation of asterisks and daggers, see Note to table B.1.

(1) See note for table B.1 column (1).

(2)–(8) refer to the following question: "Different kinds of law require different kinds of professional activities. [The respondent was then handed a card listing seven pairs of statements describing different characterizations of law practice.] Each pair represents polar opposites. If the situation in your practice is midway between poles, circle code 3: if your situation is at one or the other extreme, circle 1 or 5; if your position leans somewhat to either pole, circle 2 or 4." The proportions given in the columns are based on the two values closest to the specified extreme (i.e., either values 1 and 2, or values 4 and 5).

(2) *Percentage High in Negotiation and Advising.* This is the percentage of respondents who characterized their work in the following way: "My specialty and type of practice requires skills in negotiating and advising clients, rather than detailed concern with technical rules." This was contrasted to the following description: "My area demands skills in handling highly technical procedures rather than skills in negotiation and advising clients."

(3) *Percentage High in Technical Expertise.* This is the percentage of respondents who characterized their work in the following way: "The type and content of my practice is such that even an educated layman couldn't really understand or prepare the documents." This was contrasted to the following description: "A para-professional could be trained to handle many of the procedures and documents in my area of the law."

(4) *Percentage with High Specialization of Work.* This is the percentage of respondents who characterized their work in the following way: "The area of law in which I work is so highly specialized that it demands I concentrate in just this one area." This was opposed to the following description: "The nature of my legal practice is such that I can handle a range of problems covering quite a number of different areas of legal practice."

(5) *Percentage of High Change in Legal Substance.* This is the percentage of respondents who characterized their work in the following way: "My area requires a great deal of reading legal material in order to keep abreast of new developments." This was opposed to the following description: "Things don't change too rapidly in my area of the law, so there is little need for constant revision of my knowledge and activities."

(6) *Percentage with High Client Choice.* This is the percentage of respondents who characterized their work in the following way: "In the course of my practice I have rather wide latitude in selecting which clients I will represent." This was contrasted to the following description: "The nature of my practice is such that it is often necessary to accept clients whom I would prefer not to have."

(7) *Percentage with High Autonomy in Work.* This is the percentage of respondents who characterized their work in the following way: "One of the things that I like about my area of practice is that I can do largely whatever I like without having someone looking over my shoulder and directing my work." This was in contrast with: "In my practice of the law I work closely with more senior lawyers who provide relatively close guidance in the nature of my work."

(8) *Percentage with High Encroachment on Practice.* This is the percentage of respondents who characterized their work in the following way: "There are aspects of my professional work which are being encroached upon by other occupations." This was in contrast with: "No other occupation is engaging in the kinds of legal matters with which I am primarily concerned."

(9) *Median State Court Appearances per Month.* Respondents reported the number of their State trial and appellate court appearances per month over the past twelve months, and this is the median of those responses.

(10) *Median Federal Court Appearances per Year.* Respondents reported the number of their federal trial and appellate court appearances over the past twelve months, and this is the median of those responses.

(11) *Percentage Appearing Before Regulatory Agencies.* This is the percentage of respondents appearing before federal, state or local regulatory boards, commissions, and administrative agencies within the past twelve months.

(12) *Percentage with Law Income $40,000 or More.* This is the percentage of respondents who reported that their annual income from the practice of law was $40,000 or more. Thirteen income categories were used (see appendix A, A49).

TABLE B.3
Differentiation of Fields of Law by Practice Setting

	Number of Practitioner Respondents (1)	% Solo Practitioners (2)	% in Firms of Fewer than 10 Lawyers (3)	% in Firms of 10–30 Lawyers (4)	% in Firms of More Than 30 Lawyers (5)	% House Counsel (6)	% Government Employees (7)
A. Corporate Sector							
Large Corporate Cluster							
Antitrust (defense)	20	0*	5*	0	85**	10	0
Business litigation	31	3*	10*	19	58**	10	0*
Business real estate	41	17	17	17	14	33**	0*
Business tax	30	3*	17	7	33**	40**	0*
Labor (management)	22	5	18	14	23	27	14
Securities	22	0*	5*	5	77**	9	5
Cluster score	150	6**	11**	12	44**	24**	3**
Regulatory Cluster							
Labor (unions)	13	8	38	15	0	15	23
Patents	34	12	29	38	6	15	0*
Public utilities	29	10	14	7	10	24	34**
Cluster score	77	12*	25	22	6**	18	17
General Corporate Cluster							
Antitrust (plaintiffs)	10	10	10	20	30	0	30
Banking	33	9	15	18	27	30**	0*
Commercial	38	13	26	8	21	18	13
General corporate	133	19	28	10	21	16	3**
Personal injury (defense)	42	10	17	19*	31*	19	5
Cluster score	194	15**	25	12	24**	17	6**
Political Cluster							
(All employed by government unless respondent changed jobs during year)							
Criminal (prosecution)	15	0*	28	33**	6	0	100**
Municipal	18	0**	16	19	3*	0*	33**
Cluster score	31						62**

TABLE B.3—Continued

Differentiation of Fields of Law by Practice Setting

	Number of Practitioner Respondents (1)	% Solo Practitioners (2)	% in Firms of Fewer than 10 Lawyers (3)	% in Firms of 10–30 Lawyers (4)	% in Firms of More Than 30 Lawyers (5)	% House Counsel (6)	% Government Employees (7)
B. Personal Sector							
Personal Business Cluster							
General litigation	23	21	46*	8	21	0*	0
Personal real estate	62	56**	32	6	5**	0**	0*
Personal tax	31	22	44*	12	19	0*	0*
Probate	100	30*	37**	10	13	9	0**
Cluster score	165	34**	38**	8	12*	5**	1**
Personal Plight Cluster							
Civil rights	14	0	29	0	14	7	50**
Criminal (defense)	43	48**	25	0*	5*	0**	20*
Divorce	57	61**	35	2*	0**	0**	2*
Family	27	44**	26	4	4	4	19
Personal injury (plaintiffs)	62	37**	52**	5	2**	3**	2*
Cluster score	138	42**	36**	3**	3**	2**	13
Other Specialties	36	8	14	0*	6	8	64**
Generalists	86	27	24	9	13	21	6*
Total sample	699	21	26	10	17	14	11

NOTE: For an explanation of asterisks, see Note to table B.1
(1) See note for table B.1 column (1).
(2)–(7) refer to the average percentages for each response category of the following question:
"Which category best describes [your] job?" [The respondent was handed a card with ten types of
practice—solo, firm, federal, state, municipal/county, or military government, corporate, insurance,

banking, or railroad house counsel.] The four house counsel categories were also combined into one
category (col. (6)). All of the government categories were combined into one category (col. (7)). The
respondents practicing in law firms were then recategorized into three firm size groupings (firms
with fewer than 10 lawyers, 10 to 30 lawyers, and more than 30 lawyers) by use of responses to the
following question: "How many lawyers are in your firm/office now?"

TABLE B.4

Differentiation of Fields of Law by Law School Attended

	Number of Practitioner Respondents (1)	% Attended Elite Law Schools (2)	% Attended Prestige Law Schools (3)	% Attended Regional Law Schools (4)	% Attended Local Law Schools (5)
A. Corporate Sector					
Large Corporate Cluster					
Antitrust (defense)	20	50**	15	20	15**
Business litigation	31	39**	13	29	16**
Business real estate	41	19	12	19	50
Business tax	30	13	23	27	37
Labor (management)	22	23	23	27	27
Securities	22	45**	31	9	14**
Cluster score	151	28**	18	22*	32**
Regulatory Cluster					
Labor (unions)	13	15	23	15	46
Patents	34	18	12	32*	38
Public utilities	29	24	28	31*	17**
Cluster score	77	19	19	29**	32*
General Corporate Cluster					
Antitrust (plaintiffs)	10	40	20	10	30
Banking	33	36*	27	9	27*
Commercial	38	26	16	21	37
General corporate	135	30**	21	14	34**
Personal injury (defense)	42	9	24	17	45
Cluster score	226	27**	22*	15	36**
Political Cluster					
Criminal (prosecution)	15	0*	27	7	67
Municipal	18	22	11	11	56
Cluster score	32	12	19	9	59

TABLE B.4—*Continued*
Differentiation of Fields of Law by Law School Attended

	Number of Practitioner Respondents (1)	*% Attended Elite Law Schools* (2)	*% Attended Prestige Law Schools* (3)	*% Attended Regional Law Schools* (4)	*% Attended Local Law Schools* (5)	
B. Personal Sector						
Personal Business Cluster						
General litigation	24	8	25	12	54	
Personal real estate	62	21	10	18	48	
Personal tax	32	28	16	12	41	
Probate	100	23	12	21	44	
Cluster score	165	22	13	16	47	
Personal Plight Cluster						
Civil rights	14	43*	21	7	29	
Criminal (defense)	44	4**	11	5*	77**	
Divorce	57	11	9	12	65**	
Family	27	19	4	19	56	
Personal injury (plaintiffs)	62	8*	3**	15	74**	
Cluster score	171	12**	9**	13	64**	
Other Specialties	36	19	17	11	50	
Generalists	86	17	22	7**	52	
Total sample	699	20	17	16	45	

NOTE: For an explanation of asterisks, see Note for table B.1.

(1) See note for table B.3 column (1).

(2) *Percentage Attended Elite Law Schools.* This is the percentage of respondents who attended one of the law schools in the "elite" category. Those schools are Chicago, Columbia, Harvard, Michigan, Stanford, and Yale.

(3) *Percentage Attended Prestige Law Schools.* This is the percentage of respondents who attended one of the schools in the "prestige" category. Those schools are University of California at Berkeley, Cornell, Georgetown, New York University, Northwestern University, University of Pennsylvania, University of Virginia, and the University of Wisconsin, by far the largest number having attended Northwestern.

(4) *Percentage Attended Regional Law Schools.* This is the percentage of respondents who attended one of the law schools in the "regional" category. This category was composed of all schools not included in the elite, prestige, or local groupings. By far the most numerous in this category are graduates of the University of Illinois, with forty-eight. Next most numerous are lawyers who attended Notre Dame, with twelve in the sample.

(5) *Percentage Attended Local Law Schools.* This is the percentage of respondents who attended schools in the "local" category. These schools are De Paul University, Chicago Kent, Loyola University, and John Marshall, all located in the city of Chicago.

TABLE B.5

Differentiation of Fields of Law by Social Origins of Practitioners

	Number of Practitioner Respondents (1)	% Nonreligious Practitioners (2)	% Type I Protestants (3)	% Type II Protestants (4)	% Catholic Practitioners (5)	% Jewish Practitioners (6)	% Irish Practitioners (7)	% British (8)
A. Corporate Sector								
Large Corporate Cluster								
Antitrust (defense)	20	21	25	15	25	10*	15	15
Business litigation	31	17	10	16	42	13*	19	10
Business real estate	42	12	10	7	31	38	12	0
Business tax	30	14	10	7	23	43	10	7
Labor (management)	22	9	9	9	32	41	18	9
Securities	22	27*	36**	14	9*	14	5	14
Cluster score	151	16	15	11	29	28	13	7
Regulatory Cluster								
Labor (unions)	13	23	8	15	0*	54	0	15
Patents	34	11	26*	14	32	15**	18	12
Public utilities	29	3	17	28**	21	31	0*	0
Cluster score	77	10	19	19*	23	27	9	8
General Corporate Cluster								
Antitrust (plaintiffs)	10	0	20	30	20	20	10	10
Banking	33	9	27**	15	12*	36	0*	9
Commercial	38	11	13	5	24	47*	3	3
General corporate	135	7*	13	15	27	38	9	11*
Personal injury (defense)	42	17	7	7	55**	14**	26**	5
Cluster score	226	10	13	12	31	33	11	8
Political Cluster								
Criminal (prosecution)	15	7	7	13	53*	20	20	0
Municipal	18	6	22	6	39	28	17	17
Cluster score	32	6	16	9	44	25	16	9

% Southern & Eastern Europeans (10)	% Black Practitioners (11)	% Mixed and "American" Practitioners (12)	% Fathers Administrators (13)	% Fathers Professionals (14)	% Fathers as Lawyers (15)	% Metropolitan Origin (16)	Mean age (17)	
								Large Corporate Cluster
0	0	45	35	30	10	55*	38*	Antitrust (defense)
0*	0	42*	32	37	10	65	41	Business litigation
12	5	19	36	24	7	86	44	Business real estate
0	0	27	40	45	24	77	38*	Business tax
9	0	14	45	23	9	72	41	Labor (management)
5	0	45*	41	45	18	68	39	Securities
6*	1	30*	40	31	13	72*	41**	Cluster score
								Regulatory Cluster
8	8	0*	23	54	23	77	43	Labor (unions)
6	0**	32	58*	24	6*	41**	45	Patents
18	0	31	45	34	14	83	45	Public utilities
11	1	26	48	32	12	71	45	Cluster score
								General Corporate Cluster
10	0	50*	40	50	40*	90	37	Antitrust (plaintiffs)
3	3	30	42	35	19	72	45	Banking
11	3	26	47	24	11	76	41	Commercial
9	2	23	46	29	13	73	45	General corporate
5	2	31	29	34	12	83	40	Personal injury (defense)
8	3	27	42	30	14	75	44	Cluster score
								Political Cluster
20	7	27	20	47	13	87	39	Criminal (prosecution)
6	0	22	22	44	22	72	41	Municipal
13	3	25	22*	47	19	78	40	Cluster score

447

TABLE B.5—*Continued*

Differentiation of Fields of Law by Social Origins of Practitioners

	Number of Practitioner Respondents (1)	% Nonreligious Practitioners (2)	% Type I Protestants (3)	% Type II Protestants (4)	% Catholic Practitioners (5)	% Jewish Practitioners (6)	% Irish Practitioners (7)	% British Prac...... (8)
	B. Personal Sector							
Personal Business Cluster								
General litigation	24	13	0	4	46	33	29**	4
Personal real estate	62	8	11	10	31	39	11	5
Personal tax	32	3	25*	12	38	22	12	16
Probate	100	9	17	16	35	22*	16	5
Cluster score	165	9	12	13	35	29	15	5
Personal Plight Cluster								
Civil rights	14	29	7	21	36	7*	7	7
Criminal (defense)	44	11	5	5	34	45	20	2
Divorce	57	11	0**	5	26	56**	16	2
Family	27	15	7	15	22	37	4	11
Personal injury (plaintiffs)	62	8	2**	3*	44*	44	19	2
Cluster score	171	14	4**	8	33	42**	16	4
Other Specialties	36	22	8	11	31	28	8	3
Generalists	86	12	16	9	26	35	6*	9
Total sample	699	12	13	12	30	33	12	7

% Southern & Eastern Europeans (10)	% Black Practitioners (11)	% Mixed and "American" Practitioners (12)	% Fathers Administrators (13)	% Fathers Professionals (14)	% Fathers as Lawyers (15)	% Metropolitan Origin (16)	Mean age (17)	
								Personal Business Cluster
9	0	8	21*	42	17	87	44	General litigation
17	5	11*	37	36	20	81	52**	Personal real estate
19	6	22	47	31	22	53**	47	Personal tax
13	5	24	32	38	22*	72	51**	Probate
14	4	19	35	35	20	76	49**	Cluster score
								Personal Plight Cluster
25	14**	14	43	36	14	93	39	Civil rights
20*	2	9*	27	31	19	98**	42	Criminal (defense)
4	4**	9**	39	26	11	94**	45	Divorce
15	19**	7*	33	35	12	72	51*	Family
15	0	18	53*	13**	10	98**	43	Personal injury (plaintiffs)
16*	6**	12**	38	27	14	92**	44	Cluster score
18	6	25	36	34	20	83	41	Other Specialties
10	1	26	48	37	14	78	45	Generalists
11	2	23	40	32	15	78	44	Total sample

NOTE: For an explanation of asterisks see Note to table B.1.

(1) See note for table B.1 column (1).

(2) *Percentage of Nonreligious Practitioners*. Respondents were asked: "Do you have a religious preference? That is, are you either Protestant, Roman Catholic, Jewish, or something else?" This column is the percentage who indicated no religious affiliation or preference.

(3) *Percentage of Type I Protestants*. This is the percentage of respondents reporting that they were affiliated with one of the following Protestant denominations: Congregational, Presbyterian, Episcopal, and United Church of Christ.

(4) *Percentage of Type II Protestants*. This is the percentage of respondents reporting that they were affiliated with a Protestant denomination other than those included in column (3).

(5) *Percentage of Catholic Practitioners*. This is the percentage of practitioners who said that their religious preference was Roman Catholic.

(6) *Percentage of Jewish Practitioners*. This is the percentage of practitioners who expressed a preference for Judaism in response to the religion question or who said that they were Jewish in response to the question: "What nationality background do you think of yourself as having—that is, besides being American?"

(7) *Percentage of Irish Practitioners*. This is the percentage of practitioners indicating Irish ancestry in response to the nationality background question.

(8) *Percentage of British Practitioners*. This is the percentage of respondents indicating English, Scottish, or Welsh ancestry in response to the nationality background question.

(9) *Percentage of Northern and Western Europeans*. This is the percentage of respondents indicating, in response to the nationality background question, one of the northern or western European nations other than Ireland, England, Scotland, or Wales; predominantly Germany and the Scandinavian countries.

(10) *Percentage of Southern and Eastern Europeans*. This is the percentage of respondents indicating, in response to the nationality background question, one of the nations of southern or eastern Europe; predominantly Italy, Poland and Russia.

(11) *Percentage of Black Practitioners*. This is the percentage of respondents who were observed to be black or who identified themselves as black when asked their race (see appendix A, Question A50).

(12) *Percentage of Mixed and "American" Practitioners*. This is the percentage of respondents who indicated, in response to the nationality background question, that they were of mixed ancestry or considered themselves "only American."

(13) *Percentage with Fathers as Administrators*. This the percentage of respondents who said that their fathers were "managers or administrators" (in the categories of the U.S. Census Occupational Code) in response to the question: "Which of these categories best describes the kind of work your (father/father substitute) usually did while you were growing up?"

(14) *Percentage with Fathers as Professionals*. This is the percentage of respondents who said, in answer to the father's occupation question, that their fathers did work in the "professional and technical" category.

(15) *Percentage with Fathers as Lawyers*. This is the percentage who responded affirmatively to the question: "Was your father a lawyer?"

(16) *Percentage of Metropolitan Origin*. This is the percentage of respondents who indicated that their residence "during most of the time they were at high school" was in a large city (over 250,000) or in a suburb of such a city.

(17) *Mean Age*. This is the average age of the respondents, according to their own reports.

TABLE B.6

Differentiation of Fields of Law by Political Preference and Value Orientation

	Number of Practitioner Respondents (1)	% Republicans (2)	% Democrats (3)	% Independents (4)	Mean Score for Economic Liberalism (5)	Mean Score for Civic Libertarianism (6)	Mean Score on Religiosity Scale (7)
A. Corporate Sector							
Large Corporate Cluster							
Antitrust (defense)	20	25	40	35	3.05	3.48	2.84
Business litigation	31	33	20	47	3.14	3.33	2.74
Business real estate	41	17	43	40	3.24	3.17	2.73
Business tax	30	17	43	40	3.23	3.56*	2.47
Labor (management)	22	9	32	59	3.17	3.35	2.64
Securities	22	27	41	32	3.10	3.26	2.61
Cluster score	151	22	34	44	3.18	3.33*	2.67
Regulatory Cluster							
Labor (unions)	13	0	38	54	3.91**	3.80**	2.00*
Patents	34	32	26	41	2.93	3.11	2.76
Public utilities	29	34	34	31	3.15	3.08	3.02
Cluster score	77	27	32	39	3.21	3.21	2.75
General Corporate Cluster							
Antitrust (plaintiffs)	10	10	30	60	3.18	3.56	3.05
Banking	33	30	39	30	3.12	3.43	2.42
Commercial	38	16	47	37	3.18	3.38	2.53
General corporate	135	30**	37	33*	3.05**	3.16	2.74
Personal injury (defense)	42	24	21*	55	3.15	3.04	2.99
Cluster score	226	26*	34	39	3.11*	3.22	2.74
Political Cluster							
Criminal (prosecution)	15	7	47	47	3.36	3.31	2.67
Municipal	18	6	50	44	3.31	3.11	2.89
Cluster score	32	6*	50	44	3.31	3.18	2.78

TABLE B.6—*Continued*
Differentiation of Fields of Law by Political Preference and Value Orientation

	Number of Practitioner Respondents (1)	% Republicans (2)	% Democrats (3)	% Independents (4)	Mean Score for Economic Liberalism (5)	Mean Score for Civic Libertarianism (6)	Mean Score on Religiosity Scale (7)
B. Personal Sector							
Personal Business Cluster							
General litigation	24	9	26	66*	3.26	3.32	2.42
Personal real estate	62	23	32	42	3.17	2.88**	2.90
Personal tax	32	41**	41	19**	3.03	3.13	2.84
Probate	100	30*	29	40	3.07*	2.89**	2.96
Cluster score	165	26	30*	43	3.14	3.00**	2.85
Personal Plight Cluster							
Civil rights	14	7	64*	29	3.63*	3.60	2.64
Criminal (defense)	44	3**	64**	32	3.51**	3.56**	2.68
Divorce	57	11*	50*	39	3.26	3.22	2.53
Family	27	12	46	35	3.37	3.10	2.75
Personal injury (plaintiffs)	62	10*	50	40	3.22	3.05	2.80
Cluster score	171	9**	52**	38	3.35**	3.28	2.66
Other Specialties	36	19	39	36	3.31	3.09	2.67*
Generalists	86	25	29	45	3.09	3.10	3.01*
Practicing total	699	21	37	41	3.19	3.20	2.77
Non-practicing	78	26	39	34	3.21	3.37	2.97
Total sample	777	22	37	41	3.23	3.28	2.82

NOTE: For an explanation of asterisks see Note to table B.1.

(1) See note for table B.1 column (1).

(2) *Percentage of Republicans.* This is the percentage of respondents who indicated that they were Republicans in answer to the question: "With respect to national politics, do you usually think of yourself as a Republican, Democrat, Independent, or what?"

(3) *Percentage of Democrats.* This is the percentage who indicated a preference for the Democratic Party in response to the question concerning national political preference.

(4) *Percentage of Independents.* This is the percentage who indicated that, in national politics, they thought of themselves as independent.

(5) *Mean Score for Economic Liberalism.* This is the average score of respondents on a set of questions intended to measure attitudes on economic issues. Higher scores indicate greater disposition toward government regulation of the economy and the redistribution of wealth. For a discussion of the economic liberalism scale, see chapter 5.

(6) *Mean Score for Civil Libertarianism.* This is the average score of respondents on a set of questions intended to measure attitudes on civil liberties issues. Higher scores indicate greater support for civil libertarian values/ indicate support for wider latitude in freedom of speech, press, and so on. For a discussion of the civil libertarian scale, see chapter 5.

(7) *Mean Score on Religiosity Scale.* This is the average score of respondents on a set of questions intended to assess religious values. Higher scores indicate greater support of organized religion. For a discussion of the religiosity scale, see chapter 5.

Name Index

Subject Index

Netherlands, number of lawyers in, 20
Networks:
  among Chicago lawyers, 7–8, 211–31
  as referral system, 47
  smallest space analysis of notable Chicago lawyers, 290–99
New York City bar, analysis of, 28
New York University Law School, 16
No fault issue, 233, 312, 327
Northwestern University Law School, 16
Notable Chicago lawyers:
  characteristics of, 280–89
  defining social organization of, by respondent characteristics, 299–309
  likelihood of knowing, 277–80
  racial distribution, 276, 302
  sex distribution, 276
  smallest space analysis of networks of, 290–99
  spheres of influence of, 309–15
Notre Dame University Law School, 16

Occupational careers, 176n
Occupational prestige; see Prestige
Occupational status, 169
Office practice, distinction between litigation and, 61, 77, 328–33
Organic solidarity, 376
Organized bar; see American Bar Association (ABA); Bar association; Chicago Bar Association

Partnership(s):
  advancement of status of, 178
  and age of attainment, 179–80
  clientele of, 4
  growth of large, 16–17
Patent law, 37
  background of, 4
  as conservative legal field, 161
  distribution of legal effort in, 40, 48
  imputed characteristics of, 103
  overlap with antitrust law, 80–81
  practitioner characteristics of, 111, 117, 434–52
  prestige ranking of, 91
  referral system in, 60
  relationship between antitrust law and, 51
  as specialty, 18, 37, 43–44, 45
  as wealth-oriented field, 157
  see also Practice setting(s)/type

Patronage occupations, as distinguished from collegiate occupations, 360–65
Pennsylvania, University of, Law School, 16
People persuasion, 61
Performance-oriented standards, pressure toward development of, 168–69
Personal business cluster, 72n
  see also General litigation law; Personal real estate law; Personal tax law; Probate law
Personal characteristics, as measure of social differentiation, 65, 68
Personal client sector:
  amount of overlap between general corporate sector and, 43
  client relationships in, 380–81
  distinction between litigation and office practice in, 328–33
  distribution of legal effort in, 40, 48
  selected characteristics of lawyers in, 434–52
  size, separation, and social differentiation of lawyers and clients in, 70, 328–33
  specialization of, 52, 323–28
  total legal effort in, 42–43
  versus corporate sector, 71
Personal injury law, 72n, 327
  clients in, 4, 82
  distribution of legal effort in, 40, 48
  imputed characteristics of, 103, 106, 107, 108
  income derived from, 82n–83n
  practitioner characteristics of, 111, 113, 115, 116, 434–52
  and prestige, 91, 92, 93, 124, 127
  social differentiation within, 68
  value structure of lawyers in field, 151
  as wealth-oriented field, 157
Personal plight cluster, 72n, 378
  characterization by litigation, 378
  comparison with personal business clusters, 82n
  distribution of legal effort in, 40, 48, 78n
  ranking of, 54
  selected characteristics of lawyers in, 434–52
  social differentiation within, 70
  value structure of lawyers in, 151
Personal real estate law:
  as conservative field, 163
  distribution of legal effort in, 40, 48
  selected characteristics of lawyers in, 434–52
  value structure of lawyers in, 150

U.S. Congress, as a representative body, 244
Upward mobility, law as avenue of, 172
Urban lawyer(s), 5
  characteristics of, 20
  community involvement of, 20–21
U-shaped distribution of legal work, 47, 48, 329–30

Value orientation, differentiation of legal fields by, 451–52
Virginia, University of, Law School, 16

Wagner Act, 34
Washington, George, University of, Law School, 16

Watergate, 14
Welfare state mentality, 143–44
Westinghouse Electric Corp. v. *Kerr-McGee Corp.* (1978), 370n
White-collar crime, 371n
Wisconsin, University of, Law School, 16
Women:
  representation of, in Chicago Bar Association, 11
  representation of, in Chicago lawyers, 11
  representation of, in Chicago notables, 276

Yale University Law School, 15, 239
Yule's Q, 58n